ICCA
CONGRESS SERIES NO. 16

50TH ANNIVERSARY CONFERENCE
GENEVA, 19 - 20 MAY 2011

Wolters Kluwer
Law & Business

INTERNATIONAL COUNCIL
FOR COMMERCIAL ARBITRATION

ARBITRATION – THE NEXT FIFTY YEARS

GENERAL EDITOR:
ALBERT JAN VAN DEN BERG

with the assistance of the
Permanent Court of Arbitration
Peace Palace, The Hague

ISBN 978-90-411-3808-8

Published by:
Kluwer Law International
PO Box 316
2400 AH Alphen aan den Rijn
The Netherlands
Website: www.kluwerlaw.com

Sold and distributed in North, Central and South America by:
Aspen Publishers, Inc.
7201 McKinney Circle
Frederick, MD 21704
United States of America
Email: customer.service@aspenpublishers.com

Sold and distributed in all other countries by:
Turpin Distribution Services Ltd.
Stratton Business Park
Pegasus Drive, Biggleswade
Bedfordshire SG18 8TQ
United Kingdom
Email: kluwerlaw@turpin-distribution.com

Printed on acid-free paper.

Printed and bound by CPI Group (UK) Ltd, Croydon, CR0 4YY, United Kingdom.

Preface

ICCA Congress Series no. 16 comprises the proceedings of the ICCA 50 Geneva Conference 2011 hosted by the ICCA 50 Organizing Committee on 19-20 May 2011. The Conference marked a major milestone: the Golden Anniversary of ICCA. A warm word of thanks goes to the Committee for arranging this splendid celebration in the beautiful city of Geneva, the birthplace of ICCA.

Milestones provide a wonderful opportunity to take stock of the past and present, and to look ahead to the future. The Conference Programme was designed to do just that. Johnny Veeder's speech and a screening of video interviews with ICCA's godfathers Professor Pieter Sanders and Professor Pierre Lalive at the Gala Dinner on the eve of the Conference, placed ICCA in its historical context. The video interviews can be viewed on the ICCA website <www.arbitration-icca.org>. The first two sessions of the Conference then focused on the present with Reports and Comments on developments in commercial arbitration and investment arbitration, respectively. The third session was a Round Table discussion on the future. Eminent arbitration practitioners and scholars were invited to share their views on what the future holds for arbitration and for ICCA. I would like to extend my thanks to Session Chairs Donald Francis Donovan and Gabrielle Kaufmann-Kohler, as well as the speakers and Round Table participants.

Information on future ICCA Congresses can be found on the ICCA website <www.arbitration-icca.org>. The next ICCA Congress will be held in Singapore on 10-13 June 2012. See the ICCA website and the Singapore 2012 Organizing Committee website <www.iccasingapore2012.org> for further details. Miami will host ICCA in 2014; information on this event will be available on the ICCA website and the website of the ICCA Miami 2014 Organizing Committee <www.miamiicca2014.com>.

On behalf of ICCA I would once again like to thank the Permanent Court of Arbitration and both the former Secretary General, Mr. Christiaan Kröner, as well as Acting Secretary General, Brooks Daly, for hosting the staff of ICCA Publications at the Headquarters of its International Bureau at the Peace Palace in The Hague. The continued administrative and technical support of the entire PCA staff is greatly appreciated as well.

I would further like to thank the editorial staff of ICCA Publications for preparing this volume for publication. In addition I would like to thank Ms. Christine Passerat of Lévy Kaufman-Kohler for her cheerful assistance in collecting materials for this volume.

Albert Jan van den Berg
March 2012

TABLE OF CONTENTS

PREFACE
Albert Jan van den Berg, General Editor — v

TABLE OF CONTENTS — vii

INTRODUCTORY REMARKS
Jan Paulsson, President of ICCA — 1

WELCOME MESSAGE FROM THE SWISS FEDERAL GOVERNMENT
Simonetta Sommaruga — 3

GALA DINNER ADDRESS
V.V. Veeder
Memories from ICCA's First Fifty Years — 5

INTRODUCTION TO ICCA'S 50TH ANNIVERSARY CONFERENCE
Gabrielle Kaufmann-Kohler — 11

The Present – Commercial Arbitration as a Transnational System of Justice

Chair: **Albert Jan van den Berg**

Introduction: Albert Jan van den Berg
The Present – Commercial Arbitration as a Transnational System of Justice: Introduction to the Session — 15

Report: W. Michael Reisman and Brian Richardson
Tribunals and Courts: An Interpretation of the Architecture of International Commercial Arbitration — 17

Comment: Emmanuel Gaillard
International Arbitration as a Transnational System of Justice — 66

Comment: Luca G. Radicati Di Brozolo
The Control System of Arbitral Awards: A Pro-Arbitration Critique of Michael Reisman's "Architecture of International Commercial Arbitration" — 74

Comment: Karim Youssef
Universal Arbitration Between Freedom and Constraint: The Challenges of Jurisdiction in Multiparty, Multi-Contract Arbitrations 103

The Present – Investment Arbitration as a Governance Tool for Economic International Relations?

Chair: **Donald Francis Donovan**

Introduction: Donald Francis Donovan
The Present – Investment Arbitration as a Governance Tool for Economic International Relations? Introduction to the Session 135

Report: José E. Alvarez
Is the International Investment Regime a Form of Global Governance? 137

Comment: Bruno Simma
Foreign Investment, Human Rights and Global Governance 161

Comment: Sir Franklin Berman, KCMG, QC
The Investment Treaty Arbitrator as Agent of Global Governance 166

Comment: Anthea Roberts
The Next Battleground: Standards of Review in Investment Treaty Arbitration 170

The Future – What Will Change?

Chair: **Gabrielle Kaufmann-Kohler**
Round Table 183

Appendices

Appendix I: ICCA 50 Organizing Committee
A Brief History of ICCA 219

Appendix II: Clyde Croft
The Development of Australia as an Arbitral Seat – A Victorian Supreme Court Perspective 227
Annex I: Supreme Court of Victoria, Practice Note 2 of 2010 – Arbitration Business 255

LIST OF PARTICIPANTS 261

LIST OF ICCA OFFICERS AND MEMBERS 291

Introductory Remarks

Geneva occupies a near mythical place in the lore of ICCA. It was on the banks of the Lac Leman that a few friends, all pioneers of international arbitration, gathered as negotiators of the European Convention on International Commercial Arbitration and fell into the habit of getting together outside the formal technical deliberations to evoke broader perspectives. Some details of these initial conclaves are recounted elsewhere in this volume (see "The First Fifty Years", pp. 219-226). They were the origins of ICCA.

From the beginning, ICCA conceived itself as the forum for a dialogue of big ideas. The very first session of its very first Congress, held in Paris in 1961, was chaired by the president of the French Court of Cassation and devoted to the innovative idea of the autonomy of arbitration clauses. Perhaps it is no coincidence that the leading French judgments on that very concept followed in the wake of that debate. Other sessions dealt with such topics as the functioning and cooperation of international arbitral institutions and the notion of an "international bureau" for the selection of arbitrators and the certification of awards for enforcement. The latter was surely over-ambitious at the practical level, but nevertheless at the very least a worthwhile mental exercise to focus all minds on the art of the possible.

The success of these early Congresses – including for example the 1975 edition in New Delhi, devoted to the concept (unusual at the time) of the filling of gaps in long-term contracts – gave impetus to the ICCA publications which have become such a prominent feature in the arbitral environment.

Perhaps the principal reason why it is appropriate that ICCA's 50th anniversary be celebrated in Geneva is not so much to remember the past as to project ourselves successfully into the future. Geneva's experience with international arbitration has been long and glorious, but this has never impeded Swiss innovation – the product, as far an outsider can tell, of a healthy dialogue among practitioners, academics, lawmakers and judges. The Swiss have never rested on their laurels, but have constantly sought to refine their analysis of the law of arbitration and to improve their practical management of the arbitral process. This example is precisely the one ICCA must follow as it embarks on its second half-century, and seeks to develop effective methods of dispute resolution for the benefit of the international community, to ameliorate its programmes, to reflect the diversity of the modem world in its membership; and as it seeks to ensure – notably by encouraging the newly formed Young ICCA – that new ambitious entrants are welcomed, and are given opportunities to contribute and to thrive.

Jan Paulsson
President of ICCA

Welcome Message from the Swiss Federal Government

On behalf of the Swiss Federal Government, I am pleased to welcome you to Geneva. I wish to congratulate ICCA on its 50th anniversary and am proud that ICCA has chosen Switzerland as the venue for its celebration.

ICCA's anniversary marks half a century of commitment to advancing arbitration as a means of settling disputes in international commercial relations. Through first-rank publications and congresses, through its educational endeavors and its cooperation with UNCITRAL, ICCA has been a leading actor in the promotion of international arbitration over the last decades. Thanks to the diversity of its membership, representing all the regions of the world, ICCA has contributed to the growing acceptance and use of international arbitration both at the global level and domestically.

Switzerland boasts a long tradition in the peaceful settlement of disputes generally and in international arbitration in particular. Landmark proceedings such as the *Alabama* case, decided by an arbitral tribunal sitting in Geneva in a dispute between the governments of the United States and Great Britain in 1872, shaped – and were shaped by – this tradition. Today, Switzerland hosts international organizations active in dispute settlement such as the World Trade Organization and the World Intellectual Property Organization, the UN Compensation Commission and the Court of Arbitration for Sport, just to name a few. Each year, countless commercial parties choose Switzerland as seat of arbitration, trusting its legal environment, its modern arbitration laws and the excellence of its judiciary.

Personally, I view this heritage both as a grant of trust and as a responsibility. Switzerland remains committed to the values which international arbitration has found to be a fostering environment in the past. Also, my administration encourages developments to maintain a wise and fruitful balance between the legitimate expectations of traditional stakeholders on the one hand and new demands international arbitration will need to accommodate in the future on the other hand. In that sense, I look forward to many years of successful dialogue and shared interests between Switzerland and ICCA.

Simonetta Sommaruga
Federal Councilor
Federal Department of Justice and Police

Gala Dinner Address
Memories from ICCA's First Fifty Years

*V.V. Veeder**

It is a pleasant privilege for me to be invited to address you tonight at this anniversary dinner. Yet, I am uniquely unqualified to speak about the historical origins of the "International Arbitration Congress", later known as the "International *Committee* for Commercial Arbitration" and, since 1975, called the "International *Council* for Commercial Arbitration – or "ICCA".

I was not there at ICCA's foundation in 1961; and, strangely, the United Kingdom was not an active supporter of ICCA in its earliest days, at least not compared to specialists from France, the Netherlands, Italy and Switzerland, soon joined by India and the USSR.

The history of ICCA is also not the usual history of an arbitral institution because ICCA was not created as an institution. It is now an organization with a legal personality under international law and ICCA's Foundation, as separate body in Holland, has a legal personality under Dutch law; but ICCA was born as a concept; and so it remains with no formal constitution and no large building or home of its own. Moreover, ICCA is entirely independent of anything and everyone; and it does not work under the umbrella of any other body with different or even conflicting interests.

From its first beginnings, ICCA has been truly international; and it does not serve nationalistic, sectorial or regional self-interests. ICCA's unique status and origins as regards international arbitration requires an explanation by analogy.

In the world of chemistry, positive catalysts play a relatively small but highly significant part. These re-agents speed up a chemical reaction without being consumed by the reaction itself. In the world of international arbitration, those catalysts are ideas, both theoretical and practical, for which ICCA has provided a highly significant forum as an ideas-factory, now for half a century.

It began with meetings over lunch and dinner in 1961 a few kilometres from here, at the Relais de Chambésy on the road to Lausanne. Professor Pieter Sanders from Holland was there, as were Me Jean Robert from France, Professor Arthur Bülow and Dr.Dr.

---

* Essex Court Chambers, London; Member of ICCA.

This historical account is drawn from several sources: Piet SANDERS, *Herinneringen*, pp. 56-59; Heinz STROHBACH, "*Vom Club de Chambésy zum* International Council for Commercial Arbitration" in A. PLANTEY, K.-H. BÖCKSTIEGEL and J. BREDOW, *Festschrift für Ottoarndt Glossner zum 70. Geburtstag*, p. 417; "The I ICCA Congress 1961 (Paris)", Rev.arb (1961, no. 2); "The II ICCA Congress 1966 (Rotterdam)", Rev.arb (1966, no. 3, special); "The III ICCA Congress 1969 (Venice)", Rev.arb (1969, no. 4) pp. 133, 226, 338 et seq; "The IV ICCA Congress 1972 (Moscow), Rev.arb (1972, no. 4) pp. 426, 463 et seq; and "The V ICCA Congress 1975 (New Delhi)", Rev.arb (1975, no. 1) pp. 3, 131 et seq; and private communications from Jan Paulsson, Sergei Lebedev, Howard Holtzmann, Brigitte Stern, Alan Redfern, Jernej Sekolec, Martin Hunter, Jason Fry, Annette Magnusson and Sebastién Besson – to all of whom I express my profound recognition and gratitude (albeit that any errors here are mine alone).

Ottoarndt Glossner both from the Federal Republic of Germany and Professor Minoli from Italy. This group of like-minded friends, joined by others, became known as the "Club de Chambésy".

These founders of ICCA began with a simple proposal: to hold one or more international congresses, open to all, to consider and debate good ideas for the better conduct of international arbitration, without fear or favour – good ideas which have now, fifty years later, become indispensable to arbitration, world trade and even the rule of law.

Now, an idea can be fleeting and ephemeral – born of present circumstance and quickly forgotten. For example, at a time when the Beys of Tunis where the undisputed rulers of Tunisia, it is said that one Bey, during the early part of the nineteenth century, wished to teach the haughty ambassadors of the Western powers a lesson in humility.

He requested all three diplomats in full ambassadorial uniform to prostrate themselves on the floor of his throne room at the outset of their regular audiences. All three politely declined, on the basis that it was not a useful precedent to subject the representatives of the United States of America, France and the British Empire to such unnatural indignities. And so, at the next royal audience, they bowed their heads; but they did *not* prostrate themselves on the palace floor. The Bey's request was nonetheless repeated for the next audience; and for that audience, these proud representatives encountered an apparently insuperable diplomatic problem.

The wily Bey had built a new entrance to his throne room, a doorway less than two feet high, the better to require the ambassadors to prostrate themselves as they squeezed themselves through the new doorway – on the palace floor. But the British ambassador had an idea which was to preserve the dignity of the Empire and which he was prepared to share with his two esteemed diplomatic colleagues from France and the United States. And thus it was that the Bey of Tunis, instead of seeing the three ambassadors prostrate themselves saw, first, the feet and then the rotund behinds of the three ambassadors as they successively wiggled themselves *backwards* through the new doorway into the royal presence.

That British idea, the backward ambassadorial wiggle, however excellent at the time, is not now to be found in any book of diplomatic etiquette.

That is manifestly not so with ICCA, as the forum for ideas planned fifty years ago by the Club de Chambésy for arbitration specialists, then straddling both the massive political divisions during the Cold War and the divide between academic, professional and state practitioners, both "*privatistes*" and "*publicistes*"; and both lawyers and non-lawyers.

You will recall that in April 1961, the United States and Cuba nearly went to war over the incident at the Bay of Pigs; that in June 1961 Kennedy and Khrushchev held a most unsatisfactory summit in Vienna; and that in August 1961, the USSR and the GDR began building the Berlin Wall. Apart from ICCA's foundation, 1961 was not a good year.

ICCA's story begins, however, before 1961. The Club de Chambésy had its origins first at the United Nations Convention of 1958 in New York, attended by Professor Sanders and other members, including Professor Bülow and Dr.Dr. Glossner. The same group of friends was already working on the long-drawn-out negotiations for the European Convention on International Commercial Arbitration; and they were present when this Convention was eventually signed on 21 April 1961 in Geneva. This 1961 Geneva Convention included an Annex and Special Committee intended to provide a new framework for trade between free market economies and socialist economies in the Soviet bloc. Hence the Club's meetings at the Relais de Chambésy, with a special interest in dispute resolution for East-West Trade. If Napoleon really said: "*C'est la soupe qui fait le soldat*", then we can say that the menu of this Swiss restaurant had much to do with the making of ICCA.

Within a month of the Geneva Convention, the first ICCA Congress took place in Paris over three days in May 1961, with Jean Robert as the rapporteur-general. There were 162 delegates from 14 countries, of which 74 came from France. There were, however, only three countries from outside Western Europe: the United States of America, Turkey and Yugoslavia.

This first congress was attended by, amongst others, Professor Sanders, Professor Berthold Goldman and senior French judges. One of the papers presented to the first of its four working groups was by a young Professor Frédéric-Edouard Klein from Basel University on the separabilty of the arbitration clause (to which we shall return).

The second ICCA Congress took place in Rotterdam in 1966, with 130 delegates from 14 countries. Again, these countries were largely from Western Europe, with the addition of the United States of America, Romania and Yugoslavia. The theme of this Congress was "Arbitration and the European Common Market". Its president was Professor Sanders. It was also attended, amongst others, by Professor Pierre Lalive.

For the United Kingdom, as with the first congress, this second congress was attended by few arbitration specialists; and, of these, only two names stand out today as representatives of the ICC's National Committee for the United Kingdom. Perhaps the European theme of the Congress put others off: the United Kingdom was not then a member of the Common Market; but, in any event, there were no Wilberforces, Diplocks, Kerrs, Mustills, Littmanns or Manns. The first well-known English name was Lord Tangley, who was a mountaineer and solicitor who later became the President of the ICC Court of Arbitration. The second was Neil Pearson, a solicitor from Manchester, who attended all these early congresses.

Neil Pearson soon became better known as the chairman of the first ICC tribunal to be ordered by the English High Court, in 1972, to state its award in the form of a Special Case for the decision of the High Court, a form of *lèse-majesté* against the ICC in Paris. That was later purged by two successive English Arbitration Acts 1979 and 1986 abolishing the Special Case; but it left England in French eyes on permanent probation as still capable of refusing to enforce a valid French ICC award under the New York Convention. In fact, of course, that is today an unthinkable impossibility. (I stress the word "valid"). It seems surprisingly hard for the French to forget Clemenceau's famous judgment, for arbitration as for much else, that England "is a French colony which failed".

The third ICCA Congress took place in Venice in 1969, with delegates from twenty-six countries and chaired by Professor Eugenio Minoli (then of Modena University and the President of the Italian Arbitration Association). These twenty-six countries now included India, Poland and the USSR, together with representatives from the United Nations and the World Bank, the latter represented by Dr. Aaron Broches, as the General Counsel of the World Bank and ICSID's first Secretary-General. It was also attended from the USSR by Professor S.N. Bratus and Professor Sergei Lebedev. (We shall return to several of these names).

The fourth ICCA Congress was held in Moscow in 1972, with delegates from thirty-six countries, now covering East and West, North and South. By this time, ICCA had achieved what no other arbitral body had ever achieved: it was worldwide, inclusive, non-national, non-political, free-thinking and truly international; and it was attracting arbitration specialists from all walks of life, from both the developed and developing world: academics, practitioners, administrators, officers of state and, of course, arbitrators, both lawyers and non-lawyers, including (from London) the doyen of English commercial arbitrators, Cedric Barclay.

The fifth ICCA Congress took place in New Delhi in 1975, organized by Dr. M.N. Krishnamurthi, with delegates from forty-three countries. Here, ICCA's status and name were formalized with its Statements of Purposes and Procedures. This non-constitution, for a non-organization, was the product of negotiations first begun in Moscow conducted by Judge Howard Holtzmann (of the United States) and Professor Lebedev, designed to square the political circle between an international "organization" (which specialists from the USSR and other countries could not join without further awkward formalities) and a "network" or council (in which representatives from those countries could take part). With only minor amendments, that Statement of Purposes and Procedures still governs the workings of ICCA in its three complimentary roles:

As to ICCA Congresses, since 1975, there have been a further twenty-one ICCA Congresses, Conferences and Meetings, including tomorrow's, held in North and South America, Europe, the Middle East and Asia, but not Africa – at least not yet.

As to ICCA publications, ICCA has published a mass of specialist legal materials, collections and research. The records of its early Congresses were published in the *Revue de l'arbitrage* and also by host organizations; but since 1976, its materials have been published by Kluwer. These extend to the multi-volumed *International Handbook on Commercial Arbitration* and the ICCA *Yearbooks* and Special Series, to which we must now add the increasingly indispensable ICCA website.

ICCA's educational third role is now no less important than its other two roles, both for senior judges confronting the 1958 New York Convention and UNCITRAL Model Law and young arbitration practitioners, more skilled and more numerous than ever before.

But I come back to ICCA's function as a forum of ideas, or catalyst, working as a laboratory and not as a museum. I can take only one example tonight, an idea so simple but so necessary to international arbitration: the severability or separablity or autonomy of the arbitration clause from the substantive contract in which it is physically embedded, whereby the non-existence or invalidity of the latter does not necessarily infect the existence or validity of the former.

This doctrine of separability is, of course, a legal fiction; the product of arbitral logic which bears no foundation in fact because no commercial person considers making two quite separate, independent agreements in one contract; but, without this simple idea, there could be no effective system of arbitration for international trade but, rather, a multiplicity of proceedings in a Legal Tower of Babel with non-stop (not one-stop) adjudications. It is an idea which shows how ICCA's forum for ideas works, both in theory and practice; and why only ICCA could have worked in this way.

Let me explain. At ICCA's first congress in Paris in 1961, as recited above, one topic was the autonomy of the arbitration clause; and the report and discussion were published by ICCA. At the third congress in Venice in 1969 and the fourth in Moscow in 1972, Professor Bratus attended as one of the foremost Soviet lawyers and arbitrators. It is inconceivable that Professor Bratus and his colleagues were not exposed through ICCA to the legal developments in France, Germany, Switzerland (and elsewhere) on the separability of an arbitration clause, including the French decision in *Gosset* (1962), the US Supreme Court decision in *Prima Paint* (1967) and the Bundesgerichtshof decision of 27 February 1970.

Much later, in 1984, Professor Bratus, as an arbitrator in a Soviet arbitration in Moscow, issued an award recognizing and applying under Russian law the doctrine of separability in a case where the substantive agreement was legally invalid ab initio, thereby assuming jurisdiction over the merits of the parties' non-contractual dispute. That had never been done before by any Russian arbitrator or judge; and it was achieved as a matter of legal logic, independently from any express provision in the Russian Civil Code or Code of Civil Procedure.

In 1989, that award was then enforced under the 1958 New York Convention by the Bermuda Court of Appeal in proceedings where legal experts had testified as to the comparative laws and practices on the separability of an arbitration clause. These experts were Professor Goldman and Dr. Broches, both, of course, well-known participants in ICCA Congresses. Dr. Broches was also assisted by the former legal secretary to Professor Sanders, who was by now the General Editor of the ICCA *Yearbook*, as he is still: Professor Albert Jan van den Berg.

But this story does not end here. The successful Counsel in this Bermudian case was a well-known advocate in England, originally from South Africa, Sir Sydney Kentridge QC. In a subsequent English case argued in 1993, before the English Court of Appeal, Sydney Kentridge cited this Bermudian judgment in support of his argument on separability under English law. The Court of Appeal decided to adopt the same approach, based on the Soviet award and the expert evidence and materials cited in the Bermudian legal proceedings. That was done in England at common law, likewise as a matter of legal logic, without benefit of any statute; and the principle is now codified in Sect. 7 of the English Arbitration Act 1996.

So, an idea which was propagated in Paris at the first ICCA Congress in 1961 led to statutory recognition by the British Parliament in 1996, thirty-five years later, which is a relatively short period for arbitral history. Some might say "better late than never" (although it took France almost fifty years to codify *Gosset*); but let us rather thank ICCA and its early supporters for pursing an idea as a cause with a manifestly good effect in very different legal systems.

So much for history. As to the future, what good ideas may come from ICCA over the next fifty years, which several of you here tonight will surely celebrate in 2061? There are certain catalytic reactions which are already taking place. Let me list four:

First, there were no women at Chambésy; and there were, apparently, no women speakers at ICCA's first five congresses. Yet, in many countries now, over 50 per cent of law students are women. That change is not reflected in the composition of arbitration tribunals and senior practitioners. We do not know the identity of the first woman arbitrator in modern times; but it was certainly not before 1961. It may have been

Margaret Rutherford QC in England, or Professor Bastid in France, or Madame Simone Rozés as an ICC arbitrator or possibly Judge Birgitta Blom as an arbitrator at the SCC. Fifty years later, changes are taking place; and we shall see further changes.

Second, ICCA in 1961 was inevitably Euro-centric. Its founders made determined efforts to break the European mould, with increasing success. We shall certainly see further changes in the practice of international arbitration, particularly in Asia and Africa; and, as you will know, the next ICCA Congress in 2012 will take place in Singapore.

Third, there were few young practitioners in ICCA's early days. That has now changed with the emergence of a new young arbitral élite, with specialist education, training and experience in all forms of international arbitration, with multiple skills, multiple languages and evermore glittering résumés. These young specialists will influence significantly the future practice of international arbitration.

Fourth, there were no computers, electronic aids or e-mails for arbitrators and arbitration practitioners in 1961. Now we have not only personal computers but also iPhones, iPads, Skype and apps (as with the SIAC App). Soon, we shall each have an "EAB", an Electronic Arbitral Bag with ready access to all electronic tools and materials in an electronic super-cloud, including ICCA publications and much, much more. Our system of work is about to undergo a massive technological change.

So the future is bright both for ICCA and international arbitration, as the attendance at this anniversary event demonstrates. ICCA's positive catalyst still works. I shall stop here, because, tomorrow morning, we too must work.

Introduction to ICCA'S 50th Anniversary Conference

Gabrielle Kaufmann-Kohler[*]

The purpose of this exceptional ICCA conference is to take some distance from day-to-day issues and reflect on the future of international arbitration. For an intelligent reflection on the future, one must start by asking what the present state of arbitration is. Where have these last fifty years led us? In other words, "where are we"? Only when this question is answered, can we turn to the next one: "where are we going?" or what will the future be? What changes will it bring and how should we adapt to the future or seek to influence it?

To answer these questions, the ICCA members who have designed the program of today – and I would like to acknowledge the contribution of Donald Donovan, Albert Jan van den Berg and Jan Paulsson – have sought to gather some of the brightest contemporary minds on these issues. We are very privileged that they have all accepted our invitation. And since there are many bright minds in the audience as well, we will make sure that there is sufficient time for floor discussions.

The morning session will be devoted to "where we are" and divided in two sessions, one about commercial arbitration and one on investment arbitration. Some of you may find part of the debate somewhat theoretical. It is true that the forthcoming presentations are not about recipes of how to be a good arbitrator or a good advocate. However, they are indispensable groundwork to understand where we are and, from there, where we are going.

The afternoon session will be devoted to the future or where we are going. What changes are coming? While the morning sessions follow a traditional format of Reports and Comments, the afternoon will take the form of a round table debate with ten participants selected to represent as many different perspectives as possible.

---

* Professor, Geneva University Law School; Director, Geneva Master in International Dispute Settlement; Honorary President Swiss Arbitration Association; Partner, Lévy Kaufmann-Kohler; Member of ICCA.

The Present –

Commercial Arbitration as a Transnational System of Justice

The Present – Commercial Arbitration as a Transnational System of Justice:

Introduction to the Session

Albert Jan van den Berg[*]

Ladies and Gentlemen, Friends,

This is a glorious occasion: celebrating half a century of ICCA. Last night, we heard Johnny Veeder make a fair attempt at revisionist history writing.[1] One thing seems historically correct: what started as a club of friends in the 1960s got its final name in 1975 – "International Council for *Commercial* Arbitration", in short ICCA. Looking at the program of today, I wondered whether the name should be changed into "International Council of *Commercial and Investment* Arbitration", in short ICCIA. I discarded that idea mainly for three reasons. First, the new abbreviation posed some problems of its own. The present one, ICCA, is also the abbreviation of the International Congress and Convention Association. *Soit*. But a Google search reveals that the abbreviation of ICCIA stands, amongst other things, for International Close Combat Instructors Association. That would be heads on with the peaceful means of conflict resolution that the genuine ICCA pursues. Second, ICCA is a household brand for independent publications and congresses. The Coca Cola amongst the arbitration clubs. Third, the numbers. In terms of percentages, international commercial arbitration cases are more than 95 percent of the number of international arbitration cases. Less than 5 percent is investment arbitration. To back this up: UNCTAD reported some twenty-five new investment cases

---

* General Editor of ICCA.

1. See "Gala Dinner Address: Memories from ICCA's First Fifty Years", this volume, pp. 5-10. A contemporaneous account can be found in N. KRISHNAMURTHI, "Fifth International Arbitration Congress – New Dehli 1975", in ICCA *Yearbook Commercial Arbitration* I (1976) pp. 227-223, who writes at p. 232 under the heading "International Council for Commercial Arbitration":

   "The International Council for Commercial Arbitration which is the body for the organization of the Congresses also held their deliberations during the period of the Congress. *Born in 1969*, in Venice, with the late lamented Dr. [Eugenio] Minoli, as its first President, it was then named as the International Committee for Commercial Arbitration and had a small number of persons as its members. Its activities, range of work and membership gradually enlarged. At the Moscow Congress in 1972, the Committee was expanded to give representation to more countries.... The Committee has been functioning without a written Constitution. At New Delhi, a 'Statement of Purposes and Procedures', which is to be its Charter was adopted. Its name was also changed into International Council for Commercial Arbitration (ICCA), in recognition of its growing status." (Emphasis added.)

   Does this mean that we will have a second celebration of ICCA's 50th anniversary in Venice in 2019?

over 2010. The International Chamber of Commerce alone reported some 600 new cases over 2010. Both figures may have to be adjusted, but the 5 percent figure of investment cases is close to the mark. I don't say this to diminish the importance of the second session of our program that deals with investment arbitration. I do say it to give you a reality check. A majority of the publications and conferences today concern investment arbitration and give you the impression that that is what international arbitration is about. Reality is quite different. Arbitration still comprises in large majority commercial disputes. So, those of you who think that your career should be in investment arbitration or that the direction of your law firm should be in this area, you may be disappointed in the future. My advice is: start to concentrate on international commercial arbitration, and only if the occasion arises, venture into the territory of investment arbitration.

The subject of the present session is "Commercial Arbitration as a Transnational System of Justice". The adjective "transnational" raises the question whether international commercial arbitration can function without the national courts. We are very privileged to have here the two main protagonists of each view: with or without the national courts. Michael Reisman will give his report about the state of the art of what he believes is a distinction between primary and secondary jurisdiction (pp. 17-65). Emmanuel Gaillard will comment on it by representing to you that everything with a label "arbitration" that comes from outside of France originates from international justice (pp. 66-73). The two other distinguished commentators, Luca Radicati di Brozolo (pp. 74-102) and Karim Youssef (pp. 103-132), have their own very interesting views on the subject as well.

All these presentations may leave you with a number of questions. On one thing the presenters of the present session could agree: we will keep to our time so that the participants can ask the questions they want. So, don't blame the reporter and commentators on the brevity of their presentations. They do that in your interest. If you wish to know all the nuances, I suggest that you read their extensive report and comments in the conference materials.

Tribunals and Courts: An Interpretation of the Architecture of International Commercial Arbitration

W. Michael Reisman[*] *and Brian Richardson*[**]

TABLE OF CONTENTS

	Page
I. Introduction	17
II. The Normative Architecture of International Commercial Arbitration: The New York Convention of 1958	20
III. Recent Initiatives to Change the Control Scheme of International Commercial Arbitration	32
IV. Conclusion	64

I. INTRODUCTION

Advocates of arbitration often assume, in a type of anarcho-capitalist fantasy,[1] that arbitration is a free-standing procedure, conceptually and politically quite independent of the apparatus of the state. But international commercial arbitration, no less than arbitration within nation-states, while conducted in the sphere of private law, is a public legal creation whose operation and effectiveness is inextricably linked to prescribed actions by national courts. Anarchic or libertarian impulses may lead some to look nostalgically back to phenomena like private dispute settlement arrangements in medieval merchant associations and "Pie Powder" courts at the medieval fairs.[2] Those

---

* McDougal Professor of International Law, Yale Law School. Parts of this Report draw on previous work by the author in this area. Readers who wish to consult more detailed discussions of many of the points here may find them in W. Michael REISMAN, *Systems of Control in International Adjudication and Arbitration* (1992); and W. Michael REISMAN, "Reflections on the Control Mechanism of the ICSID System" in Emmanuel GAILLARD, ed., *IAI Series on International Arbitration No. 6. The Review of International Arbitral Awards,* at p. 197 (2010). The authors acknowledge the contributions of Heide M. Iravani to several sections of this report, as well as extremely helpful comments from John Barkett and Albert Jan van den Berg.

** Yale Law School, J.D. 2011.

1. Murray N. ROTHBARD, *Power and Market*, 4th edn. (2006) p. 4, p. 10 (noting, by way of introduction, that "the Argentinean ... lives in a state of 'anarchy,' of non-government, in relation to the citizens of Uruguay – or of Ceylon. And yet the private citizens of these and other countries live and trade together without getting into insoluble legal conflicts." He continues: "a truly free market is totally incompatible with the existence of a State".).

2. See, e.g., Amalia KESSLER, "Enforcing Virtue: Social Norms and Self-Interest in an Eighteenth-Century Merchant Court", 22 Law and History Rev. (2004, no. 1) p. 71; Harold J. BERMAN and Felix J. DASSER, "The 'New' Law Merchant and the 'Old': Sources, Content, and Legitimacy" in Thomas E. CARBONNEAU, ed., *Lex Mercatoria and Arbitration*, (1990) Ch. 2; *Select Cases Concerning the Law Merchant* p. 23, p. 46, p. 49 (edited for the Selden Soc. by Charles Gross, 1908-1932); Wyndham Anstis BEWES, *The Romance of the Law Merchant* (1923); Charles Gross, "The Court of Piepowder", 20 Q.J. Econ. (Feb. 1906) p. 231 at pp. 231-249; Frances M. BURDICK,

who wish to think of arbitration without any role for government can say that these medieval arbitrations were truly independent of the state; they may also point to the felicitous fact that most contemporary international arbitration awards seem to win voluntary compliance. But how much voluntary compliance with adverse awards would occur if there were no courts in the background poised to enforce them? As for those courts, how willing would they and the governments (whose instruments they are) be to co-sign a "blank check" for enforcement if their own public interests were not assured? Arbitration tribunals and national courts are certainly very different but they are inseparable. How they are joined is the essential, the existential question of all forms of arbitration.

The anarcho-capitalist fallacy also tends to ignore the essentially democratic basis of all legal arrangements in modern societies.[3] Legal arrangements which fail to win significant constituencies will be doomed to failure or compelled to change. In commercial arbitration, the outcomes of this political process are usually registered in adjustments in judicial practices with respect to the arbitral process, but its sources are almost always to be found in pressure from larger social formations. We believe that this is key to understanding the current initiatives to secure "fairness in arbitration", but it is evident in many other areas of public disagreement about some aspect of the structure and scope of private decision and its proper relation to the institutions of public power.

Any legal system that has elected to permit, much less encourage, arbitration has to decide how to structure the relationship between private arbitral tribunals and public courts. The analogy of freedom to contract here can be misleading, for the issue is not the freedom to fashion private arrangements in what Hart conceived as the moral sphere, and Lasswell and McDougal "the civic order".[4] It is, rather, the availability of *public* power to compel compliance with these private arrangements, whatever their content, when one party to them defects from its agreement.[5]

Each government's posture with respect to private decision procedures reflects two concerns: first, how much to control its substance without "killing" it, i.e., denying its citizens a freedom many wish and denying itself the economies attendant on the privatization of any governmental function. Second, how much to control its procedures to ensure that private decision-makers execute their delegation without falling prey to moral hazard.

"What is the Law Merchant?", 2 Columbia L. Rev. (Nov. 1902) p. 470.

3. We do, however, take the point that the tension between arbitration "worldviews" can often be overdrawn. See John M. BARKETT and Jan PAULSSON, "The Myth of Culture Clash in International Commercial Arbitration", 5 Fla. Int'l U. L. Rev. (2009) p. 1.

4. See generally H.L.A. HART, "Are There Any Natural Rights?", 64 Phil. Rev. (1955) p. 175; and Harold D. LASSWELL and Myres S. MCDOUGAL, *Jurisprudence for a Free Society: Studies in Law, Science, and Policy*, vol. 1 (1992) pp. 365-368.

5. Here the idea of arbitration has the feature of realist criticism of property rights; while there is a contract between parties in any arbitration, it is always *endorsed* by the state. See Felix S. COHEN, "Dialogue on Private Property", 9 Rutgers L. Rev. (1954) p. 357 at pp. 373-374: "Suppose we say, that is property to which the following label can be attached. To the world: Keep off X unless you have my permission, which I may grant or withhold. Signed: Private Citizen[.] Endorsed: The state."

Clearly, the decision to externalize some competences to make decisions which will be enforced by the operation of state power must be accompanied by putting some controls in place to address the ever present problem of moral hazard. This is a constant challenge in every delegation of power. Without such controls, limited power would become unlimited and rational actors would have little incentive to turn to arbitration. Alternatively, *excessive* control by courts would obviate the advantages of private dispute resolution. After all, why arbitrate if the winner must then "sue on the award", i.e., after the award has been rendered the dispute must be litigated all over again in court?

Thus the relationship between private commercial arbitration and national courts tasked with the responsibility of enforcement must seek, in the most general terms, to accommodate two sometimes-competing interests: fairness and finality. In the normative space bounded by these interests, a range of possible relationships varying in scope of delegation, control mechanisms and enforcement arrangements can be imagined; any comparative examination of the treatment of domestic arbitration *within* nation-states boasting of developed legal systems illustrates this diversity.

Even though domestic and international commercial arbitration use the same vocabulary and the same essential techniques, the normative space for experimentation in international commercial arbitration is more constrained than in domestic arbitration. In transnational contracts, each rational party seeks to deal with the uncertainty of the rules of jurisdictional allocation in public international law: in the absence of an agreement on where disputes will be heard, either party may be able to find a willing forum which will take its case and, it hopes, tilt in its favor. Since each party is concerned that the other may move first, there is an inherent pressure to litigate, if only to preempt the other from suing in a court more favorable to it. But by adopting an arbitration clause which is internationally enforceable and which ensures a pre-agreed neutral decision-maker, the latent conflict-generating dynamic and the consequent threat of a rush to the "wrong" courthouse is contained. The point is that international commercial arbitration has a *problematique* different from its domestic counterpart and the legal matrix for its operation must be assessed in terms of its own context and challenges.

Each government's decision about its posture with respect to private decision-making for its domestic or non-international disputes will be determined by national values, national legal culture and the relative political power of internal constituencies. But *transnational* private decision, while using many of the same arbitral techniques which resonate to the same values, must also address other problems.

Modern governments encourage their citizens to engage in foreign economic activities but the prospect of their having to litigate in foreign courts could deter them from engaging in foreign ventures. And not without reason: many national courts lack independence, impartiality or high levels of some legal skills. So the provision for and support of arrangements for private decision, while essentially a matter of choice domestically, is actually *required* when the focus shifts outward to transnational economic exchanges which the state wishes to encourage.

When a government devises an arrangement between *domestic* arbitral tribunals and its own courts, it is operating within a single judicial institution of whose strengths and weaknesses it is aware. In transnational exchanges, by contrast, a large number of national court systems are involved and their strengths, weaknesses and cultural values vary widely. The national courts of some of the states participating in the arrangements may come close to being paragons of judicial virtue. The national courts of others do not. No surprise then that the interstate collaboration in establishing a common arrangement for the relation between arbitral tribunals and courts produces arrangements that may differ from their respective domestic arbitral arrangements and may even differ from their other conflicts of law or private international law arrangements.

When a government devises an arrangement between its domestic arbitral tribunals and its own courts, it is ordinarily contemplating a transaction within a single "judicial space", *viz.*, its own territory and jurisdiction. By contrast, in transnational exchanges, relevant events as well as phases of arbitration may take place in the judicial spaces of many states. Award enforcement may engage a number of different jurisdictions simultaneously or sequentially; the absence of uniformity and treatment in them poses a concern that does not arise in domestic arbitration.

In this paper, we first describe the distribution of competences between national courts and arbitral tribunals in the authoritative system of international commercial arbitration since 1958. These components are, of course, familiar to this audience but, as we explain, we believe that together they reflect a cogent strategy for ensuring the efficient operation of international commercial arbitration. We then briefly examine six initiatives, some undertaken by states' legislatures, some by their courts, some by private parties, and some by scholars, which have sought to change or respond to challenges to the internationally prescribed relationship between arbitral tribunals and courts. Some of these initiatives are recent, some of earlier vintage. Some, we will suggest, may address and offer sound remedies to obstacles that have emerged to the efficient functioning of the relationship as designed in 1958, while others may threaten it.

II. THE NORMATIVE ARCHITECTURE OF INTERNATIONAL COMMERCIAL ARBITRATION: THE NEW YORK CONVENTION OF 1958

The effectiveness of private international commercial arbitration depends on substantial and predictable governmental and intergovernmental support. In any arbitral system, states, through their courts, can, according to the particular legal arrangement in place, play a role *before* the arbitration commences, *during* the arbitration, or *after* an award has been rendered. Two of these points, the "before" and "after", are critical for the effectiveness of any system of arbitration, be it domestic or international. The third point, the "middle", is anodyne in domestic arbitration, but can prove problematic for international commercial arbitration.

An arbitration clause between parties from different jurisdictions will only be effective if the courts in *all* relevant jurisdictions will refuse to exercise judicial jurisdiction over the case – other, perhaps, than to compel, on request, the reluctant party to repair to arbitration. Thus neither party will be able to ignore the arbitration clause and try to shunt the dispute to what it believes to be a court favorable to it. At the other end of the arbitral process, parties are unlikely to invest the time and money necessary to prosecute an arbitration if, upon award, the loser cannot be compelled to honor it at the place where it has assets. In the course of an arbitration, actions necessary to prosecute the arbitration and orders that a tribunal may issue, but which it will be unable to implement, may require the support of national courts – either at the place of arbitration or elsewhere.

Legal planning tries to take account of what may go wrong, but principally is animated by a healthy skepticism about human nature and assumes the omnipresence of the "bad man". Since an unscrupulous party can exploit differences in the various pertinent jurisdictions' legal arrangements, opportunities to frustrate an international commercial arbitration abound. National courts may become unwilling tools in such efforts, yet they are also the critical and indispensable defense against them. But national courts would not be effective without the aid of two coinciding elements:

(1) international agreements among all the pertinent jurisdictions, establishing common arrangements to compel arbitrations to which parties have contractually committed themselves and to enforce the awards that ensue; and
(2) domestic legislation in support of arbitration in the various jurisdictions which is compatible with the international arrangements.[6]

The building materials available to the architects of the international commercial arbitral system are limited. They have had to adapt and channel the cooperation of the only agencies which are readily available: national judicial systems. The Convention on the Recognition and Enforcement of Foreign Arbitral Awards, signed in New York in 1958 (New York Convention), is the most comprehensive and, until now, successful effort to do this.[7] It locates its control mechanism in the national courts of its States Parties, while at the same time seeking to limit that control on the assumption that if national courts delve too far into the substance of the disputes in the "before", "middle" or "after" phases, they may be prone to favor their native sons over the invariably foreign counterparty. The Convention has been adopted by 146 states,[8] and for all intents and purposes, that part of the world which is most actively engaged in international commercial arbitration operates under its regime.[9]

The New York Convention applies to foreign awards, which include awards rendered abroad as well as awards rendered within the state in which enforcement is sought if the state chooses to characterize them as "non-domestic". Art. I(1) provides:

> "This Convention shall apply to the recognition and enforcement of arbitral awards made in the territory of a State other than the State where the recognition and enforcement of such awards are sought, and arising out of differences between

6. See, e.g., Australian International Arbitration Act and Australian International Arbitration Amendment Act 1989; Korean Arbitration Act; Swiss Law on Private International Law; Swiss Law on Private International Law (Arbitration, Jurisdiction) Amendment of 6 Oct. 2006.
7. Convention on the Recognition and Enforcement of Foreign Arbitral Awards, 21 U.S.T. 2517, T.I.A.S. No. 6997, 330 U.N.T.S. 38 (hereinafter New York Convention).
8. Status, 1958 Convention in the Recognition and Enforcement of Foreign Arbitral Awards, available at <www.uncitral.org/uncitral/en/uncitral_texts/arbitration/NYConvention_status.html>.
9. For early experiments, see Geneva Protocol on Arbitration Clauses (1923); Geneva Protocol for the Pacific Settlement of International Disputes (1924); Geneva Convention on the Execution of Foreign Arbitral Awards (1927).

persons, whether physical or legal. It shall also apply to arbitral awards not considered as domestic awards in the State where their recognition and enforcement are sought."

Art. I(2) extends the reach of the Convention to both ad hoc arbitrations as well as awards emanating from "permanent arbitral bodies".

With regard to arbitration agreements meeting the requirements of Art. I, the Convention obliges the courts of any contracting state to compel arbitration if a party to a written agreement to arbitrate that satisfies the personal and material requirements of the Convention seeks instead to initiate court action in its territory, and the would-be defendant – the other party to the arbitration agreement – insists upon its right to arbitration. Art. II(3) provides:

> "The Court of a Contracting State, when seized of an action in a matter in respect of which the parties have made an agreement within the meaning of this article, shall, at the request of one of the parties, refer the parties to arbitration, unless it finds that the said agreement is null and void, inoperative or incapable of being performed."

Note that there is no obligation to compel arbitration if the arbitration agreement invoked is "null and void, inoperative or incapable of being performed".[10]

At the back-end of the process, the Convention provides for the recognition and enforcement of awards that qualify under its terms. Art. III provides:

> "Each Contracting State shall recognize arbitral awards as binding and enforce them in accordance with the rules of procedure of the territory where the award is relied upon, under the conditions laid down in the following articles. There shall not be imposed substantially more onerous conditions or higher fees or charges on the recognition or enforcement of arbitral awards to which this Convention applies than are imposed on the recognition or enforcement of domestic arbitral awards."

The technical requirements referred to in Art. III are set out in Art. IV.[11] The other,

---

10. The national court which has been petitioned may also refuse recognition and enforcement, even when there is an agreement, if it finds that its own law does not permit arbitration of the subject matter of the dispute. These exceptions should not be interpreted as weakening the regime. By providing explicit and carefully bounded safety valves for precisely those arbitral matters which national legal systems would find difficult to compel or enforce, they greatly reinforce expectations of enforceability of all the other matters (and they are the vast majority) in this regime. See discussion infra.

11. Art. IV states:

> "1. To obtain the recognition and enforcement mentioned in the preceding article, the party applying for recognition and enforcement shall, at the time of the application, supply:
> (*a*) The duly authenticated original award or a duly certified copy thereof;

less technical conditions, which have the potential for allowing the national legal values of the enforcement arena to intrude into the decision of the arbitrator, do not exclude the application of national law, but insulate the foreign award from discrimination by requiring that whatever conditions the national court imposes be no more onerous than those set out in the Convention.[12]

The Convention's conditions are set out in Art. V. As part of its enforcement system, the Convention establishes grounds on which a national court in which recognition or enforcement is sought may deny the request. The first paragraph of Art. V provides:

> "1. Recognition and enforcement of the award may be refused, at the request of the party against whom it is invoked, only if that party furnishes to the competent authority where the recognition and enforcement is sought, proof that:
> (*a*) The parties to the agreement referred to in Article II were, under the law applicable to them, under some incapacity, or the said agreement is not valid under the law to which the parties have subjected it or, failing any indication thereon, under the law of the country where the award was made; or
> (*b*) The party against whom the award is invoked was not given proper notice of the appointment of the arbitrator or of the arbitration proceedings or was otherwise unable to present his case; or
> (*c*) The award deals with a difference not contemplated by or not falling within the terms of the submission to arbitration, or it contains decisions on matters beyond the scope of the submission to arbitration, provided that, if the decisions on matters submitted to arbitration can be separated from those not so submitted, that part of the award which contains decisions on matters submitted to arbitration may be recognized and enforced; or
> (*d*) The composition of the arbitral authority or the arbitral procedure was not in accordance with the agreement of the parties, or, failing such agreement, was not in accordance with the law of the country where the arbitration took place; or
> (*e*) The award has not yet become binding on the parties, or has been set aside or suspended by a competent authority of the country in which, or under the law of which, that award was made."

In addition to these grounds, Art. V(2) sets out two additional justifications for refusing to enforce:

(*b*)The original agreement referred to in Article II or a duly certified copy thereof.
2. If the said award or agreement is not made in an official language of the country in which the award is relied upon, the party applying for recognition and enforcement of the award shall produce a translation of these documents into such language. The translation shall be certified by an official or sworn translator or by a diplomatic or consular agent."

12. Thus Sect. 208 of the United States Federal Arbitration Act (FAA) provides that the law for domestic arbitration, in Chapter 1, "applies to actions and proceedings brought under this chapter to the extent that chapter is not in conflict with this chapter or the Convention as ratified by the United States".

> "2. Recognition and enforcement of an arbitral award may also be refused if the competent authority in the country where recognition and enforcement is sought finds that:
> (*a*) The subject matter of the difference is not capable of settlement by arbitration under the law of that country; or
> (*b*) The recognition or enforcement of the award would be contrary to the public policy of that country."

The two additional grounds, set out in Art. V(2), function, in our view, as safety valves. A national court petitioned to enforce may refuse to do so, not because the award fails to meet some of the international standards of the Convention, but because its enforcement would offend the court's fundamental domestic policies. These safety valves, by making explicit what national courts would probably be pressed to do anyway under endogamous political pressure, make adherence to the Convention easier and may actually reinforce expectations of enforceability. To be precise, they are not, in our view, grounds of nullity but rather grounds for non-enforcement, a distinction which acquires importance in reference to the differences between primary and secondary forums in the scheme of the Convention; we will turn to this in a moment. They are of less interest to us and seem to have proved to be comparatively less important in the history of the Convention than are the alternative grounds that constitute the international control system.

The regime in Art. V is both an enforcement mechanism and a policy statement about the proper scope of arbitral control. Incorporating, as it does, the courts of many different but coarchical national jurisdictions for particular types of disputes that are expected to involve more than one jurisdiction, it must evince as well a private international law system of allocation of competence. This allocative function of international law is necessitated whenever separately organized political communities (often describing themselves as "sovereign") are incorporated into larger interactive processes, such that a significant number of persons, things and events may become subject to simultaneous or sequential regulation by different communities. By allocating among the various states or state-groupings competences to make and apply law for these persons, things and events, and recognizing and by giving effect to the proper application of those competences, private international law makes possible productive processes of interaction and exchanges between individuals and entities from different communities.

This point bears emphasis. Because international commercial arbitration is a transnational phenomenon, it is always an event which by definition is subject to the simultaneous or sequential competences of at least two states. Hence a clear allocation of national competences, as they relate to the regulation of arbitration, is also required. The New York Convention establishes the conditions under which an arbitral event in one jurisdiction will be given full effect in another jurisdiction. But here, as well as in other areas, the control mechanism for the system of allocation is also important. That is the function of Art. V. The grounds of Art. V, which are to be applied by the national courts of States Parties in reciprocal fashion, constitute critical components of the international control system.

Now it is obvious that, in this scheme, an exceedingly fine balance must be struck between arbitral autonomy on the one hand, and the role of national judicial review, on the other, in order for arbitration to remain both an effective and credible method of legal recourse. Too much autonomy for the arbitrators creates a situation of moral hazard. If abuses occur – and the theory of moral hazard holds that they will in the absence of controls – national courts will become increasingly reluctant to grant what amounts to a preferred, fast-track enforcement of awards. But too extensive and searching national judicial review that begins to approximate appeal will transfer real decision power from the arbitration tribunal, selected by the parties in order to be non-national and neutral, to a national court whose party neutrality may be significantly less.

To navigate between these two extremes, the Convention, as we see it, establishes two tiers of review competence, making a distinction between so-called "primary" or "venue" jurisdictions and "secondary" or "enforcement" jurisdictions.[13] Traditionally, the place of arbitration was called the forum and its law, the *lex loci arbitri*. Since those terms are closely related to other functions performed by this venue, a different, though hardly arcane term has been used to refine the focus on the operation of the control system. "Primary" jurisdictions refer to those in which the arbitration was sited and the award was rendered, or (perhaps anachronistically)[14] those whose law governed the award – in other words, the state where the arbitration took place, "the arbitration state", or the state whose law governed the arbitration, the "law state". "Secondary" or "enforcement" jurisdictions include any other jurisdiction, subject to the Convention, in which enforcement is sought.

The carefully prescribed and limited grounds for reviewing an award set out in the Convention serve to restrain secondary jurisdictions – those jurisdictions which a hypothetical loser of a valid award could search out in an effort to undo the award's intended effect, or which an unscrupulous winner of a defective award could seek in order to win enforcement. But the legal effects which the Convention assigns to the national judicial acts of the primary and secondary jurisdictions differ significantly.[15] The

13. Jan Paulsson has criticized the treatment of the distinction we are about to defend. See Jan PAULSSON, "Arbitration in Three Dimensions", Transnat'l Disp. Mgmt. (April 2010) at pp. 1, 7 (arguing that "US federal courts of appeal have invented a distinction of 'primary/secondary' jurisdictions in terms of controlling awards, and assigned the 'primary' appellation to the country where awards are rendered. These US courts have stated that this is their understanding of the New York Convention, which in fact nowhere mentions these terms. It is very difficult to see why their use is helpful, let alone necessary.") We shall elaborate our defense of the primary/secondary distinction in the material that follows.

14. We discuss Professor van den Berg's proposal, in this regard, infra at pp. 62-64.

15. For a concise summary of American courts' articulation of this view, see, e.g., *Yusuf Ahmed Alghanim & Sons v. Toys "R" Us, Inc.*, 126 F.3d 15, 23 (2d Cir. 1997) ("[T]he Convention mandates very different regimes for the review of arbitral awards (1) in the state in which, or under the law of which, the award was made, and (2) in other states where recognition and enforcement are sought. The Convention specifically contemplates that the state in which, or under the law of which, the award is made, will be free to set aside or modify an award in accordance with its domestic arbitral law and its full panoply of express and implied grounds for relief.... However, the Convention is equally clear that when an action for enforcement is brought in a foreign state, the state may refuse to enforce the award only on the grounds explicitly set forth in Art. V of the Convention."). See also *Gulf Petro Trading Company, Inc. v. Nigerian Nat. Petroleum Corp.*, 512 F.3d 742, 746 (5th Cir. 2008). Not surprisingly, national courts and legal scholars have evinced

secondary jurisdiction may only decide whether or not to *enforce* the award. There are not to be any "nullificatory" consequences for decisions in secondary jurisdictions: they are limited to the question of enforcement and only in that secondary forum and have no wider radial effects. By contrast, nullificatory (as opposed to non-enforcement) consequences of decisions in primary jurisdictions have a universal effect. In terms of the dynamic of the Convention, once an award has been set aside in a primary jurisdiction, it is not – as we understand the architecture of the Convention – supposed to be enforceable anywhere else.

Once a venue (or a governing law) is selected, the Convention assigns to these jurisdictions a primacy with regard to the validity of the ultimate award. If an award is rendered, let us say, in Switzerland and is nullified under Swiss law, it is not supposed to be enforced in any other jurisdiction. Otherwise, there would be no difference between primary and secondary fora; and, instead of finality, there would be an incentive to flout it. However, if the award is rendered in Switzerland but *enforcement* is refused in France, where the award debtor has property, the French judgment should have no effect outside of France, even if it explicitly bases itself on a ground of nullity which would have nullified the award everywhere had it been rendered in a primary jurisdiction. The award creditor may still seek enforcement in any other jurisdiction which is party to the Convention. The critical difference between primary and secondary fora, then, is the radius of effects of their respective decisions. As opposed to the nullification of the hypothetical award in Switzerland, which should have universal effect, a putative nullification in France should have no effect beyond France.[16]

---

different positions which we will consider below.

16. A comparable primacy is given to the *law* under which the award was made. This means that if the award were rendered in Switzerland but under, let us say, Indian law (a mix of venue and law available to the parties), and the award were subsequently nullified by an Indian court, that nullification, like nullification in Switzerland, would terminate the validity of the award in all other jurisdictions.

This, while theoretically cogent, may be anachronistic in practice. In terms of the logic and dynamics of a control system, the assignment of primacy coordinately to a legal system whose law the parties had chosen but which has no other connection with the arbitration is puzzling. Control under the New York Convention essentially involves policing procedure and not substance. Thus, a US federal district court in the Southern District of New York ruled, in interpreting the New York Convention, that "the competent authority of the country under the law of which, [the] award was made refers exclusively to procedural and not substantive law, and more precisely, to the regimen or scheme or arbitral procedural law under which the arbitration was conducted, and not the substantive law of contract which was applied in the case". *International Standard Electric Corporation v. Bridas Sociedad Anonima Petrolera Industrial y Comercial*, 745 F.Supp. 172, 178 (S.D.N.Y. 1990).

The court explained its view as follows: "Any suggestion that a Court has jurisdiction to set aside a foreign award based upon the use of its domestic, substantive law in the foreign arbitration defies the logic both of the Convention debates and of the final text, and ignores the nature of the international arbitral system." *Ibid.*, at 177. This particular judgment appears to be a clarification, if not a refinement, of the control system, and the court's approach has been accepted by the Second Circuit Court of Appeals as well as district courts in other jurisdictions. See, e.g., *Yusuf Ahmed Alghanim & Sons, W.L.L. v. Toys "R" Us, Inc.*, 126 F.3d 15, 20 (2d Cir. 1997); *Four Seasons Hotels & Resorts v. Consorcio Barr, S.A.*, 267 F.Supp.2d 1335, 1346 (S.D. Fla. 2003); *Steel Corp. v.*

For a control system like that established in the New York Convention to work, the primary and secondary assignments must be mandatory. Because of the language in the English text of the Convention, the control system has appeared to some to be optional rather than imperative. The text may not be as permissive as some have suggested. It reads, "recognition and enforcement of the award *may* be refused" but may be refused "only" if there is proof of a defect, as detailed by the Convention. The French text, which is equally authentic, suggests that the control system is mandatory,[17] as does the Spanish text.[18] Textual discrepancy between equally authentic languages is not uncommon in multilingual treaties, for the discretionary power intended and expressed in English by "may" is more difficult to convey in some other languages, and the combination of "may ... only", which is, at once, permissive and restrictive, is not easily rendered in many other languages. But focus on text is not the only basis for international legal interpretation.

The New York Convention is a treaty and, as such, falls to be interpreted according to international law, whose interpretative canons are codified in the Vienna Convention on the Law of Treaties (VCLT).[19] The VCLT provides, in brief, for interpretation in good faith in accordance with the plain meaning of the terms of the instrument, read in context, taking account of the major purposes of the drafters, legislative history and subsequent practice.[20] While text is primary, an interpretation which is only textual is

---

Int'l Steel Servs., 2006 U.S. Dist. LEXIS 52464 (W.D. Pa. 2006).

See infra, pp. 62-64 et seq., discussing Professor van den Berg's proposal for a "new" New York Convention.

17. The relevant part of the French text states: "*1. La reconnaissance et l'exécution de la sentence ne seront refusées, sur requête de la partie contre laquelle elle est invoquée, que si cette partie fournit à l'autorité compétente du pays où la reconnaissance et l'exécution sont demandées la preuve*[.]"

18. The relevant part of the Spanish text provides: "*1. Sólo se podrá denegar el reconocimiento y la ejecución de la sentencia, a instancia de la parte contra la cual es invocada, si esta parte prueba ante la autoridad competente del país en que se pide el reconocimiento y la ejecución*[.]"

19. See Vienna Convention on the Law of Treaties, adopted 23 May 1969, U.N. Doc. A/CONF./39/27 (1969), reprinted in 63 Am. J. Int'l L. (1969) p. 875.

20. Art. 31 of the VCLT provides:

"1. A treaty shall be interpreted in good faith in accordance with the ordinary meaning to be given to the terms of the treaty in their context and in the light of its object and purpose.
2. The context for the purpose of the interpretation of a treaty shall comprise, in addition to the text, including its preamble and annexes:
(a) any agreement relating to the treaty which was made between all the parties in connection with the conclusion of the treaty;
(b) any instrument which was made by one or more parties in connection with the conclusion of the treaty and accepted by the other parties as an instrument related to the treaty.
3. There shall be taken into account, together with the context:
(a) any subsequent agreement between the parties regarding the interpretation of the treaty or the application of its provisions;
(b) any subsequent practice in the application of the treaty which establishes the agreement of the parties regarding its interpretation;
(c) any relevant rules of international law applicable in the relations between the parties.
4. A special meaning shall be given to a term if it is established that the parties so intended."

not complete. A single provision must be read in the "context" of the rest of the instrument, and, of course, one should seek to accommodate the different but equally authentic language versions in international treaty interpretation, as prescribed by Art. 33 of the VCLT in accordance with the objects and purposes of the treaty.

The English text's arguable allowance of judicial discretion should not, in our view, be taken as an invitation for extended national judicial action. (Fear of just such an *abus de droit* accounts for one of the initiatives to vary the control system; we consider it below.) In keeping with our understanding of the architecture of the Convention, we suggest that the discretionary part of Art. V ought to be understood as a policy decision by the drafters to adopt what has been called elsewhere a "material violation" rather than "technical discrepancy" approach.[21] A realistic system requires that the national court seized of the case be allowed to reserve for itself some prudential discretion to refuse enforcement when the discrepancy that has been raised against enforcement is superficially technical but nevertheless suggests a deeper defect in the ratiocination of the tribunal.

A coherent control theory and a proper interpretation of the texts *require* the national jurisdictions implicated in the arbitration to perform, as the case may be, a primary or secondary control function under Art. V. While that obligation is subject to local interpretation and, inevitably, some variation, the Convention's function as a common matrix for a shared control system would be defeated if there were no such core obligations. Assurances of the performance of primary control functions permit responsible agencies in the secondary states to lend state power to the enforcement of actions that are otherwise privately effected, comparatively unregulated and substantially unchecked. These issues are at the core of one of the initiatives that we will consider.

Some leading scholars have urged an interpretation that would effectively transform the obligations imposed on the primary jurisdiction into matters of discretion. Their objective of this revision is usually to deal with specific miscarriages of justice. Strictly as a textual matter one can press this argument, but international treaty interpretation may not, as said, look only to the text. Moreover, if the regime we have described is optional, it is difficult to see why this part of the treaty was drafted.

The distinction between primary and secondary jurisdictions is, we submit, central to the control system of the New York Convention and has been an important reason for the attractiveness of the regime to its various consumers. Limiting the radial effects of decisions in secondary jurisdictions provides an important protection for the winner and vindicates one of the key reasons for going to international arbitration. Parties initially agree to a jurisdiction for their arbitration in order to avoid the potential bias of a particular national court or courts which might have a predilection for its own national or affiliate. But arbitration is not an autonomous system, as we stated at the outset; its functioning is inextricably linked to national courts. Because there is no international arbitral sheriff to enforce an award, those same national courts that could be skirted in the earlier phases must then be recruited for enforcement once an award is rendered.

21. See W. Michael REISMAN, *Systems of Control in International Adjudication and Arbitration* (1992) pp. 70-71.

And because the loser's national courts may be called on to enforce if the loser, as is likely, keeps substantial assets there and because one of the common purposes of arbitration is to allow the parties to stay out of each other's courts insofar as possible, it is necessary to design a system which confines the radial effects of the res judicata of these secondary enforcers to their own fora in order to avoid the possibility of frustrating the entire arbitration. Otherwise, there would be an ever-present danger that the loser might retreat to its own national courts, there to try to secure the nullification of the award or the enforcement of an award that had been annulled in the primary forum and then to use that judgment as a defense everywhere else.

Confining to a maximum of two (and, in the Van den Berg projet, to one) the jurisdictions which can be "primary" in a particular case is critical to the control scheme. Without the primary-secondary jurisdictional distinction, all States Parties to the New York Convention would be jurisdictionally equal. If any of the 146 fora of the Convention enjoyed the power accorded to primary jurisdictions, the unscrupulous arbitration loser could quickly abandon the neutral forum upon which both parties had agreed and seek a favorably inclined jurisdiction. It could secure a full "nullification" there and even if it could not use it as a defense to enforcement in all other fora, it could continue to frustrate attempts to enforce or continue to try to enforce an award that was annulled.

But this control system must also have a primary jurisdiction in order to anticipate the converse peril. If no forum enjoyed the nullificatory power with universal effect accorded to primary jurisdictions under the Convention, the winner of a defective award could fail in enforcement in any forum and still continue to go to others in an effort at enforcement, harassing the other party and forcing it either to settle for a nuisance value factored by the number of jurisdictions in which it could be pursued, or to expend great amounts of time and effort to block and block again enforcement efforts without ever securing a terminal annulment. Such undesirable effects are limited if only a primary jurisdiction has the capacity to nullify an award *erga omnes.* (The problem of the primary jurisdiction, itself, acting in ways manifestly violative of the role assigned to it in the Convention, which we concede is not hypothetical, and which accounts for some of the proposed changes to the architecture of international commercial arbitration, will be taken up in what follows.)

There are, in our view, good reasons to entrust a particular primary jurisdiction with this exclusive power. It has been selected either by both of the parties or, in the absence of such a designation, by the arbitrators they appointed and to whom they delegated this choice. Presumably neither party, acting rationally in its own interest, is likely to agree to a venue which it feels would discriminate against it in favor of its adversary. As a result, the dynamics of this sort of selection process work to ensure that the primary jurisdiction itself is likely to be less prone to bias than others, in the sense that fewer of its interests should be engaged in the case than those of other possible jurisdictions. This imports burdens, but there are also benefits. The primary jurisdiction is also the beneficiary of the invisible trade benefits of the arbitration and, as such, may reasonably be asked to shoulder the comparatively greater transactional costs of supervision. Of course, each primary forum's nationals can rely on systemic reciprocity: they will have the benefit of a comparably regulated level of judicial supervision when they agree to other states as the venue for arbitration.

No discussion of the architecture of international commercial arbitration can now ignore the brilliant exposition of Emmanuel Gaillard in his *Legal Theory of International Arbitration*. In contrast to accounts that are laconic about the role of state power in arbitration, it is one of the distinctive virtues of Professor Gaillard's work to pair his vision of a freestanding transnational arbitral order with an acknowledgement of the theoretical imperative to describe a relationship between private arbitral tribunals and public courts.

Professor Gaillard focuses our attention on what he calls arbitration's "juridicity",[22] an evocative term whose import is not entirely clear. This "juridicity" is elaborated by looking outward from the arbitrator's observational perspective, and organizing the representations from that vantage point into a vision of a normative system. It is thus an internal "theory of law" rather than, as we propose, an external "theory *about* law".[23] From the internal point of view of the arbitrator, Professor Gaillard argues that international commercial arbitration has evolved from the archaic "monolocal" representation, and, then, from a comparatively more progressive "Westphalian" representation, into a freestanding transnational system rooted only in the authority of the international public order. What should now be apparent to the reflective contemporary arbitrator who but looks in the right place is a new coherent representation: a transnational legal order, unfettered by the outmoded features of the New York Convention model.

While Professor Gaillard praises the Westphalian acknowledgement that the coordinated views of a plurality of states can help to underwrite an effective juridical theory of international arbitration, he proposes an approach that looks beyond mere plurality to "contemplate the *collectivity* of states".[24] According to Professor Gaillard, his method "essentially factors in the arbitrators' perspective"[25] to arrive at a juridical account of arbitration based on a "majoritarian" rule of recognition that can stand on its own bottom apart from states.[26] This rule of recognition affords Professor Gaillard's representation of the transnational legal order its claim to authority.[27]

But this majoritarian move encounters problems: a great many countries have national laws that directly refute the transnational autonomy of international arbitration (indeed, the critical empirical premise of Gaillard's critique of Westphalian "lex executionism" is that many states have passed legislation implementing the New York Convention that

22. Emmanuel GAILLARD, *Legal Theory of International Arbitration* (2010) p. 15 ("The … representation, which the author of this Course favors is that which recognizes an autonomous character to international arbitration, viewed as having generated an authentic legal order: the arbitral legal order.").

23. Harold Dwight LASSWELL and Myres Smith MCDOUGAL, *Jurisprudence For a Free Society*, vol. 1 (1992) p. 39.

24. Emmanuel GAILLARD, supra fn. 22, at p. 37 (emphasis added).

25. *Ibid.*, at p. 35.

26. *Ibid.*, at pp. 47-48.

27. Gaillard argues that his majoritarian principle for discerning the correct representation of international arbitration is precisely the same as that contemplated by Art. 38 of the Statute of the International Court of Justice: just as Art. 38 directs the Court to distill general principles, the idea of Gaillard's approach "is to ascertain the prevailing trend within national laws…". *Ibid.*, at p. 48.

is actually arbitration-averse).[28] The avowed "majoritarianism" of this approach overcomes this impediment by deeming the aspirational aspects of the theory as emergent, or even settled, rules of decision by virtue of having been thought by arbitrators deciding individual cases.

It is Professor Gaillard's view that the more-modern Westphalian representation and the most-modern transnational representation present "no theoretical bar to the recognition in a given State of an award set aside in another", even if the award is vacated by the supreme court of the forum.[29] On this view it is only the archaic monolocal representation that accords any weight to the decision of a forum state to vacate an award.[30] While the Westphalian and transnational representations each come to the right result in Professor Gaillard's view, an added virtue of the transnational representation is its "comfort to the courts of the place of enforcement that [an award] exists autonomously, irrespective of its recognition in *any* national legal order...".[31]

We plead guilty to "Westphalianism". Because an international arbitration, as a

---

28. Professor Gaillard views his transnational representation as one of several options. But according to Gaillard, history is marching towards the transnational representation: "[n]ational legal orders are thus gradually abandoning the idea that the source of validity of arbitral awards necessarily lies in the legal order of the seat ... and moving towards the conception ... of an arbitral legal order". *Ibid.*, at p. 66.

29. *Ibid.*

30. *Ibid.*, at pp. 135-136.

31. *Ibid.*, at p. 136 (emphasis added). One finds compelling evidence of the continued vitality of the two orthodoxies Gaillard criticizes, as well as evidence of the importance of Gaillard's work in modern arbitration law, in the complicated and developing story of the fate of the award in the *Dallah v. Pakistan* ICC arbitration (*Dallah Real Estate and Tourism Holding Company v. The Ministry of Religious Affairs, Government of Pakistan (Respondent)* [2010] UKSC 46 (appeal taken from EWCA Civ)). Called upon to enforce an ICC award in the United Kingdom, in late 2010 the UK Supreme Court interpreted Art. V(1)(*a*) of the New York Convention, as implemented by Sect. 103(2)(b) of the English Arbitration Act of 1996, to require the Court to apply French law to the question of whether the jurisdiction of the arbitral tribunal extended to Pakistan. (In the contract at issue, a purpose-built trust, rather than the government of Pakistan, was the formal signatory of the agreement.) The Supreme Court explicitly set to one side the issues raised by Gaillard's theory – including the argument that "transnational law is part of French law" – in favor of a "common intention" test drawn from its own reading of French law. *Ibid.*, at paras. 15-16 ("In the light of the common ground between the parties, it is also unnecessary to engage with the competing representations of international arbitration lucidly discussed in Gaillard's *Legal Theory of International Arbitration*.... Whatever the juridical underpinning or autonomy of their role from the viewpoint of international arbitrators, the present case involves an application to enforce in the forum of a national court, subject to principles defined by Sect. 103 of the 1996 Act and Art. V of the New York Convention, upon the effect of which there is substantial, though not complete, agreement between the parties now before the Supreme Court."). The Court thus applied the law of the seat to hold the arbitration agreement unenforceable in the United Kingdom. However, on 17 February 2011, the Paris Court of Appeal came to the opposite conclusion, holding the ICC award enforceable in France. Significantly, the French court parsed the same set of facts to come to the conclusion that Pakistan, by its behavior during the negotiation and termination of the contract, considered itself to be the true party to the contract despite the formalism of the trust named as party to the agreement. See Judgment of *Cour d'appel* [CA] [regional court of appeal] Paris, 17 Feb. 2011

transnational phenomenon, is always an event that is subject to the simultaneous or sequential competences of the judicial institutions of at least two states, arrangements that carefully allocate those competences as they relate to the regulation of arbitration is required.[32] The Convention, as a public international law regime that *allocates* jurisdiction, establishes the conditions under which an arbitral event in one jurisdiction will be given full effect in another jurisdiction. By allocating among the various states competences to make and apply law for these persons, things and events, and recognizing and giving effect to the proper application of those competences by individual states, the Convention makes possible processes of interaction and exchanges between individuals and entities from different communities under expectations of neutral adjudication of disputes.

In dwelling upon the essential distribution of competence in the Convention system between primary and secondary jurisdictions, and in dwelling upon the arbitration control system's conflicting interests in assuring both a fair and a final process, we have emphasized that the accomplishments of the New York Convention are hard-won realistic and pragmatic successes. It is necessary to *distribute* jurisdictional competences between primary and secondary fora so that states find the arbitration system attractive enough to continue to sustain the regime and enforce awards sometimes adverse to its nationals. But just as important as this need to secure ongoing state consent to the Convention regime is the need to assure *predictability* in the arbitral order for the good of parties seeking to consummate cross-border contracts. In this second aspect, a well-functioning control system for international commercial arbitration is enormously valuable.[33]

III. RECENT INITIATIVES TO CHANGE THE CONTROL SCHEME OF INTERNATIONAL COMMERCIAL ARBITRATION

That is, in brief, our interpretation of the normative architecture of international commercial arbitration as set forth in the New York Convention. We see it as a complex systemic relationship between national courts and private arbitration tribunals in which national courts have decisive but nonetheless carefully defined roles. The regime has worked remarkably well since 1958 and can be seen as a significant contribution to the global commercial system. But no legal arrangement is fixed or permanent; a constant

32. See also Jan PAULSSON, "Arbitration in Three Dimensions", Transnat'l Disp. Mgmt. (April 2010) at p. 1 (arguing that "Inasmuch as [French proposals for an international arbitral order] ultimately seek to establish this order by positing its recognition by the very state orders from which they claim autonomy, their idea is circular and in effect no more than a dressed-up variant of ordinary horizontal pluralism. But the model of horizontal pluralism fails to account for important orderings of arbitral activity. Arbitration in modern society is accurately perceived as a complex, three-dimensional form of pluralism, in which legal orders (i) are not exclusively those of states and (ii) frequently overlap."). We shall elaborate our defense of the primary/secondary distinction in the material that follows.

33. We discuss the importance of "predictability" in our assessment of the lex mercatoria challenge to the New York Convention. See infra at pp. 41-42.

dialectic operates in law in democratic systems when parties with different interests stress or challenge existing arrangements. In some instances the challenge is successful and the arrangement adjusts; in others, the *status quo ante* prevails and is maintained; courts applying law recognize and accommodate this process.

In the recent decision in the *Case Concerning the Dispute Regarding Navigational and Related Rights* (Costa Rica v. Nicaragua) (the *San Juan River* case), the International Court of Justice (ICJ) observed:

> "[W]here the parties have used generic terms in a treaty, the parties necessarily having been aware that the meaning of the terms was likely to evolve over time, and where the treaty has been entered into for a very long period or is 'of continuing duration', the parties must be presumed, as a general rule, to have intended those terms to have an evolving meaning."[34]

That is certainly the situation with respect to the New York Convention. But there is a peculiar passivity in the ICJ's statement; the Court neglected to explain *its* own active role in determining which putative changes, urged in the ongoing legal dialectic, are to be endorsed and incorporated as conducing to the eufunction of the treaty regime in the face of new circumstances and which putative changes are to be rejected. Change is not, per se, "good" or "bad". Evaluations turn upon the consequences of specific changes in terms of the eufunction of the system of which they are a part, including the achievement of that system's goals.

This point is critical. For all of our admiration for the New York Convention, we are not suggesting, after the fashion of constitutional "originalists" in the United States, that legal arrangements must be maintained with a zealous, religious-like devotion, exactly as they were conceived. Nor are we suggesting, as implied by the ICJ in the *San Juan River* case, that eufunctional changes automatically self-identify and are accepted. Because contexts change and political power changes, challenges change and goals change; juridical management – whether performed judicially or doctrinally – is a creative and not a merely curatorial responsibility. As we will see, some aspects of the various types of initiatives address real problems, though the extent to which every one of them answers the specific challenge it addresses without causing collateral damage to the system is uncertain. Some of the initiatives do indeed pose threats to the eufunction of the system. That is the critical question with respect to the various challenges which have been presented to the architecture of international commercial arbitration since its inception.

We propose to briefly examine and appraise a number of challenges:

(1) the failure to apply Art. II strictly: the use of anti-arbitration injunctions;
(2) attempts to limit arbitrators' competence: the implications of *Stolt-Nielsen* in the United States;
(3) the use of "manifest error of law" in American courts and its implication for international commercial arbitration in the United States;

34. Judgment of 13 July 2009 at para. 66, available at <www.icj-cij.org>.

(4) the erosion of respect for Art. V's distinction between primary and secondary national courts;
(5) attempts to transform the newer institutions of international investment arbitration into courts of last appeal for international commercial awards; and, finally,
(6) a "new" New York Convention.

Although many of these putative changes have been and will continue to be initiated by private parties acting in their own interests, it is in the very nature of law that each has a *universalizing* potential. The fact that they may have initially been pressed for special interests in a single case does not impeach them as candidates for systemic change *erga omnes*, insofar as they may contribute to the eufunction of the international arbitral system.

1. *Failure to Apply Art. II of the New York Convention Strictly and the Use of Anti-arbitration Injunctions*

The first challenge to the control regime of international commercial arbitration that we shall discuss occurs when national courts attempt to use their power to interfere with an arbitration in ways incompatible with the New York Convention. The so-called anti-arbitration injunction, as it has emerged in practice, is a species of anti-suit injunction or order, issued by a domestic court against a party (or arbitrators), enjoining the initiation or continuation of an arbitration. Anti-arbitration injunctions may be directed in personam against one or both of the parties to the arbitration, against the arbitrators themselves or against the arbitral institution under which the arbitration is proceeding.

In general terms, when there is an agreement to arbitrate, all the States Parties to the New York Convention are expected to close their own doors to adjudication of the dispute and to refer the parties to arbitration unless the agreement to arbitrate is "null and void, inoperative or incapable of being performed". Those are the only grounds on which such decisions may be taken. Art. II does not, in terms, accord a national court of a state party any authority over the arbitration tribunal itself.[35] Other objections to jurisdiction fall to be decided by the arbitration tribunal by operation of the *competence-competence* principle.

May a state party's courts arrogate the competence assigned to the arbitral tribunal by doing *more* than what is prescribed in Art. II?

In domestic commercial arbitrations, how national courts exercise a supervisory jurisdiction at this "before" phase is of no concern to international law (unless, of course, a serious human rights violation might be involved). Art. II of the New York Convention is not concerned with and does not restrict the range of permissible actions of national courts with respect to *domestic* arbitrations. So national arrangements in which courts exercise a more extensive and/or intensive supervisory jurisdiction over domestic arbitrations are of no moment to international law. In various jurisdictions, however, respondents in *international* commercial arbitrations (and latterly in international

35. The FAA does purport to convey such a discretion, which raises an interesting interpretive challenge for US courts.

investment disputes) have sometimes tried to use this technique to arrest arbitral proceedings brought against them, for reasons that go beyond the three grounds to which national courts are confined under the New York Convention. In some instances, anti-arbitration injunctions are deliberately obstructionist of arbitration, pursued in sympathetic local courts and aimed at disrupting the parties' agreed-upon dispute resolution mechanism. But their use is not limited to jurisdictions that are deemed hostile to international commercial arbitration.

Courts in the United States have issued anti-arbitration injunctions against foreign commercial arbitral proceedings;[36] English courts have recognized the possibility of issuing such orders[37] and have issued anti-arbitration orders against English-seated international arbitrations.[38] Canadian courts have also claimed (and exercised) the authority to issue anti-arbitration injunctions against international arbitrations (including arbitrations seated abroad).[39]

---

36. *Hall v. Norcom*, 750 F.2d 1547 (11th Cir. 1985); *Société Generale de Surveillance v. Raytheon European Mgt. & Sys. Co.*, 643 F.2d 863 (1st Cir. 1981); *Shinto Shipping Co. v. Fibrex & Shipping Co.*, 572 F.2d 1328 (9th Cir. 1978) (concluding injunction against arbitration was not warranted on the facts); *Masefield AG v. Colonial Oil Indus., Inc.*, 2005 WL 911779 (S.D.N.Y. 2005) (enjoining arbitration of question whether non-signatories were bound by arbitration clause on grounds that there was no clear and unmistakable agreement to arbitrate jurisdictional issues and that there was no basis for concluding that non-signatories were bound by arbitration agreement).

Some US circuit courts have rejected the argument that the FAA prohibits injunctions barring arbitration. See, e.g., *Re Y&A Group Sec. Lit.*, 38 F.3d 380 (8th Cir. 1994) (rejecting the argument that the FAA precludes injunction against arbitration); *SATCOM Int'l Group plc v. ORBCOMM Int'l Partners, LP*, 49 F.Supp.2d 331, 342 (S.D.N.Y. 1999), *aff'd*, 205 F.3d 1324 (2d Cir. 1999) (it "should follow [from FAA's power to compel arbitration] that the court should have a concomitant power to enjoin arbitration where arbitration is inappropriate"; "A failure to [order the arbitration to be suspended] would frustrate the goals of arbitration, since there would be a delay and increased expense as the parties litigated in both fora."); *L.F. Rothschild & Co. v. Katz*, 702 F.Supp. 464 (S.D.N.Y. 1988) (asserting power to enjoin arbitration); *In re Bd. of Directors of Hopewell Int'l Ins. Ltd*, 238 B.R. 25 (S.D.N.Y. Bankr. Ct. 1999) (enjoining any arbitration against insurance company subject to foreign insolvency administration).

37. *Elektrim SA v. Vivendi Universal SA*, [2007] EWHC 571 (Q.B.); *Allied Marine Ltd. v. Vale do Rio Doce SA*, [1985] 1 WLR 925 (English Court of Appeal) (possibility of anti-arbitration injunction).

38. See, e.g., *Republic of Kazakhstan v. Istil Group Inc.*, [2007] EWHC 2729 (Comm.) (Q.B.) (enjoining the continuation of an English-seated international arbitration on grounds that an earlier English court decision held that no valid arbitration agreement bound the parties to the arbitration). See also *National Navigation Co. (NNC) v. Endesa Generacion SA*, [2009] Lloyd's Rep. 666 (holding, in spite of ECJ ruling that English courts should not grant anti-suit injunctions against arbitrations proceeding in other EU member states, that English courts retained a power to grant declaratory relief from arbitration).

39. *Lac d'Amiante du Canada Ltee v. Lac d'Amiante du Quebec Ltee, J.Q.* (Quicklaw) No. 5438 (Quebec Court of Appeal, 19 Nov. 1999) (enjoining foreign arbitration on grounds that right to arbitrate had been waived; rejecting contrary jurisdictional determination by arbitral tribunal).

In recent years, Indian[40] and Pakistani[41] courts have issued injunctions against both parties *and* arbitrators, purporting to enjoin arbitral proceedings sited abroad. Under Indian law, an anti-arbitration injunction may be issued where it is shown that the arbitral proceedings were oppressive and vexatious and would constitute an abuse of the process of law, as defined under Indian law.[42] Pakistani courts enjoined an arbitration that was alleged to have been initiated in bad faith and where the dispute was non-arbitrable and subject to the exclusive jurisdiction of the Pakistani courts under Pakistani law.[43] And while it has been said that anti-suit (and anti-arbitration) injunctions are unknown in civil jurisdictions,[44] courts and tribunals in Brazil,[45] Ethiopia[46] and Indonesia[47] have recently issued injunctions against foreign arbitrations.

American and British courts have expressed a greater reluctance than some other jurisdictions in issuing anti-arbitration injunctions. British courts have reaffirmed their discretion to issue these injunctions, but have required a "high degree of probability" that the arbitration would prejudice a legal or equitable right of one of the parties,[48] and have

---

40. *Union of India v. Dabhol Power Co.*, IA No. 6663/2003 Suit No. 1268/2003 (Delhi High Court 2004). But see *CDC Fin. Serv. (Mauritius) Ltd. v. BPL Comms.*, (2003) SCC 140, 144 (Indian S. Ct.).
41. *SGS v. Pakistan*, 19 Arb. Int'l p. 182 (Pakistan S.Ct. 2002)(2003); *The Hub Power Co. v. Pakistan WAPDA*, 16 Arb. Int'l p. 439 (Pakistan S.Ct. 2000)(2000). See Michael KERR, "Concord and Conflict in International Arbitration", 13 Arb. Int'l (1997) p. 121 at p. 137 (describing Pakistani anti-suit injunctions against arbitrations seated in Singapore and England).
42. *Union of India v. Dabhol Power Co.*, IA No. 6663/2003 Suit No. 1268/2003 (Delhi High Court 2004).
43. *SGS v. Pakistan*, 19 Arb. Int'l, 182 (Pakistan S.Ct. 2002) (2003); *The Hub Power Co. v. Pakistan WAPDA*, 16 Arb. Int'l 439 (Pakistan S.Ct. 2000) (2000).
44. Emmanuel GAILLARD, "The Misuse of Antisuit Injunctions", N.Y.L.J., 1 Aug. 2002, at p. 3.
45. Judgment of 3 June 2003, *Companhia Paranaense de Energia (Copel) v. UEG Arauncaria Ltda.*, 21 R.D.B.A. 421 (Curitiba Court of First Instance). See also Clavio VALENÇA FILHO and Joao BOSCO LEE, "Brazil's New Public-Private Partnership Law: One Step Forward, Two Steps Back", 22 J. Int'l Arb. (2005, no. 5) p. 419; Mauricio GOMM FERREIRA DOS SANTOS, "Arbitration in Brazil", 21 J. Int'l Arb. (2004, no. 6) p. 453.
46. Partial Award in ICC Case No. 10623, 21 ASA Bull. (2003) p. 59.
47. See *Karaha Bodas Co., L.L.C. v. Perusahaan Pertambangan Minyak Dan Gas Bumi Negara*, 335 F.3d 357, 363 (5th Cir. 2003) ("On 27 August 2002, while the matter was still under ... review [in the Fifth Circuit], the Central Jakarta District Court concluded that it had primary jurisdiction under the New York Convention and annulled the Award on grounds that it was contrary to the Convention and Indonesian arbitration law. The Indonesian court also permanently enjoined KBC from seeking to enforce the Award and imposed a fine of $500,000 for each day that KBC violated the Indonesian injunction.") (describing an unpublished Judgment of 1 April 2002, *Persusahaan Pertambangan Minyak Dan Gas Bumi Negara v. Karaha Bodas Co.* (District Court of Central Jakarta).
48. See *Midgulf International Group Ltd. v. Groupe Chimiche Tunisien*, [2010] 1 C.L.C. 113; *Youell v. Kara Mara Shipping Co.*, [2000] 2 Lloyd's Rep. 102 ("On an application to restrain foreign proceedings ... the applicant must show to a high degree of probability that its case is right, and it is entitled as of right to restrain the foreign proceedings.") See generally Hakeem SERIKI, "Anti-Suit Injunctions, Arbitration, and the Non-EU perspective: Some Recent Developments", 14 Int'l Arb. L. Rev. (2011) p. 19.

required parties to seek the injunction promptly.[49] In the United States, federal courts have tended to grant anti-arbitration injunctions only in the most exceptional circumstances.[50] Such reluctance can be partially explained by the fact that the Federal Arbitration Act (FAA) implements a public policy in favor of arbitration and in part by the relatively cautious approach that US courts take towards anti-suit injunctions generally.

US courts have typically declined to issue injunctive relief against participation in arbitral proceedings that are subject to the New York Convention. Some US courts have gone further and held that they altogether lack the power to enjoin a foreign arbitration subject to the New York Convention.[51] (We would add that this was *not* the conclusion reached in the Southern District of New York in 2010 and the Second Circuit in 2011: Ecuador had filed a motion to stay an UNCITRAL investment arbitration brought by Chevron under the US-Ecuador Bilateral Investment Treaty or BIT. Until that time, no federal court had stayed a BIT arbitration; all arbitral proceedings which have been stayed have been purely commercial in nature. While the district court denied Ecuador's motion for the injunction and granted Chevron's motion to dismiss, it did *not* do so on the grounds that it lacked the authority to enjoin the arbitration from proceeding, acknowledging that within the Southern District of New York, there is a split among the judges as to whether a federal court has the authority to enjoin an arbitration. The

---

49. See *Transfield Shipping Inc. v. Chiping Xinfa Huayu Alumina Co. Ltd.*, [2009] EWHC 3642 at [79] (denying an injunction after noting that the application "comes forward very late in the day" and that the problems complained of by the applicant "would have been avoided if an application had been made much earlier...".) (*citing Verity Shipping SA v. Chartworld Shipping Corp. (The Skier Star)*, [2008] 1 Lloyd's Rep. 652). See Hakeem SERIKI, supra fn. 48 at pp. 25-26.

50. Compare *Raytheon Eng'rs & Constructors, Inc. v. SMS Schloemann-Siemag AG*, 2000 WL 420866 (N.D. Ill. 2000) (granting a preliminary injunction – on $150,000 surety bond – to prevent an ICC arbitration because, after review of the contract at issue, "the relevant language yields the unescapable conclusion that Raytheon is not required to arbitrate this dispute"); *Am. Life Ins. Co. v. Parra*, 25 F.Supp.2d 467 (D. Del. 1998) (apparently enjoining foreign arbitration, subject to New York Convention); *SATCOM Int'l Group plc v. ORBCOMM Int'l Partners*, LP, 49 F.Supp.2d 331 (S.D.N.Y. 1999), *aff'd*, 205 F.3d 1324 (2d Cir. 1999) (preliminary injunction against international arbitration, subject to New York Convention, seated in United States); and *Masefield AG v. Colonial Oil Indus., Inc.*, 2005 WL 911779 (S.D.N.Y. 2005) (preliminary injunction against ICC arbitration, subject to New York Convention, seated in United States) with *URS Corp. v. Lebanese Co. for the Dev. and Reconstr. of Beirut Central District SAL*, 512 F.Supp.2d 199, 209 ("URS primarily relies on four cases to support its position that this court can enjoin a foreign tribunal proceeding abroad under the FAA. This authority is not persuasive. The *Masefield* and *Satcom* courts both granted preliminary injunctions against proceeding arbitrations. *Satcom* involved an arbitration agreement that fell under the New York Convention, while *Masefield* involved an arbitration before the ICC. Significantly, and despite their international nature, both the arbitrations in *Masefield* and *Satcom* were initiated in the United States. The fact that the arbitrations took place on US soil vested the district courts with primary jurisdiction over those proceedings.").

51. See *URS*, *supra* fn. 50, at 208-210 ("comity and the purposes of the New York Convention do not support issuing an injunction against a foreign arbitral proceeding"); *Ibid.*, at 208 ("the FAA does not authorize an injunction against a foreign arbitral proceeding"; "the French courts have primary jurisdiction over the pending arbitration [seated in France] and this court declines to extend its jurisdiction over those extraterritorial waters by enjoining the ongoing arbitration in France".).

Second Circuit recently affirmed this decision, but preserved the question of "whether federal courts have the power to stay arbitration under the FAA (or any other authority) in an appropriate case" because it "is an open question in [the second] circuit".)[52] English courts, on the other hand, have not hesitated to assert the power to issue anti-arbitration injunctions but have expressed reluctance actually to do so.[53]

Regardless of how "cautious" US and British courts might be in issuing anti-suit injunctions, the overall impact of this body of law raises complex issues for international arbitral tribunals, to whom the anti-arbitration injunction may be directed. These issues have been put into sharp relief by a current example: Belize, which is not party to the New York Convention, recently amended its Supreme Court of Judicature Act[54] to dictate that:

> "Notwithstanding any other law or rule of practice to the contrary but without prejudice to the power of Court to punish for contempt in accordance with Part 53 of the Supreme Court (Civil Procedure) Rules 2005 by way of committal and seizure of assets, every person, whether in Belize or elsewhere, who disobeys or fails to comply with an injunction, or an order in the nature of an injunction, issued by the Court (whether such injunction was issued before or after the commencement of this Act), shall be guilty of an offence and shall be punished in accordance with the Summary Procedure of the Court, and in every such case, any rule of court relating to the unlimited jurisdiction of the Court shall apply."[55]

This means that arbitrators who ignore the injunction and issue an award in a case that has been enjoined by a Belize court may be tried for contempt; if they are given notice of such charges and fail to appear before the court, they may be tried for the charges in

52. See *Republic of Ecuador v. Chevron Corp.*, 2010 U.S. Dist. LEXIS 25487, No. 09 Civ. 9958 (LBS) (S.D.N.Y. 16 Mar. 2010), *aff'd*, 126 F.3d 15 (2d Cir. 2011). See also *Westmoreland Capital Corp. v. Findlay*, 100 F.3d 263, 266 n. 3 (2d Cir. 1996) (preserving the question of courts' authority to stay arbitration under the FAA, because in this case subject-matter jurisdiction was lacking).

53. See, e.g., *Elektrim SA v. Vivendi Universal SA*, [2007] EWHC 571 (Q.B.) (finding, by analogy to English doctrine regarding an injunction to restrain *proceedings* in a foreign court, that English courts may have residual power to issue anti-arbitration injunctions where an arbitration is "an infringement of a legal or equitable right of a party" or "the ends of justice require an injunction to restrain foreign proceedings that are vexatious or oppressive". The court concludes, however, that "the scope for the court to intervene by injunction before an award is made by arbitrators is very limited".). For greater analysis, see Gary BORN, *International Commercial Arbitration* (2011) p. 739.

54. The legislative amendment came about as part of Belize's attempt to avoid an expropriation claim by a large private investor commenced pursuant to the UK-Belize BIT. See "BIT Arbitration Filed in Belize Telecoms Nationalization Dispute", 2(20) Inv. Arb. Rep. (21 Dec. 2009) available at <www.iareporter.com>. Belize obtained injunctive relief from its own courts to restrain the arbitration and enacted the aforementioned legislation in a further attempt to deprive any final arbitration award of ultimate validity and effect in Belize.

55. Belize Supreme Court of Judicature (Amendment) Act, 2010, Sect. 106A.

absentia. (The amendment also states that any award made by an arbitral tribunal in disregard of an injunction "shall be wholly void and the Court shall have jurisdiction to vacate any such award".[56])

Now one may be inclined to dismiss the Belize statute as comic opera, as did Lord Ellenborough when, in the first decade of the nineteenth century, he asked with regard to one of Belize's neighbors: "Can the island of Tobago pass a law to bind the rights of the whole world?"[57] In 1808 that was a rhetorical question. In the twenty-first century, the world is much more globalized and interdependent. One state's arrogation of new power, whether in its maritime boundaries, its claim to preemptive military action or its jurisdiction, is likely to generate a mimetic process in which other states make comparable claims until what may have commenced as an aberration becomes state practice.[58] So the answer to Lord Ellenborough's question is now far less certain. The national institutionalization of an anti-arbitration competence – whether by legislation or judicial fiat – poses a serious threat to the efficacy of the international commercial arbitral system.

As for the law on this matter, no less an authority than Judge Schwebel has said that the notion of an anti-arbitration injunction "appears to violate conventional and customary international law, international public policy and the accepted principles of international arbitration".[59] Consistent with this view, in Switzerland, anti-arbitration injunctions are considered irreconcilable with the principle of *competence-competence*,[60] a central tenet of international arbitration, which dictates that it is the arbitral tribunal that has the competence to decide, in the first instance, its own jurisdiction.

We believe that Judge Schwebel has precisely stated the international legal standard and the Swiss approach epitomizes its correct national implementation: the issuance of an injunction against an arbitration subject to the New York Convention on any ground other than those of Art. II is inconsistent with and undermines its basic legal framework. Anti-arbitration orders which are not compliant with Art. II, by interfering with the ability of parties to give effect to their obligations under the New York Convention and

---

56. *Ibid.*, Sect. 106A(8).

57. *Buchanan v. Rucker*, 103 Eng. Rep. 546 (1808).

58. See W. Michael REISMAN and Andrea ARMSTRONG, "The Past and Future of the Claim of Preemptive Self-Defense", 100 Am. J. Int'l L. (Jul. 2006) p. 525.

59. Stephen M. SCHWEBEL, "Anti-Suit Injunctions in International Arbitration: An Overview" in Emmanuel GAILLARD, ed., *Anti-Suit Injunctions in International Arbitration* (2005) p. 5. See also Emmanuel GAILLARD, "The Misuse of Antisuit Injunctions", N.Y.L.J., 1 Aug. 2002, at p. 2; Georgios PETROCHILOS, *Procedural Law in International Arbitration* (2004) p. 105 ("It is far from settled that such injunctions should be regarded as a proper remedy at all, in particular under the New York Convention.").

60. See Judgment of 2 May 2005, 23 ASA Bull. pp. 728-737 (Geneva Court of First Instance) (2005). Other authorities are similar. See generally Hakeem SERIKI, supra fn. 48. See also Frédéric BACHAND, "Must an ICC Tribunal Comply with an Anti-Suit Injunction Issued by the Courts of the Seat of Arbitration? – Comment on *Salini Construttori SpA v. Ethiopia*", 20 Int'l Arb. Rep. (2005, no. 3) p. 47; Marco STACHER, "You Don't Want to Go There – Antisuit Injunctions in International Commercial Arbitration", 23 ASA Bull. (2005) p. 640; Emmanuel GAILLARD, "The Misuse of Antisuit Injunctions", N.Y.L.J. (1 Aug. 2002) at p. 3.

by purporting to strip tribunals of their competence, violate the Convention's obligation of judicial non-interference in the arbitral process. This is so whether the order is issued by a court in the venue (which would appear to be the proper forum) or otherwise.

That said, one cannot deny the plenary competence of the primary jurisdiction to issue such injunctions. Where the primary jurisdiction enjoins an arbitration, secondary fora are bound to enforce these decisions. Where secondary fora do so, the injunction is limited in effect to the secondary forum's domestic courts. This is a consequence – and a cost – of the differential distribution of competences by the New York Convention. Primary fora which capriciously exercise their competence to enjoin arbitration will, we assume, be shunned and, thus, experience the economic costs that follow.

The most recent manifestation of otherwise legitimate national practices which could threaten the efficacy of the international system is to be found in the "Arbitration Fairness Act". It has been introduced in both houses of Congress to amend the FAA and gone through a series of iterations. The House version of the Act (H.R. 1020) has been discharged by House Judiciary Subcommittee on Commercial and Administrative Law; the Senate version (S.931) is pending before the Senate Judiciary Committee. If enacted, the bill would invalidate pre-dispute arbitration agreements for employment, consumer and franchise disputes. The bill is ostensibly intended to offer greater protection to consumers and employees who are subject to adhesion contracts. But some have cautioned that the bill could have unintended effects for international commercial arbitration in the United States. The version of the bill introduced by the House of Representatives[61] provides, in relevant part, the following amendment to Chapter 1, Sect. 2 of the FAA:

> "(b) No pre-dispute arbitration agreement shall be valid or enforceable if it requires arbitration of–
> (1) an employment, consumer, or franchise dispute; or
> (2) a dispute arising under any statute intended to protect civil rights.
> (c) An issue as to whether this chapter applies to an arbitration agreement shall be determined by Federal law. Except as otherwise provided in this chapter, *the validity or enforceability of an agreement to arbitrate shall be determined by the court, rather than the arbitrator*, irrespective of whether the party resisting arbitration challenges the arbitration agreement specifically or in conjunction with other terms of the contract containing such agreement." (Emphasis added.)

Similarly, the Senate version of the bill[62] proposes to add the following text to the end of the U.S. Code on arbitration:

> "*Sect. 402. Validity and enforceability*
> (a) In General – Notwithstanding any other provision of this title, no predispute arbitration agreement shall be valid or enforceable if it requires arbitration of an employment, consumer, franchise, or civil rights dispute."

---

61. For full text, See <www.opencongress.org/bill/111-h1020/text>.

62. For full text, See <www.govtrack.us/congress/billtext.xpd?bill=s111-931>.

In our view, this is a debate about national policy and the efficiency of domestic arbitration which does not concern international commercial arbitration. But the legislation could breach US obligations under the New York Convention and undermine the system of review afforded to national courts under the established control regime: the proposed amendments appear to reverse federal jurisprudence on separability and *competence-competence* with respect to arbitration in general, even though they purport to limit the bill's effects to the categories of parties that the legislation seeks to protect.[63] For example, under the new legislation, federal courts might refuse to refer a matter to arbitration, despite the limited scope of the "null and void exception" of Art. II – or, ironically, they might use the terms of the legislation to declare an otherwise valid agreement to arbitrate "null and void" simply because the arbitration concerns a consumer, employment or franchise dispute – even were it part of an international transaction. If the legislation in one form or another is enacted, precisely how such inconsistencies between it and US obligations under the New York Convention will be accommodated, as well as the way in which US courts will deal with conflicts between an international obligation and a later-in-time statute, is not cause for optimism.

2. National Courts' Attempts to Limit Arbitrators' Competence and the Problem of Non Liquet

In the much discussed *Stolt-Nielsen* case,[64] Justice Alito, writing for the Court, addressed the question of the law to be applied by the arbitrator and, by implication, the law-generative competence of international commercial arbitration tribunals.

> "Because the parties agreed their agreement was 'silent' in the sense that they had not reached any agreement on the issue of class arbitration, the arbitrators' proper task was to identify the rule of law that governs in that situation. Had they engaged in that undertaking, they presumably would have looked either to the FAA itself or to one of the two bodies of law that the parties claimed were governing, *i.e.*, either federal maritime law or New York law. But the panel did not consider whether the FAA provides the rule of decision in such a situation; nor did the panel attempt to determine what rule would govern under either maritime or New York law in the case of 'silent' contract."[65]

But the arbitrators did not do that.

> "Instead, the panel based its decision on post-*Bazzle* arbitral decisions that 'construed a wide variety of clauses in a wide variety of settings as allowing for class arbitration'. App. to Pet. for Cert. 49a—50a. The panel did not mention

63. See, e.g., Edna SUSSMAN, "The Proposed U.S. Arbitration Fairness Act: A Threat to U.S. Business", 18 Am. Rev. Int'l. Arb. (2009) p. 455; Mark KANTOR, "Legislative Proposals Could Significantly Alter Arbitration in the United States", 74 Arb. (2008) pp. 444-452.

64. *Stolt-Nielsen S.A. et al. v. AnimalFeeds International Corp.*, 559 U.S.—, 130 S.Ct. 1758 (27 April 2010).

65. *Ibid.*, at p. 8.

> whether any of these decisions were based on a rule derived from the FAA or on maritime or New York law." (footnote deleted) [66]

Justice Alito found this to be beyond the competence of the tribunal.

> "Rather than inquiring whether the FAA, maritime law, or New York law contains a 'default rule' under which an arbitration clause is construed as allowing class arbitration in the absence of express consent, the panel proceeded as if it had the authority of a common-law court to develop what it viewed as the best rule to be applied in such a situation. Perceiving a post-*Bazzle* consensus among arbitrators that class arbitration is beneficial in 'a wide variety of settings', the panel considered only whether there was any good reason not to follow that consensus in this case. App. to Pet. for Cert. 49a—50a. The panel was not persuaded by 'court cases denying consolidation of arbitrations', [footnote deleted] by undisputed evidence that the Vegoilvoy charter party had 'never been the basis of a class action', or by expert opinion that 'sophisticated, multinational commercial parties of the type that are sought to be included in the class would never intend that the arbitration clauses would permit a class arbitration'. (footnote deleted) *Ibid.*, at 50a—51a. Accordingly, finding no convincing ground for departing from the post-*Bazzle* arbitral consensus, the panel held that class arbitration was permitted in this case. App. to Pet. for Cert. 52a. The conclusion is inescapable that the panel simply imposed its own conception of sound policy." (footnote deleted)[67]

The tribunal had ignored "the two bodies of law that the parties claimed were governing" and, instead, had relied on arbitral awards as a sort of arbitral *jurisprudence constante*, even though those awards were inconsistent with the relevant federal and New York case law.

In terms of our analysis, Justice Alito was correct on two issues but incorrect on a third. First, he was correct in insisting that where parties have specified the applicable law, it is the law to be applied. That, in our view, is part of the implicit covenant not only between the parties to the contract but also between the international commercial arbitration regime and states and their courts. This does not preclude the application of business practices if they are consistent with the principles of the applicable national law or decision by reference to lex mercatoria (whatever it is) or decision ex aequo et bono, insofar as the parties have elected or authorized their tribunal to repair to one of those.

In our view, Justice Alito was also correct in rejecting the law-generative power of international commercial arbitral awards, even when those awards purport to apply the national law which the parties had designated as the applicable law. *Stare decisis* is a system of judicial law-making within a judicial hierarchy.[68] In that sense international

66. *Ibid.*, at pp. 8-9.

67. *Ibid.*, at pp. 9-11.

68. See generally Mirjan R. DAMAŠKA, *The Faces of Justice and State Authority* (1986) pp. 29-44.

commercial (as, perhaps, opposed to international investment)[69] arbitral awards are not "precedential". Even if one were to assume that they are, as do proponents of lex mercatoria, they are not systematically reported; the haphazard way in which they come to notice should raise serious doubts as to how representative of actual decision trends those fragments that become public are.

But we think that Justice Alito overstated the limits of tribunals in criticizing the panel for acting "as if it had the authority of a common-law court to develop what it viewed as the best rule to be applied in such a situation". Certainly a panel may not ignore the applicable law (which is itself a statement of the authoritative policy of the state concerned) in favor of "its own conception of sound policy". That would be a self-authorization of a power to decide ex aequo et bono. But where there is a real *lacuna* in the applicable law, a tribunal would be remiss were it to issue a *non liquet*, yet that would seem to be the implication of Justice Alito's holding. In the circumstances, we would expect that the tribunal should indeed apply "its own conception of sound policy". But, unlike a common-law judge's ruling, that holding would not be precedential.

3. *Do All National Practices Which Are Inconsistent with International Arrangements Harm the System?*

Some jurisdictions have decided, for national policy reasons, to install more heightened judicial supervision over domestic arbitration. From the perspective of international commercial arbitration, that is a matter of indifference. But if these national practices are transposed to international awards by courts functioning as secondary fora, they could threaten the balance of competences between courts and tribunals that the Convention establishes.

For example, federal courts in the United States will not typically review the merits of an arbitral award; ordinary errors of fact or law do not constitute grounds to disturb an otherwise valid award.[70] This principle applies with equal force to foreign arbitral awards. By way of the FAA, federal courts have the authority to vacate a domestic award where:

> "(1) It was procured by corruption, fraud, or undue means.
> (2) Where there was evident partiality or corruption in the arbitrators, or either of them.

---

69. W. Michael REISMAN, "Law, International Public Policy (So-called), and Arbitral Choice in International Commercial Arbitration" in *International Arbitration 2006: Back to Basics?* ICCA Congress Series no. 13 (2007) p. 849 at pp. 853-854 (hereinafter *ICCA Congress Series no. 13*).

70. See, e.g., *United Paperworkers Int'l Union v. Misco, Inc.*, 484 U.S. 29, 38 (1987) ("Because the parties have contracted to have disputes settled by an arbitrator chosen by them rather than by a judge, it is the arbitrator's view of the facts and of the meaning of the contract that they have agreed to accept. Courts thus do not sit to hear claims of factual or legal error by an arbitrator as an appellate court does in reviewing decisions of lower courts."); *Burchell v. Marsh*, 58 U.S. 344, 349 (1855) ("If an award is within the submission, and contains the honest decision of the arbitrators, after a full and fair hearing of the parties, a court of equity will not set it aside for error, either in law or fact.").

> (3) Where the arbitrators were guilty of misconduct in refusing to postpone the hearing, upon sufficient cause shown, or in refusing to hear evidence pertinent and material to the controversy; or of any other misbehavior by which the rights of any party have been prejudiced.
> (4) Where the arbitrators exceeded their powers, or so imperfectly executed them that a mutual, final, and definite award upon the subject matter submitted was not made."[71]

That enumeration tracks Art. V of the New York Convention. However, at different times courts in the United States have recognized judicially and contractually created grounds on which courts may decline to enforce or vacate arbitral awards: (1) where enforcement of the arbitration would violate "public policy";[72] (2) where the parties have entered into an agreement providing for more extensive judicial review; and (3) where the arbitrator "manifestly disregarded" applicable law. The first of these three possible grounds for vacatur or non-enforcement, while not found in the FAA, does not vary from the regime of the New York Convention, for it has an analogue in Art. V. The latter two may vary from the international regime; as such, they raise the question of their contribution to the operation of the Convention.

Should parties be able to contract for expanded post-award judicial review?[73] Some US courts were historically willing to uphold such provisions;[74] others were not.[75] Prior to a recent decision on the matter by the US Supreme Court, three federal courts of appeal had enforced clauses that expanded the scope of review. In *Gateway Technologies v. MCI Telecommunications Corp*,[76] the Fifth Circuit upheld an arbitration clause stating that the "arbitration decision shall be final and binding on them both, except that errors of law shall be subject to appeal".[77] In justifying its decision, the Court stated, "Such a contractual modification is acceptable because, as the Supreme Court has emphasized, arbitration is a creature of contract and the FAA's pro-arbitration policy does not operate without regard to the wishes of the contracting parties."[78]

71. 9 U.S.C. Sect. 10(a) (2000).

72. See, e.g., *W.R. Grace & Co. v. Local Union* 759, 461 U.S. 757, 766 (1983).

73. See, e.g., Christopher R. DRAHOZAL, "Standards for Judicial Review of Arbitral Awards in the United States: Mandatory Rules or Default Rules?", 16 Int'l Arb. Rep. (2001, no. 3) p. 27; Victoria HOLSTEIN, "Co-Opting the Judicial Review of Arbitral Awards Through Contract", 12 World Arb. & Med. Rep. (2001) p. 276; Hans SMIT, "Contractual Modification of the Scope of Judicial Review of Arbitral Awards", 8 Am. Rev. Int'l Arb. (1997) p. 147.

74. See, e.g., *Harris v. Parker College of Chiropractic*, 186 F.3d 790 (5th Cir. 2002); *New England Utils. v. Hydro-Quebec,* 10 F.Supp.2d 53, 62-64 (D. Mass. 1998).

75. See, e.g., *Kyocera Corp. v. Prudential Bache Trade Servs.*, 299 F.3d 769 (9th Cir. 2002), *vacating en banc, LaPine Tech. Corp. v. Kyocera Corp.*, 130 F.3d 884 (9th Cir. 1997); *Bowen v. Amoco Pipeline Co.*, 254 F.3d 925, 932 (10th Cir. 2001); *Chicago Typographical Union v. Chicago Sun-Times, Inc.*, 935 F.2d 1501, 1505 (7th Cir. 1991).

76. *Gateway Technology v. MCI Telecommunications Corp.*, 64 F.3d 993 (5th Cir. 1995).

77. *Ibid.*, at 995.

78. *Ibid.*, at 996.

Similarly, in *La Pine Technology v. Kyocera*, the Ninth Circuit enforced the parties' agreement, which provided for review to determine whether there was "substantial evidence" and "legal error". The majority held that the expanded review authorized in the arbitration agreement was not inconsistent with the FAA and that it had to be enforced because of the federal policy requiring enforcement of arbitration agreements "according to their terms".[79] The Fourth Circuit, in an unpublished opinion, agreed.[80]

By contrast, the Seventh, Eighth and Tenth Circuit Courts of Appeals rejected attempts by parties to allow for judicial review broader than that provided in the FAA.[81] In *Bowen v. Amoco Pipeline Co.*, the Tenth Circuit found unenforceable a clause giving the parties the right to appeal an award to the district court "on the grounds that the award is not supported by the evidence" because it threatened "to undermine the policies behind the FAA".[82] This view was also adopted by the Eighth Circuit in *UHC Management Co. v. Computer Sciences Corp.*[83]

This split among the circuit courts of appeals regarding the validity of agreements providing for heightened judicial review of arbitral awards was taken up by the Supreme Court in *Hall Street Associates v. Mattel*.[84] The Court held that Sect. 10 of the FAA's statutory grounds for vacatur were exclusive and that the "statutory grounds for prompt vacatur and modification may [not] be supplemented by contract".[85] The Court went on to find, however, that "to rest this case on the general policy of treating arbitration agreements as enforceable as such would be to beg the question, which is whether the FAA has textual features at odds with enforcing a contract to expand judicial review following the arbitration".[86] The Court concluded that the FAA's language mandatorily required confirmation of awards, subject only to limited grounds for vacatur set forth in Sect. 10.[87]

Although *Hall Street* said that parties cannot contract to expand judicial review, it left open the possibility that parties might obtain expanded judicial review of arbitration awards via some means other than the FAA, stating that federal law does not preclude "more searching review based on authority outside the [federal] statute".[88] Such language has contributed to speculation that the case management authority assigned to trial judges under Federal Rule of Civil Procedure 16 might permit parties to obtain a form of

79. *LaPine Technology v. Kyocera*, 130 F.3d at 888.

80. *Syncor International Corp. v. McLeland*, 1997 U.S. App. LEXIS 21248, 1997 WL 452245 (4th Cir. 1997) (unpublished).

81. See, e.g., *Bowen v. Amoco Pipeline Co.*, 254 F.3d 925 (10th Cir. 2001); *UHC Management Co. v. Computer Sciences Corp.*, 148 F.3d 992, 998 (8th Cir. 1998); *Chicago Typographical Union v. Chicago Sun-Times*, 935 F.2d 1501 (7th Cir. 1991).

82. *Bowen*, 254 F.3d at 930, 935.

83. *HC Management Co. v. Computer Sciences Corp.*, 148 F.3d at 998.

84. 128 S.Ct. 1396 (2008).

85. *Ibid.*, at 1400.

86. *Ibid.*, at 1404.

87. *Ibid.*, at 1405.

88. *Ibid.*, at 1406.

expanded review if such agreements are reached during the course of the proceedings.[89]

Hall Street concerned a domestic arbitration. May parties to an international arbitration, subject to the New York Convention, elect a forum that assigns an "appellate", rather than review, competence to its courts? On the one hand, the parties would have knowingly consented to it; on the other, such appellate review is, on its face, not consistent with the conception of Art. V and could lead to a modulation to "intrinsic" review. In fact, some jurisdictions still allow this.[90]

Hall Street also addressed the continuing viability of the "manifest disregard" doctrine as a standard of judicial review of arbitral awards. The phrase "manifest disregard" originates from dicta in *Wilko v. Swan*,[91] where the Court remarked that "the interpretations of the law by the arbitrators in contrast to manifest disregard are not subject, in the federal courts, to judicial review for error in interpretation".[92] This seemed to imply that "manifest disregard", as opposed to a mere erroneous "interpretation", of the applicable law could be subject to judicial review and justify the vacatur of an award. Since *Wilko*, the Supreme Court has still not defined "manifest disregard", as will be discussed below, but most lower federal courts over the years prior to *Hall Street* had adopted some variant of a formulation by the Second Circuit:

> "In order to vacate for manifest disregard, a court must find that the arbitrators knew of a governing legal principle yet refused to apply it or ignored it altogether.... Moreover, the law ignored by the arbitrators must be well defined, explicit, and clearly applicable if the award is to be vacated."[93]

The Sixth Circuit remarked, to similar effect, that "[t]o merit reversal, the award must fly in the face of clearly established legal precedent.... Arbitrators act in manifest disregard if (1) the applicable legal principle is clearly defined and not subject to reasonable debate; and (2) the arbitrators refused to heed that legal principle."[94]

Unsurprisingly, this standard was seldom satisfied, particularly where the law

89. See, e.g., Stuart M. WIDEMAN and Donald Lee ROME, "Judicial Remands of Challenged Awards: Legal and Procedural Issues after *Hall Street*", Disp. Res. J., Nov. 08-Jan. 09 at pp. 50, 57.

90. The UNCITRAL Model Law has initiated a trend away from judicial review of the merits of arbitral awards, but several jurisdictions, including Australia, China, Ireland and New Zealand, continue to allow for it. See Gary BORN, *International Commercial Arbitration* (2009) pp. 2647-2648.

91. *Wilko v. Swan*, 346 U.S. 427 (1953), overruled on other grounds by *Rodriguez de Quijas v. Shearson/American Express, Inc.*, 490 U.S. 477 (1989).

92. *Wilko*, 346 U.S. at 436-437.

93. *Folkways Music Publishers, Inc. v. Weiss*, 989 F.2d 108, 112 (2d Cir. 1993) (citations and internal quotation marks omitted).

94. *Jacada (Europe) Ltd. v. Int'l Marketing Strategies, Inc.*, 401 F.3d 701, 713 (6th Cir. 2005) (citations and internal quotation marks omitted); see also *San Martine Compania de Navegacion v. Sagueney Terminals, Ltd.*, 293 F.2d 796, 801 (9th Cir. 1961) (emphasizing that "manifest disregard of the law must be something beyond and different from a mere error in the law or failure on the part of the arbitrators to understand or apply the law" and that "it might be present when arbitrators understand and correctly state the law, but proceed to disregard the same").

allegedly disregarded by the arbitrators was foreign and therefore often less familiar to US federal judges than to the arbitrators.[95] In a seminal Second Circuit decision, *I/S Stavborg v. National Metal Converters, Inc.*,[96] a dispute arising out of a charterparty agreement governed by Spanish law, the court found the award of the majority of the arbitrators "clearly erroneous both in logic and result" but nevertheless affirmed the award because "even though erroneous the arbitral majority here was not irrationally so".[97] In another decision, *Duferco International Steel Trading v. T. Klaveness Shipping A/S*,[98] the Second Circuit observed that since 1960, when it first mentioned the "manifest disregard" standard, it had "vacated some part or all of an arbitral award" on this basis in only "four out of at least 48 cases where [it] applied the standard".[99]

The Fifth Circuit, like the Second Circuit, traditionally recognized "manifest disregard of law" as a valid ground for vacatur, but seldom applied the doctrine. In one case the Fifth Circuit adopted verbatim the Second Circuit's test,[100] stating that "manifest disregard of law":

> "clearly means more than error or misunderstanding with respect to the law. The error must have been obvious and capable of being readily and instantly perceived by the average person qualified to serve as an arbitrator. Moreover, the term 'disregard' implies that the arbitrator appreciates the existence of a clearly governing principle but decides to ignore or pay no attention to it."[101]

Another formulation offered by the Fifth Circuit was a two-step test, which applied where one party asserted "manifest disregard":

> "First, where on the basis of the information available to the court it is not manifest that the arbitrators acted contrary to the applicable law, the award should be upheld.
>
> Second, where on the basis of the information available to the court it is manifest that the arbitrators acted contrary to the applicable law, the award should

95. See *Brandeis Intsel Ltd. v. Calabrian Chemical Corp.*, 656 F.Supp. 160, 167 (S.D.N.Y. 1987) ("It is one thing to ask an American judge to hold American arbitrators guilty of a manifest disregard of American law. It is quite another to ask an American judge to determine whether foreign arbitrators manifestly disregarded the internal, substantive law of a foreign nation by which the parties agreed in their contract to be bound. That seems to me a slippery slope upon which American judges should not embark, in clear derogation of the public policy underlying the Convention.").

96. 500 F.2d 424 (2d Cir. 1974).

97. *Ibid.*, at 429, 431.

98. 333 F.3d 383 (2d Cir. 2003).

99. *Ibid.*, at 389.

100. *Prestige Ford v. Ford Dealer Computer Services, Inc.*, 324 F.3d 391 (5th Cir. 2003).

101. *Ibid.*, at 395 (quoting *Merrill Lynch, Pierce, Fenner & Smith, Inc. v. Bobker*, 808 F.2d 930, 933-934 (2d Cir. 1986)).

be upheld unless it would result in significant injustice, taking into account all the circumstances of the case, including powers of arbitrators to judge norms appropriate to the relations between parties."[102]

This latter formulation introduced an additional hurdle to the application of the doctrine. Whereas, under the Second Circuit's test, "manifest disregard" could justify vacatur where the result reached by the arbitrators, among other things, was incorrect, the Fifth Circuit test further suggested that error per se would not be enough to warrant setting aside the award. The error must have "result[ed] in significant injustice" in view of the totality of the circumstances and of arbitral discretion to "judge norms appropriate to the relations between parties".

But in *Hall Street*, as already mentioned, the Supreme Court stated that the FAA's four grounds for vacatur are "exclusive".[103] Without directly addressing whether the manifest disregard doctrine would henceforth be precluded as a ground for vacatur, the Court merely speculated as to whether the term "manifest disregard" was meant to name a new ground for review, or whether it merely referred to the Sect. 10 grounds collectively, rather than adding to them. Nor did the Court clarify the matter in its most recent arbitration case, *Stolt-Nielsen S.A. v. Animalfeeds International Corp*,[104] which we discussed earlier. Since *Hall Street*, it is therefore unsurprising that there has been extensive controversy within the arbitration community over whether the case did away with the "manifest disregard" of law doctrine.[105] Lower courts remain split on the issue,[106] and five courts of appeals have now expressed their views.

The First Circuit, the first appellate court to comment on *Hall Street*, views the opinion as holding that manifest disregard "is not a valid ground" for vacating an arbitration award.[107] The Fifth Circuit reached the same conclusion in *Citigroup Global Markets Inc. v. Bacon*,[108] in which the court concluded that the Supreme Court's

---

102. *Sarofim v. Trust Co. of the West*, 440 F.3d 213, 217 (5th Cir. 2006) (citation and internal quotation marks omitted).

103. *Hall St. Assoc. v. Mattel Inc.*, 128 S.Ct. 1396, 1403 (2008).

104. 130 S.Ct. 1758, 1768 n. 3 (2010) ("We do not decide whether 'manifest disregard' survives our decision in *Hall Street Associates, L.L.C. v. Mattel, Inc.*, 552 U.S. 576, 585 (2008), as an independent ground for review or as a judicial gloss on the enumerated grounds for vacatur set forth at 9 U.S.C. Sect. 10.").

105. See, e.g., *The Householder Group v. Caughran*, 576 F.Supp.2d 796, 800 (E.D. Tex. 2008); See also *Prime Therapeutics LLC v. Omnicare Inc.*, 555 F.Supp.2d 993, 999 (D. Minn. 2008); *Robert Lewis Rosen Assocs., Ltd. v. Webb*, 566 F.Supp.2d 228, 233 (S.D.N.Y. 2008).

106. *Coffee Beanery, Ltd. v. WW, L.L.C.*, 300 Fed. Appx. 415, 2008 U.S. App. LEXIS 23645, *10-11 (6th Cir. 2009) (Hall Street "significantly reduced the ability of federal courts to vacate arbitration awards for reasons other than those specified in 9 U.S.C. Sect. 10, but it did not foreclose federal courts' review for an arbitrator's manifest disregard of the law"); See also *Qorvis Comms., LLC v. Wilson*, 549 F.3d 303 (4th Cir. 2008) (noting *Hall Street* and considering a manifest disregard challenge to an arbitration award but rejecting that challenge); Hiro N. ARAGAKI, "The Mess of Manifest Disregard", 119 Yale L.J. Online (2009) p. 1 at p. 5 (*Hall Street* "leaves manifest disregard and other common-law vacatur standards fully intact".).

107. *Ramos-Santiago v. UPS*, 524 F.3d 120, 124 n. 3 (1st Cir. 2008).

108. 562 F.3d 349 (5th Cir. 2009).

description of the FAA Sect. 10 grounds as "exclusive" means that manifest disregard of the law "is no longer an independent ground for vacating arbitration awards under the FAA".[109]

On the other hand, the Sixth Circuit has held that *Hall Street* merely "reduced" the ability of courts to vacate awards on grounds other than those specified in FAA Sect. 10 but "did not foreclose" review for manifest disregard of the law,[110] reasoning that the Supreme Court's "hesitation to reject" the manifest disregard standard would make it "imprudent" to jettison "such a universally recognized principle". But underscoring the difficulties posed by *Hall Street*, a different Sixth Circuit panel subsequently noted that the Supreme Court opinion "casts some doubt on the continuing vitality" of the manifest disregard standard.[111]

The Ninth Circuit has similarly held that *Hall Street* did not undermine a court's authority to vacate arbitration awards for manifestly disregarding the law.[112] However, the Ninth Circuit views manifest disregard as subsumed within FAA Sect. 10(a)(4), which authorizes vacatur where the arbitrators exceed their powers. According to such an approach, manifest disregard is not a non-statutory ground; it is merely another way in which arbitrators can exceed their powers.

The Second Circuit also has found that the manifest disregard standard survives *Hall Street*, but with the caveat – similar to the approach taken by the Ninth Circuit – that the standard can no longer be considered a non-statutory ground of judicial review. Instead, it is to be considered "a mechanism to enforce the parties' agreements to arbitrate".[113] But, as before *Hall Street*, the Second Circuit continues to insist that an arbitration award will be vacated on that basis only in "exceedingly rare" instances.

From the systemic perspective which we take, the issue of manifest disregard is an entirely national affair. The grounds on which a national court sets aside an award arising out of a *domestic* agreement to arbitrate should be of no import to *international* commercial arbitration, which operates under its own treaty-based regime. The real issue of concern is whether, in the face of *Hall Street* and the decisions following it, US courts may be willing to set aside *international* arbitral awards under the manifest disregard doctrine.[114] For that ground, which is not found in the New York Convention,

109. *Ibid.*, at 350.

110. *Coffee Beanery, Ltd. v. WW, L.L.C.*, 300 F.3d App'x 415, 418 (6th Cir. 2008).

111. *Grain v. Trinity Health, Mercy Health Servs. Inc.*, 551 F.3d 374, 380 (6th Cir. 2008).

112. *Comedy Club, Inc. v. Improv West Assocs.*, 553 F.3d 1277 (9th Cir. 2009).

113. *Stolt-Nielsen SA v. AnimalFeeds Int'l Corp.*, 548 F.3d 85, 95 (2d Cir. 2008), later overruled on other grounds, 130 S.Ct. 1758 (2010).

114. Art. I(1) of the New York Convention states:

> "This Convention shall apply to the recognition and enforcement of arbitral awards made in the territory of a State other than the State where the recognition and enforcement of such awards are sought, and arising out of differences between persons, whether physical or legal. It shall also apply to arbitral awards not considered as domestic awards in the State where their recognition and enforcement are sought."

would disturb the focus on extrinsicity that characterizes the control mechanism of the Convention.

Similar to the systemic concern about anti-arbitration injunctions, were US courts to expand Art. V to include the "manifest disregard" doctrine, other courts, by the well-known process of *mimesis* in customary international law,[115] could arrogate a comparable power and the confined review of the New York Convention would evolve into appeal. From a systemic perspective, the most realistic way to tackle this incipient problem is by cabining the radius of effects: the architecture of international commercial arbitration can accommodate expanded interpretations of Art. V when they issue from the *primary* forum for it has been selected by the parties; application of the "manifest disregard" ground would be inappropriate where the courts of a secondary forum invoke them.

4. *Defections from Obligations Under the New York Convention: Failure to Respect the Distinction Between Primary and Secondary National Courts*

National prescriptions limiting or extinguishing parties' rights to seek annulment of international arbitral awards may also threaten the efficacy of the New York Convention. In 1985, Belgium legislated its courts out of any post-award control function for international commercial arbitrations taking place within its jurisdiction. The critical section of the law of 27 March 1985, which added a new sub-paragraph to Art. 1717 of the Belgian Code, provided:

> "The courts of Belgium may be seized of a request for annulment only if at least one of the parties to the dispute decided by the arbitral award is either a physical person having Belgian nationality or residence, or a legal entity created in Belgium or having a branch or any other establishment in Belgium."

Under that amendment, Belgian courts could not perform any post-award control function within the scheme of the New York Convention. They could assist the arbitration prior to award, but were then legislatively paralyzed at the point at which an award would be rendered; that is exactly the instant at which the control function of the Convention is needed. Belgium's 1985 amendment was a take-it-or-leave-it offer. If parties chose Belgium as the venue of arbitration, they knew that Belgian courts were statutorily excluded from performing the control function of a primary jurisdiction under the New York Convention.

In 1999 Art. 1717(4) was once more amended, stating in pertinent part:

> "The parties may, through an express declaration in the arbitration agreement or through a later agreement, exclude any action for the annulment of an arbitrator's award when neither of them is either a natural person with a Belgian citizenship or a residence in Belgium, or a legal person having its main establishment or having a branch there."

115. See W. Michael REISMAN and Andrea ARMSTRONG, "The Past and Future of the Claim of Preemptive Self-Defense", supra fn. 58.

Apparently motivated by considerations similar to those that impelled Belgium to amend its law, the Swiss arbitral bar lobbied for and succeeded in securing a comparable regime. The international arbitration statute in Chapter 12 of the Swiss Law on Private International Law is also problematic from the standpoint of the control scheme in the New York Convention. Art. 192, according to an unofficial translation, provides:

> "1. If neither party is domiciled, nor has its habitual residence or place of business in Switzerland, the parties may expressly agree in the arbitration agreement or in a subsequent written agreement, to waive their right to challenge an arbitral award before the Swiss courts; they may also waive their right only with respect to one or some of the grounds set forth at Art. 190(2).
>
> 2. When the parties have waived all recourse against the award and when its enforcement is sought in Switzerland, the New York Convention on the Recognition and Enforcement of Foreign Arbitral Awards of 10 June 1958 shall apply by analogy."

The controls afforded by Art. V of the New York Convention only operate if enforcement is sought in Switzerland and, then, only "by analogy". One would assume that most international arbitrations taking place in Switzerland will concern foreign assets. But the essential self-interest of the Swiss regime is highlighted by Art. 192(2). If an international award involves assets in Switzerland, the Swiss legislature says that, parties' wishes notwithstanding, Switzerland still merits a control system.

The 1999 amendment to the Belgian law and the Swiss legislation pose an additional hazard. Consider the implications of the Swiss version. If the parties have agreed in the original arbitration clause to waive the jurisdiction of the Swiss courts, they simply surrender the international control function otherwise provided by primary national courts. But if they have not, and one party presses for such a waiver after the dispute has arisen, the party that does not wish to surrender that control reassurance will find itself in an awkward and potentially damaging position. The party pressing for waiver will be implying complete confidence in the arbitrator or arbitrators; the party resisting waiver, however diplomatic it may try to be, will appear to be doing the opposite. The party pressing for waiver is also promising to insure the arbitrator against the embarrassment of being criticized and reversed by a Swiss or Belgian court. The party resisting waiver is withholding those important professional indulgences.

Lest one think that these are risks that can be avoided by deciding the waiver issue beforehand, bear in mind that even if the parties agree not to waive in the arbitration clause, either party may raise the issue again once the tribunal has been installed. And lest one think that these risks can be avoided by not selecting Switzerland, in particular, as the venue, it is important to remember that this is not an option for the innumerable arbitration clauses in extant commercial contracts.

Thus, non-Swiss and non-Belgian parties are statutorily authorized to waive either some or all of the grounds for annulment specified. A few other arbitration statutes are similar, providing expressly that (typically foreign) parties may waive or limit the grounds for annulling an international arbitral award.[116] The English Arbitration Act 1996 offers a slight variation of this model, permitting exclusion clauses, by which parties waive their rights to judicial review of the substance of the arbitral award.[117] English law does not, however, allow broader waivers of the right to set aside an arbitral award for either jurisdictional objections or serious irregularity affecting the tribunal or the proceedings.[118] And although the United States has no such legislation, a limited number of US courts have permitted parties to waive judicial review of arbitral awards in an action to vacate, provided that the waiver is clear and explicit.[119]

Some have argued that the sort of unsupervised award contemplated by the Belgian and Swiss laws might not be enforceable in secondary jurisdictions under the Convention. Others have insisted that it is. But we would suggest that the question is not one of enforceability by a secondary jurisdiction, as such, but of the absence of operational finality of international commercial awards. Assume that an award which is the product of arbitral misconduct is issued by a tribunal sitting in Belgium or Switzerland, and it is brought for enforcement to the United States. As the secondary enforcer under the New York Convention, the American court is still empowered to examine the allegations of the defendant in terms of Art. V of the Convention and to refuse enforcement if it finds that the facts sustain one of them. However, the US judicial action will not constitute a nullification *erga omnes*, as would a comparable action in the primary jurisdiction. So the "winner" may continue to pursue enforcement in other fora.

Given the fact that decisions of secondary jurisdictions taken under Art. V have no effect beyond their boundaries, the elimination of the operational finality of foreign awards that was a function of the New York Convention will be felt in each successive jurisdiction in which enforcement is sought. Thus, the problem is not merely an increase in the burden of a single secondary jurisdiction. It is, in the aggregate, an increase in the burdens of all potential secondary jurisdictions, each of which may now be required to refuse enforcement for a defective award that could and should have been nullified in the primary jurisdiction.

---

116. See, e.g., Swedish Arbitration Act, Sect. 51; Tunisian Arbitration Code, Art. 78(6); Turkish International Arbitration Law, Art. 15(A)(2). However, national arbitration legislation in some developed jurisdictions provides that agreements waiving or restricting the parties' rights to seek annulment of an award are unenforceable. Egyptian Arbitration Law, Art. 54(1); Italian Code of Civil Procedure, Art. 829(1); British Columbia Commercial Arbitration Act, Sect. 31(1)(b).

117. English Arbitration Act 1996, Sect. 69(1); Robert MERKIN, *Arbitration Law*, para. 22.10 (2004 and Update 2007).

118. English Arbitration Act 1996, Sect. 68, Sect. 4(1), Schedule 1.

119. See, e.g., *Roadway Package Sys., Inc. v. Kayser*, 257 F.3d 287, 293 (3d Cir. 2001) (parties may "opt-out of the FAA's off-the-rack vacatur standards"); *Gramling v. Food Mach. & Chem. Corp.*, 151 F.Supp. 853 (W.D.S.C. 1957); David R. FOLEY, "Agreements Precluding Review of Awards: Are They Now Enforceable in US Courts?", 15 Int'l Arb. Rep. (2000, no. 5) p. 29. See also *MACTEC, Inc. v. Gorelick*, 427 F.3d (10th Cir. 2005) 821, 830 (upholding arbitration agreement's "waive[r of] the right to appellate review over district court decisions" regarding vacatur of award). Note that it can be argued that these decisions run contrary to the US Supreme Court's decision in *Hall Street*, discussed above, which held that the FAA's standards for judicial review of arbitral awards are exclusive and cannot be expanded by contract.

5. *Crossovers: Investment and Human Rights Tribunals as Supervisory Courts of Appeal in International Commercial Arbitration*

As we have seen, a critical strut supporting the architecture of international commercial arbitration is the assurance of the finality of arbitral awards once they have undergone the limited scope of extrinsic review available under the New York Convention on the Recognition and Enforcement of Foreign Arbitral Awards.[120] The keystone of this normative structure is the national court of the primary forum; that court is the agent of control and it has been given the ultimate say as to the validity of the award. Of late, however, this control system is in danger of being trumped, as disappointed litigants try to override it and its extrinsic criteria of review by crossing over to different international decision systems. These other systems may have different assignments as well as criteria of decision which differ from those prescribed in the New York Convention.

Litigants who had won international commercial arbitral awards only to see them annulled or unenforced in primary national fora have invoked relevant BITs in order to initiate investment arbitrations against the states whose courts issued the annulments, on the ground that the states' judiciaries' actions or inactions violated some of the protections afforded foreign investors under BITs and/or customary international law. Given that the adherences to the New York Convention (146) and the adherences to the Washington Convention[121] (147) are roughly congruent and that there are some 2,700 BITs, there are many opportunities for crossovers. Disappointed award creditors have also turned to international human rights courts for comparable relief, alleging violations of the applicable human rights instrument.

Thus, international commercial arbitration, on the one hand, and international investment arbitration and human rights adjudication, on the other, are intersecting. If the trend continues, the latter may displace the national court of the primary jurisdiction as the final decision-maker with respect to the validity of an international commercial arbitral award.

In a system such as international law, in which lawyers are always in search of hospitable forums, crossovers are not unprecedented. In the *Socobelge* case, Belgium espoused the claim of a Belgian company that had won an international commercial arbitration award against Greece with which Greece had not complied.[122] But that took place long before the New York Convention had established the contemporary international commercial arbitral system. In any event, the initiative was unsuccessful as the Permanent Court of International Justice was unwilling to invade the res judicata of

120. Convention on the Recognition and Enforcement of Foreign Arbitral Awards, 10 June 1958, 330 U.N.T.S. 3.

121. Convention on the Settlement of Investment Disputes between States and Nationals of Other States, 18 Mar. 1965, 575 U.N.T.S. 159.

122. *Société Commerciale de Belgique* (Belg. v. Greece), 1939 P.C.I.J. (ser. A/B) No. 78 (June 15). See generally W. Michael REISMAN, *The Supervisory Jurisdiction of the International Court of Justice: International Arbitration and International Adjudication*, 258 *Recueil Des Cours* 1 (1997) pp. 233-252.

the award. In the *SPP* case,[123] the claimant successfully crossed over from ICC to ICSID arbitration, but in that case, the ICC tribunal had found itself without jurisdiction.[124]

In the recent case of *Saipem v. Bangladesh*, Saipem, an Italian company, had initiated ICC proceedings against Petrobangla, a state-owned entity and party to the underlying contract. The venue of the arbitration was Bangladesh so Bangladeshi courts were the primary forum. After the ICC tribunal dismissed Petrobangla's jurisdictional challenges as well as a number of other procedural requests, Petrobangla sought the revocation of the tribunal's authority in Bangladeshi national courts. Various local courts in Bangladesh issued anti-arbitration injunctions purporting to revoke the ICC tribunal's authority and staying the arbitration proceedings. Despite those injunctions, the ICC tribunal continued with the arbitration and eventually delivered a final award, which was promptly declared unenforceable by the Supreme Court of Bangladesh. As Bangladesh was the seat of the arbitration, the Supreme Court claimed, as it could, that it had the legal authority to annul the ICC award under the New York Convention.

Saipem then initiated ICSID proceedings under the Italy-Bangladesh BIT, claiming that the interference by the local judiciary with the ICC arbitration constituted an expropriation under international law, inasmuch as Bangladesh had deprived it not only of its right to arbitrate any disputes with Petrobangla, but also its right to payment of the amounts due under the contract as determined by the ICC award.

In the jurisdictional phase of the ICSID arbitration, the ICSID tribunal had to decide whether a dispute arising from the ICC Award could be considered to have arisen directly from the investment – i.e., the underlying contract – according to both the ICSID Convention and the BIT. (Art. 25(1) of the ICSID Convention requires, as a condition for jurisdiction ratione materiae, that a dispute "aris[e] directly out of an investment".) Under Art. 1(1) of the BIT, investment was defined as "any kind of property". The tribunal held:

> "[T]he notion of investment pursuant to Article 25 of the ICSID must be understood as covering all the elements of the operation, that is not only the ICC Arbitration, but also *inter alia* the Contract, the construction itself and the Retention Money. Hence, in accordance with previous case law, the Tribunal holds that the present dispute arises directly out of the overall investment."[125]

123. *Southern Pacific Properties (Middle East) Limited v. Arab Republic of Egypt* (ICSID Case No. ARB/84/3) Award, 8 ICSID Rev.—Foreign Inv. L.J. (1993, no. 2) p. 328.

124. *SPP (Middle East) Limited v. Arab Republic of Egypt*, 22 I.L.M. (1983) 752.

125. *Saipem v. Bangladesh* (ICSID Case No. ARB/05/7), Decision on Jurisdiction (2007) at para. 114 (internal citations omitted).

The tribunal found that the that broad definition included the contract,[126] but it declined to go so far as to say that the ICC award itself would have constituted an investment.[127]

The tribunal also rested its conclusions in the first phase of the proceedings on the fact that the BIT provided ICSID jurisdiction for claims alleging expropriation, as well as the observation that under international law, judicial action could result in an expropriation[128] and immaterial rights could be the object of expropriation.[129] Because Saipem's claims were based on the allegation that Bangladesh had breached the New York Convention in a way which contravened the protections afforded in Art. V of the BIT, the tribunal found that they had a firm basis in the BIT, as opposed to being mere "contract claims dressed up as treaty claims".[130] The tribunal insisted that its role was not to "enforce" the ICC award or to serve as a supranational appellate body but rather to rule exclusively on treaty breaches, whatever their nature.[131] But here the tribunal may have protested too much. Its disclaimer notwithstanding, the remedy which Saipem sought was enforcement of an award which had been annulled by a primary national forum, a remedy which was being prayed from what amounted to a supranational appellate body.

In the merits phase, the tribunal found that the Bangladeshi Supreme Court's decision setting aside the ICC award constituted "a taking of the residual contractual rights arising from the investments as crystallized in the ICC Award",[132] and thus met the definition of unlawful expropriation under the applicable BIT:

> "In respect of the taking, the actions of the Bangladeshi courts do not constitute an instance of direct expropriation, but rather of "measures having similar effects" within the meaning of Article 5(2) of the BIT. Such actions resulted in substantially depriving Saipem of the benefit of the ICC Award. This is plain in light of the decision of the Bangladeshi Supreme Court that the ICC Award is 'a nullity'. Such a ruling is tantamount to a taking of the residual contractual rights arising from the investments as crystallised in the ICC Award. As such, it amounts to an expropriation within the meaning of Article 5 of the BIT."[133]

In contrast to the actions of the courts, the tribunal determined that the conduct of Petrobangla, the state-owned counterparty, did not qualify as a "taking", because, in the

126. *Ibid.*, at para. 122.
127. *Ibid.*, at para. 128 ("[T]he Tribunal does not need to make a final ruling on Saipem's additional argument that the arbitration agreement contained in the Contract constitutes a 'right of a financial nature accruing by law or by contract' within Article 1(1)(e) of the BIT....").
128. *Ibid.*, at paras. 131-132.
129. *Ibid.*, at para. 130 ("rights under judicial decisions are protected property that can be the object of an expropriation").
130. *Ibid.*, at paras. 139-141.
131. *Ibid.*, at paras. 155-158.
132. *Saipem v. Bangladesh* (ICSID Case No. ARB/05/7), Award (2009) at para. 129.
133. *Ibid.*

tribunal's view, Petrobangla's acts were not governmental in nature. As a result, the only actions at stake in the arbitration were those of the courts of Bangladesh. Regarding those actions, the tribunal considered whether the taking or deprivation was "substantial":

> "[G]iven the very peculiar circumstances of the present interference, the Tribunal agrees with the parties that *the substantial deprivation of Saipem's ability to enjoy the benefits of the ICC Award is not sufficient to conclude that the Bangladeshi courts' intervention is tantamount to an expropriation. If this were true, any setting aside of an award could then found a claim for expropriation, even if the setting aside was ordered by the competent state court upon legitimate grounds*." (Emphasis added.)

But that was hardly the end of the matter. The tribunal proceeded to distinguish between illegitimate and legitimate supervision on the part of the national court: "the actions of (or the actions attributable to) Bangladesh must be 'illegal' in order to give rise to a claim of expropriation".[134]

Applying that criterion, the tribunal found that, although the Bangladeshi courts were entitled to assert jurisdiction to hear the complaint of Petrobangla against the ICC arbitration, and although it was not evident that the Bangladeshi courts acted in collusion or conspired with Petrobangla, the Bangladeshi court's finding of misconduct and the revocation of the ICC tribunal's authority constituted "a grossly unfair ruling".[135] For those reasons, and because the Bangladeshi courts also declined to consult the ICC arbitrators during the process of revoking their authority, taking for granted "what Petrobangla falsely presented",[136] the tribunal found that "the Bangladeshi courts exercised their supervisory jurisdiction for an end which was different from that for which it was instituted and thus violated the internationally accepted principle of prohibition of abuse of rights",[137] as well as Art. II of the New York Convention.[138]

Saipem, for all the hedging in its holding, is far-reaching in its implications. It adapts the mechanisms of international investment law, as expressed in bilateral investment treaties, to serve as the criterion for a review of the lawfulness of the performance by national courts of their responsibilities under the New York Convention.

In *Romak v. Uzbekistan*,[139] a recent case at the Permanent Court of Arbitration, the tribunal was asked to determine whether an Uzbekistan court's refusal to enforce an arbitral award constituted a breach of the relevant BIT. Romak, a Swiss company, and several other companies specializing in the trading of grain, entered into a set of contracts for the supply of wheat. As a result of the inability to obtain payment for the deliveries, Romak initiated arbitration under the auspices of the Grain and Feed Trade Association (GAFTA) against its Uzbek counterparty and won an award for the value of

---

134. *Ibid.*, at para. 134.
135. *Ibid.*, at para. 155.
136. *Ibid.*, at para. 157.
137. *Ibid.*, at para. 161.
138. *Ibid.*, at para. 167.
139. *Romak S.A. v. Uzbekistan*, PCA Case No. AA 280, Award (2009).

the 40,000 tons of wheat that Romak had delivered. But Romak's attempts to enforce the award in several countries, including Uzbekistan, all failed.

Uzdon, the government-controlled Uzbek company which was ordered to pay damages, appealed the award to the GAFTA Board of Appeals but the appeal was rejected as untimely. Subsequently, Uzdon turned to the High Court of Justice in London to contest the award, as English law had been designated as the applicable law by the GAFTA tribunal. Despite the High Court of Justice's refusal to vacate the award, the Uzbek government insisted that it would not enforce it, contending that "the decision was biased and had been rendered against the wrong party, as Odil, [another, privately held Uzbek company] was in fact responsible for paying Romak".[140]

Art. IV of the New York Convention prescribes that "the party requesting enforcement should present all corresponding documents to the court of the country where the respondent is located". When Romak applied to the Commercial Court of the City of Tashkent for recognition and enforcement of the GAFTA Award, the Court returned the application to Romak because, first, Romak had not provided a translation of the award into Uzbek, the court's official language and, second, Romak had submitted no evidence to the Court that Uzdon had been duly notified of the appointment of the arbitrators as required by Art. V(1)(*b*) of the New York Convention. Romak appealed the Commercial Court's decision; the Appellate Jurisdiction of the Tashkent Commercial Court confirmed the decision of the lower court. Thus, unlike the situation in *Saipem*, the *Romak* award was never actually annulled; it merely went unenforced by the Uzbek courts.

Having failed under the New York Convention regime, Romak tried to cross over to the international investment law regime by initiating arbitration against Uzbekistan under Art. 9 of the Switzerland-Uzbekistan BIT. Romak's submissions were classic investment law claims. It alleged that Uzbekistan's refusal to enforce the award constituted a violation of the mother of all grounds in investment arbitration, the fair and equitable treatment standard. Specifically, Romak contended that Uzbek courts, in refusing to enforce the GAFTA award on the basis of Art. IV of the New York Convention, misapplied the Convention, as Art. V sets out the exclusive grounds for refusing recognition and enforcement of an award. Moreover, Romak averred that a claimant "*should be allowed to complete the conditions for such a request during the proceedings*".[141] Such an improper interpretation and application of the New York Convention constituted a breach of the BIT's "umbrella" clause, which guaranteed the enforcement of arbitral awards. Romak also claimed that the conduct of the Uzbek courts was incompatible with Art. 3 of the BIT, which is intended to ensure a secure investment environment, the promotion of investments, and fair and equitable treatment before Uzbek courts.[142] Like Saipem, Romak claimed that the Uzbek courts' conduct resulted in the expropriation of

140. *Ibid.*, at para. 62.

141. *Ibid.*, at para. 134.

142. *Ibid.*, at para. 135.

its contractual rights, either directly or indirectly, and that the Uzbek courts' refusal to enforce the GAFTA award destroyed Romak's rights and the commercial value of its investment, constituting expropriation.[143]

Some of Romak's claims were appellate in nature, such as its contention that the Uzbek courts' decision to refuse enforcement of the GAFTA award contained "*gross defects in its substance*", which resulted in a denial of justice and a violation of principles of international law, and that, in contravention of Uzbekistan's international obligations, "the Uzbek courts imposed two unreasonable obstacles preventing the enforcement of the GAFTA Award: the obligation to provide an Uzbek translation of the GAFTA Award (although Russian is commonly used by the courts), and the refusal to grant an extension in order to have the GAFTA Award translated into Uzbek".[144] And, of course, Romak claimed that, together, these acts amounted to unjustified, unfair and inequitable treatment prohibited under Art. 3 of the BIT and, "by virtue of the MFN Clause[,] under Art. 2(c) of Annex B to the Uzbekistan-Italy BIT. Alternatively, Romak submit[ted] that it was denied justice under customary international law, giving rise to corresponding liability under the BIT."[145]

For the *Romak* investment tribunal, as for its counterpart in *Saipem*, international investment ratione materiae jurisdiction turned on whether Romak was an "investor" and whether the dispute submitted to arbitration related to an "investment" within the meaning set forth in the BIT. Romak argued that the award was an "investment" under the treaty, whose broad definition included "every kind of asset" having economic value;[146] it was the owner of a "claim to money", including rights under the Romak Supply Agreement and the GAFTA award.[147] Uzbekistan, also relying on the *Saipem* decision, argued that an arbitral award can be considered an investment only to the extent that the underlying transaction could be defined as an investment, and that the sale of goods contract underlying the original dispute did not itself constitute an investment.

Although the BIT's definition of investment was comprehensive,[148] the tribunal

---

143. *Ibid.*, at para. 136.
144. *Ibid.*, at para. 137.
145. *Ibid.*, at para. 138.
146. *Ibid.*, at para. 101.
147. *Ibid.*
148. Art. 1 states, in pertinent part:

> "For the purpose of this Agreement: …
> (2) The term 'investments' shall include every kind of assets and particularly:
> (a) movable and immovable property as well as any other rights in rem, such as servitudes, mortgages, liens, pledges;
> (b) shares, parts or any other kinds of participation in companies;
> (c) claims to money or to any performance having an economic value;
> (d) copyrights, industrial property rights (such as patents, utility models, industrial designs or models, trade or service marks, trade names, indications of origin), technical processes, know-how and goodwill;
> (e) concessions under public law, including concessions to search for, extract or exploit natural resources as well as all other rights given by law, by contract or by decision of the authority in

rejected Romak's argument that it "should simply confirm that the Claimant's assets fall within one or more of the categories listed in Article 1(2) of the BIT, thus sponsoring a construction of the BIT that puts special emphasis on the literal words in the list of Article 1(2)".[149] According to the tribunal, such an interpretation "would eliminate any practical limitation to the scope of the concept of 'investment'. In particular, it would render meaningless the distinction between investments, on the one hand, and purely commercial transactions, on the other."[150] The tribunal reasoned that

> "the mechanical application of the categories found in Article 1(2) would create, *de facto*, a new instance of review of State court decisions concerning the enforcement of arbitral awards. Under the scenario advocated by Romak, any award rendered in favor of a national of a Contracting Party (even one rendered in a purely commercial arbitration procedure) would be considered a '*claim to money*' or, arguably – as pleaded by Romak – a '*right given by decision of the authority*'. The refusal or failure of the host State's courts to enforce such an award would therefore arguably provide sufficient grounds for a *de novo* review – under a different international instrument and on grounds different from those that would normally apply – of the State courts' decision not to enforce an award."[151]

Having addressed and rejected the implication of the *Saipem* holding, the *Romak* tribunal evaded actually applying it, by finding that the underlying transaction was not an investment and that it could not be transformed into a qualifying investment by molting into an arbitral award.

> "The Arbitral Tribunal need not rule in abstract whether an arbitral award in itself can be considered an investment under the BIT, a matter which should be analyzed in light of the meaning of the term 'investment' as it has been determined by this Arbitral Tribunal, and which is necessarily dependent on the specific facts of the case.
>
> ... [T]he GAFTA Award is so inextricably linked to the Romak Supply Agreement that any determination as to whether Romak holds an investment under the BIT cannot be made without reference to the entire economic transaction that is the subject of these arbitral proceedings. The GAFTA Award merely constitutes the embodiment of Romak's contractual rights (as determined by the GAFTA Arbitral Tribunal) stemming from the wheat supply transaction entered into by Romak. If the underlying transaction is not an investment within the meaning of the BIT, the mere embodiment or crystallization of rights arising thereunder in an arbitral award cannot transform it into an investment."

---

accordance with the law."

149. *Romak*, at para. 178.

150. *Ibid.*, at para. 185.

151. *Ibid.*, at paras. 186, 210-211 (italics in original).

Thus the *Romak* tribunal disallowed jurisdiction ratione materiae by looking to whether the underlying transaction met the criteria of an investment.[152] In fact, the BIT's definition of investment was expansive and this was not an ICSID case implicating Art. 25(1) of the Washington Convention. Had the underlying transaction conformed to the definition of an investment, it is not clear whether the tribunal would have accepted jurisdiction and ordered Uzbekistan to pay damages for its failure to enforce the GAFTA award. From an investment law perspective, however, there is no material difference between the fact that *Romak* arose from the host state's failure to enforce a commercial arbitral award while in *Saipem*, there was an outright annulment.

One final investment law decision illustrates the potential reach of *Saipem*'s novel holding, and the importance of taking a moment to appraise *Saipem*'s potential effect. In the recent ICSID Award in *GEA v. Ukraine*,[153] the tribunal was asked to deem an ICC award, as well as a settlement agreement, to be "investments" under the relevant BIT, and to characterize Ukraine's failure to give effect to either the award or the settlement an act tantamount to expropriation. The claimants seized upon the language of *Saipem* to argue that Ukraine's non-enforcement of the ICC award was "a travesty of justice applying a discriminatory law to avoid enforcement of GEA's award under the New York Convention such that their refusal to recognize GEA's ICC award is tantamount to expropriation".[154]

The tribunal found unpersuasive the claimant's characterization as "investments" the ICC award and the settlement agreement. With a nod to *Romak*, the tribunal acknowledged that "it is not so much the term 'investment' in the ISCID Convention than the term 'investment' *per se* that is often considered as having an objective meaning in itself...".[155] And nodding to *Biwater v. Tanzania*,[156] the tribunal noted the resistance to an inflexible *Salini*-type standard for investment among tribunals, and found persuasive reasons to adopt a pragmatic definition of "investment", respectful of the broad definitions of investment to be found in many BITs. But, crucially, the tribunal noted that however this interpretive debate is resolved, "neither the Settlement Agreement nor the Repayment Agreement – *in and of themselves* – constitute 'investments' under [the BIT] or (if needed) Art. 25 of the ICSID Convention".[157]

The *GEA* tribunal was sensitive to the systemic costs of overlooking the differences between distinct arbitral regimes. Noting that neither settlements nor arbitral judgments are "investments", the tribunal identified the critical difference in kind between the regimes of investment law and international commercial arbitration.

---

152. For a different view, see W. Michael REISMAN and Anna VINNIK, "What Constitutes an Investment and Who Decides?" in Arthur ROVINE, ed., *Contemporary Issues in International Arbitration and Mediation: The Fordham Papers 2010* (2011).

153. *GEA Group Aktiengesellschaft v. Ukraine* (ICSID Case No. ARB/08/16) (2011).

154. *Ibid.*, at p. 62 (internal quotation marks omitted).

155. *Ibid.*, at p. 40.

156. *Biwater Gauff (Tanzania) Ltd. v. Tanzania* (ICSID Case No. ARB/05/22) Award (2008).

157. *Ibid.*, at p. 46.

> "[T]he fact that the Award rules upon rights and obligations arising out of an investment does not equate the Award with the investment itself. In [our] view, the two remain analytically distinct, and the Award itself involves no contribution to, or relevant economic activity within, Ukraine such as to fall – *itself* – within the scope of ... the BIT or ... [the ICSID] Convention."[158]

The tribunal quoted, without adopting, the respondent's argument that "creat[ing] an appellate jurisdiction for the recognition and enforcement of awards ... would undermine the present international legal system for the recognition and enforcement of arbitral awards".[159] Though these systemic considerations were not adopted as the *ratio* for decision, the tension between these considerations and the claimant's construction of *Saipem*'s rule against "egregious" non-enforcement seemed to play a role in the tribunal's decision in favor of the respondent.

Crossovers from international commercial arbitration may also be possible to human rights courts. In 2010 the European Court of Human Rights issued a judgment regarding Serbia's non-enforcement of a commercial arbitral award. In *Kin-Stib and Majkić v. Serbia*, the applicants complained under Art. 1 of Protocol No. 1 of the European Convention for the Protection of Human Rights and Fundamental Freedoms (ECHR)[160] about the partial non-enforcement of an arbitral award that had been rendered in 1996 against a Serbian company in the Foreign Trade Arbitration Court of the Yugoslav Chamber of Commerce.

Art. 1 of Protocol No. 1 states:

> "Every natural or legal person is entitled to the peaceful enjoyment of his possessions. No one shall be deprived of his possessions except in the public interest and subject to the conditions provided for by law and by the general principles of international law.
>
> The preceding provisions shall not, however, in any way impair the right of a State to enforce such laws as it deems necessary to control the use of property in accordance with the general interest or to secure the payment of taxes or other contributions or penalties."

Accepting jurisdiction over the matter, the ECHR noted:

> "[A] 'claim' can constitute a 'possession', within the meaning of Article 1 of Protocol No. 1, if it is sufficiently established to be enforceable.... It further recalls that it is the State's responsibility to make use of all available legal means at its disposal in order to enforce a binding arbitration award providing it contains

158. *Ibid.*, at p. 47.
159. *Ibid.*, at p. 63.
160. Protocol to the Convention for the Protection of Human Rights and Fundamental Freedoms, Art. 1, 20 March 1952, 213 U.N.T.S. 262.

> a sufficiently established claim amounting to a possession.... Finally, the State must make sure that the execution of such an award is carried out without undue delay and that the overall system is effective both in law and in practice."[161]

The Court found that the Serbian courts had not taken "the necessary measures to fully enforce the arbitration award in question and have not provided any convincing reasons for that failure".[162] As such, the ECHR found Serbia to be in violation of Art. 1, Protocol No. 1 and ordered the government to compensate the applicants accordingly.

Four cases in which disappointed consumers of the justice afforded by national courts under the New York Convention or national arbitration statutes turned to other international systems hardly constitute a trend. Yet given the ingenuity of lawyers, these cases – different in facts and applicable law but all concerned with the appraisal of the performance of national courts under the New York Convention – may portend a unique variation of the architecture of international commercial arbitration. Do they mean that the assignment of the crucial role to the courts of the primary forum is shifting to other public international institutions who will now exercise a higher, quasi-appellate role? Each case came about when parties were either unable to enforce an arbitral award, or when an award had been annulled altogether by the primary forum or it refused to execute it. The acceptance by investment tribunals and international human rights courts of jurisdiction over treaty claims arising from the non-enforcement or annulment of commercial arbitral awards could dramatically change the control regime governing international commercial arbitration in terms of authorized decision makers, legal criteria and, not the least, the total time required to conclude an international commercial arbitral proceeding.

Would such a shift in control help or hinder the operation of the New York Convention? On the one hand, the prospect of a new level of jurisdiction capable of appraising national courts' performance of their competences under the New York Convention in terms of *international law* may increase accountability by incentivizing those courts to comply with the Convention in the enforcement of commercial arbitral awards and to annul or refuse enforcement of awards only in those circumstances permitted by the Convention. But crossovers also have the potential to extend the process of international commercial arbitration, often touted for its speed and economy, for additional months, if not years.

6. *A "New" New York Convention? The Van den Berg Projet*

The dean of the New York Convention, Professor Albert Jan van den Berg, has drawn upon several of the discontinuities that have emerged over fifty years of interpretation and application of the Convention to suggest some amendments to the architecture of international commercial arbitration. To this end, he has created a hypothetical "New

---

161. *Kin-Stib and Majkić v. Serbia*, ECHR, Application no. 12312/05 (2010), at para. 83.
162. *Ibid.*, at para. 85.

York Convention 2.0".[163] Together with his explanatory Report, the text of Professor van den Berg's new New York Convention is an important contribution to the useful debate about the architecture of international commercial arbitration.

With the caveat in mind that change in the law should not come from the pen of an arbitrator, this draft convention, if adopted through legitimate legislative processes, settles many of the anomalous features of the 1958 New York Convention that have been commented on. They merit comment.

Given our analysis regarding the importance of maintaining the distinction between primary and secondary fora in Art. V, the draft convention makes explicit what is already clear: Art. V adjusts the first paragraph of the English text ("enforcement may be refused") to make clear that it is a mandatory formulation ("enforcement *shall* be refused"). Because the ambiguity of Art. V's mandatory language has detained several interpreters, codifying the mandatory character of Art. V "alleviate[s] the need to deal with the question under article V(1) ... whether the introductory language of the grounds for refusal of enforcement should be permissive.... [It] is unambiguous by being mandatory."[164]

The projet also disposes of an anachronism in Art. V: the duality of the primary forum. It does away with the primary co-competence assigned to the court "under the law of which, [an] award was made".[165] In its place, the primary forum is defined exclusively as "an arbitral appeal tribunal or a court in the country where the award was made".[166] As we discussed earlier, the 1958 Convention's allocation of primary competence to both the domestic court of the seat and the system whose law the parties had chosen is puzzling given that selection of that law does not, in itself, mean that the parties intended to assign any role to the courts of that legal system.[167] The new Art. V(3)(f) would remove this anomaly, in our view to the benefit of the system.

One provision of Professor van den Berg's new proposal is likely to encounter resistance from the states who are meant to sign it, and, in our view, with reason. It would change Art. V (2)(*b*) (which allows courts to refuse enforcement where doing so "would be contrary to public policy") so that national courts are permitted to resist awards on public policy grounds only insofar as considerations of *international* public policy are implicated. International public policy originally functioned to enable courts whose national public policy might have prevented enforcement of Convention awards to replace it with a more permissive international version which allowed enforcement.

---

163. See Albert Jan VAN DEN BERG, "The Miami Draft", available at <www.newyorkconvention.org/draft-convention> (hereinafter the Miami Draft).

164. Albert Jan VAN DEN BERG, "Explanatory Note: Hypothetical Draft Convention on the International Enforcement of Arbitration Agreements and Awards", para. 75

165. New York Convention, Art. V(1)(*e*).

166. The Miami Draft, Art. (V)(3)(f).

167. See supra fn. 16.

Over time, however, it has transformed into a ground for denying enforcement. In our view, its vagueness makes it a problem. If public policy is "an unruly horse", international public policy is a wild, unbroken one.[168]

IV. CONCLUSION

The New York Convention established a carefully designed allocation of competences between international commercial arbitral tribunals and national courts; the latter were tasked with facilitating the initiation of arbitration and the enforcement of ensuing awards as well as with providing a carefully gauged measure of control. In the course of the half century in which the Convention has operated, the application of the Convention by a wide range of national courts has hewed remarkably closely to the original normative architecture.

But no legal arrangement can claim the finality of the proverbial Decrees of the Medes and the Persians. In the dialectical process of all law, demands for change and challenges are continuous. Some resulting changes improve on existing arrangements; some undermine them; some transform them into something radically different from what they had been.

We do not contend that changes in the architecture of international commercial arbitration are, per se, "good" or "bad". Such evaluations turn upon the consequences of specific changes in terms of the eufunction of the system of which they are a part, including the achievement of that system's goals. But we do submit that the architecture of the New York Convention reflects a coherent and realistic system. Some changes to the system governing international commercial arbitration address real problems, while others are themselves problematic for the regime. National courts, which allow expanded review beyond that prescribed by the Convention when serving as a primary forum seem to be system-neutral but the mimetic dynamic in international law may lead to wide adoption of the practice with unintended consequences. Legislation stripping parties of the right to a primary forum of review may disturb the system as will anti-arbitration injunctions for grounds not found in the Convention.

The creation of a limited "supervisory-supervisory" role for investor-state arbitral tribunals over the performance by national courts of their responsibilities under the New York Convention, while extending the resolution of commercial disputes, may actually increase the accountability of States Parties and incentivize national courts to comply with the Convention in the enforcement of commercial arbitral awards; international human rights courts performing a comparable function may do the same. Since they are not other "national" courts and insofar as they do not (at least for investment tribunals) undertake a de novo review of the dispute, they avert a critical concern of the New York Convention.

168. See generally W. Michael REISMAN, "Law, International Public Policy (So-called), and Arbitral Choice in International Commercial Arbitration" in *ICCA Congress Series no. 13*, p. 849.

But that is not the only possible outcome of these initiatives. Excessive supervisory-supervisory jurisdiction over national courts' powers of enforcement and annulment as prescribed by the Convention could change the allocation of competences under the regime. The extent to which this last innovation would solve the problem of abuse of power by primary fora remains uncertain.

International Arbitration as a Transnational System of Justice

*Emmanuel Gaillard**

TABLE OF CONTENTS

	Page
I. Introduction	66
II. The Representations of International Arbitration	67
III. The Role of the 1958 New York Convention	71

I. INTRODUCTION

International arbitration is increasingly recognized as a transnational system of justice, if not a genuinely autonomous legal order, sometimes labeled as the arbitral legal order.[1] This evolution, however, continues to generate robust controversies on the extent of autonomy of international arbitration from national legal systems and the role, if any, that the seat of the arbitration should have over the arbitral process.

This pervasive debate suggests that the longstanding relationship between autonomy and international arbitration is still ill-defined to some extent. It also demonstrates that considerations of autonomy, without more, cannot provide answers to certain more fundamental and practical questions ubiquitous in international arbitration, such as questions related to applicable law, procedure and the enforcement of awards.

A more fundamental approach is to examine the reasons for the sharp divergence in views between those who root international arbitration in a national legal system and those who recognize the transnational character of the process. These differences cannot be explained solely by considerations of autonomy, or by focusing on isolated practical aspects of international arbitration. Instead, one must consider the source (or sources) of validity and legitimacy of the arbitral process and the ensuing award. In this respect,

* Professor of Law, Paris XII University; head of the International Arbitration Group, Shearman & Sterling LLP; Member of ICCA.

1. For a discussion on the evolution and usage of the expression "arbitral legal order", see Emmanuel GAILLARD, *Legal Theory of International Arbitration* (Martinus Nijhoff Publishers 2010) pp. 38-46. On the recognition in certain jurisdictions of the existence of an arbitral legal order, see Dominique HASHER, "The Review of Arbitral Awards by Domestic Courts – France" in Emmanuel GAILLARD, ed., *IAI Series on International Arbitration, No. 6. The Review of International Arbitral Awards* (Juris 2010) p. 97 ("The French concept of arbitration is based on the premise that there is an arbitral legal order, which is distinct from the legal order of individual States.... It is this arbitral legal order – and no national legal order – that confers juridicity to arbitration."); Jean-Pierre ANCEL, "The Decree of 13 January 2011: Increasing the Efficiency of Arbitration in France", *The 13 January 2011 Decree, The New French Arbitration Law* (Paris the Home of International Arbitration, 2011) p. 9 (noting that the French view of international arbitration law is based on "the recognition of the existence of a truly autonomous arbitral legal order"); Ugo DRAETTA, Report given at the Seminar *Journée d'étude en l'honneur de Giorgio Shiavoni : La résolution des différends commerciaux en Méditerranée : quel rôle pour l'arbitrage?*: "*L'arbitrage international est-il une fonction publique?*" (Camera Arbitrale di Milano, 27 June 2011).

three visions of international arbitration appear to constitute a dividing line, each having a distinct theoretical ground as well as entailing extremely concrete practical consequences. These visions will be described below (II), before further consideration is given to the role of the 1958 New York Convention[2] in this debate (III).

II. THE REPRESENTATIONS OF INTERNATIONAL ARBITRATION

There are three competing visions of international arbitration, defined by what their proponents consider to be the source of legitimacy of the phenomenon: the monolocal vision, the Westphalian vision and the transnational vision.[3] These visions, mental constructs or representations,[4] strongly influence the views held on a number of questions ranging from whether the arbitrators are empowered to determine their own jurisdiction, the conduct of the arbitral proceedings, the determination of the law applicable to the merits of the dispute, or the fate of the resulting arbitral award, including the controversial question of whether an award set aside in the country of the seat of the arbitration may nevertheless be enforced in other jurisdictions.

This Comment will focus on dispelling two common misunderstandings that go to the heart of both the philosophical underpinnings of the representations of international arbitration and their practical consequences: First, none of these representations suggests that international arbitration does not ultimately derive its legitimacy or validity from states (*1*). Second, whether or not one is conscious of their existence, these representations carry major practical consequences for all the players in the field of international arbitration, not just arbitrators (*2*).

1. The Source of the Legitimacy and Validity of International Arbitration

The three representations of international arbitration are defined by what they hold to be the source of legitimacy of international arbitration, namely what is the arbitrator's source of power to adjudicate. This assumption carries far-reaching implications for how one views the entirety of the arbitral process.

The first and most traditional view is the monolocal vision, which considers the sole source of legitimacy and validity of international arbitration to be the law of the seat of the arbitration, or as proponents of this view might say, the "country of origin". In this

2. Convention on the Recognition and Enforcement of Foreign Arbitral Awards, done in New York on 10 June 1958 (hereinafter the New York Convention or the Convention). As of 30 September 2011, 146 states were parties to the New York Convention. The membership status is available at: <www.uncitral.org/uncitral/en/uncitral_texts/arbitration/NYConvention_status.html>.

3. See generally Emmanuel GAILLARD, *Legal Theory of International Arbitration*, fn. 1 above. See also Emmanuel GAILLARD, "Three Philosophies of International Arbitration" in Arthur W. ROVINE, ed., *Contemporary Issues in International Arbitration and Mediation: The Fordham Papers 2009* (Martinus Nijhoff Publishers 2010).

4. For an analysis of the notion of representation from a cognitive science perspective, see Emmanuel GAILLARD, "The Representations of International Arbitration", Journal of International Dispute Settlement (2010) pp. 1-11.

vision, the seat of the arbitration is more than a location chosen for convenience or neutrality; it provides the exclusive basis for the binding nature of the arbitration. Consequent to this view, if the arbitration is taking place in Mexico it is a Mexican arbitration, even if the dispute is between a French company and an American company, and governed by Swiss law. If these diverse parties are allowed to arbitrate, it is because the Mexican legal order has given a preauthorization to do so. The resulting award is considered a Mexican award.

The second representation is the Westphalian vision, which considers that if international arbitration is a legitimate process, it is because there are a number of states that are prepared to recognize the legitimacy of an adjudication process based on the common intent of the parties, as well as the binding nature of the resulting award. This vision is a radical departure from the monolocal view in two respects. First, the arbitral process is no longer preauthorized, but rather legitimized *a posteriori* if an award meets the enforcing state's criteria. Second, this view considers that international arbitration can derive its legitimacy from a plurality of legal systems, including the state or states of enforcement. Under this representation, the law of the seat is just one amongst other potentially relevant legal systems, and the seat itself is considered more as a physical location where the arbitration is held as opposed to a legal forum defining the extent of the arbitrators' role, just as it would for a local court. This vision of judicial plurality is best described as Westphalian because it is based on a model in which each state has an equally legitimate title to decide for itself the conditions under which it will consider as valid the arbitration process and the ensuing award as worthy of enforcement.[5]

The third representation, the transnational vision, goes one step further than the Westphalian approach to contemplate the states collectively, rather than individually. This representation recognizes the source of legitimacy of arbitration as rooted in the views developed collectively by the community of nations through instruments such as the 1958 New York Convention, the UNCITRAL Model Law and numerous guidelines which express a common view as to how an arbitration should be conducted so as to be recognized as a legitimate means of adjudication. In other words, in this vision, the source of validity and legitimacy of the arbitral process is found in the collective normative activity of states. This representation also corresponds to international arbitrators' strong perception that they do not administer justice on behalf of any particular state, but that they play a judicial role for the benefit of the international community.

Some have mistaken this transnational representation to be a vision of judicial anarchy. Michael Reisman has suggested that "[a]dvocates of arbitration often assume ... that arbitration is a free-standing procedure, conceptually and politically quite independent of the apparatus of the state". He goes on to describe these advocates as "[t]hose who

5. For an example of this approach, see, e.g., Arthur von Mehren, who eloquently described at a lecture given in Tel Aviv in 1986 the ambulatory nature of arbitration and the fact that, unlike a judge, the arbitrator has no lex fori: Arthur T. VON MEHREN, "Limitations on Party Choice and the Governing Law: Do They Exist for International Commercial Arbitration?" (The Mortimer and Raymond Sackler Institute of Advanced Studies, Tel Aviv University, 1986).

wish to think of arbitration without any role for government".[6] This suggestion confounds the notion of an autonomous legal order with an a-national legal order, which would be characterized by a rejection of or opposition to national legal systems.[7] In contrast, the transnational vision considers that international arbitration is anchored in the collectivity of legal systems. As such, this vision of judicial collectivism embraces rather than rejects the laws derived from national legal systems.

Thus, none of the three representations described above suggests that international arbitration promotes a system of international justice that is "floating in the transnational firmament",[8] entirely divorced from the national legal systems of states. Instead, the relevant question in understanding these three views is *which* state, *or states*, provides the relevant source of legitimacy and validity for the arbitration agreement, the arbitral process and the ensuing award.

2. *Practical Consequences of the Representations*

The competing visions of international arbitration do not merely nourish a theoretical debate, they translate into highly practical consequences. They influence not only how arbitrators address various aspects of an international arbitration, but also the approach taken by all other players in the field, including parties, counsel and national judges.

Of course, the representations have significant consequences for arbitrators, and for the arbitrations over which they preside. For example, in choosing the applicable law,[9] an arbitrator adhering to the first representation and sitting in Mexico will consider he or she is bound by Mexican choice of law rules. An arbitrator adopting the Westphalian vision would not shy away from selecting, amongst the various conflict of laws rules at play, the choice of law rule which he or she considers appropriate to the arbitration at hand. An arbitrator adhering to the transnational representation will be more prone to look to the international trend for the determination of the relevant choice of law rule

6. W. Michael REISMAN and Brian RICHARDSON, "Tribunals and Courts: An Interpretation of the Architecture of International Commercial Arbitration", this volume pp. 17-18.

7. In contrast to the transnational representation of international arbitration, the doctrine of lex mercatoria stemmed from a more critical view of national legal systems, arising out of the perceived inadequacy of those systems to address disputes arising in a global commercial environment, and through its selectivity, constituting a form of "legal Darwinism". See Eric LOQUIN, "*Où en est la lex mercatoria?* in "*Souveraineté Étatique et Marchés Internationaux à la Fin du 20ème Siècle. A Propos de 30 Ans de Recherches du CREDIMI. Mélanges en l'Honneur de Philippe Kahn* (Litec 2000) at p. 26; Eric LOQUIN, "*Les règles matérielles internationales*" in Collected Coursesof the Hague Academy, volume 322 (2006) Sect. 503; for a discussion of this idea, see Emmanuel GAILLARD, *Legal Theory of International Arbitration*, fn. 1 above, at pp. 46-47.

8. Another example of this misperception of a transnational philosophy is *Bank Mellat v. Helliniki Techniki SA*, where Kerr LJ stated that: "[d]espite suggestions to the contrary by some learned writers under other systems, our jurisprudence does not recognise the concept of arbitral procedures floating in the transnational firmament, unconnected with any municipal system of law" [1984] 1 QB 291, 301.

9. For a detailed discussion on the consequences of the representations of international arbitration on applicable procedure and rules of law, see Emmanuel GAILLARD, *Legal Theory of International Arbitration*, fn. 1 above, pp. 93-134.

or, in appropriate cases, the rule which reflects the consensus of nations to resolve a particular substantive issue. Like the Westphalian arbitrator, this transnational arbitrator does not consider himself or herself bound by the Mexican choice of law rules simply because he or she is sitting in Mexico. Unlike the Westphalian arbitrator who views himself or herself as having unfettered discretion, however, an arbitrator adopting the transnational vision looks to the trend developed by the international community as guidance. Whereas the Westphalian vision is characterized by a margin of unpredictability, the transnational view aims at promoting certainty through its endorsement of majoritarian principles and its rejection of idiosyncratic or outdated rules of law.

This example of the choice of the law applicable to the merits of the dispute illustrates the far-reaching effects the representations can have on arbitrators, and how they may in turn have a significant impact on the outcome of the arbitration itself. The same is true for all the other players in the field of international arbitration. To take another example, these representations greatly influence national courts, such as when a court is asked to enforce an arbitral award that was set aside in the country of the seat of the arbitration. National courts adopting a monolocal view will consider an award rendered in Mexico as a Mexican award, even if none of the parties is Mexican, and will treat it as they would a local judgment issued by Mexican courts. Consequently, if the award is set aside in Mexico, there is nothing to recognize in another state.

Courts with a Westphalian view will not necessarily adhere to the way an award rendered in Mexico is treated by the Mexican legal system. They would not consider a Mexican court's determination that an award issued in Mexico was not valid, for instance for the arbitrators' failure to comply with a local procedural rule, as having an absolute extraterritorial legal effect. They consider that they are free to make their own determination as to whether such failure should lead to the rejection of the award as a binding legal instrument. Thus, English courts may enforce an arbitral award that Mexican courts have held as being invalid, or vice versa.

Courts adhering to the third, transnational representation accept the same result for different reasons. They will look to what constitutes a valid award by international standards, such as those set forth in the New York Convention. Their adherence to these international standards does not suggest that these courts exercise no control over the recognition of the award in their own national legal system. To the contrary, the New York Convention has preserved the discretion of every legal system to decide for itself, based on the collective guidelines set forth in the Convention and its own standards, whether or not an award meets the conditions of recognition and enforcement.[10] In this respect, national legal systems continue to shape international arbitration, both through their adherence to collective standards and their development of national jurisprudence on arbitration when exercising their discretion within those standards.

---

10. From a procedural point of view, Art. III of the New York Convention provides that "[e]ach Contracting State shall recognize arbitral awards as binding and enforce them *in accordance with the rules of procedure of the territory where the award is relied upon*" (emphasis added). In other words, the standards according to which an award "shall" be recognized are those of the country where recognition and enforcement are sought.

III. THE ROLE OF THE 1958 NEW YORK CONVENTION

Because of its crucial role in the development of international arbitration during the past fifty years, the 1958 New York Convention provides a forceful illustration of the question whether international arbitration can be viewed as a transnational system of justice.

The rules established by the New York Convention represent a collective, pro-enforcement movement by the international community. Despite the Convention's relatively straightforward approach to promoting enforcement by limiting the grounds of review for enforcement of arbitral awards, it has been interpreted by some as creating a jurisdictional hierarchy between national legal systems reviewing awards. This interpretation is not only unfounded in the text of the Convention, but is also contrary to the Convention's fundamental objectives.

One proponent of this idea, Michael Reisman, has argued that the New York Convention creates a "normative architecture" of international arbitration, dispatching competence to "two tiers of review competence, making a distinction between so-called 'primary' or 'venue' jurisdictions and 'secondary' or 'enforcement' jurisdictions".[11] This view suggests that the Convention establishes, on the one hand, a primary jurisdiction, that of the seat of the arbitration – regardless of the other criterion adopted by the Convention, that of law chosen by the parties to govern the arbitration – and, on the other hand, a secondary jurisdiction (or secondary jurisdictions) at the place (or places) of enforcement.

In reality, the objective of the New York Convention is much more straightforward. It is to facilitate the recognition and enforcement of arbitral awards, not to dispatch relative competence to national legal systems. The idea that the New York Convention would place the seat of the arbitration at the top of a jurisdictional hierarchy for enforcement purposes is counter to its fundamental objectives.[12] If accepted, it would shift the focus from the award itself, which is the subject matter of the Convention, to the judicial process surrounding the award in the country where it was rendered, and would fly in the face of one of the greatest achievements of the New York Convention. Indeed, one must recall that the drafters of the Convention set out to abolish the requirement of double exequatur, which governed enforcement under the 1927 Geneva Convention on the Enforcement and Recognition of Foreign Arbitral Awards. Until 1958, awards had to be rubber-stamped by courts at the seat of the arbitration before they could be enforced elsewhere. Thus the 1927 Geneva Convention recognized the "country of origin" as having primary competence to determine whether an award was valid. It did, at the time, organize the world into a primary jurisdiction, that of the seat, and secondary jurisdictions. The drafters of the New York Convention intended

11. W. Michael REISMAN and Brian RICHARDSON, "Tribunals and Courts: An Interpretation of the Architecture of International Commercial Arbitration", this volume p. 25).

12. It is also contrary to the letter of the Convention, which places the seat and the law under which the award is made on the same footing (see Art. V(1)(*e*) of the Convention). Thus if the Convention were to be seen as allocating jurisdictions between countries, which it does not, it would have created primary jurisdictions (plural), not a primary jurisdiction.

precisely to move away from this anti-enforcement system, and adopt a system where review of awards for enforcement would be limited to the grounds defined in the Convention.[13] The abolition of double exequatur has massively been applauded since 1958 as a major step towards a pro-enforcement system. That the drafters of the Convention moved away from the notion that the seat of the arbitration is somehow the controlling state, does not suggest that no state would have control over the arbitral process; rather, they shifted the authority to review awards for enforcement to the states at the place (or places) of enforcement.

For this reason, the Convention does not address at all the extent of review of arbitral awards for the purposes of annulment at the seat of arbitration. It does not say, for instance, that the seat should have a maximum of five, six or eight grounds to annul. There is no breach of the Convention if, for instance, courts in the United States review an award for "manifest disregard of the law" for the purposes of *annulling* an award rendered in the United States. If, on the other hand, a state were to review an arbitrator's "manifest disregard of the law" for the purposes of *enforcing* an award falling within the ambit of the Convention, it would be in breach of the Convention.

Conversely, the Convention does not prevent the state of enforcement from being more permissive as to the grounds set forth in the Convention, which represent the maximum standard of review acceptable under the Convention when a country is requested to recognize and enforce an arbitral award.[14] If a state reviews the merits of the dispute, it breaches the Convention. If a state uses a ground other than those set out in the Convention to deny enforcement, it breaches the Convention. But if a state chooses to enforce awards according to more liberal standards, it is free to do so. More specifically, the Convention does not prohibit a state from enforcing an award which has been set aside at the seat of the arbitration, or in the country of the law governing the arbitration.[15] As such, any positions taken by the courts of the seat with respect to the validity of the award do not have a binding effect in other legal systems.

Widespread acceptance of the New York Convention by states thus evidences a shift away from the traditional paradigm that grants unwarranted discretion to the seat of

---

13. See, e.g., Art. VII(2) of the New York Convention, which states that "[t]he Geneva Protocol on Arbitration Clauses of 1923 and the Geneva Convention on the Execution of Foreign Arbitral Awards of 1927 shall cease to have effect between Contracting States on their becoming bound and to the extent that they become bound, by this Convention".

14. This fact is made clear by the New York Convention's more-favorable-right provision under Art. VII(1), which expressly provides that courts must pay heed to domestic laws that are more favorable than the Convention: "The provisions of the present Convention shall not ... deprive any interested party of any right he may have to avail himself of an arbitral award in the manner and to the extent allowed by the law or the treaties of the country where such award is sought to be relied upon." A number of domestic courts have exercised this discretion by applying more favorable provisions of domestic law. See Emmanuel GAILLARD, "The Relationship of the New York Convention with Other Treaties and with Domestic Law" in Emmanuel GAILLARD and Domenico DI PIETRO, eds., *Enforcement of Arbitration Agreements and International Arbitral Awards* (Cameron May 2008) at pp. 70-71, 76-86.

15. For a more detailed analysis of enforcement of arbitral awards set aside at the seat in relation to the three representations of international arbitration, see Emmanuel GAILLARD, "The Representations of International Arbitration", New York Law Journal (4 October 2007).

arbitration. By giving some discretion to the national legal systems at the place (or places) of enforcement to review arbitral awards, the Convention appears at the very least to accommodate the Westphalian representation of international arbitration. But the Convention is primarily a declaration of the overarching international standards to which contracting states agree to adhere, the boundaries within which they will exercise their discretion. In this way, the Convention exemplifies the normative, collective activity of the states in which the legitimacy and validity of the transnational arbitral legal order is anchored.

The Control System of Arbitral Awards: A Pro-Arbitration Critique of Michael Reisman's "Architecture of International Commercial Arbitration"

*Luca G. Radicati di Brozolo**

TABLE OF CONTENTS Page

I. Introduction: The Shortcomings of a Two-Tier Control Conception of International Commercial Arbitration 74
II. No Primary Control Jurisdiction of the Courts of the Seat Under the New York Convention 77
III. The Recognition of Foreign Vacatur Judgments Under Domestic Rules: An Alternative Legal Basis for a Primary Control System? 87
IV. Primary Jurisdiction Control and Policy Options 89
V. The Importance of Supervisory-Supervisory Jurisdiction 100
VI. Conclusion: The Proper Balance of the Respective Roles of Arbitration and of the State of the Seat 101

I. INTRODUCTION: THE SHORTCOMINGS OF A TWO-TIER CONTROL CONCEPTION OF INTERNATIONAL COMMERCIAL ARBITRATION

The relationship between arbitration and national law and national courts is inevitably at the heart, or in the background, of every discussion on arbitration.[1] Professor Reisman's insightful and multifaceted analysis of what he terms the "normative architecture of international commercial arbitration", which focuses on this issue, is therefore thought-provoking. From a practical standpoint it is pertinent because it underscores the impact of States and of national law on international arbitration. So is

---

* Professor, Catholic University of Milan; Partner, Bonelli Erede Pappalardo, Milan-London; Chair, International Bar Association Subcommittee on the Recognition and Enforcement of Arbitral Awards.

This paper was the basis for the author's intervention as discussant of the Report by Professor W.M. Riesman (W.M. REISMAN and B. RICHARDSON, "Tribunals and Courts: An Interpretation of the Architecture of International Commercial Arbitration") this volume, pp. 17-65, which is a development of W.M. REISMAN and H. IRAVANI, "The Changing Relation of National Courts and International Commercial Arbitration", The Am. Rev. of Int'l Arb. (2010) p. 1.

1. For further analysis of the issue by this author see Luca G. RADICATI DI BROZOLO, "The Impact of National Law and Courts on International Commercial Arbitration: Mythology, Physiology, Pathology, Remedies and Trends", *Cahiers de l'arbitrage*/The Paris Journal of International Arbitration (2011) p. 663; Luca G. RADICATI DI BROZOLO and Loretta MALINTOPPI, "Unlawful Interference with International Arbitration by National Courts of the Seat in the Aftermath of *Saipem v. Bangladesh*" in M.Á. FERNÁNDEZ-BALLESTEROS and David ARIAS, eds., *Liber Amicorum B. Cremades* (La Ley 2010) p. 993.

its message of caution to parties, practitioners and scholars alike, who too often discount the role of the State in international arbitration. That role, instead, remains as central and indispensable as ever even today. Arbitration cannot exist and operate as a legal mechanism for the settlement of disputes, domestic and international, unless it is tolerated and supported by States.

Michael Reisman's analysis is less convincing on the conceptual level, insofar as it addresses the function of the State of the seat of the arbitration and especially of its control over awards, notoriously one of the most complex and controversial topics in international arbitration. Reisman rationalizes that function in a "control scheme" of arbitration based on "two tiers of review competence" of awards by State courts, consisting of a "primary" (or "venue") jurisdiction and of a "secondary" (or "enforcement") jurisdiction. The "normative architecture of international commercial arbitration", which would posit this scheme, is held to derive from the 1958 New York Convention.

At the risk of oversimplification, Reisman argues that the primary jurisdiction, i.e., the State of the seat, has the right and almost the duty to exercise a supervisory jurisdiction over arbitrations that take place on its territory and on the resultant awards. The enforcement jurisdiction, for its part, must have due regard for the decisions of the primary jurisdiction.[2] This leads Reisman to view critically those national provisions that limit or extinguish the rights of parties to seek annulment as well as the "permissive" interpretation of Art. V(1)(*e*) of the New York Convention according to which States are entitled to enforce international awards even if annulled in the State of the seat. Professor Reisman is equally disapproving of the emerging "supervisory-supervisory" jurisdiction, which consists essentially in the review of the respect of the New York Convention and of fundamental rights under arbitration in the context of international adjudication, especially under investment treaty arbitration. This development is portrayed as a potential source of conflict with the control structure alleged to be designed by the New York Convention and liable to impact negatively on the expeditiousness of the arbitration process, which is regarded as one of the main features of arbitration.

Reisman's theorization thus, on the one hand, accords with the more traditional views of international arbitration and of the role of the State of the seat and of its decisions. As a growing and authoritative body of thinking has shown over the years, that vision is by no means the only possible one, nor even necessarily the preferable one. At the same time Reisman's normative architecture appears to envisage an overriding role for public international law, which finds no basis in the only legal instrument which purports to apply to arbitration on a worldwide level. The New York Convention at best permits an attribution of competences such as that portrayed by Reisman, but certainly does not mandate it.

2. This centralized vision of international arbitration is clearly at the antipodes of that of Emmanuel Gaillard, who identifies the basis of international arbitration in what he defines as the arbitral legal order and favors a decentralized conception of its control by State courts: see E. GAILLARD, *Legal Theory of International Arbitration* (Martinus Nijhoff 2010).

This Comment presumes neither to add significantly to the ample body of reflection on this classic topic, and in particular to the views of the proponents of a less narrow view of the relations between arbitration and the State of the seat,[3] nor to propose theoretical or philosophical visions. Rather, given the theme of this Conference it will focus on the policy implications, having due regard to the current legal framework.

In the perspective of favoring greater efficiency in the transnational system of justice, in which arbitration will always necessarily play a central role, I will weigh in for loosening the umbilical cord between awards and the jurisdiction of the seat. I will argue that, contrary to Reisman's vision, the New York Convention does not lay down a formal control structure of international arbitration and specifically that it does not provide for a "primary control" of awards by the jurisdiction of the seat. I will also discuss other possible legal or policy bases for according a primary role to that jurisdiction and conclude that a nuanced approach is called for in the present state of the law of arbitration in the different national legal systems.

Precisely because of the different levels of protection of international arbitration in today's environment, Professor Reisman's skepticism as to supervisory-supervisory jurisdiction will also be analyzed critically.

3. It is likewise not intended to go over the legal underpinnings and the strengths and weaknesses of the individual decisions on the subject of the enforceability of awards annulled at the seat, which have been the subject of abundant research. The resilience of this topic is demonstrated by the *Yukos* saga in its most recent developments in the Netherlands and in England (see fn. 41 below) and by the recent judgment of the *Arbitrazh* Court of Kemerovo Oblast (Russia) of 20 July 2011, *Ciments Français v. Sibirskiy Cement and Istanbul Cimento*, Case No. A27-781/2011 (overturned on appeal on 5 December 2011).

This subject was the topic of an earlier ICCA Congress: *International Arbitration and the Courts: The Never Ending Story*, ICCA Congress Series no. 12 (2001) (hereinafter *ICCA Congress Series no. 12*), wherein see Pierre MAYER, "Revisiting *Hilmarton* and *Chromalloy*", p. 165. To limit references to some of the most recent works, which contain all further citations, see Sylvain BOLLÉE, note in Rev. arb. (2009) p. 557; Jan PAULSSON, notes in Rev. arb. (2006) p. 796 and Rev. arb. (2007) p. 559; Philippe PINSOLLE, "The Status of Vacated Awards in France: the *Cour de Cassation* decision in *Putrabali*", Arbitration International (2008) p. 277; Alexis MOURRE, "*A propos des articles V et VII de la Convention de New York et de la reconnaissance des sentences annullées dans leur pays d'origine après les arrêts Termo Rio et Putrabali*", Rev. arb. (2008) p. 263; Christopher KOCH, "The Enforcement of Awards Annulled in Their Place of Origin", J. of Int'l Arb. (2009) p. 267; Nadia DARWAZEH, "Article V(1)(*e*)" in Herbert KRONKE, Patricia NACIMIENTO, et al., eds., *Recognition and Enforcement of Foreign Arbitral Awards: A Global Commentary on the New York Convention* (Kluwer 2010) p. 301; Talia EINHORN, "The Recognition and Enforcement of Foreign Judgments on International Commercial Arbitral Awards", *Yearbook of Private International Law* (2010) p. 43. For comprehensive overviews see H. GHARAVI, *The International Effectiveness of the Annulment of an Arbitral Award* (London 2002); Gary BORN, *International Commercial Arbitration* (Kluwer 2009) p. 2701 and, for a thorough analysis of the theoretical implications, Sylvain BOLLÉE, *Les méthodes du droit international privé à l'épreuve des sentences arbitrales* (Economica 2004); Horatia MUIR WATT, note in Rev. arb. (2006) p. 700.

II. NO PRIMARY CONTROL JURISDICTION OF THE COURTS OF THE SEAT UNDER THE NEW YORK CONVENTION

1. *The Scope of the Convention and of the Exceptions to the Obligation to Recognize Awards*

To assess the proper role of the courts of the seat in international commercial arbitration it is useful to begin with a brief recapitulation of the purpose and scope of the New York Convention, which is the cornerstone of international arbitration in today's world. It is trite that, without the Convention, we would not have international arbitration as we know it.[4]

As is well known, there is an ongoing debate on the conception of international commercial arbitration and its "normative" underpinning according to the New York Convention, and the extent to which the latter can accommodate also a non-territorialist notion of arbitration. Unquestionably the Convention assumes that arbitration may have a foundation in national law and that States, and in particular the one of the seat,[5] have control over it. That is obvious from many provisions, starting from the first sentence of Art. I(1) which refers to awards "made in the territory of a State", and especially from the famous reference to the setting aside of the award "in the country in which, or under the law of which, the award was made" in Art. V(1)(*e*).

At the same time the Convention does not appear to rule out the possibility that awards may be disconnected from the law of a given State. Support for this position can be found in the much commented second sentence of Art. I(1), which includes in the definition of awards subject to the Convention those that are "not considered as domestic awards" in the country of enforcement, viewing them as a different category with respect to awards made in the territory of another contracting State.[6]

This debate is not of itself of great practical value to the present discussion. What is more relevant is an analysis of the New York Convention's substantive provisions. The Convention lays down only two obligations for States. The first one, contained in Art. II, is to recognize arbitration agreements and to compel arbitration. The second one, contained in Art. III, is to recognize arbitral awards as binding and to enforce them. Both obligations are subject to certain conditions: as to arbitration agreements, that the subject matter is arbitrable (Art. II(1)) and that the agreement is not "null and void, inoperative

---

4. Most of the questions approached here have been the subject of a vast and articulate literature well known to arbitration specialists and no attempt will be made here to consider specifically all the different theories and nuances.

5. This currently used expression does not appear in the Convention.

6. The fact that this expression is different from the one "under the law of which" used in Art. V(1)(*e*) can be taken as an indication that the two provisions refer to different concepts and that Art. I(1) can indeed be interpreted as a reference to non-national awards. For an analysis of the different positions on this point and for further citations see J.-F. POUDRET and S. BESSON, *Comparative Law of International Arbitration* (London 2007) p. 813; G. BORN, *op. cit.*, fn. 3, p. 184. See also the contributions by Eduardo SILVA ROMERO, Fernando MANTILLA-SERRANO and Albert Jan VAN DEN BERG in Guido TAWIL and Eduardo ZULETA, eds., *El arbitraje comercial internacional, Estudio de la Convención de Neuva York con motivo de su 50° aniversario* (Abeledo Perrot 2008) respectively pp. 90, 102 and 110.

or incapable of being performed" (Art. II(3)); as to awards, the conditions of Art. V. If these conditions are not satisfied, States are not bound to enforce arbitral agreements or awards. The two obligations are imposed respectively on the State before whose courts an arbitration agreement is invoked, generally in support of a stay of jurisdiction in an action on the merits of a dispute alleged to be covered by the arbitration agreement,[7] and on the State requested to enforce an award.

Beyond this, the Convention is silent and leaves States free as to how they regulate arbitration. It does not provide for a harmonized regime of arbitration,[8] such as the one contemplated in particular by the 1961 Geneva Convention, nor does it lay down detailed rules even for the functioning of the two obligations that it does lay down (for instance, the definition of arbitrability or the requirements of validity of arbitration agreements). Likewise, the Convention does not contemplate a mechanism for its harmonized application, such as the one of preliminary references to the Court of Justice of the European Union.[9]

In spite of its limited scope, the Convention has had an extremely significant impact on the development of the law of arbitration in the Contracting States. This has been essentially the product of the competition between legal systems unleashed by it. The obligation imposed on Contracting States to recognize agreements for arbitration abroad, in combination with the obligation to enforce foreign awards, has the practical effect of allowing parties to commercial transactions to opt out of a given legal system and to opt into the arbitration system of their choice simply by designating the seat of the arbitration, whilst at the same time allowing them to obtain the desired effects within the legal system they opted out of. As a consequence of this, many States that initially adhered to a more interventionist, or less liberal, approach in matters of arbitration have been induced to evolve towards more liberalized regimes. This has resulted in a broad convergence between the arbitration regimes of many diverse legal systems, and to a very broad acceptance of the role of party autonomy and of the wisdom of limiting court control over arbitral proceedings and awards. Likewise, most States now consider the seat of the arbitration as the connecting factor between an arbitration and their legal systems and recognize the freedom of the parties to make this choice.

Of course, this has not brought about a true harmonization. Predictably there still exist divergences, at times significant ones, between different legal systems even as to how they apply apparently similar rules, including those of the New York Convention, as well as in their overall attitude towards arbitration.

---

7. The question may be raised whether the obligation to recognize arbitration agreements under Art. II applies also to other States, e.g., those that might presume to interfere with arbitration by means of anti-suit injunctions or to pass judgment on the validity of an arbitration clause in declaratory actions.
8. For an interesting discussion of the harmonizing influence of the New York Convention, see G. BORN, *op. cit.* fn. 3, p. 91.
9. For similar considerations see Herbert KRONKE, "Introduction" in Herbert KRONKE, Patricia NACIMIENTO, et al., eds., *op. cit.*, fn. 3, p. 1.

2. *The Enforcement of Awards and the Respective Roles of the "Primary" and "Secondary" Control Jurisdiction Under the Convention*

Leaving aside the theoretical debate on the New York Convention's conceptual roots, and having regard only to the obligations it lays down, it is difficult to deny that with respect to awards the Convention is concerned only with secondary jurisdiction, i.e., with the jurisdiction of the State where enforcement is sought.

On this point, as mentioned above, it imposes an unequivocal obligation to recognize and enforce non-domestic awards, unless they fail to satisfy the conditions of Art. V. These conditions are obviously intended as exceptions to that fundamental obligation, which therefore ceases to operate in their presence. In such situations, the State regains the freedom not to enforce non-domestic awards that it would have absent the Convention.

The scope of the enforcing State's obligation under the Convention is limited also in the opposite direction. Not only does such obligation not bind that State to recognize awards that fail to satisfy the conditions of Art. V; conversely, it does not bind it to refuse recognition and enforcement when those conditions are not satisfied. To read into Art. V an obligation to refuse enforcement in the presence of those conditions would be in sheer contrast with both the letter and the rationale of the Convention. As to the letter, the language of the initial part of Art. V(1) is explicitly permissive in the English text (recognition and enforcement "*may* be refused"), but is not prescriptive even in the French and Spanish texts ("*ne seront refusés que*"; "*sólo se podrá denegar*").[10] As to the rationale, the aim of the New York Convention is obviously not to limit the pre-existing freedom of States to treat non-domestic arbitral awards as favorably as they please, nor to harmonize the conditions for recognition and enforcement. What the Convention intends to do is to lay down an obligation to enforce awards, which would otherwise not exist, without however imposing it in situations where it would normally be unpalatable for States to have to enforce owing to the lack of certain minimum requirements generally considered intrinsic to arbitration and to awards. Such requirements are identified with the conditions set out in Art. V(1)(*a*)-(*d*).[11]

Put otherwise, the New York Convention is not about curtailing the freedom of States to recognize awards, but about curtailing their freedom *not* to recognize awards.

The lack of prescriptive value of the list of exceptions in Art. V is confirmed by Art. VII(1), which allows Contracting States to avail themselves of provisions of their own domestic law that are more permissive with regard to the treatment of awards.[12]

---

10. This language (which translates into "will only be refused if") simply indicates that the list of grounds for refusal of enforcement is exhaustive, and that accordingly no other grounds are permitted. It does not require that enforcement be denied in the presence of those grounds.

11. If one views the conditions of Art. V as exceptions to the obligation to enforce an award, it appears very clear, contrary to Reisman's opinion (W.M. REISMAN and H. IRAVANI, "The Changing Relation of National Courts and International Commercial Arbitration", Am. Rev. of Int'l Arb. (2010) p. 1 (hereinafter, "The Changing Relation")), why the regime of Art. V was drafted.

12. Considering that the conditions of Art. V(1)(*a*)-(*d*) reflect the basic requirements of an enforceable award, the freedom to enforce awards that do not meet the requirements of Art. V is particularly relevant in cases that fall under para. 1(*e*), as will be discussed below. However, such freedom can

The obligation laid down by Arts. III-V is addressed to the State of the secondary jurisdiction, to use Reisman's terminology, and is the only one deriving from the Convention that relates to awards. The Convention does not lay down any rules addressed to the State of the seat as such, unless by coincidence that State is also the one where the recognition of an arbitration agreement is sought, either in support of an objection to jurisdiction on the merits of a dispute or in the form of a declaratory judgment on the invalidity of an arbitration agreement. As a matter of fact, the Convention does not specifically consider the seat State. It says nothing about "primary control jurisdiction" over awards, both as regards ancillary jurisdiction in support of arbitration and as regards supervisory jurisdiction over the validity of awards.

In laying down the obligation to enforce awards, the Convention has in mind only the circulation of the awards, and thus essentially the interest of the parties to the arbitration, with no regard whatsoever to the putative interest of the State of the seat to have its annulment decisions respected abroad. Clearly the State of the seat would have no title to claim a violation of the Convention if its annulment decisions were not respected by other Contracting States.

The seat State can acquire a role at most when it comes to deciding which awards benefit from the obligation of recognition. This is where the famous discussion on the object of the Convention could become relevant. The Convention does seem to presuppose that arbitrations will ordinarily have a seat or at least a country of origin (in the sense of "the country in which, or under the law of which" the award was made in Art. I(1)), nor that the seat State has the power to exercise jurisdiction to review and set aside awards. In relation to such cases it seems to consider the award as originating from that State's legal system, as evidenced in particular by Art. V(1)(*e*).

However, as indicated above, the Convention also accepts that an award may not be considered as originating from a given national legal system. Whatever meaning of the second sentence of Art. I(1) the drafters may have had in mind, the language is sufficiently supple to comprehend also awards not stemming from a specific legal system.[13] Even if the Convention is held to have been principally concerned with awards having the "nationality" of a given legal system, it is fair to assume that it was not adopting a prescriptive stance on this point. It was merely taking stock of the normal factual situation and adhering, somewhat uncritically, to the prevailing view of the time, which assumed that awards are necessarily the product of a given legal system to which they remain inextricably tied.

Be that as it may, even the question of what awards the Convention applies to and are entitled to recognition thereunder is not necessarily directly relevant to the one at issue here, which is that of the role to be attributed to the courts of the seat in the international circulation of awards.

---

become relevant even in relation to the basic conditions, for instance if the enforcing State wants to apply its own standards to verify the existence of such conditions rather than those laid down in the Convention (for example by applying its own law instead of the law applicable under letters (*a*) and (*d*) of para. 1).

13. This is now admitted by A.J. VAN DEN BERG, "*La aplicación de la Convención de Neuva York de 1958 a laudos no nacionales*" in G. TAWIL and E. ZULETA, *op. cit.*, fn. 6, at p. 116.

On this point it is significant that the Convention does not establish how the State of the seat is to be identified. Specifically, it is silent as to how to resolve those situations where there may be doubts as to where the award was made, in particular where more than one State can consider the award as having been made on its territory (or under its law) and where, conversely, no State considers the award as stemming from it. Likewise, it is not clear which forum would have primary control jurisdiction over awards "not considered as domestic awards" in the enforcement State. Furthermore, situations are conceivable where it may be objectively difficult to establish whether an award has a "nationality",[14] since it is not impossible for a given award, so to speak, to fall through the cracks between different legal systems, possibly through no intention of the parties.[15] The silence of the Convention would be surprising if the seat were entrusted by it with such an important competence as the primary control over awards.

The Convention is thus concerned with the circulation of the final product, the award, with little regard to its origin and nature, to the role that States may have played in its coming into being and to the effects attributed to it by them.

It therefore seems inescapable that, on a proper interpretation in light of the rules of the Vienna Convention on the Law of Treaties, the New York Convention contemplates neither an allocation of jurisdiction between States with primary and secondary jurisdiction nor a two-tier review competence over arbitral awards by national courts.[16]

3. *The Article V(1)(e) Exception*

The conclusion that the Convention does not attribute a "primary jurisdiction" to the seat might appear contradicted by the Art. V(1)(*e*) exception, which famously permits the refusal of enforcement to awards that have been set aside by the courts of the country of origin. A correct understanding of this provision shows this not to be the case.

a. The status of vacated awards

As indicated above, Art. V(1)(*e*) is just one of the exceptions to the obligation to recognize non-domestic awards listed in Art. V and therefore does not oblige States to refuse enforcement when the award has been annulled in the State of origin. Equally importantly, that provision implies nothing about the nature and the effects of such an annulment.

The view that the mere setting aside of the award renders it per se unenforceable is heavily influenced by the belief that an award somehow stems from, or is part of, the legal system of the State of the seat and that its annulment by that State essentially

---

14. In this respect arbitral awards are obviously fundamentally different from judgments, the origin and nationality of which can never be in doubt.

15. See for instance the well-known case decided by the Svea Court of Appeal, 28 February 2005, *Titan Corp. v. Alcatel*, in ICCA *Yearbook Commercial Arbitration* XXX (2005) p. 139. Although this decision has been superseded by the Swedish Supreme Court, 12 November 2010, *Rosinvestco UK Ltd v. The Russian Federation* (case No. Ö 2301-09), the possibility of a similar approach being taken in the future by other courts cannot be ruled out.

16. This position has, instead, been followed by the well-known decision *TermoRio v. Electranta*, 487 F.3d 928 (D.C. 2007) which clearly is inspired by Reisman's thinking.

obliterates it, leaving nothing to enforce.[17] That view, espoused also by Reisman,[18] reflects conventional wisdom, but is based on a petition of principle.

The fallacy of that position is demonstrated firstly by the 1961 Geneva Convention, which in certain conditions permits the recognition of awards annulled in the State of origin, thereby proving that the award continues to exist and is capable of having effects even after its annulment. Further confirmation comes from the fact that even the proponents of according deference to foreign annulment decisions, including Reisman, admit that the annulment does not preclude enforcement when it is in some way the product of abuse.[19]

Secondly, that view is unconvincing because it tends to equate the award with a judgment of the courts of the seat State.[20] A court judgment is intrinsic to the legal system of which the court is a judicial organ, and indeed it is a product of that system. Its effects and destiny depend wholly on that law. It is therefore natural that it cannot be recognized or enforced abroad if it ceases to be effective in that legal system (for instance if it has been annulled or quashed by a higher court).

For awards the position is completely different. An award is first and foremost the product of the will of the parties and of the activity of the arbitrators, who are agents of the parties and not organs of any State, including the State of the seat. Of course, the will of the parties and the powers of the arbitrators alone are not capable of conferring legal effects on the award, at least in the legal systems of States.[21] For that to be the case, it is necessary that the award's legal existence and effects be recognized by States. In the absence of the New York Convention, each State is free to decide whether to recognize an award, wherever and however made, and what effects to attribute to it. In this respect an award is akin to a contract, which is not a part of any legal system and, once entered into, lives a life of its own and is capable of being assessed as to its validity and effects by each legal system according to its own rules.[22]

The State of the seat is not in a fundamentally dissimilar position with respect to the award compared to other States. Normally, the legal system of the seat will provide assistance and support to the arbitral proceedings and will be prepared to review the

---

17. As is well known, this position was pugnaciously argued by F.A. MANN, "Lex Facit Arbitrum" in *Liber Amicorum Martin Domke* (1967) p. 157.

18. The view that awards are not part of the legal system of the seat is, however, convincingly contested even by authors who do not subscribe to the position defended here: see for instance the two works by S. BOLLÉE, *op. cit.*, fn. 3 and H. MUIR WATT, *op. cit.*, fn. 3.

19. W.M. REISMAN and H. IRAVANI, "The Changing Relation", *op. cit.*, fn. 11, p. 32.

20. An alternative reasoning for giving weight to the decisions of the court of the seat rests on a conflicts of laws approach positing that those decisions embody the law of the seat which, it is sometimes argued, would be the law governing the award. This approach is at odds with the modern tendency to avoid a strict conflicts of laws methodology in matters concerning arbitration in favor of relying on substantive rules.

21. The fact that, as postulated for instance by E. GAILLARD, *op. cit.*, fn. 2, awards might produce effects in a hypothetical arbitral legal order is irrelevant to their ability to produce effects in State legal systems.

22. This analogy is noted also by W.W. PARK, "Duty and Discretion in International Arbitration" in *Arbitration of International Business Disputes – Studies in International Arbitration* (2006) p. 189.

award. Nevertheless, this does not make the award a decision, or a creature, of that State. And even if the legal system of the seat does consider the award a product of its legal system, that does not affect the nature of the award from the viewpoint of other legal systems nor the freedom of every other State to deal with it as it thinks fit.

If this is clear, the effects in other States of the annulment of awards by the courts of the State of the seat become equally evident. The analogy with contracts is again useful. The annulment of a contract, or the removal of its effects, by the courts of one State[23] is certainly capable of having effects also in the legal system of other States. This, however, does not occur per se, because the contract is wiped out of existence by the decision of the court, but occurs only if the effects of the relevant judgment are granted some form of recognition in other States. In the same way, unless the award is improperly assimilated to a court judgment, its annulment by the courts of one State, including the one of the seat, does not of itself deprive the award of its existence. The annulment is simply the act of a State, which purports to deprive the award of its legal validity and effects, but whose consequences, like those of any judgment of a court, are limited to the territory of the State from which the judgment emanates. The annulment notwithstanding, the award continues to exist, were it only as a physical document (*un chiffon de papier* to use Pierre Mayer's expression), and as such remains capable of being submitted for enforcement by the courts of any other country. Any State before which it is presented retains the power, and the right, to attribute to the arbitrators' decision whatever value and effects it wishes according to its own law.

b. Refusal of recognition of vacated awards and recognition of foreign vacatur

In light of the above, to postulate that the setting aside of an award by the State of the seat renders it unenforceable abroad is tantamount to suggesting that the State of enforcement is bound by an obligation automatically to recognize and give effect to the foreign setting aside judgment, with no opportunity to review it.

Such a supposition would be in stark contrast with generally accepted principles and practice regarding the international circulation of judgments. Absent specific obligations deriving from international agreements, States are not required to recognize and enforce foreign judgments, and are allowed to make recognition conditional on any substantive and procedural requirement foreseen by their respective domestic laws. In practice States are often reluctant to recognize foreign judgments, especially without a possibility to review them.

A departure from this principle for judgments annulling arbitral awards definitely cannot be inferred in the absence of an unambiguous obligation deriving from a treaty. There is no doubt that, despite Art. V(1)(*e*), the New York Convention lays down no such obligation. It would indeed be counter-intuitive to imagine that the Convention, whose purpose is to favor the circulation of awards, would have surreptitiously introduced an obligation not only to recognize foreign judgments, but specifically those judgments that potentially interfere with arbitration because they set aside awards,

23. Clearly the State whose courts pass judgment on the validity of a contract, and whose judgment may or may not be recognized in other States, can be any State, regardless of the links between the contract and that State.

regardless of the grounds for doing so.[24] Such an inference is particularly inconceivable given the absence of uniform standards on the review of awards by the court of the seat. In such a situation an obligation to recognize foreign setting aside judgments would result in the lowest common standard.

c. *The proper scope of Article V(1)(e)*

What then is the reason for the presence of Art. V(1)(*e*) in the Convention? In part it is probably the result of an uncritical adhesion by the drafters to the view that assumes an intrinsic connection between awards and the legal order of the seat. In other words, by allowing States to refrain from enforcing awards vacated at the seat, Art. V(1)(*e*) is mindful of the concerns of those for whom, at the time and still nowadays, giving effect to such awards appears unacceptable and even inconceivable. In a more positive light, the provision can also be seen as a flexible tool that the Convention makes available to the enforcement courts, allowing them to take for good the decisions of the seat which may have had a first look at the award. As will be shown below, in many situations that can be a sensible policy choice.

4. *No Obligation of Supervisory Jurisdiction over Awards, State Practice and the Position of the Parties*

The finding that the logic of the New York Convention does not contemplate a dual control structure of international arbitration is relevant also to assess the law and practice of those States that, in certain circumstances and to a variable extent, refrain from exercising control over international arbitrations that take place on their territory.

The Convention is neutral as to the control over awards by the State of origin. Just as it does not impose any particular deference by other States to the decisions of the jurisdiction of the Seat, it neither forbids the exercise of a control function by that jurisdiction (or for that matter by any other jurisdiction)[25] nor does it require that such a function be exercised. Incidentally, such control would not be justified if no deference

---

24. This is all the more inconceivable because the Convention irrefutably does not require the recognition of pro-arbitration judgments of the seat State, i.e., those that uphold the validity an award and could thereby shield it from a refusal of recognition in other States.

25. Whist annulment jurisdiction is usually exercised by the seat State, there are instances where courts of a State other than that of the seat entertain setting aside actions in relation to awards purportedly having certain links to that State. A notable example is India. This practice is often criticized, but it is questionable that it violates any rule or principle. In particular the New York Convention does not lay down any criteria on annulment jurisdiction. At most it could be argued that an annulment by a court other than one of the seat could conflict with the Convention if it results in an obstacle to enforcement in that State. The issue was touched upon in a recent investment arbitration (*White Industries v. India*, UNCITRAL award of 30 November 2011, para. 10.4.11, <www.iareporter.com>) where the tribunal was confronted with the issue of the compatibility with a bilateral investment treaty of the actions of the Indian courts which, inter alia, entertained a setting aside action in relation to an award rendered in Paris. The tribunal did not decide the point, but the award contains a long footnote (fn. 69) setting out the unconvincing position of one arbitrator who deemed such a practice illegal on the strength of certain national cases, the writings of A.J. van den Berg and even the New York Convention.

is required to be given to the decisions of the forum of the seat. There is thus no basis in the Convention to criticize[26] States that adopt a more hands-off approach to the control of international arbitration.[27] Such a policy can be dictated by a variety of reasons, from the belief in the need to give proper deference to party autonomy, to the desire to attract foreign arbitrations, to the desire not to overburden the local judiciary with the supervising of proceedings lacking a sufficiently close link to the forum. All of these are compatible with the Convention, nothing in which condemns a legislative or jurisprudential approach inspired by such criteria and leading to a lax control on arbitrations on their territory. There is likewise no legal basis for criticizing a more intrusive approach to the review of awards.

This said, the empirical evidence is that the prevailing attitude amongst States is still, on the one hand, to exercise jurisdiction over arbitrations seated in their territory and, on the other hand and perhaps more importantly, to defer to the decision of the court of the seat when it comes to deciding whether to refuse enforcement to awards annulled in the State of origin.[28]

It is for this purely practical reason that the parties to arbitration are in a different position from States and enforcing courts. The parties cannot lightly disregard the law and the courts of the State of the seat, even if they have no particular interest in the effects of the award in that State. The law and the courts of the seat can have a decisive influence on the arbitration that, in the current state of play, will normally be respected by the enforcement courts elsewhere in the world, despite the lack of any legal or overarching policy considerations for doing so. Consequently, where they are in a position to do so, the parties should exercise great care in choosing the seat, in order to ensure that their arbitration will be subject to the degree of primary jurisdiction control that they view as suitable to their needs.

---

26. Such criticism is an integral part of Reisman's theory: see W.M. REISMAN and H. IRAVANI, "The Changing Relation", *op. cit.*, fn. 11, p. 23; W.M. REISMAN and B. RICHARDSON, "Tribunals and Courts: An Interpretation of the Architecture of International Commercial Arbitration" (hereinafter "Tribunals and Courts"), this volume, pp. 17-65.

27. The most notorious provisions which allow the parties to exclude any review of arbitral awards, subject to an express waiver, are Art. 192(1) of the Swiss Law on Private International Law, Art. 1717(4) of the Belgian Code Judiciaire, Art. 51 of the Swedish Arbitration Act and, most recently, Art. 1522 of the French Code of Civil Procedure. Whilst under the first three provisions the waiver is permitted only for arbitrations where none of the parties are resident in the country of the seat, the French provision contains no such limitation. As noted by E. GAILLARD and P. DE LAPASSE, "*Le nouveau droit de l'arbitrage interne et international*", Dalloz (2011) p. 171, these provisions are a step in the direction of the approach that leaves the control of the award solely to the country of enforcement.

28. It is only from this empirical perspective, and not for any cogent legal or logical reason, that one has to recognize that in today's world the law of the seat has a central role in arbitration (see L.G. RADICATI DI BROZOLO, "The Impact of National Law and Courts on International Commercial Arbitration", *op. cit.*, fn. 1, p. 667). The role of the seat would greatly diminish if less deference were accorded to judgments setting aside awards, as advocated here.

5. *The Nature of International Arbitration and of Arbitral Awards*

To hold that the New York Convention does not provide for "primary jurisdiction review" – in that it neither mandates control over arbitration by the State of the seat nor requires the annulment at the State of the seat to be recognized extraterritorially – does not involve any profound implications as to the theory and foundations of international arbitration.

In particular it does not amount to espousing the theory of stateless arbitration or of arbitration grounded on a non-national legal system or to discounting the role of national law and courts in the life of arbitration. It does not imply that arbitral awards are any more "stateless" than international contracts that do not draw "intrinsic" binding force from any individual legal system, but are valid and binding in all those legal systems that are prepared to consider them effective (and, it is worth adding, only in those legal systems).[29]

In other words, recognizing that vacatur at the seat is not entitled to dispositive extraterritorial authority as to the validity of the award at the enforcement stage is by no means equivalent to indulging in an "anarcho-capitalist fantasy",[30] according to which international arbitration would live in a legal no-man's land, nor that parties need no longer reckon with national legal systems and courts. Likewise it does not mean giving absolute prevalence to party autonomy over the sovereignty of States or require resorting to theories of arbitral awards rooted in a transnational arbitral legal order.[31] As underscored above, arbitration remains as firmly dependent on State support as ever. Parties will always depend on the recognition by courts of their arbitration agreements if they are to be permitted to resort to arbitration and to avoid litigation in national courts. The courts of the seat will have to be taken into consideration at least to the extent that it is intended that the award will be effective there and when assistance in the constitution and functioning of the tribunal is required.[32] And, of course, State support will always be required for enforcement.

The conclusion as to the proper role of the courts of the seat amounts to drawing the consequences from the fact that arbitral awards are worthless without the support of States, but also that such support need not necessarily come from the seat State, since the award is not a "product" of that legal system.[33] Each State is free to assess an award according to its own principles, obviously respecting the requirements of the New York

29. See Pierre MAYER, "*Réflexions sur la notion de contrat international*" in *Mélanges en l'honneur de Pierre Tercier* (Schultess 2008) p. 873.

30. To borrow the expression of W.M. Reisman, "Tribunals and Courts", this volume, p. 17.

31. According to the theory of E. Gaillard and Ph. Pinsolle.

32. One could query whether the courts of the seat will be as amenable to provide their support to the arbitration if their decisions on the validity of the arbitration will not be accorded universal recognition. In this case the intervention by the courts of third States, according to the model of French law codified in the latest reform of international arbitration (Art. 1505(4) of the Code of Civil Procedure), could provide a useful backup.

33. The fact that, unlike contracts, awards aim to settle disputes and in that respect are akin to judgments is not of itself a reason to postulate that they be must be rooted in a national legal system.

Convention, so that the award can live and have effects in all States that are prepared to recognize it, regardless of its origin and vicissitudes, and independently of whether it is accorded effect by the "home" State.

The fact that most States are prepared to grant a broad measure of deference to the assessment of awards by the seat State does not change this, as it does not change the fact that, regardless of the validity accorded to the award in the seat State, its circulation elsewhere will always depend on the explicit recognition by other States.

III. THE RECOGNITION OF FOREIGN VACATUR JUDGMENTS UNDER DOMESTIC RULES: AN ALTERNATIVE LEGAL BASIS FOR A PRIMARY CONTROL SYSTEM?

Having seen that a two-tier control system of awards that allocates primary and secondary competence to the courts respectively of the seat State and of the enforcement State is not foreseen by the New York Convention, it is worth investigating whether such a dual control system might have other legal underpinnings.

The point of departure for such an investigation is the fact that, as mentioned, albeit without being required to do so under the Convention, States tend almost *a priori* to refuse to recognize or enforce awards annulled at the seat, thereby according considerable deference to foreign annulment judgments. Since such judgments do not undermine the existence of the award itself, the question is whether the refusal to recognize annulled awards may derive from an obligation to recognize foreign annulment judgments.

Such an obligation does not stem from an international source. Even within the tight-knit European Union system of cooperation in jurisdictional matters there is no obligation to recognize foreign vacatur judgments, since arbitration is excluded from the ambit of the Brussels I Regulation.[34] The question, therefore, is whether such an obligation can derive from the domestic rules on the recognition of foreign judgments. Most States indeed have elaborate systems for the recognition of foreign judgments and, since vacatur judgments are after all a type of judgment, those rules could in principle be applicable to them.[35]

The rules on the recognition and enforcement of foreign judgments vary from State to State. They may provide for an automatic recognition or they may submit it to a specific procedure. Recognition can be raised as a principal question or arise as an incidental one in other proceedings, including proceedings for the enforcement of the award, if in such proceedings the defense is raised that the award has been annulled by a foreign judgment. Normally foreign judgments are recognized without review of the merits, provided that the enforcement court is satisfied that they comply with basic

34. L.G. RADICATI DI BROZOLO, "Arbitration and the Draft Revised Brussels I Regulation: Seeds of Home Country Control and of Harmonization?", Journal of Private International Law (2011) p. 423.

35. It is usually held that there can be no question of recognition of foreign judgments granting enforceability to foreign awards (as, for that matter, to foreign judgments granting recognition to the judgments of third States) on the principle that *exequatur sur exequatur ne vaut*.

procedural requirements and are consistent with the public policy of the forum. A usual additional requirement is that the issuing court exercised its jurisdiction on the score of connecting factors considered acceptable by the recognizing State (*compétence indirecte*). The application of the latter requirement to vacatur judgments would tend to rule out the possibility of recognizing judgments issued by States other than that of the seat.[36]

The point is whether these rules can (or should) be applied to foreign annulment judgments. One important reason for hesitation has to do with the fact that the application of the rules on the recognition and enforcement of foreign judgments to setting aside judgments, with the consequence that such judgments would be treated as ordinary foreign judgments, would not in principle be beneficial to the enforcement of awards. More often than not it would entail the recognition and enforcement of such judgments, thereby precluding the recognition of the awards. That is because the normal approach to the recognition of judgments is increasingly favorable to recognition, in that it excludes the review of the merits and predicates a very sparing use of the public policy filter. The result is that, by virtue of those rules, a foreign setting aside judgment could be refused recognition only exceptionally, notably if the foreign court violated basic procedural rules or possibly some fundamental principle, which can be gleaned from the New York Convention, e.g., the obligation to give effect to and enforce arbitration agreements.[37]

Absent such exceptional circumstances, the foreign setting aside judgment would usually have to be recognized. The prohibition of review of the merits would in fact preclude a refusal of recognition of the judgment on the grounds of a mere divergence, albeit even a serious one, between the annulment standards of the seat State and those of the enforcing State, or even any assumed international standard, such as those foreseen by the UNCITRAL Model Law. Likewise, the lack of conformity between the standards for annulment applied by the State of the seat and other more broadly recognized standards would rarely qualify as a violation of public policy according to the more modern approach to the recognition of foreign judgments (and for that matter of arbitral awards).

The result could therefore well be that foreign annulment judgments would ordinarily be recognized, with the consequence that the annulments of awards by foreign courts will be upheld, and the awards will not be recognized.

From a practical point of view this solution would essentially amount to introducing a form of primary control of awards by the court of the seat such as that advocated by Reisman, albeit with a fundamental difference. The difference would be that such a system would be a voluntary one, in which the deference accorded to the review of awards by the courts of the seat and to their annulment decisions would be the result of

---

36. That is because most States tend to consider the State of the seat as the one having jurisdiction over setting aside actions.

37. For instance if the award has been annulled on the basis of a completely arbitrary and idiosyncratic decision as to the inexistence or invalidity of the arbitration agreement: see ICSID Award in Case No. ARB/05/7 of 30 June 2009, *Saipem v. Bangladesh*, as to which see L.G. RADICATI DI BROZOLO and L. MALINTOPPI, *op. cit.*, fn. 1.

the application of national rules on the recognition of foreign judgments, and not a mandatory system purportedly imposed by the New York Convention.

This is in essence the situation that prevails nowadays, when courts indeed do tend to refuse to recognize awards annulled at the seat, even though in doing so they do not always distinguish clearly between the simple refusal to recognize the award as a result of its annulment, on the one hand, and the recognition of the foreign annulment judgment on the other hand. The effect of this approach is that foreign awards are refused enforcement even when, absent annulment at the seat, they would be entitled to recognition in the forum, because they fail to meet the criteria for refusal of enforcement of Art. V(1)(*a-d*) of the New York Convention or those of the local law of the enforcing State.

IV. PRIMARY JURISDICTION CONTROL AND POLICY OPTIONS

1. *Introduction*

As discussed in the previous section, a mechanism for the control of international arbitration based on attributing to the courts of the seat a primary jurisdiction to review awards, which precludes the international circulation of annulled awards, is conceivable, although perhaps not precisely on the terms envisaged by Professor Reisman. Such a control scheme is not mandatory under the New York Convention, and it is debatable whether it is even truly compatible with the overall purpose and spirit of the Convention. However, it is permissible under the Convention and feasible, since enforcement courts have the ability to defer to foreign annulment decisions.

There are two ways in which the enforcing jurisdiction can defer to foreign vacatur. Courts and national legislators looking for an easy way out of the conundrum have to look no further than Art. V(1)(*e*) of the New York Convention, which allows them to refuse recognition by virtue of the mere fact that the award has been suspended or vacated abroad, without any further questions. Courts more prone to reflection and that realize that the foreign annulment is not *per se* dispositive of the issue would have to consider whether to recognize the effect of the foreign annulment judgment according to their domestic rules on recognition of foreign judgments.

The debate must therefore center on the merits of following either one of these courses.

2. *Reasons for Deferring to Foreign Vacatur*

The policy reasons for deferring to the review of the courts of the seat are well known. The one most widely cited is uniformity of solutions. As to the other reasons, Professor Reisman like other commentators purports that control by the primary jurisdiction is important because, by providing for an up-front control of the award, it allows other courts to rely on that control and to grant fast-track enforcement of awards in secondary jurisdictions.[38] He also highlights that the absence of a nullificatory power with universal effect would allow the winner of a defective award to continue to seek enforcement in countless secondary jurisdictions, thereby unjustifiably harassing the other party.[39] The opportunity to eliminate an award once and for all by challenging it immediately at the seat also allows the party convinced of the award's defectiveness to achieve legal certainty up front, without having to await the enforcement stage, possibly years later, to raise its grounds for complaint. Although this position is expressed with regard to the system that Reisman sees as mandated by the New York Convention, the same policy considerations could apply if the control by the primary jurisdiction were to be ensured as a result of voluntary deference to its decisions by the courts requested to enforce.

A further concern could be deference to the putative will of the parties whenever the seat of the arbitration, whose courts have set aside the award, has been chosen by the parties.

Furthermore, it is sometimes said that a review of awards at the seat can serve to boost confidence in arbitration and to avoid a backlash against it, on the part both of prospective users and of States, whose amenability to trust arbitration, and therefore to accept arbitral awards, would depend also on the existence of a form of control at the seat.

3. *The Case Against Automatic Deference to First-Tier Review by the Courts of the Seat*

Whilst understandable, the policy reasons in support of recognizing absolute nullificatory powers to the court of the seat are not cogent. The arguments are similar to those against inferring an obligation to recognize foreign annulments from Art. V(1)(*e*). It is in fact questionable whether attributing a pre-eminent role to the courts of the seat is justified in a situation where, despite increasing convergence, arbitration laws and cultures, and court practices, around the world continue to differ significantly.[40] As mentioned, this is a consequence of the fact that, save for the fundamental obligations of Arts. II and III, the New York Convention leaves States free as to how they govern arbitration, and specifically as to the mechanisms for the control of awards and the grounds for annulment and standards of review. The inescapable result, which is perfectly legitimate from the perspective of the Convention, is that certain States adhere to much stricter (one could say less arbitration-friendly) standards than others. Those countries will be more prone to annul awards that would, instead, be considered perfectly valid and enforceable from the perspective of more arbitration-friendly systems.

In such conditions, automatically acknowledging extraterritorial effect to annulment decisions, even on a voluntary basis pursuant to domestic law, has the practical effect that the countries with the most restrictive standards are able to impose their own standards on others, thereby preventing the enforcement of awards in countries that adopt a more open approach. This outcome is not necessarily desirable or justified from an arbitration law perspective, which is that of the New York Convention. The *Yukos* case, in its

38. W.M. REISMAN and H. IRAVANI, "The Changing Relation", *op. cit.*, fn. 11, p. 8.

39. *Ibid.*, p. 12.

40. See Section II.*1* above.

Dutch[41] and English[42] ramifications, relating to the refusal of enforcement of an award set aside in Russia due to the alleged partiality of the courts of the seat, is a prototypical example of a case where according automatic deference to a foreign legal system's appreciation of an award would appear scarcely justified.

It is not without interest that the difference in attitudes towards arbitration is one of the principal reasons why any solution going beyond the New York Convention is problematic even within a relatively homogeneous area like the European Union. As indicated above,[43] in that context the idea of bringing arbitration under the umbrella of Regulation (EC) 44/2001, and in particular ensuring the circulation of annulment judgments between member States, is encountering very significant and on the whole well-deserved opposition, partly predicated on possible clashes with obligations arising under the New York Convention.[44] It is conceptually inconceivable to extrapolate in the international context something that is still unacceptable to many even within a tight-knit environment like the EU.

Furthermore, until significant divergences persist in the approach to arbitration between different States, there is no evidence that admitting a first-tier review of the award by the courts of the seat would entail the possible positive by-product of such an approach. That would consist in enforcement States relying also on the positive assessment of the award by the primary jurisdiction, and in particular on the rejection of challenges to the validity of the award. In that case, the deference to the "primary" jurisdiction would have a significant upside in that it could simplify or accelerate the review process under Art. V of the Convention at the enforcement stage. For the moment this development is unrealistic, since courts with a less favorable attitude towards arbitration will presumably remain reluctant to give particular weight to the lack of annulment by courts of more arbitration-friendly seats. This means that, in a non-homogeneous environment, deferring to the review of the courts of the seat can only go to the detriment of arbitration, and never to its advantage.

Additionally, the policy in favor of giving finality to the annulment of a defective award, with a view to achieving legal certainty and avoiding harassment of the winning party in the annulment proceeding by means of repeat attempts at enforcement, is defensible only where the annulment occurs on grounds that are universally shared. The danger of such harassment is not necessarily greater than the danger of giving universal effect to annulments that are unjustified according to more widely accepted standards

---

41. Amsterdam Court of Appeals, 28 April 2009, in Rev. arb. (2009) p. 557, annotated by S. BOLLÉE and in Stockholm International Arbitration Review (2009) p. 219, annotated by Eric SCHWARTZ. The judgment was upheld by the Dutch Supreme Court, Judgment of 25 June 2010, in *Yearbook* XXXV (2010) p. 423: see Martin LEIJTEN and R. SCHELLAARS, "The *Yukos* Awards: Enforcement of Awards Annulled at the Place of Arbitration", Paris Journal of International Arbitration (2010) p. 1155; A.J. VAN DEN BERG, "Enforcement of Arbitral Awards Annulled in Russia", J. of Int'l Arb. (2010) p. 179.

42. *Yukos Capital v. OJSC Rosnef Oil Company* [2011] EWHC 1461 (Comm).

43. See fn. 34 and corresponding text.

44. E.g., where the annulment is based on grounds involving the arbitration agreement and which could be viewed as denying effects to the latter in violation of Art. II of the Convention.

or, worse, arbitrary. The interests of finality need not necessarily trump those of avoiding unwanted annulments.

From the viewpoint of arbitration law, therefore, a remissive or blind approach by enforcement courts towards foreign annulments, such as that somewhat irresolutely permitted by Art. V(1)(*e*) of the New York Convention and which translates into a blanket deference to a first level of control of awards by the courts of the seat, is a setback for arbitration and in principle not good policy. Absent broad consensus on annulment standards, such an attitude does not serve arbitration well, nor does it serve the interests of those States that value arbitration and its contribution to international commerce and to a neutral, efficient and fair settlement of disputes.[45]

4. *The Case for a Nuanced Approach*

Failing any international legal obligation, conceptual reason[46] or overarching policy argument to consider annulments of awards at the seat dispositive of the issue of their enforceability in other countries, and given the drawbacks of such a solution, there is scope for further considerations as to the wisdom of a different approach.

The first, and most straightforward, approach would obviously consist simply in an absolute refusal to take foreign annulments into consideration. It could be held that this solution has some merit also in terms of efficiency, in that it too can to a certain extent avoid a duplication and lengthening of procedures. In the traditional scheme, there is a first recourse to the courts of the seat by the losing party (which may be just as tactical and vexatious as multiple enforcement proceedings), for the duration of which the enforcement proceedings can be stopped, and arguably even should be, if one believes that logical precedence ought to be given to the annulment proceedings.[47] If the annulment proceedings are inconclusive, there will have to be a second set of proceedings in the enforcement State. It is true that there may be a plurality of enforcement procedures, which would be avoided by a definitive annulment. The number of cases in which there is such a multiplicity of enforcements is probably not very high. The trade-off in terms of efficiency between taking foreign annulment into account and not doing so is therefore a matter for debate.

Disregarding annulment at the seat would also have no downside in terms of safeguarding universally acknowledged fundamental interests and avoiding abuses by arbitrators and parties alike. The safeguard of such interests is ensured by the enforcing court's power to verify the conditions for enforceability listed in Art. V(1)(*a*)-(*d*) of the Convention. A two-tier control system is thus not indispensable even for this reason.

---

45. Also the argument based on the usefulness of a review of awards at the seat to avoid a backlash against arbitration in the fear of an "arbitration unbound" makes sense only insofar as such a review is based on acceptable standards, as discussed further in this paper.

46. In particular, the notion that non-domestic awards would somehow be part of the legal system of the State of the seat, and therefore cease to exist if annulled by the courts of that State, thereby becoming intrinsically unenforceable, which has been exposed as completely fallacious.

47. This is clearly permitted by Art. V(1)(*e*) which permits refusal of enforcement also if the award has not become binding or has been suspended.

Incidentally, there is an analogy between admitting the possibility of dispensing with the review of awards by the courts of the seat and the abolition by the New York Convention of the double-exequatur mechanism, which was premised on the assumption that the intervention of the State of the seat is unnecessary to ensure the international circulation of awards.

Whatever the merits of denying outright any relevance to foreign vacatur at the enforcement stage,[48] such an inelastic solution clearly goes against current mainstream thinking and may be viewed as excessive.

A more balanced approach is perhaps suggested by the New York Convention itself. As recalled above, the Convention lays down in Art. V(1)(*a*)-(*d*) what are generally considered the minimum requirements that an award must satisfy and accordingly allows States to insist on their satisfaction at the enforcement stage. Not coincidentally, those same requirements are often considered to be the only ones that justify annulment, as evidenced by the fact that they are replicated in Art. 34 of the UNCITRAL Model Law. Deferring to foreign annulments, whether relying on Art. V(1)(*e*) or on other legal basis, may therefore make sense for the enforcing State if the grounds for the annulment of the foreign award coincide with those of Art. V(1)(*a*)-(*d*), or in any case are similar to grounds for annulment admitted by its own law. This will be especially true if there is also a convergence as to the way in which such standards are applied in practice by the annulling court. In such circumstance refusal of enforcement simply based on prior annulment may be justified in the interest of avoiding the repetition of the review process before the enforcing court and therefore on grounds of efficiency.[49]

Refusal of enforcement based on annulment at the seat makes less sense from the standpoint of the enforcement State if annulment at the seat occurred on grounds which are not common to the two States. This of course includes public policy, since the public policy of the seat need not necessarily overlap with that of the enforcing State. It may appear all the more devoid of justification when the seat lacks any particular connection to the subject matter of the dispute, which it often does.

From the perspective of the most efficient circulation of awards, which is the primary aim of the New York Convention, deference to foreign annulment decisions would therefore seem justified only where the grounds for annulment (and the concrete approach to their application) coincide with those for refusal of enforcement or, at most, with those of the enforcing State.

5. *Other Considerations*

The question is whether there are further considerations in favor of recognizing a more significant role to the primary control jurisdiction.

48. This, as is well known, is the French position which is understandably subject to considerable criticism (see for instance S. BOLLÉE, Rev. arb. (2009) p. 557).

49. It is less justified if the annulment is based on the grounds of Art. V(2), since these are specific to the law of each State.

a. The interests of the State of the seat

In theory it could be held that, in deciding whether to allow a measure of deference to the control by the seat over arbitral awards, some consideration should be had for the interests of the State of the seat itself. However, as already noted, there seems to be no reason to take such putative interest into account. It is first of all questionable whether States always have any particular interest in having their decisions recognized in other jurisdictions, other than perhaps purely as a matter of principle or of prestige. This by itself can hardly be reason enough for other States to defer to such decisions and for overriding other possible considerations. This is all the more true given that there is not necessarily a connection between the State of the seat and the dispute decided by the award, and that the State's control jurisdiction over the arbitration is not "intrinsic", but is usually a mere consequence of the choice of the venue by the parties.

b. The rules on the recognition of foreign judgments

A second possible justification for taking into consideration the review of awards by the primary jurisdiction, and therefore foreign annulment decisions, is that this would accord with the general approach to the recognition of foreign judgments.

As noted above, the application of the ordinary rules on the recognition of foreign judgments to judgments annulling arbitral awards would entail that such judgments would normally be recognized, except possibly when they are seriously flawed. That, in turn, could lead to the refusal of enforcement of awards deserving recognition if assessed only against the standards of the Convention and of the enforcing State.

Hence, there is a tension between two competing policies, the recognition of arbitral awards and the recognition of foreign judgments. Giving prevalence to the latter, thereby hindering the recognition of arbitral awards, would not be in direct conflict with the New York Convention which, as discussed above, admits an exception to the obligation to recognize awards if these have been annulled in the State of origin. However, to do so leads to a paradox, given that the recognition of awards is the subject of an international convention, whilst the recognition of foreign judgments is not, and actually encounters significant resistance on the part of States. This is witnessed by the notorious failure of the Hague Conference on Private International Law's attempts to draft a worldwide convention on the recognition of judgments.[50]

The policy in favor of the circulation of international arbitral awards evidenced by the near-universal acceptance of the New York Convention, and the obligations under international law that flow from it, is a powerful element militating for a special treatment of foreign annulment judgments and against applying the ordinary rules on recognition of judgments to them. Those considerations can influence domestic principles on the recognition of foreign judgments. Specifically they can lead to broadening the grounds for refusal of recognition of foreign annulment judgments, to the point of permitting refusal of recognition (and thus of allowing the enforcement of the annulled award) even where the grounds of annulment are not outrageous, but simply fail to comport with those admitted by the enforcement State.

50. Not even the more modest Hague Convention on Forum Selection Agreements of 30 June 2005, (2005) ILM 1294, has entered into force.

This amounts to saying that the recognition and enforcement of foreign annulment judgments in this forum should be subject to a lex specialis.

The conclusion that foreign judgments dealing with arbitration, and specifically annulment judgments, deserve to be treated differently from other judgments, is consistent with the fact that, even within the European Union, judgments annulling arbitral awards do not benefit from the ordinary treatment accorded in Member States to judgments of other Member States under the Brussels I Regulation regime. It is also consistent with the fact, recalled above, that judgments that reject challenges to awards in vacatur proceedings are usually not recognized automatically abroad even when they have decided on grounds contemplated by the New York Convention.

c. *The expectations of the parties*

A more delicate question is whether granting deference to foreign annulment decisions may be justified by reference to the will or expectations of the parties.

The classic response is that, since the parties are free to choose the venue of their arbitration, they have the power to avoid the less arbitration-friendly fora and thus unwanted annulments, thereby diminishing the "nuisance power" of States with "abnormal" annulment standards. In any event, where, as is true in most cases, the seat has been agreed by the parties (directly or indirectly), there is an arguable case that the choice was made also relying on the local annulment standards. Following this reasoning, deference to the foreign annulment would be in line with the agreement and expectations of the parties. Even ignorance or weak bargaining power on the part of the parties could not be invoked as a justification to relieve them of their bargain.[51]

Against this it can be argued that, also if the parties were, or should have been, aware of the local vacatur standards and can therefore be held to have agreed by implication to be bound by them, such standards, and in particular their application by the courts, may be difficult to gauge in advance, and annulments can be unpredictable. In some cases, therefore, postulating an obligation to give effect to the decisions of the courts of the seat simply because the parties agreed to seat their arbitration there may go too far and appear unjustifiably harsh.

At times it will be questionable that the choice of the seat truly implied the intention to be bound by decisions of the local courts under local annulment standards, particularly where in practice that may render the agreement to arbitrate worthless.[52] Although rigorous evidence is lacking, anecdotal evidence seems to indicate that parties, at least those not from the State of the seat, are often surprised by annulments that do not conform to the more internationally recognized standards.[53] The high degree of

51. This point is made also by W.W. PARK, *op. cit.*, fn. 22.

52. This is particularly true given that, as often happens, standards for review that may appear perfectly satisfactory on paper, are applied in a way that appears at a minimum surprising or unforeseeable.

53. There would be scope for empirical research, for example, on the extent to which in annulment proceedings involving awards opposing a foreign party to a domestic one, or at least one from a more homogeneous background, the outcome tends to be favorable to the latter (the *Bechtel* case referred to in fn. 58 below might be on point).

uncertainty surrounding the US "manifest disregard of the law" standard is only one example of the fact that the choice of the venue of the arbitration cannot necessarily be taken as an acceptance of the outcome of annulment proceedings based on the vagaries of local law.[54]

Insisting on according near automatic deference to annulments coming from the courts of the seat, simply because the seat has been designated by the parties, and even where the designation is a take-it-or-leave-it proposition,[55] amounts partially to defeating one of the principal purposes of recourse to arbitration. A fundamental feature of arbitration is that it puts dispute settlement in transnational transactions on a level playing field and eliminates home court advantages and more generally affords an instrument to reduce to the utmost the intervention of State courts in transnational disputes.[56] To place excessive weight on assumed party expectations bears some similarity to claiming that judgments of a foreign court must be recognized in the forum whenever the foreign court's jurisdiction was based on a choice of forum agreement.[57]

It is meaningless to refer to the expectations of the parties on an abstract level. Expectations are bound to vary significantly depending, inter alia, on the origin and sophistication of the parties and whether they come from a homogeneous legal background, as well as on the business and geographic context in which the arbitration agreement is entered into. It is fair to assume that generally the parties will be unwilling to relinquish entirely the possibility of relying on States for assistance in the functioning of the arbitration and for some measure of control over the award. It is less clear to what extent they are prepared to accept the review where this is not predictable as to its legal premises and actual application or does not conform to standards that are generally accepted, or at least shared by them in the given circumstances. One may also question the degree of correlation between the designation of a seat for its supervisory functions and an effective, as opposed to a merely hypothetical, acceptance of that jurisdiction's standards for review of the award, particularly if they are unforeseeable or non-standard.

---

54. See for instance Hiro ARAGAKI, "The Mess of Manifest Disregard", Yale L. J. Online (2009).

55. This is almost invariably the case when one of the contracting parties is a State or a public entity (for example, see Art. 16(1) of the Procedural Rules on Conciliation and Arbitration of the the contracts financed by the European Development Fund, *OJ* 283 of 31 December 1990, p. 1). In such cases the only option for the party that is wary of the seat is to forego conclusion of the contract. If arbitration is subject to the absolute power and discretion of the courts of the seat, recourse to arbitration as a means of dispute settlement alternative to recourse to the courts becomes a fiction.

56. The normal desire of the parties to transnational business dealings to reduce the scope of State intervention in the settlement of disputes has little to do with an illusion of denationalizing such dealings or, worse, with a desire to engage in illegal conduct. Usually it is based on the belief that arbitration is better attuned to the needs of transnational relations because it ensures greater neutrality of the process, a higher level of finality and a greater ability than litigation in domestic courts to deal with the complexities and peculiarities of transnational disputes. All this is defeated if broad deference is given to the decisions of the seat courts at the annulment stage.

57. Requiring blind deference to local annulment standards only because the seat has been agreed by the parties can also be analogized to requiring the respect of limitations to the capacity of States or State entities to enter into arbitration agreements dictated by local law because the parties have chosen that law. As is well known, this position has been abandoned decades ago.

Put otherwise, from the fact that, according to the opinion prevailing today, the designation of the seat for its supervisory function entails the possibility of its intervention also at the review stage, it does not necessarily follow that that is what the parties really want or expect in all circumstances. To imply the acceptance of the seat's standards of review from the choice of the seat is often a legal fiction. It is true that it is a common legal technique to deduce consent from the mere acceptance of a contractual provision. The justification of resorting to such a legal fiction is, however, questionable if the parties' assumed intention in designating the seat is used as the primary basis for relying on the decisions of foreign courts and thereby of jeopardizing their fundamental intention, which was to resort to arbitration in lieu of going before domestic courts.

It is difficult to draw hard and fast conclusions on this point, because the application of the law inevitably must rely on presumptions. However, these considerations indicate that great caution must be exercised in justifying deference to foreign annulments on the basis of party expectations.[58]

6. *The Suggested Standard*

There is thus no overriding policy reason dictating a strict, or even a presumptive, deference to the setting aside of arbitral awards at the seat in the present state of arbitration.

Certainly under the New York Convention and arguably, in most cases, under their respective rules on the recognition of foreign judgments, States enjoy a broad latitude as to whether to enforce arbitral awards annulled abroad.

Given the absence of any intrinsic reason for treating awards differently from contracts or of any foregone right of the courts of the seat to have their decisions respected abroad, eliminating one layer of control of awards (i.e., that of the seat) neither breeds anarchy nor subverts traditional legal thinking and models. Likewise, it does not downplay the importance of national law in the system of international arbitration. Even if one believes that considerations of comity which may prescribe respecting foreign judgments should apply also to annulment judgments, there are equally compelling reasons for upholding the effects of party autonomy and of arbitral

58. This is all the more true where the seat has not been chosen by the parties, but has been designated by a third party, especially a domestic court. A further reason for not placing excessive weight on the expectations of the parties is that at the outset even the party that eventually will challenge the award at the seat will often not have any bona fide expectation as to availability of the particular ground of annulment subsequently invoked by it, given that the grounds invoked for the challenge and upheld by the courts for setting aside are often haphazard. To take the well-known example which was the subject of *Cour d'Appel de Paris*, 29 September 2005, *Direction générale de l'aviation civile de Dubai v. Bechtel*, Rev. arb. (2006) p. 695, one might wonder whether, *ex ante*, even the party that eventually invoked it was reasonably entitled to expect that the formality for the taking of oaths by witnesses would be applicable in the case at bar and would be considered so essential that failure to abide by it would justify annulment by the courts of the seat.

awards. Pre-eminent amongst these is the existence of an international regime aimed precisely at favoring the circulation of awards.[59]

Nor can it seriously be contended that an up-front review by the courts of the seat is indispensable for the respect of the fundamental interests of fair and just arbitration and of the parties. Such interests can be adequately protected at the enforcement stage by virtue of the grounds for refusal of enforcement of Art. V of the New York Convention,[60] which are recognized to embody the minimum standards.

Conversely, there are reasons for not ignoring foreign annulments systematically. These are essentially the same as those invoked by Reisman and others who postulate the need to refuse enforcement to annulled awards, and which have to do primarily with ensuring consistency and finality of outcomes. The fact that those reasons do not justify a blanket refusal of recognition of foreign annulments, or even according particular deference to such annulments, does not mean that such considerations should not be borne in mind where possible.

The conclusion can therefore only be that, in deciding whether to grant enforcement to an award annulled at the seat or, put otherwise, to recognize a foreign judgment having annulled an award, national courts are entitled – or should be allowed –[61] to exercise a broad margin of discretion, without taking as a given the decision of the State of the seat. In exercising this discretion, enforcing courts should bear in mind the interests of finality of arbitration. These would dictate that foreign annulments of awards be taken into account as a bar to enforcement only if in line with the grounds of Art. V(1)(*a*)-(*d*) and V(2)[62] of the New York Convention or with other grounds found in the law of the enforcing State, regardless of whether the grounds for annulment that are denied extraterritorial effects do not rise to the level of egregious misbehavior capable of being characterized as a violation of the Convention.[63]

This said, and because of the pre-eminent role of party autonomy in arbitration, when deciding whether to take into account an annulment of the award at the seat, the enforcement courts should also attempt to pay due regard to the parties' expectations on a case-by-case basis. In particular, they should insofar as possible seek to ascertain whether the choice of the seat was specifically inspired by confidence in the local courts' review standards and by a desire that annulment under such standards have definitive and extraterritorial effect. Admittedly the parties' intentions on this point, as on many

59. The spirit of the New York Convention supports the conclusion that courts other than those of the seat have a free-standing obligation under the Convention to assess issues of validity and scope of arbitration agreements and awards and to resolve these issues consistent with the Convention itself, irrespective of the determinations of the court of the seat, which would have to be disregarded if they are incorrect, or at least blatantly incorrect (G. BORN, *op. cit.*, fn. 3, p. 2925 et seq.).

60. Obviously excluding para. 1(*e*).

61. In some domestic legal systems there is no discretion for courts to recognize annulled awards. This is for instance the case in Italy, pursuant to Art. 840 of the Code of Civil Procedure.

62. And in the latter case only if the notions of public policy and arbitrability adopted by the annulling court are in line with those generally accepted in international arbitration and in the State of enforcement.

63. As was found to be the case in *Saipem v. Bangladesh* (fn. 37 above).

others, may not always be easy to identify and courts must rely on presumptions. These, however, should not weigh too heavily towards assuming an intention to defer to annulment standards that are not widely shared.

That is a matter that the parties would be well advised to consider when drafting their arbitration agreement, although there is little evidence that they do so in practice. At that point they could state whether they agree that any setting aside by the courts of the seat will have extraterritorial effect, thereby preventing the enforcement of the award abroad, or whether instead they want to be free to seek enforcement in other States despite annulment by the courts of the seat.

To sum up, the underlying question is whether, in the presence of a conflict between an arbitral decision and a court decision, there is any reason to give greater weight to the latter as a matter of principle. The answer should be negative. Given the well-developed, consistent and widely accepted body of rules and principles concerning arbitration, courts should be permitted to assess awards and foreign judgments relating to arbitration on their respective merits and to decide which are more in line with such principles.

A nuanced approach such as the one advocated here[64] might well lead to greater deference being given to annulments by the courts of internationally consolidated arbitration venues than to those by courts with a patchier track record in matters of arbitration. This should not be a cause for concern. One may even reflect on whether such a standard for deference to foreign annulments might not have a beneficial effect on less arbitration-friendly courts. It could act as an incentive for them to embrace internationally recognized standards, thereby increasing the competitiveness of their respective countries for the seating of arbitrations.[65]

A focused consideration of the review of awards by the courts of the seat would have even more significant pro-arbitration effects if applied not one-sidedly, i.e., only to annulment judgments, but in a broader perspective, i.e., also to judgments rejecting challenges. There is indeed no reason to defer to foreign judgments at the enforcement stage when they set aside an award (albeit only where the standards are satisfactory, as advocated here) and not to do so, instead, when they uphold an award, if the grounds for rejecting the challenge are the same as those invoked to contest enforcement and are applied in an equally satisfactory manner. Such an approach would streamline the recognition procedure and be beneficial for the circulation of awards.

---

64. There is increasing acceptance of the idea that foreign annulments cannot be given absolute effect and of the wisdom of a selective approach: see for instance N. DARWAZEH, *op. cit.* fn., 3, p. 343; S. BOLLÉE, *Les méthodes*, *op. cit.*, fn. 3, p. 259 and Rev. arb. (2009) p. 561; C. KOCH, *op. cit.*, fn. 3, pp. 291-292; Dana FREYER, "The Enforcement of Awards Affected by Judicial Orders of Annulment at the Place of Arbitration" in E. GAILLARD and D. DI PIETRO, eds., *Enforcement of Arbitration Agreements and International Arbitral Awards* (Cameron May 2009) p. 757. See also Sect. 4-16(b) of Preliminary Draft No. 5 (1 September 2011) of the Restatement of the Law Third of the U.S. Law of International Commercial Arbitration which permits non-enforcement of an award set aside at the seat "if the judgment setting it aside is not entitled to recognition under the principles governing the recognition of judgments in the court where such relief is sought, or in other extraordinary circumstances".

65. Indeed, whilst it is true that parties usually are not prepared to accept outlandish annulments, they usually value rigorous and predictable review on limited grounds.

There is particular merit in this solution because, different from when the New York Convention was adopted, in some contexts the circulation of arbitral awards has become more complicated than that of judgments. In particular within the European Union, judgements benefit from automatic recognition, unlike awards under the New York Convention and most national laws. From this standpoint, within the European Union recourse to court litigation has become more attractive than recourse to arbitration.

V. THE IMPORTANCE OF SUPERVISORY-SUPERVISORY JURISDICTION

Professor Reisman views with concern the emergence of a new level of control over international arbitration in the form of a review by international courts, in particular investment tribunals or the European Court of Human Rights, of the legality of State acts purportedly interfering with international arbitration. He sees this as displacing the final authority of the courts of "primary jurisdiction" and posing a risk of prolonging arbitral proceedings.[66]

This concern is unfounded for several reasons. First, as discussed above, there is no overriding principle prescribing that any particular deference be accorded to the decisions of the primary forum on the validity of awards. Such deference is justified (but not mandatory) only where the annulment is the result of a review in keeping with standards shared by the country of enforcement or with unequivocal expectations of the parties. In the absence of a clearly defined scheme of control of arbitration conferring a role on the courts of the seat, there is therefore no reason for concern that a new level of control would subvert the present order of things.

Second, and more importantly, there are many instances where States, be they the one of the seat or other States, interfere with arbitration in what can appear to be violations of their international obligations, foremost amongst which those deriving from the New York Convention. Until *Saipem v. Bangladesh*[67] and the other recent pronouncements of international courts and tribunals,[68] it seemed that almost nothing could be done about this, because the Convention does not provide for a mechanism to

---

66. W.M. REISMAN and B. RICHARDSON, "Tribunals and Courts", this volume, pp. 17-65; W.M. REISMAN and H. IRAVANI, "The Changing Relation", *op. cit.*, fn. 11, p. 32.

67. See fn. 37 above.

68. For a discussion of these matters and of the relevant case law see L.G. RADICATI DI BROZOLO, "The Impact of National Law and Courts", *op. cit.*, fn. 1; L.G. RADICATI DI BROZOLO and L. MALINTOPPI, "Unlawful Interference with International Arbitration", *op. cit.*, fn. 1. An interesting recent addition to this case law is *White v. India* (fn. 25 above) which dealt with the legality under a bilateral investment treaty of the actions of the Indian courts in setting aside and enforcement actions in relation to a foreign award. The tribunal decided that the Indian judicial system's inability to deal with the investor's enforcement action in a timely fashion constituted a breach of India's "voluntarily assumed obligation of providing [the investor] with 'effective means' of asserting claims and enforcing rights" (para. 11.4.19), for which it awarded compensation to the investor. In reaching this decision the tribunal went as far as to decide that, having regard to the New York Convention, the award which was the subject of the enforcement action pending before the domestic courts was "enforceable under the laws of India" (para. 14.2.66).

ensure its proper application by States. The only practical remedy was to disregard the illegal interferences, where the parties and arbitral tribunals could get away with it.

In such a context the prospect of an intervention by international courts and tribunals can only be welcomed. It can serve to hold States accountable for violations of the New York Convention and more generally of the rights accruing from arbitration, with an overall positive impact on the furtherance of the rule of law in international arbitration. The decisions of these higher instances can also improve the understanding of the obligations of States in this respect and to give more flesh to them.

This said, there is no likelihood of a widespread intervention by such courts and tribunals liable to result in a generalized prolonging of arbitration proceedings, as feared by Reisman. The jurisdictional barriers for access to this form of justice (the existence of an appropriate international treaty conferring jurisdiction to review these State behaviors, the possibility to characterize the arbitral award as investment,[69] to name just two) are such that only seldom will that form of review and justice be available. Given the frequency with which States still defer to the decisions of the courts of the seat, this is more of a cause of regret than of satisfaction.

VI. CONCLUSION: THE PROPER BALANCE OF THE RESPECTIVE ROLES OF ARBITRATION AND OF THE STATE OF THE SEAT

Professor Reisman's conceptualization of the system of international commercial arbitration comports with mainstream thinking and with current State practice on the role of the courts of the seat, rationalizing it in a coherent theoretical framework.

Nevertheless, in envisaging a control system of arbitration that entrusts to the courts of the seat primary supervisory jurisdiction over arbitrations and awards, this vision reads more into the New York Convention than seems possible having regard to its text as well as to its purpose and scope. The conception of international arbitration as relying on a crucial role for the courts of the seat is tantamount to introducing into the system a form of "home country control" (to borrow the terminology of EU law).[70] In the absence of a broad international consensus on the ground rules of arbitration and in particular on the grounds for annulment, such a model is even less warranted on a worldwide level than it is within the European Union. Professor Reisman's vision is therefore at best premature, in that it assumes a trust in the courts of the seat that is not justified in the light of the diverging attitudes toward arbitration throughout the world.[71]

---

69. See ICSID Case No. ARB/08/16, *GEA Group v. Ukraine* of 31 March 2011 in which, contrary to *Saipem v. Bangladesh* (fn. 37 above) but on somewhat different facts, it was held that an arbitral award was not an investment. This decision is criticized in *White v. India* (fn. 25 above) as "an incorrect departure from the developing [investment treaty] jurisprudence on the treatment of arbitral awards" (para. 7.6.8).

70. For some parallel consideration on developments within the European Union see L.G. RADICATI DI BROZOLO, "Arbitration and the Draft Revised Brussels I Regulation", *op. cit.*, fn. 34.

71. It is not by chance that in the European Union the model of home country control, and the related concept of mutual trust between the legal systems of the different Member States, presupposes a certain level of harmonization of the rules in the Member States.

For the moment[72] the preferable course seems to be for each State to decide on its own whether to grant enforcement to non-domestic arbitral awards, obviously in the respect of the obligations laid down by the New York Convention. Deference to foreign annulment decisions should be accorded only on a selective, reasoned and ad hoc basis. The enforcing court should give effect to a foreign annulment only if it considers it justified in the particular circumstances, and having regard to the commonality between the standards of review of awards at the place of enforcement and the concrete standards applied by the vacating court, as well as to the true expectations of the parties.

Considering that today foreign annulment decisions are still almost systematically dispositive of the validity of non-domestic awards, albeit for reasons that cannot be shared, a widespread recognition that Art. V(1)(*e*) has no prescriptive force may amount to a step away from the control structure in place today. However, such a step would be more a step forward than a step back in the direction of a proper allocation of jurisdiction between States with regard to arbitration.

Evidently this conclusion militates heavily against any proposal to modify the New York Convention by rendering mandatory the ground for refusal of recognition of arbitral awards contemplated by Art. V(1)(*e*).[73] It could be acceptable only in a completely different world characterized by a much greater convergence in the standards of review of arbitration and, possibly, with a central authority to monitor the correct application of such standards. This is hardly in the cards for the near future.

Downplaying the role of the seat of the arbitration, at least when it leads to annulments unjustified according to international standards, would bring about a more efficient system of transnational justice. Such a system would avoid a two-tier control and allow sidestepping the intervention of courts that may be less arbitration-friendly than those of the countries where enforcement of the awards is sought. Conversely, in the interest of increasing the effectiveness of arbitration it would be equally important that foreign judgments validating non-domestic awards be given greater weight internationally, obviously where the standard of review conforms with internationally accepted ones.

The emergence of a supervisory-supervisory jurisdiction over international arbitration, limited as it may be, is not in contrast with the present structure of international commercial arbitration. It can exercise a useful function of restraint over States, instilling greater respect for the obligations to recognize agreements to arbitrate and awards, and thereby the proper functioning of arbitration.

---

72. Still today annulments, and the standards on which they are based, are very often tainted by a very local perspective, which cannot be prevented, but does not justify recognition abroad.

73. See Albert Jan VAN DEN BERG, "Hypothetical Draft Convention on the International Enforcement of Arbitration Agreements and Awards, Explanatory Note" in *50 Years of the New York Convention*, ICCA Congress Series no. 14 (2009) (hereinafter *ICCA Congress Series no. 14*) p. 649. And this even assuming that the principle of an amendment of the New York Convention were a viable idea, which it is not for the reasons convincingly laid out by E. GAILLARD, "The Urgency of Not Revising the New York Convention" in *ICCA Congress Series no. 14*, p. 689; V.V. VEEDER, "Is There a Need to Revise the New York Convention" in E. GAILLARD, ed., *The Review of Arbitral Awards*, IAI Forum, Dijon, 2008 (Juris) p. 183. See also Catherine KESSEDJAN, "*En revenant de Dublin: L'éventuelle réforme de la Convention de New York*", 26 ASA Bulletin (2008) p. 644.

Universal Arbitration Between Freedom and Constraint: The Challenges of Jurisdiction in Multiparty, Multi-Contract Arbitrations

*Karim Youssef**

TABLE OF CONTENTS | Page

I.	Introduction: The Changing Relation of National Courts and International Arbitration in Multiparty, Multi-Contract Contexts	103
II.	Arbitrators: Between the Ideal of Equity and the Constraints of Law	105
III.	National Courts: Changing State of Mind and Degree of Control	111
IV.	Changing Rules of the Game: The Making of *a* Law of Complex Arbitrations	113
V.	The Qualitative Element of the *Juge Naturel*: Dealing with the Challenges	118

I. INTRODUCTION: THE CHANGING RELATION OF NATIONAL COURTS AND INTERNATIONAL ARBITRATION IN MULTIPARTY, MULTI-CONTRACT CONTEXTS

Beyond "change", nothing less than a revolution has taken place in the relation of national courts and international arbitration in the field of complex arbitrations.

Expansive practices of jurisdiction in the last decades (in particular, the so-called "extension" of the arbitration agreement to non-signatories or to related contracts)[1] brought a serious challenge to the idea that national courts are the natural judge of international commerce. The enforcement of arbitration beyond the scope of formal reference has informally, but fundamentally, modified the structure of the theory of international jurisdiction which is based on the *exceptionalism* of private justice. Arbitral justice turned, in fact, into the default justice of international commerce. The shy contractual creature which only fifty years ago was struggling for recognition has emerged, today, as a transnational commercial justice that hosts the large majority of

---

* Partner, Head of Middle East Arbitration, Amereller Legal Consultants; Associate-Professor of Private Law, Cairo University School of Law. The views expressed in this material do not necessarily reflect those of AMERELLER LEGAL CONSULTANTS or its clients, and are exclusively those of the author.

This Comment is based on the author's *Consent in Context, Fulfilling the Promise of International Arbitration: Multiparty, Multi-Contract and Non-Contract Arbitration*, 2nd edn. (West 2011 (Preface by Jan PAULSSON)), (hereinafter, "*Consent in Context*"). It also builds on reflections made in "The Limits of Consent: The Right or Obligation to Arbitrate of Non-Signatories in Groups of Companies" in B. HANOTIAU and E. SCHWARTZ, eds., *Dossier of the ICC Institute of World Business Law No. VII: Multiparty Arbitration* (ICC publications 2010) (hereinafter, "Limits of Consent").

1. The term refers, *lato sensu*, to cases where tribunals assert jurisdiction in cases where the claimant did not sign an arbitration agreement or the respondent did not accept expressly or implicitly the jurisdiction of the tribunal.

international commercial disputes, and stands side by side in pacific coexistence with state justice. If the last three centuries were an era of nation-states and state justice, the last decades have inaugurated a historical revival of international commercial arbitration in the image of the earlier days of glory of the institution in the trade fairs of Middle Ages Europe.

As the developments to follow will show, the gradual (re-)construction of a global arbitral justice has had a direct effect on consent to arbitrate or the requirement that those who may be compelled to arbitrate must have consented, which is the legal and conceptual foundation of arbitration. The effect goes to the manner of assessment of consent and its relative role as basis of jurisdiction.

1. *Four Challenges*

The modern renaissance of universal arbitration and contemporary practices of jurisdiction in complex settings have given rise to a number of serious challenges to the classic regulation of arbitration and to those who apply it. These challenges are:

1. the rise of pragmatic and equitable considerations in the context of a general sophistication of decision-making processes and methods;
2. the declining relevance of the classic regulation of arbitration rooted in the writing requirement and contractual interpretation;
3. the mounting uncertainty of outcomes;
4. the development of practices of compelling non-consenting parties to arbitrate or compelling consenting parties to arbitrate beyond the scope of submission.

2. *Four Issues*

These challenges face arbitral tribunals, courts and even international parties with difficult questions which lie on the borderline of black-letter law and subjacent practical and equitable considerations in the particular case.

1. *For arbitral tribunals*: How to honor the jurisdictional necessities of complex arbitrations in the age of global commerce, while operating in a legal environment that is protective of consent and often also of formalism?
2. *For national courts*: How to exercise control in a manner which neither dismisses practical considerations, nor flushes legalism out of the system of control and causes a potential backlash in terms of the parties' desire to arbitrate?
3. *The governing rules*: In the midst of the mounting uncertainty of outcomes in the individual case, what are the "rules" governing issues of jurisdiction in multiparty multi-contract settings? Can these "rules" be rationalized, if possible, in terms of the classic regulation of arbitration?
4. *For the parties*: In the face of their partially diminished jurisdictional autonomy, how can international parties re-exercise their freedom to arbitrate, and manage jurisdictional exposure, in ways which would tie the hands of arbitrators and courts?

This Comment proposes that workable – and reasonable – solutions to the jurisdictional challenges raised by complex arbitrations are not necessarily inconsistent with rigorous decision-making methodology or with the *tronc commun* of arbitration norms. To cater for the growing complexity of assessing jurisdiction, solutions may be sought, in a back-to-basics approach,[2] which re-introduces legalism and consent, without necessarily sacrificing subjacent considerations of efficiency and equity.

II. ARBITRATORS: BETWEEN THE IDEAL OF EQUITY AND THE CONSTRAINTS OF LAW

1. *The Simple Picture: Consensual Analysis as the Rule*

Consent is the touchstone of jurisdictional assessment in complex arbitrations,[3] regardless of the form of extension or the fact setting. Questions of extension in groups of contracts settings are resolved, as a general matter, by consensual analysis. "[A]rbitrators generally proceed by analyzing the parties' intentions to accept or refuse to submit the entire group of contracts concluded between the same parties to a single arbitration agreement contained in one of these contracts."[4] Similarly, the so-called group of companies doctrine,[5] despite its economic premise, is predominantly consent-based, in most accounts.[6]

The predominance of consensual analysis in arbitral decision-making is obviously a natural penchant. It is also, partly, a consequence of the way arbitrators rule on jurisdiction. They usually avoid a conflict of laws approach, and decide on the scope of their jurisdiction directly by interpretation of the parties' intentions, outside any system of national or international norms. Arbitrators are also less inclined than national courts

2. See generally, Albert Jan VAN DEN BERG, ed., *International Arbitration 2006: Back to Basics?* ICCA Congress Series no. 13 (2007) (hereinafter *ICCA Congress Series no. 13*).

3. "In most cases, courts and arbitral tribunals still base their determination of the issue on the existence of a common intent of the parties and, therefore, on consent." Bernard HANOTIAU, "Non-Signatories in International Arbitration: Lessons from Thirty Years of Case Law" in *ICCA Congress Series no. 13*, pp. 341-358 at p. 343.

4. Daniel COHEN, "*Arbitrage et Groupes de Contrats*", Rev. Arb. (1997) p. 482.

5. See *Dow Chemical*, ICC Case No. 4131 (1982), ICCA *Year Book Commercial Arbitration* IX (1984) p. 131 at p. 136. The arbitration clause signed by companies of a corporate group binds other companies of the group "which by virtue of their role in the conclusion, performance, or termination of the contracts containing said clauses, *and in accordance with the mutual intention of all parties to the proceedings*, appear to have been veritable parties to these contracts...". (Emphasis added.)

6. "It is not so much the existence of a group that results in the various companies of the group being bound by the agreement signed by only one of them, but rather the fact that such was the true intention of the parties." Emmanuel GAILLARD and John SAVAGE, eds., *Fouchard, Gaillard, Goldman on International Commercial Arbitration* (Kluwer 1999) at para. 500 (hereinafter *Fouchard, Gaillard, Goldman*). See also ICC Case No. 10758 (2000), 16 ICC Ct. Bull. (no. 2) pp. 94-98; JDI (2001) p. 1171. "If the Claimant had intended [the non-signatory] to be a party to either the Contract or its arbitration clause, it could have so insisted at that time." For a more extensive analysis of the exact dosage of consent in the group of companies doctrine, see generally, "Limits of Consent", fn. * above.

to venture into unchartered jurisdictional territories and depart from well-established jurisdictional principles to comply with their legal duty to render an award that is enforceable, inter alia, jurisdiction-wise.

However, closer analysis of case law reveals a different and more complex scene. The traditional simplicity of a jurisdictional exercise conducted under the exclusive rule of consent has faded; and the assessment of jurisdiction has become more complicated in a variety of ways, which are explored – and analyzed – in the following sections.

2. *Changing Processes of Decision-Making*

a. *Inadequacy of the classic regulation of arbitration*

In the age of global commerce, arbitral tribunals are often faced with complex economic structures and realities that they simply cannot ignore (such as the existence of a group of companies, or a global economic operation which is implemented *via* a group of interconnected contracts, etc.).

At the same time, the basic law of international arbitration (the 1958 New York Convention and typical UNCITRAL-based arbitration laws) does not deal by specific rules with multiparty or multi-contract proceedings. Therefore, third-party issues are treated, as a general matter, under the *droit commun*.[7]

The classic regulation of arbitration, rooted in the requirements of consent and writing, is indifferent to economic realities (such as the factual or legal nexus among independent legal entities or among autonomous instruments) and insensitive to considerations of equity which may *arise in the specific case*. It is based on consent as a per se rule. The classic simple yes-no question, whether a written arbitration agreement exists, is often simplistic and fails to reflect the true complexity of the jurisdictional issues which arise in complex arbitrations.

To reach workable solutions to complex problems (in terms of equity and efficacy *in the specific case*), tribunals had to depart sometimes from black-letter law, strict legal rigor and conventional methods of decision-making. While the search for the parties' intent remains predominant, a more *practical* methodology is noted in decision-making, one that is less focused on the automatic and per se application of consent and traditional legal rules.

b. *Practical imperatives and post-modernist approaches to jurisdiction*

In terms of technical aspects of decision-making in complex settings, it seems that, not infrequently, strict legalism gives way to a complex weighting of all the specific circumstances of the case in view of reaching a decision on the utility and fairness of compelling a non-signatory or extending jurisdiction beyond the formal scope of submission. Interpretation of the parties' intent is also often made with the economies of the transaction in mind.

7. For example, the Egyptian Arbitration Law provides that "the expression 'the two parties to the arbitration' when used in this Law shall denote the parties to the arbitration, whatever their number may be". (Art. 4.3, Law No. 27 for 1994 promulgating the Law Concerning Arbitration in Civil and Commercial Matters, as last amended by Law No. 8/2000 in ICCA *International Handbook on Commercial Arbitration* (hereinafter *Handbook*) Supp. 36 (November 2002)).

In fact, analysis of case law shows that decisions to extend would typically take place in cases where restricting the tribunal's jurisdiction to the formal scope of the arbitration agreement would be inefficient or unjust. A decision is made on whether and to what extent the practical considerations of the specific case could justify bending legal rules.

c. Contextual decision-making: Consent and context

Analysis of case law also shows that the rule of consent applies less *per se* and more *in context*. Every search for implicit consent is contextual by nature, and the general context of the dispute is normally taken into account when ascertaining the existence and scope of consent to arbitrate.

But, in some cases, the *specific context* of the jurisdictional inquiry (for example, the existence of an economic group, or the involvement of non-signatories in the contract containing the arbitration clause) would exercise a distorting effect on the process of searching for consent, and the intellectual process of decision-making is modified. The contextual elements would play a role which goes beyond merely ascertaining consent, and contribute *directly* to the decision to extend or not to extend. A tribunal or court may take these elements not merely as indication of consent, but as self-standing elements that feed, in their own right, the decision to extend or not to extend, within a larger context of complication of the process of ruling on jurisdiction.

ICC Case No. 9517[8] illustrates this approach. The tribunal listed the elements which it took into consideration in ruling on jurisdiction. The "*intention of the parties as regards rights of non-signatories to participate in the arbitration agreement*" was merely one of them. It noted that:

> "... [T]he question whether persons not named in an agreement can take advantage of an arbitration clause incorporated therein is a matter which *must be decided on a case-to-case basis*, requiring a close analysis of *the circumstances in which the agreement was made, the corporate and practical relationship existing on one side and known to those on the other side of the bargain, the actual or presumed intention of the parties as regards rights of non-signatories to participate in the arbitration agreement, and the extent to which and the circumstances under which non-signatories subsequently became involved in the performance of the agreement and in the dispute* arising from it." (Emphasis added.)

In some cases, contextual elements could even justify the exclusion of consent altogether; but context must be compelling to justify such an outcome.[9]

8. 30 November 1998, unpublished, cited in B. HANOTIAU, "Lessons from Thirty Years of Case Law", fn. 3 above, at pp. 351-352.

9. Marc Blessing explains: "All individual elements of a case will have to be weighted very carefully, respecting the basic principle of the privity of contract and the clear notion that legal entities are distinct from each other and that, therefore, such fundamental principles cannot easily be removed by an arbitral tribunal unless very specific circumstances demand such a removal." Marc BLESSING, "Extension of the Arbitration Clause to Non-Signatories" in *The Arbitration Agreement – Its Multifold Critical Aspects*, ASA Special Series (1994, no. 8) pp. 151-164 at p. 160.

d. Global assessment of jurisdiction

The difference between the usual scenario (consent as *the* criteria of jurisdiction, and the jurisdictional exercise is limited to looking for *indices* of its existence), and the modified intellectual process (consent is merely *an* element of jurisdictional assessment, and together with context contributes *directly* to decision-making) may seem slim. However, the conceptual and technical leap is fundamental and should not be underestimated.

The jurisdictional exercise is no longer limited to consensual analysis, but transcends consent, and is fundamentally more sophisticated, in terms of decision-making by reference not to one, but to a number of criteria and factual elements.

On the level of technique, the intellectual analysis moves from being a single-minded exercise whose sole purpose is to find consent to a more complicated endeavor that is both more global in its purpose, and less legalistic in its nature.

Tribunals ruling in this fashion would usually proceed with a global factual assessment of all subjective and objective elements (including the parties' intent, the existence of an economic group, the existence of a single global economic transaction, the involvement in the contract and the appearance that all these elements may have created in the minds of third parties), which contributes to forming their mind in view of reaching a decision on whether to extend or not to extend.

e. The emergence of a rule of reason

The development of more sophisticated patterns and methods of decision-making suggests that the per se rule of consent has been replaced, in part, by a *rule of reason*. When ruling on extension, tribunals (and courts) reason less in terms of *norms* (the consent, writing and *privity* requirements), and more in term of *effects* of extension (or its absence) *in the particular case*. Extension may be ordered, notwithstanding the fact that consent has not been found or has not been searched for, to honor considerations that are deemed worthy to prevail, in the particular case, over a single-minded and abstract search for *ex ante* consent.

The emergence of a *règle de raison* has been identified by commentators analyzing case law in complex settings. In order to assess the effects of particular outcomes, the decision to extend or not to extend is often made under a *what-if-not* scenario. Hanotiau explains: "It seems that at least in a great number of cases, a good test to decide whether an 'extension' of the clause is appropriate is to determine whether the same solution would be justified if the situation were reversed."[10]

The *what-if-not* assessment is, itself, made in a global fashion which takes into account all the relevant factual elements of the dispute.

f. Ruling on jurisdiction ex aequo et bono

These different patterns of decision-making (and in particular those which involve the global assessment of all relevant contextual elements) also necessarily involve a measure of equitable thinking that is hard to ignore. The decision to extend or not to extend is made not only by reference to legal rules, but also by reference to whether extension is "appropriate", "fair" or even "wise" in the particular case. "Concerns of equity often

10. Bernard HANOTIAU, "Lessons from Thirty Years of Case Law", fn. 3 above, at p. 353.

underlie the reasoning of courts and, even more, of arbitral tribunals."[11] These concerns seem to *compete* in the minds of arbitrators and courts with fundamental principles of arbitration law (consent, writing and *privity*), and at times prevail. "[T]he equities that appear from the underlying facts are likely to be far more important to the outcome than which theory of law is advanced."[12]

Interestingly, when courts and tribunals exclude the normal application of arbitration law to accommodate economic realities or to take into account considerations that are deemed more *just,* the "equities" of the case are not mere *dicta*. They constitute an integral part of the *legal* reasoning of courts and tribunals.

In US case law, concerns of practicality and efficiency are often explicit. The arbitration agreement "would be of little value if it did not extend to [the non-signatory]".[13] In the context of groups of contracts, it was held that the arbitral proceedings based on identical clauses were consolidated, in the absence of the parties' consent, because inter alia the "efficient and speedy resolution of disputes was clearly among the desired effects of [the Arbitration Act]".[14] The Fifth Circuit has even applied veil-piercing and alter ego theories "in the name of equity".[15]

One also finds explicit reference to considerations of efficiency in French case law concerning the so-called *involvement in performance*. In *Sté V 2000 v. Sté Project XJ 220 ITD et autre*,[16] the Paris Court of Appeal relied on considerations of good administration of justice to justify extension. The Court allowed a non-signatory company involved in the performance of the contract containing the arbitration clause to arbitrate "so that all legal and economic aspects of the dispute are brought before the arbitrator".[17]

Equitable considerations seem to also play a role in cases involving non-signatory States.[18] The tribunal, in the *Westland* case, noted at the end of the award: "Finally, mention must be made of the practical reasons and considerations of equity which have motivated the arbitrators in this matter, *quite apart from the legal ground*."[19] (Emphasis added.)

---

11. Bernard HANOTIAU, "Problems Raised by Complex Arbitrations Involving Multiple Contracts — Parties — Issues: An Analysis", 18 J. Int'l Arb. (2001, no. 3) p. 278.
12. John M. TOWNSEND, "Non-signatories and Arbitration", 3 ADR Currents (1998) p. 19 at p. 23.
13. *Pritzker v. Merrill Lynch, Pierce, Fenner & Smith*, 7 F.3d 1110, 1122 (3d Cir. 1993).
14. *Sociedad Anonima De Navegacion Petrolera v. CIA. De Petroleos De Chile S.A.*, 634 F.Supp. 805, 1986 A.M.C. 1995 (S.D.N.Y. 1986).
15. "Courts will apply the alter ego doctrine and hold a parent corporation liable for the actions of its instrumentality in the name of equity when the corporate form is used as a sham to perpetrate a fraud." *Bridas S.A.P.I.C. v. Government of Turkmenistan*, 447 F.3d 411, 416 (5th Cir. 2006).
16. Paris Court of Appeal (1st Ch.), 7 Dec. 1994, Rev. Arb. (1996, no. 2) pp. 245-249, Case note, Ch. JARROSSON, Rev. Arb.(1996, no. 2) pp. 250-258.
17. *Ibid.*, at p. 250.
18. George Rosenberg seems to suggest that jurisdictional assessment in these cases depends more on the balance of policy considerations at stake, than on the strict application of general contract law and the interpretation of the will of the parties. George ROSENBERG, "State as Party to Arbitration", 20 Arb. Int'l (2004, no. 4) p. 387 at p. 398
19. ICC Case No. 3879, Interim award of 5 March 1984, *Yearbook* XI (1986) p. 127 at p. 132.

There is reason to believe that rationales of practicality and equity, which can sometimes come to the surface of legal reasoning, are often implicit in the minds of tribunals and courts and play a mind-setting role, but are simply part of the *unsaid*.[20]

The intellectual processes of decision-making described above are complex. They involve balancing the outcomes dictated by legal rules with possible deviations therefrom which may be required by considerations of equity and efficiency. The extent to which equitable considerations would be outcome determinative is, in turn, influenced, or at least should be influenced, by other practical considerations, including how much support there is in the facts and the law for the arbitrators' equitable outcomes, and hence the extent to which the arbitrators would need to depart from their duty to render an enforceable award in order to reach the intended outcome.

g. *The transition towards realist decision-making*[21]

It has been argued that a latent equitable inclination is identifiable in arbitral decision-making as a general matter, and even in the rulings of all judges. The contemporary *glissement* from legal to practical concerns described above transposes this inclination to the domain of jurisdiction. It creates an environment where it seems that decisions on the *scope* of jurisdiction are, de facto, rendered, at least in part, ex aequo et bono. Moral norms that arbitrators sometimes apply to the merits, in the silence of or even against a legal rule,[22] seem to exercise today an incontrovertible influence on the intellectual process of decision-making on jurisdiction in complex settings.

This *post-modernist* methodology puts in evidence a decisional environment where strict legalism is excluded, as well as conforming with a predetermined set of rules. It evokes conceptions similar to those advanced by Carl Schmidt or Oliver Wendell Holmes, Jr., of a "legal system" defined not as *normative*, i.e., as a set of rules, but as a *process* of reaching a decision which is essentially pragmatic, utilitarian or even at times, regrettably, arbitrary.[23]

3. *The Necessity of a Decision Justified in Law*

The changing face of jurisdictional assessment, in terms of methods of decision-making and applicable rules, creates the impression that arbitrators and courts rule on complex jurisdictional questions ex aequo et bono, and, as a matter of fact, may do as they please with respect to assessing jurisdiction. That is simply not the case. Arbitrators are not authorized to rule on jurisdiction *in equity*. They must render a decision on jurisdiction that is justified *in law*. They are bound to do so, even if they were empowered to act as amiables compositeurs. A decision to compel a non-signatory to arbitrate, to expand the reach of an arbitration clause to cover a global economic transaction or to consolidate otherwise-independent proceedings may (or may not) be motivated by pragmatic considerations, but must in all cases be justified in a legally acceptable fashion.

---

20. Daniel COHEN, Rev. Arb. (1997) at p. 499.
21. See Karim YOUSSEF, *Consent in Context*, fn. * above, at Sect. 8.12.
22. Pierre MAYER, "*La Règle Morale dans l'Arbitrage International*" in P. BELLET, *Etudes offertes à Pierre Bellet* (Litec 1991).
23. Bruno OPPETIT, *Theorie de l'Arbitrage*, pp. 125-126.

This tension between a liberating intellectual process and the constraints of law imprints the process of ruling on jurisdiction with unique complexity. Arbitrators are under the duty to give *legal* reasons for outcomes which may have been justified, in fact, by considerations of equity and practicality. Arbitrators must also justify their decision by reference to the legal framework of international commercial arbitration, although this framework would not necessarily support a decision to extend or a liberal approach to jurisdiction in the particular case.

III. NATIONAL COURTS: CHANGING STATE OF MIND AND DEGREE OF CONTROL

1. *From Competition* with *to Competition* for *Arbitration*

The flourishing of liberal approaches to jurisdiction and the construction of a global arbitral justice could not have happened without the acquiescence, if not the active encouragement and participation of national courts.[24]

In the last three decades, the classic judicial perception of arbitration as ouster of court jurisdiction has faded, and a dramatic shift in judicial attitudes has taken place in a number of jurisdictions.[25] The reasons for this shift are complex but include the growing awareness by national courts of their own limitations in litigating complex international disputes. The US Supreme Court has, as early as the 1970s, developed a doctrine of *necessity* of international arbitration in international transactions.[26]

The development of arbitration, in turn, created a spiral of accelerated expansion which fueled even more liberal judicial attitudes. With its universal development, international arbitration has become a major *business* subject to competition in itself and less of a competitor. Instead of competing *with* arbitration to retain jurisdiction over international disputes, national courts started to compete *among themselves* to attract more arbitral business.

24. For an explanation of the public international law foundation of international commercial arbitration, see W. Michael REISMAN, W. Laurence CRAIG, William PARK and Jan PAULSSON, *International Commercial Arbitration – Cases, Materials and Notes on the Resolution of International Business Disputes* (Foundation Press 1997) p. lxxix.

25. The US Supreme Court underlined this basic truth as a fundamental basis for the federal policy in favor of international arbitration. If arbitration is "to take a central place in the international legal order, national courts will need to 'shake off the old judicial hostility to arbitration,' and also their customary and understandable unwillingness to cede jurisdiction of a claim arising under domestic law to a foreign or transnational tribunal". *Mitsubishi Motors Corp. v. Soler Chrysler-Plymouth, Inc.*, 473 U.S. 614, 638, 105 S.Ct. 3346, 3359-3360, 87 L.Ed.2d 444 (1985).

26. See *Scherk v. Alberto-Culver Co.*, 417 U.S. 506, 94 S.Ct. 2449, 41 L.Ed.2d 270, Fed. Sec. L. Rep. (CCH) P 94593 (1974). "A parochial refusal by the courts of one country to enforce an international arbitration agreement" would frustrate "the orderliness and predictability essential to any international business transaction." at 506-507.

2. *Relinquishing Control*

a. *Loose control of the gate to arbitration*

Regulatory competition fueled attitudes of significant liberalism, and at times explicit arbitral bias. Bias manifests, inter alia, in a general restraint in the exercise of judicial control,[27] and materializes into a less strict policing of the gate to arbitration: consent. Arbitration agreements are given face value effect, and arbitral awards rendered for or against non-signatories or involving claims made under related contracts are enforced. National courts conceive judicial principles of extension which exceed the standards of the New York Convention, and exercise control by reference to these more liberal rules.

On the level of technique, a full control of jurisdictional findings, one which reviews also the facts upon which a finding of consent has been made or otherwise extension was ordered, is dispensed with. Art. VII(1) of the New York Convention is invoked as a license to develop liberal *local standards of extension*, or to avoid the rigorous application of domestic mandatory rules which require consent in writing, voluntary consolidation or extension only with the parties' consent.

The French *règles matérielles* of extension constitute a good example. Over the last two decades, French courts have invented an entire arsenal of judicial principles which govern the scope of the arbitration agreement, and its extension beyond that scope. These principles complement, and often apply *in lieu* of the fundamental rule of consent. In the field of extension to non-signatories, for example, a *jurisprudence constante* of the Paris Court of Appeal considers the involvement in the contract per se as a self-standing basis of jurisdiction[28]

b. *Judicial self-negation*

Beyond encouragement, post-modernist approaches to jurisdiction involve some form of judicial self-negation. Arbitration agreements are not only fully enforced, they are *over*-enforced."[M]any national courts not only help international arbitration but appear anxious to externalize a larger amount of the disputes that are formally within their jurisdiction",[29] that is in cases where the dispute or part of it should remain in court. This is the case when national courts compel (or accept compelling) arbitration beyond or absent the requirement of consent. They, in fact, defer to arbitration beyond the *logical* and *conceptual* limit of the arbitration system.

Self-negation has, at times, culminated in the relation of national courts and international arbitration being governed by a principle of *subsidiarity.*[30] The principle is one of the pillars governing the relationship of the European Union to its States. As applied to jurisdictional questions in complex arbitrations, the principle would dictate that national courts may only assert jurisdiction if the arbitral tribunal cannot rule on *all*

---

27. See in this sense W.M. REISMAN, W.L. CRAIG, W. PARK and J. PAULSSON, fn. 24 above, p. lxxviii.

28. See *Sté Ofer Brothers v. The Tokyo Marine and Fire Insurance Co Ltd et autres*, Paris CA (1st Ch. Suppl.) 14 February 1989, Rev. Arb. (1989) p. 691. *Orri v. sté des Lubrifiants Elf Aquitaine,* Paris CA (1st Ch. Suppl. D), 11 January 1990, Rev. Arb. (1992, no. 2) pp. 95-98.

29. W.M. REISMAN, W.L. CRAIG, W. PARK and J. PAULSSON, fn. 24 above, at p. lxxvii.

30. See Laurent GOUIFFÈS, "*L'Arbitrage International Propose-t-il Un Modèle Original de Justice?*" in *Recherches sur l'Arbitrage en Droit International et Comparé*, (L.G.D.J. 1997) p. 55.

aspects of the dispute, because of the limitations imposed on third-party involvement or consolidation of claims under the applicable mandatory norms.

French courts have described their own jurisdiction, when in addition chosen by the parties in the form of a forum selection clause, as "subsidiary" to arbitration.

> "*[L]a clause attributive de juridiction a seulement pour objet de conférer une compétence subsidiaire aux juridictions étatiques dans le cas, où pour une raison quelconque, les arbitres ne seraient pas saisis ou ne pourraient statuer et ne saurait être interprétée comme vidant la clause compromissoire de son contenu.*"[31]

IV. CHANGING RULES OF THE GAME: THE MAKING OF *A* LAW OF COMPLEX ARBITRATIONS

1. *Social Engineering*

The development of complex and new jurisdictional settings created the typical gap between law and society, between arbitration law and the needs of complex arbitral settings, which calls for change in legal rules.[32] "[T]he law of arbitration cannot ignore these situations [complex arbitrations] which have become the norm in present day international commerce."[33] It had to adapt.

The result was a major undertaking of judicial and arbitral *social engineering,* in the sense Roscoe Pound intended the term to be used.[34] A cumulative body of case law resulted in the gradual, but substantial, re-writing of arbitration law governing jurisdiction and the differentiation of a distinct body of exceptions to the classic regulation of arbitration rooted in an unqualified rule of consent.

2. *Jurisdictional Uncertainty and the Problem of Identifying the "Rules" Governing Jurisdiction in Complex Settings*

a. *The loss of uniformity: The New York Convention dépassée*

The general body of arbitration law is largely uniform, thanks to the universal reach of the New York Convention and the universal inspiration of the UNCITRAL Model Law on International Commercial Arbitration.[35] In sharp contradistinction, the emerging "law" of complex arbitration is far from uniform. It consists mainly of judicial and arbitral

31. Paris, 1ère Ch. D, 11 January 1995 (*Ste' Brigif*) (unreported).

32. Alan WATSON, *Society and Legal Change*, 2nd edn. (Temple University Press 2001) pp. 87-88.

33. Horacio A. GRIGERA NAON, ed., Committee on International Commercial Arbitration, Complex Arbitrations (Multi-Issue, Multi-Party, Multi-Contract): First Interim Report of the Sixty-Sixth Conference of the International Law Association, Buenos Aires Conference 1994, (ILA, London 1994) footnote 1, p. 690.

34. Roscoe POUND, *Social Control Through Law* (Transaction Publishers 1996) p. 46 et seq.

35. The minimum standards of the New York Convention constitute one of the most uniform branches of international commercial law. The New York Convention counts 146 States Parties, and hence comes close to some of the most fundamental treaty law since 1945, such as the Convention on the Prevention and Punishment of the Crime of Genocide, New York, 9 December 1948, which currently has 142 Parties.

trends which are formulated beyond the baseline of the New York Convention. This, in fact, is the crux of the revolution in the relation of national courts and international arbitration. The reconstruction of arbitration, as global commercial justice, has required serious legal groundwork. National courts have remodeled the public international law foundation of international commercial arbitration, mainly by relying either on the permission of Art. VII(1) for free progress in legal rules or, generally, on the spirit of the Convention as merely providing minimum standards which may be exceeded. "The New York Convention is a treaty for the enforcement of arbitration agreements and awards and not the reverse."[36]

National laws present very significant divergences with respect to issues of extension or consolidation. The differences exist between the traditional jurisdictions and the developing ones. While the latter adhere to international standards, the former exceed them (hence the descriptive *post-modernist*).

The differences also exist among the developed jurisdictions. For example, the United States and France present two very different styles of legislating beyond international standards for complex arbitrations.

b. Uncertainty

The law of complex arbitrations is characterized by uncertainty. Normative uncertainty is inevitable in a decentralized process of adaptation and development of the law, and a decision-making state of mind bent on the resolution of specific problems in individual cases. Uncertainty is also hard to avoid in a decisional environment characterized by a significant relaxation in control, and dominated by the pursuit of utilitarian goals and the application of pragmatic methods in pursuit of these goals.

Additionally, the identification of the applicable law to matters of extension or consolidation raises difficult issues which are largely unsettled. Once identified, the *content* of the applicable rules is often difficult to ascertain, due to constant normative change. For example, normatively speaking, if *a* group of companies doctrine exists, there is not one, but many.[37] Similarly, in French law, judicial statements and restatements of various principles of extensions are being constantly produced, shaping and re-shaping the content of the law.[38] Therefore, even a relatively recent snapshot of

36. Adam SAMUEL, "Arbitration Clauses Incorporated by General Reference and Formal Validity Under Article II(2) of the New York Convention" in Ph. FERRARI, et al. , eds., *Études de Procédure et d'Arbitrage en l'Honneur de Jean-Francois Poudret* (Lausanne 1999) p. 505 at 507.

37. See for a detailed analysis of the evolution of case law, "Limits of Consent", fn. * above, and in particular at pp. 82 et seq.

38. In the aftermath of the *Dow* award – which conceived the group of companies doctrine (*Yearbook* IX (1984) pp. 131), French courts emphasized the existence of an economic group as an element that necessarily affects decision-making. See for example, the Pau Court of Appeal, 26 November 1986, Rev. Arb. (1988) p. 154. Then, only a few years after it had confirmed the *Dow* award, the Paris Court of Appeal shifted focus to the involvement in the contract containing the arbitration clause, regardless of the existence of a "*réalité économique unique*", which remained more as a *façade* rather than as a condition of extension. In turn, the relative importance of involvement in the contract has itself varied significantly in case law. At times, it was considered as a mere *indice* of consent; at others it was erected into a self-standing basis of jurisdiction.

case law in a particular legal system may not necessarily reflect the *current* state of case law.

Another by-product of *case-by-case* law-making is that the "rules" governing jurisdiction often also apply *retroactively*. New or modified rules are "invented" by courts or tribunals and applied at the same time in the particular case.

Finally, there is often not *one* right answer to a specific jurisdictional problem raised in the context of complex arbitrations. Although the principle which would govern the third-party problem in a particular case is largely dictated by the nature of the legal rapport and the facts of the case, more than one legal basis or approach to jurisdiction may be available for the parties, the tribunal or the court to "shop" from. For example it has been argued that "[a]ssignment issues in United States arbitration law are often decided by applying other legal theories".[39] The party seeking extension may therefore (and often does) invoke more than one ground of extension *interchangeably*, with the hope that extension would be compelled at least based on one of them: for example, in *Copropriété Maritime Jules Verne et autres v. Société ABS American Bureau of Shipping et autre.*[40] The defendant before French courts – the American Bureau of Shipping – invoked simultaneously four different principles to justify compelling the plaintiffs (the owners of the *TAG HEUER* yacht) to arbitrate: agency, third-party beneficiary, involvement of the owners in the performance of the classification agreement, and the doctrine of accessory.[41]

c. *Risks*

These different manifestations of uncertainty combine to make it increasingly difficult for international parties involved in complex proceedings to identify with reasonable certainty what "rules" *will* govern the assessment of jurisdiction by arbitrators or its control by courts. A backlash seems inevitable. The unpredictability of the law could develop into a "*sociological defect*" which would put into question the desirability of arbitration for international parties, and risks turning the seemingly unstoppable expansion of arbitration into a spiral of self-defeating regression. Specifically, as a result of the mounting jurisdictional uncertainty, voluntary enforcement of awards[42] may already be declining.[43]

39. James M. HOSKING, "The Third Party Non-Signatory's Ability to Compel International Commercial Arbitration: Doing Justice Without Destroying Consent", 4 Pepp. Disp. Resol. L.J. (2004) p. 469.

40. Cass. Civ. (1st Chamber) no. 937, 26 June 2001. Rev. Arb. (2001, no. 3) pp. 529-530.

41. See for more details, *Consent in Context*, fn. * above, Sect. 9:22 "Interchangeability of Principles of Extension and Rule Shopping".

42. A fairly general estimate was that about 90 percent of awards are enforced spontaneously. See Quentin TANNOCK, "Judging the Effectiveness of Arbitration Through the Assessment of Compliance with and Enforcement of International Arbitration Awards", 21 Arbitration International (2005, no. 1) p. 71 at pp. 76-77.

43. "[V]oluntary compliance with the majority of awards, which previously looked fairly predictable, is now increasingly in question. The efficacy of the New York Convention has faded." Charles H. BROWER and Jeremy K. SHARPE, "The Coming Crisis in the Global Adjudication System", 19 Arbitration International (2003, no. 4) p. 415 at p. 418.

3. *Cosmopolitan Law?*

a. *Emerging jurisdictions and the dilemma of modernity*

Post-modernist approaches to jurisdiction face emerging jurisdictions with an elementary dilemma. Just as they have fully received minimum international arbitration standards (which are based on the writing requirement), they find themselves faced with liberal trends, coming from the traditional jurisdictions, which exceed those same standards, and often are inconsistent with them.

Courts in emerging jurisdictions would be naturally inclined to apply the recently adopted regulation or international standards, rather than set them aside. By rejecting liberal trends, or by refusing to enforce awards against non-parties, courts in rising jurisdictions are simply applying the universally agreed legal regime of arbitration and could not be accused of parochialism. Adherence to the letter of arbitration law signals a legal system intolerant of jurisdictional uncertainty and respectful of party autonomy and legitimate expectations. On the downside, it also signals a reduced ability to accommodate complex arbitrations, and the possible perception of a less competitive or less "modern" arbitration site.

However, the regulatory gap between developed and developing arbitral *fora* seems to be closing in at an accelerated rate. Case law from developing jurisdictions suggests that the reception of various practices of extension and assimilation of their techniques occurs in developing arbitral jurisdictions faster than in the leading ones, which first pioneered this evolution. Popular sites in developing jurisdictions, such as Mexico, Cairo, Dubai, Singapore and Kuala Lumpur are places where modernity and tradition, liberalism and classicism meet and interact.

b. *Reception of post-modernist approaches in emerging jurisdictions*

With few exceptions, strict formalist approaches to jurisdiction remain the rule in emerging jurisdictions. The writing requirement is mandatory in typical UNCITRAL-based jurisdictions; and so, *a priori,* there is little room to discuss extension practices, by consensual analysis or, indeed, at all.

On occasion, however, developing jurisdictions show signs of significant liberalism, by reason of regulatory competition or the process of global pollination built in a universal practice of arbitration. They receive, and at times even invent, judicial trends that are usually found only in the traditional jurisdictions. Two decisions of the Egyptian and the Polish Supreme Courts are analyzed briefly.

In *Khatib Petroleum Services International Co. v. Care Construction Co. and Care Services Co.,*[44] the Egyptian Court of Cassation formulated its own principle of extension in group of companies' settings.[45] The Court confirmed the annulment of an award rendered in ad hoc proceedings administered by the Cairo Regional Centre (CRCICA),[46] and dismissed the mere existence of a corporate group as sufficient basis for extension of the obligation to arbitrate to non-signatory companies of the group.

---

44. Case no. 4729 of Judicial year 72, 22 June 2004. For the full text and commentary, see Karim YOUSSEF, "The Group of Companies Doctrine in Egyptian Law", 3 SIAR (2007) pp. 103-113.
45. See, "Limits of Consent", fn. * above, at p. 91et seq.
46. Case no. 212 of 2001.

However, the Court did not exclude the possibility of extension, and in fact formulated its own principle of extension. The Court held:

> "... [A]rbitration agreements are of relative effect, and may not be invoked except against the parties who have consented thereto. Therefore, the mere fact that one of the parties to the arbitration proceedings is a company member of a corporate group, in which a parent company holds in the capital of its member entities, is not by itself sufficient basis to hold the parent company bound by the contracts concluded by other companies of the group, and which may contain arbitration clauses; *unless evidence is submitted that the parent company was involved in the performance of these contracts, or has caused by its conduct, confusion as to the identity of the member of the corporate group contracting with the third party, in such a way that it has become difficult to distinguish the wills of the companies involved.*"[47] (Emphasis added.)

The following is noteworthy about the Court's decision:

– The Court simply omitted any reference to the writing requirement, which is mandatory under the Egyptian arbitration law.
– The Court reiterated that consent, and its consequence, *privity,* is the fundamental rule in jurisdictional assessment.
– The Court formulated a double basis for extension in groups of companies. A non-signatory parent company may be compelled to arbitrate if it was involved in the performance of the contracts entered into by its subsidiaries (which contain an arbitration clause), or if it caused, by its conduct, confusion "as to the identity of the member of the corporate group contracting with the third party".
– This principle of extension may be classified as even more "liberal" than the *Dow* award, which is said to have invented the group of companies doctrine. *Khatib* does not refer to the parties' intentions, unlike *Dow* which refers explicitly to the "*common intentions of the parties*" as the main basis for extension.

Similarly, an important decision of 1998 of the Polish Supreme Court held, in the context of an assignment of the arbitration agreement, that arbitral jurisdiction is assessed "on the basis of an arbitration agreement, and not the parties to it".[48] In other words, the scope ratione personae of the arbitration agreement is determined by reference to its scope ratione materiae. The arbitral tribunal has jurisdiction over the legal rights that are covered by the arbitration agreement, regardless of the parties to these rights.[49] Thus, a change in the subjects of the relationship, by assignment or other forms of transfer of rights, would not affect the jurisdiction of the tribunal. This organic

47. K. YOUSSEF, fn. 44 above, at pp 105-106.
48. See Polish Supreme Court, 3 September 1998, I CKN 822/97.
49. The Court founded its decision on Art. 698(2) of the Polish Code of Civil Procedure which requires that the subject of the dispute or of a legal relation resulting in a dispute, or a potential dispute, is specified in the arbitration agreement.

conception of the arbitration agreement dictates that the arbitration clause simply travels with the substantive right(s).

V. THE QUALITATIVE ELEMENT OF THE *JUGE NATUREL*: DEALING WITH THE CHALLENGES

1. *Directions for Solutions*

A back-to-basics approach would reinforce the arbitrators' duty to give legal reasons for their jurisdictional findings, and to render an award that is enforceable jurisdiction-wise. It would require national courts to exercise rigorous control of the arbitrators' rulings on their jurisdiction in complex settings, and to re-introduce applicable law methodology in their decision-making processes, which would bring about the application of national contract law to arbitration agreements. Finally, a back-to-basics approach would invite international parties to take a pro-active approach and re-appropriate their partially expropriated jurisdictional autonomy by managing the scope of possible exposure to extension practices.

2. *Arbitrators: The Need for Creative Legalism*

a. *Giving reasons*

For the reasons explained above, the duty of the arbitrators to give *legal* reasons for their jurisdictional findings in complex settings has become a difficult task. The exact contours of the duty to give reasons obviously depend on the fact setting and the legal principles invoked to justify extension; but the following basic remarks can be made:

– Where extension is decided by consensual analysis (which is the majority of the cases), an often elaborate and fact-intensive interpretation exercise must be undertaken in order to ascertain the existence of consent.[50]

– Advancing economic, equitable or pragmatic rationales for extension is not necessarily exclusive of giving *legal* reasons. Arbitrators must make explicit the *necessity* of extending the scope of arbitral jurisdiction or of compelling non-signatories, that is to show the elements of fact and of law that would render the expansive (or more liberal) solution *compelling,* and the opposite solution manifestly unjust or impracticable (for example, the existence of a serious risk of conflicting awards and/or court decisions, the risk of a *déni de justice*). The factual elements would include, for example, the exact economic scope of the broader transaction in question, the involvement in performance of non-

50. See ICC Final Award in Case No. 7453 (1994), *Yearbook* XXII (1997) pp. 107-124, para. 10

> "It is now necessary to apply the law to the facts as found. It is a fundamental principle that any arbitration must be founded on the consent of all the parties thereto and the consent must be recognized as such by law. Especially in an international arbitration, such as this, *the consent of each party must be unambiguously demonstrable if any resulting Award is to be safely enforceable.* [citing *SPP v. Egypt*] Consent here falls to be tested by the law governing the agreement to arbitrate which, I hold, is the Federal Arbitration Act, 9 U.S.C.A. 1 et seq." (Emphasis added.)

signatories, the relationship of ownership or control among corporate entities belonging to the same group.
– The attempt should be made to root equitable outcomes in some applicable principle of law such as good faith, estoppel or *l'apparence*, which is usually possible, as explained below.

In view of producing an award on jurisdiction that is sufficiently reasoned *in law*, decision-making processes which take into account equitable considerations may also involve some form of *reverse reasoning*. A decision on jurisdiction is reached, prima facie, based on the global assessment of all relevant elements and the equities of the case; the decision then being confirmed by reference to applicable legal principles. Hanotiau goes as far as arguing that:

> "Concerns of equity and good administration of justice are not foreign to the decisions of judges and arbitrators. *One is occasionally tempted to wonder whether equity is not in some cases the paramount consideration and all the legal theories advanced to justify the tribunal decision, ex post facto creation*."[51] (Emphasis added.)

As suggested earlier, international arbitrators more likely take into consideration both consent and context, equitable considerations and black-letter law in a global fashion in reaching their decision on jurisdiction.

b. The duty to render an enforceable award jurisdiction-wise[52]

The duty to give reasons is part of the arbitrator's legal duty to render an enforceable award, including jurisdiction-wise.[53] Compliance with this duty, in complex jurisdictional settings, is a complicated exercise. First, there is the difficulty inherent in reducing to pure legal reasoning a composite intellectual process of decision-making. Then, there is jurisdictional uncertainty. Because rules change, arbitrators often decide on jurisdiction by reference to a set of rules that is different from that by reference to which courts will exercise control. In other words, the rules of the game change, as the game plays. It is also often difficult to identify *a* "right" answer to the jurisdictional issue. Case law differs, substantially, from one jurisdiction to the other, and is often in constant metamorphosis within the same jurisdiction. In addition, rendering an award which deals with third parties or matters which fall outside the scope of submission involves a major departure from the traditional way of discharging the duty, which is to ensure basic compliance with the New York Convention.[54]

To discharge their duty of enforceability when ruling on complex jurisdictional questions,

51. Bernard HANOTIAU, "Problems Raised by Complex Arbitrations", fn. 11 above, p. 253 at p. 258
52. See *Consent in Context*, fn. * above, Sects. 14:8-14:12.
53. See, for example, the ICC Arbitration Rules Art. 35 "[T]he Court and the Arbitral Tribunal ... shall make every effort to make sure that the award is enforceable at law."
54. See Martin PLATTE, "An Arbitrator's Duty to Render Enforceable Awards", 20 Journal of International Arbitration (2003, no. 3) p. 307 at p. 308

– Tribunals need to be aware of the simple fact that, notwithstanding the mounting complexity of jurisdictional assessment and the abundance of legal principles which may come to apply to extension scenarios, consent remains *the* rule. It follows that arbitrators must base their decisions, by default, on consensual analysis in order to find whether extension should be ordered.
– To this effect, the tribunal must identify, in detail, the factual elements from which tacit consent was derived.
– Tribunals must also verify that the applicable legal principle of jurisdiction (for example, veil piercing, accessory, group of companies doctrine, etc.) is recognized in the jurisdictions in which enforcement is most likely to take place (for instance, the country of citizenship of the award debtor, its main place of business or the place of performance of the contract). To this end, tribunals have sometimes adopted flexible and pragmatic approaches to applicable law. In ICC Case No. 5721,[55] the tribunal engaged in a comparative law analysis, and verified that the legal basis for extension is recognized under the legal systems that had the closest connection to the arbitral process.

> "In the United States ... the concept of lifting the corporate veil is justifiable wherever the principle of limited liability gives rise to situations which are wholly unjust. In Swiss Law ... [t]he *Durchgriff* theory is based upon the prohibition against abuse of law ... a company's independence should only be disregarded in exceptional cases, where it is used fraudulently, that is contrary to the principle of good faith....
>
> Egyptian law does not contradict these general principles. It too attaches decisive importance to the principle of good faith and punishes any abuse of the law...."

– If the tribunal bases its decision to extend (or not to extend) on a basis other than consent, its reasons must involve stating the following:

• The alternative *basis of jurisdiction* vis-à-vis non-signatories or related contracts (the principle of assignment, third-party beneficiary, veil piercing, etc.)
• The *source* of the applicable norm (national law, general principles of law or the lex mercatoria).
• The *factual* elements which support the application of the principle of extension (for example, the elements indicating the involvement in performance, or, when extension is decided by application of veil piercing, alter ego, or *apparence,* evidence of the confusion of assets, the basis for legitimate reliance or control of corporate entities).
• In cases of extension to non-signatories, the tribunal would need, in addition, to verify the non-signatory's "position" (for instance, as assignee, or third-party beneficiary) which gives him the right or the obligation to arbitrate. Extension would command a preliminary ruling that the non-signatory is, indeed, an assignee or a third-party beneficiary.

---

55. ICC Case No. 5721, in Sigvard JARVIN, Yves DERAINS and Dominique HASCHER, eds., *Collection of ICC Arbitral Awards 1986-1990* (Kluwer/ICC Publishing 1994), p. 401 et seq.

3. *National Courts: Finding the Juste Milieu of Control*

a. *Retrieving control*

Relinquishing judicial control of the arbitrators' decision on their jurisdiction[56] challenges the very core of an international order composed of sovereign states.[57] It is also inconsistent with the nature of the arbitrators' mandate as a limited delegation of power.[58] "Arbitrators ... can never have the final word on their jurisdiction, since the extent of their authority is the very issue presented to courts asked to enforce arbitration agreements or awards."[59] Judicial control of jurisdictional findings is therefore simply a logical and legal necessity.

b. *The standard of review at the jurisdictional threshold*

i. *Excès de pouvoir* as the conceptual foundation of control

An initial hurdle that national courts face in exercising control is how to orchestrate the theory of *excès de pouvoir*, which is the conceptual foundation of judicial control,[60] with expansive approaches to jurisdiction. The simple answer is that *excès de pouvoir* continues to be the benchmark by reference to which control is exercised, even in cases where arbitral jurisdiction is asserted beyond the original scope of submission. US courts apply the principle *excess of mandate* through the prism of the general principle of extensive interpretation, which reigns in federal case law. "A reviewing court examining whether arbitrators exceeded their powers must resolve all doubts in favor of arbitration."[61]

ii. De novo control of jurisdictional findings

National courts do not always exercise a full *de novo* review of the jurisdictional findings of the arbitrators. The issue is exacerbated because there is disagreement about what "de novo" review means. A de novo review is one which involves a full re-assessment of both the legal basis of extension and the facts upon which a finding of consent, or on which a decision to extend, has been made. The lack of de novo review is due, at least in part, to the prevailing *modus operandi* of the arbitral tribunal when ruling on jurisdiction. Specifically, the search for consent reduces the jurisdictional function to a matter of contractual interpretation, which could undermine in the minds of courts the need to

---

56. Exclusion of all judicial control of the arbitrators' determination of their jurisdiction did exist, but usually did not survive. For example, before 1998, German law accepted the so-called "*Kompetenz-Kompetenz* clauses" which authorized the arbitrators to rule on their jurisdiction in first and *last* resort. In 2005, the Federal Supreme Court ended this practice. (13 January 2005, III ZR 265/03). The Court held that such clauses are inconsistent with the 1998 Arbitration Law. National courts would always have *final* say on arbitral jurisdiction.
57. See Kenneth C. RANDALL and John E. NORRIS, "A New Paradigm for International Business Transactions", 71 Wash. U. L.Q. (1993) p. 599
58. See W. Michael REISMAN, *Systems of Control in International Adjudication and Arbitration* (Duke University Press 1992) p. 2.
59. William J. PARK, "Determining Arbitral Jurisdiction: Allocation of Tasks between Courts and Arbitrators", 8 Am. Rev. Int'l Arb. (1997) p. 133 at p. 145.
60. See W. Michael REISMAN, fn. 58 above, at p. 6.
61. *Apache Bohai Corp. LDC v. Texaco China BV*, 480 F.3d 397 (5th Cir. 2007).

exercise control. In the decision which confirmed the *Dow* award, the Paris Court of Appeal noted: "The arbitrators ... are *exclusively* empowered to interpret the aforementioned contracts...."[62] (emphasis added), and therefore, their interpretation, correct or incorrect, stands.

This approach is conceptually flawed. The absence of control, in fact-intensive inquiries such as ascertaining the intent of the parties, means that arbitrators are given, at least partially, *final* say over their jurisdiction; which is something they cannot have. In addition, relinquishing control under the cover of deference to contractual interpretation confuses jurisdiction and merits. The arbitrators' interpretation is final only when it relates to the merits. As part of the jurisdictional inquiry, interpretation exercises must be reviewed de novo. In *SNCFT v. Sté Voith* (in which the tribunal rendered a negative decision on jurisdiction), the Paris Court of Appeal held that: "To exercise its control, the court must find all the elements of law and fact to appreciate the scope of the arbitration agreement."[63]

c. *The need to re-introduce applicable law methodology*

Analysis of case law reveals *two* prevailing trends with respect to how tribunals and courts deal with issues of applicable law in in cases involving extension issues. First, the process of *identification* of applicable law is often simply omitted from the demarche of decision-making by arbitrators. This is the case, in particular, when tribunals rule on extension by analysis of consent. They simply interpret the parties' intentions, and the nature of the jurisdictional exercise dispenses with the need to identify an applicable law or system of norms by reference to which interpretation is made.

In some cases, applicable law methodology is often simply excluded altogether. In group of companies settings, for example, the arbitrators would usually proceed with a global factual assessment of jurisdiction and examine closely the structure of the entities of the group.[64] Ideally, however, the applicable corporate law should be identified in order to determine the relevance of the existence of an integrated economic structure, its effect, if any, on the application of legal rules, and the extent to which the corporate veil may be lifted.[65]

Second, there seems to be a general tendency among national courts in favor of the application of the lex fori to issues of jurisdiction. The application of the lex fori may be conceptualized under some sophisticated form, such as the French substantive norms of private international law. It may also derive, more naturally, from the application of

62. Paris Court of Appeal, 21 October 1983, Rev. Arb. (1984) p. 98.

63. Paris Court of Appeal (1st Ch. C.), 26 October 1995, Rev. Arb. (1997) p. 555.

64. Marc BLESSING, "The Law Applicable to the Arbitration Clause" in *Improving the Efficiency of Arbitration Agreement and Awards: 40 Years of Application of the New York Convention*, ICCA Congress Series no. 9 (1999) pp. 168-188 at p. 177.

65. In *Eurosteel Ltd v. Stinnes AG* (Com Ct, [1999] All ER (D) 1394), the English court provided a model of identification of applicable law, in a scenario of merger. The court held that the arbitration agreement is transmitted by succession to the non-signatory company in which the signatory entity merged. The court distinguished between German law which governed the conditions and regime of the merger, as the law of the place of incorporation, and English law which governed the assignment of the arbitration agreement, being the law of the place of arbitration; and applied each in its own domain.

domestic norms of contract interpretation (for example, the United States). In both cases, the lex fori does not apply as the outcome of a conflict method, but *en tant que tel.* The lex fori also seems to apply in all generality.[66] For example, US courts seem to invariably apply domestic standards of veil piercing, not only when exercising control, but also when acting as enforcing courts, to re-assess findings of arbitral awards rendered under a foreign law.[67]

However, analysis of consent should not dispense with the necessity to follow applicable law methodology. Interpretation cannot be made in a void; it must be conducted in accordance with *some* system of norms. Although general principles of interpretation of intent exist, national laws provide very different solutions to key questions, such as: What are the acceptable forms of expression of consent? What are the rules which govern the interpretation of arbitration agreements? Are these rules different from the rules which govern contractual interpretation in general? And finally, what are the conditions and scope of application of third-party principles to contracts in general, and to arbitration agreements, in particular?

On the other hand, the direct application of the lex fori is also simplistic. It disregards the degree of complexity that governing law issues in extension or consolidation contexts may reach.[68] The exclusion of applicable law methodology is also obviously counterintuitive in international contexts. The lex fori would apply beyond the limits of applicable law, and notwithstanding the possibility of a contrary outcome under the law which would otherwise govern the question of jurisdiction.[69] For this reason, the French substantive norms methodology has been criticized as a form of *legal imperialism*.[70] While it is difficult to see more light in the French method, French courts could otherwise be seen as messengers who spread a *different,* and perhaps more *sensible,* approach to difficult questions, one which is more suited to the needs of global commerce, the fact, in any event, is undeniable that spreading one's views on legal issues beyond the limits of applicable law is simply inconsistent with the rising cosmopolitan spirit of international arbitration.

4. *The Governing Rules: Re-introducing Legalism*

a. *Consent as default principle*

Solutions to the problems of identifying what "rules" govern jurisdiction should also be sought in a back-to-basics approach. Decision-makers need not forget that, despite the complication of jurisdictional assessment and the emergence of a multitude of approaches and rules governing jurisdiction, consent remains *the* rule and the pillar of the system of

66. Jean-François POUDRET, "*L'originalité du Droit Français de l'Arbitrage au Regard du Droit Comparé*", *Bull. d'information de la Cour de Cassation*, no. 589, 15 December 2003.

67. See *Sarhank Group v. Oracle Corp.*, 404 F.3d 657 (2d Cir., 2005) (Second Circuit rejected the enforcement of an award rendered against a non-signatory US parent by application of Egyptian Law).

68. See *Consent in Context*, fn. * above, Sect. 9:1 et seq.

69. See in this sense Daniel COHEN, Rev. Arb. (2001) pp. 769-770.

70. *Fouchard, Gaillard, Goldman*, fn. 6 above, pp. 230-231 no. 438; and Jean-François POUDRET and Sebastien BESSON, et al., *Comparative Law of International Arbitration*, 2nd edn. (Sweet & Maxwell 2007) p. 149 no. 182.

international arbitration. On the other hand, legalism needs to be reintroduced. Decision-makers should not short-circuit applicable law methodology in pursuit of utilitarian goals and global assessment of jurisdiction. They should also remember that the law governing arbitration agreements includes, in addition to arbitration law, national contract law.

b. The application of national contract law

Supported by the universal fiction of *separability*, arbitration agreements were considered, both conceptually and normatively, *sui generis*. The common treatment of arbitration agreements excluded the application of general contract law to them. Today, however, another old code of the relation of national courts and international arbitration has decayed. The exorbitant nature of arbitration agreements has faded, due to the generalization of their use and the rise of arbitration as the *natural judge* of disputes arising under international contracts. The application of general contract law to arbitration agreements is not only conceptually but also legally justified. It is consistent with, and in fact brings back to center stage, applicable law methodology. Today, in a number of jurisdictions, arbitration agreements are increasingly treated as *ordinary* contracts, which brings about the now-accepted principle that general contract law applies *mutatis mutandis* to arbitration agreements.

i. Comparative perspectives

United States law is a model in this respect. It solves the third-party problem, as a general matter, by reference to ordinary principles of contract law.[71] Contract law principles generally applicable to arbitration include agency, third-party beneficiary, assignment, subrogation, succession, good faith, fraud, alter ego and veil piercing.

General contract law applies to arbitration agreements in the same way it does to ordinary contracts. There is a caveat, however. Its application is "subject to the policy favoring arbitration".[72] This means that "[i]f there are deviations from such standard contract doctrine, they should be in the direction of arbitrability".[73]

French courts, on the other hand, are less systematic about treating the arbitration agreement as an ordinary contract. Depending on the case, the arbitration agreement is treated as a *sui generis* agreement or under the *droit commun*. For example, French contract law is, as a general matter, hostile to admit exceptions to *privity*. However, French courts have compelled non-signatories to arbitrate, in group of companies, based on the *principe de l'apparence*,[74] the theory of *contrat de fait*[75] and fraud.[76] Case law also

71. "Arbitration is contractual by nature.... It does not follow, however, that under the [Federal Arbitration] Act an obligation to arbitrate attaches only to one who has personally signed the written arbitration provision. This court has made clear that a non-signatory party may be bound to an arbitration agreement if so dictated by the 'ordinary principles of contract and agency'." *Thomson-CSF, S.A. v. American Arbitration Ass'n*, 64 F.3d 773, 776 (2nd Cir. 1995).

72. Ian MACNEIL, Richard SPEIDEL and Thomas STIPANOWICH, *Federal Arbitration Law: Agreements, Awards and Remedies Under the Federal Arbitration Act* (Little, Brown 1994) Sect. 18.7.1.1.

73. *Ibid.*

74. Paris Court of Appeal, 7 October 1999, Rev. Arb. (2000) p. 288 (D. Bureau) "*Les circonstances de la négociation, de la conclusion et de l'exécution du contrat ayant créé pour l'un des contractants la croyance légitime qu'une société, avec qui elle avait delà traite' dans le passe', était également partie à ce contrat bien*

developed judicial doctrines of extension such as the groups of contracts doctrine or the group of companies doctrine, which derogate from the *droit commun*. On occasion, narrow interpretation resurfaces. The French *Cour de cassation* excluded extension to a non-signatory, based on Art. 1165 of the Code Civil (on *privity* of contracts).[77]

ii. National contract law and consent

The application of general contract law involves, in most cases, a consensual determination of jurisdiction. However, this is not always the case. The application of national contract law is premised on the treatment of the arbitration agreement as an ordinary contract, and hence on the exclusion of distinct arbitration rules which are built on the basis of a requirement of an autonomous consent to arbitrate. The application of national contract law to extension and third-party issues involves a jurisdictional exercise which is largely *indifferent* to consent. The applicable principle applies *in its own right*, and no systematic consensual analysis is undertaken. A finding of implied consent is neither necessary, nor indeed sufficient to operate extension. The application of third-party principles results in a basis of jurisdiction embodying various degrees of consent,[78] depending on the extent of objectivity built in the particular principle of extension. This contractual approach also "seems to focus as much on equitable considerations after the conclusion of the contract as on discerning the intent of the parties ex ante".[79]

c. *General principles of law*

i. General principles in the sense of Art. 38 of the Statute of the International Court of Justice

General principles of law in the sense of Art. 38 of the Statute of the International Court of Justice constitute another way of accommodating the needs of international commerce and the changing nature of jurisdictional assessment, while maintaining legal rigor in the methods of decision-making. Considerations of equity or practicality, which sometimes underlie or at least influence the decision to extend or not to extend, can usually be

qu'étant pas signataire, la convention d'arbitrage a un effet obligatoire pour cette dernière conformément au principe de l'apparence applicable aux relations du commerce international." (Emphasis added.)

75. See, for example, Cass. com., 20 November 1990, Bull. inf. stés 1991, at p. 99.

76. See Cass. civ. (1st Chamber) 11 June 1991 (*Orri*), Rev. Arb. (1992) pp. 74-75.

77. Cass. Com., 14 January 2004, Note Olivier CACHARD, Rev. Arb. (2004) pp. 356-358. See also Ahmed S. EL-KOSHERI, "Enforcement of Awards – Some Additional Problems" in *New Horizons in International Commercial Arbitration and Beyond*, ICCA Congress Series no. 12 (2005) p. 339. See in particular his reference to *Misk v. A.V.C. Shipping*, Paris Court of Appeal, 26 June 2003, where French courts annulled an arbitral award that extended the arbitration agreement to a non-signatory based on agency.

78. See James M. HOSKING, "The Third Party Non-Signatory's Ability to Compel International Commercial Arbitration", fn. 39 above, p. 469 at p. 486.

79. Noah RUBINS, "Group of Companies Doctrine and the New York Convention" in Emmanuel GAILLARD and Domenico DI PIETRO, eds., *Enforcement of Arbitration Agreements and International Arbitral Awards: The New York Convention in Practice* (Cameron May 2008) at p. 460.

rooted in general principles of law such as fraud, good faith,[80] the prohibition against contradicting oneself to the detriment of others,[81] or *l'apparence*. These principles contain latent considerations of justice which would affect decision-making, without sacrificing legalism.

In terms of technical basis for application, general principles of law may apply as part of the otherwise applicable national contract law, since these principles also typically constitute general *domestic* contract principles in the majority of legal systems. They may also come to apply *as is*, that is either as part of the lex mercatoria, or as *self-standing* principles which do not necessarily require a conflict methodology to root their application.

ii. A new generation of principles of jurisdictional lex mercatoria[82]

Additionally, decades of case law on extension issues have produced an emerging body of exceptions to the traditional regulation of international arbitration. A number of these exceptions have become so widely used that they have sedimented into general principles of arbitration law which gradually displaced, in complex settings, the traditional principle of jurisdiction based on the existence of a written agreement to arbitrate, which is increasingly limited to simple arbitration settings.

Courts and tribunals apply these general principles in the name of different systems of norms: usages of international commerce, principles of the lex mercatoria, general principles of the law of international arbitration, or even under the clothing of equitable principles, such as *estoppel*. Regardless of their label, these principles are the creation of international tribunals and, to some extent national courts, to alleviate the rigor of arbitration law and adapt it to jurisdictional necessities, giving them the spirit of a growing body of jurisdictional lex mercatoria. From this standpoint, the genesis of the law of complex arbitrations is similar, in the process of its elaboration, to the development of a more sophisticated old English law based on principles of equity that differentiated from the common law of the land to govern situations in which the application of common law yielded results that were wholly unjust.

Although these principles cannot claim to be of universal application, they are emerging as generally recognized in comparative arbitration law. They are:

a. Consent as a general and sufficient basis of jurisdiction

The first among these principles is the rule of consent, or the search for the parties' intentions, regardless of whether they have consented *in writing*. Subject to national mandatory requirements of form, the principle is widely accepted today, as a general and

80. See Marc BLESSING, "Extension of the Arbitration Clause, fn. 9 above, at p. 162. "Again the 'heart' of all the above notions or doctrines clearly is the bona fides principle, respectively the requirement to act in good faith and the notion that positions or defenses which stand in contradiction to the exigencies to act in good faith will not deserve legal (or arbitral) protection."

81. Emmanuel GAILLARD, "*L'Interdiction de se Contredire au Détriment d'autrui Comme Principe Général Du Droit Du Commerce International*", Rev. Arb. (1985) p. 241.

82. See *Consent in Context*, fn. * above, Sect. 12-1 et seq.

sufficient basis of jurisdiction. Its operation often complements the scope of arbitral jurisdiction which is originally established based on a written arbitration agreement.[83]

One finds formulations of the rule of consent in landmarks. In the *Westland* award, the tribunal held solemnly:

> "Everything depended on the intention expressed by the parties in the arbitration clause. It is *necessary and therefore sufficient, in principle that they wished to bind themselves* for the arbitrators to have jurisdiction at the same time in respect of them all and for one of them to be able to initiate proceedings against all the others within one set of arbitration proceedings."[84] (Emphasis added.)

Consent is most often implied from conduct. The direct involvement of a non-signatory in the contract containing the arbitration clause may indicate acceptance of all its provisions including the arbitration clause.[85] This principle finds frequent application in group of companies' contexts and gave birth to one of arbitration's most famous – and most controversial doctrines.[86] The extension of the arbitration clause contracted by a parent company to members of the corporate group has also been authoritatively cited as a principle of the lex mercatoria.[87]

Although the principle of consent is very widely recognized, substantial differences exist among national laws with respect to how much formalism is excluded, how consent is found, how it is interpreted and what modes of expression of consent are accepted.[88]

b. The general transmission of the arbitration agreement with the substantive right(s)

Transmission of the arbitration clause by *accessory* is another principle of arbitration law which is becoming of universal application. Its main domain of application concerns cases of assignment, subrogation and succession. The arbitration clause is considered as an accessory of the substantive rights, by analogy to security interests.[89] It circulates freely, and is transferred to whoever receives the substantial rights, independently, in most

83. "[R]eview of the theories, principles and procedures employed to bind non-signatories, reveals – perhaps unsurprisingly – that the 'touchstone' for this determination is whether or not the relevant entities consented to arbitrate with one another." James M. HOSKING, "Non-Signatories and International Arbitration in the United States: The Quest for Consent", 20 Arbitration International (2004, no. 3) p. 289 at p. 303.

84. *Westland*, ICC Interim Award of 5 March 1984, Case No. 3879, *Yearbook* XI (1986) p. 127 at p. 133

85. See Cass. com., 17 October 1961, Bull. civ. III, no. 361; Rev. Arb. (1961) p. 233.

86. In most accounts, the group of companies doctrine is consent-based. The existence of an integrated economic structure is merely an *indice* of consent, and does not constitute a self-sufficient basis to compel or entitle to extension.

87. See Michael MUSTILL, "The New Lex Mercatoria" in Maarten BOS and Ian BROWNLIE, eds., *Liber Amicorum for Lord Wilberforce* (Clarendon Press 1987) p. 176.

88. See in this sense, James M. HOSKING, fn. 83 above, p. 289 at p. 303.

89. See Daniel GIRSBERGER and Christian HUASMANINGER, "Assignment of Rights and Agreement to Arbitrate", 8 Arbitration International (1992, no. 2) p. 121 at p. 138

cases,[90] from any inquiry into whether consent to arbitrate exists. Transmission is accepted, even in contracts with a very pronounced *intuitus personae* character, for instance, partnership agreements.[91]

The principle of transmission of the arbitration agreement along with the substantive right(s) transcends legal cultures. It is the rule, rather than an exception in European jurisdictions.[92] Common-law jurisdictions also use language similar to the continental doctrine of "accessory". The arbitration agreement is "*collateral*" or "*ancillary*" to the underlying contract.[93] The principle also transcends different degrees of arbitral development. Courts in emerging jurisdictions routinely enforce arbitration agreements vis-à-vis transferees and enforce awards doing the same.

Finally, the principle of transmission transcends legal techniques and principles of implementation. A number of legal principles bring it into play[94] (such as assignment, subrogation, merger, third-party beneficiary, succession, and the French judicial theories of chains or strings of contracts). In 2000, the French *Cour de Cassation* formulated the principle of transmission in the broadest terms: "*La clause d'arbitrage international s'impose à toute partie venant aux droits de l'un des contractants.*"[95] The court instated a principle of extension that is indifferent from consent (the principle of transmission is *automatic)*. The language used is also indifferent to the particular legal principle operating the transmission.

c. Narrow interpretation no more: The emergence of a general principle of extensive interpretation

With pervasive contemporary practices of extension, narrow interpretation,[96] or the principle according to which doubt as to the scope of the arbitration agreement is interpreted in favor of the default jurisdiction of national courts, seems to be a relic of a more classic period of international arbitration.[97] An emerging principle of extensive interpretation of arbitration agreements is now identifiable in arbitral awards, civil law, common law and, in some jurisdictions, has even been made the subject of an express legislative provision.

---

90. In some cases, the transmission of the arbitration agreement is made conditional upon some inquiry into the parties' intentions. See *Consent in Context,* fn. * above, Sect. 5:12.
91. See Otto SANDROCK, "'Intra' and 'Extra-Entity' Agreements to Arbitrate and their Extension to Non-Signatories Under German Law", 19 Journal of International Arbitration (2002) p. 423 at p. 441-442.
92. French, German and Swiss courts regularly admit the automatic transmission of the arbitration clause with the substantive right or underlying contract in cases of assignment of rights, assignment of contracts or transfer of contractual positions.
93. *Bremer Vulkan Schiffbau und Maschinenfabrik v. South India Shipping Corporation* [1981] AC 909.
94. V. GHESTIN, "*La Transmission des Obligations en Droit Positif Français*" in J. DABIN, *Travaux des journées d'études juridiques* Bibl. Louvain, Vol. XII (Bruylant 1980) at p. 4.
95. Cass. civ. (1st Chamber) 8 February 2000, *Defre' nois*, 2000.721; Rev. Arb. (2000) p. 281.
96. "*Les clauses compromissoires sont d'interprétation stricte.*" See ICC award No. 2138 (1974), JDI (1975) p. 934.
97. Classically, one of the cornerstones of the classic regulation of arbitration, narrow interpretation stems from the general *privity* of contracts. It is also conceptually rooted in the fundamental right to the *juge naturel.*

α. Awards
A rule of liberal interpretation can be found in early, as well as more recent, ICC awards. The tribunal, in ICC case no. 1434, ruled that strict interpretation should be set aside with respect to the decision to compel non-signatories "... unless it is established, in a given case, that a formalistic interpretation is necessary and corresponds to the parties' true intention, interpreted in good faith and in the spirit of the transaction".[98] Similarly, in ICC case no. 6000, the tribunal held that:

> "[I]t is largely admitted that by virtue of a usage of the international trade, where a contract, including an arbitration clause, is signed by a company which is a party to a group of companies, the other company or companies of the group which are involved in the execution, the performance and/or the termination of the contract are bound by the arbitration clause, *provided the common will of the parties does not exclude such an extension*." (Emphasis added.)[99]

The effect of extensive interpretation is dramatic. Extension to non-signatory members of the group becomes the rule, not the exception. The basic structure of international jurisdiction is reversed, and arbitration prevails *by default*.

β. National laws
Nevertheless, the rules governing the interpretation of arbitration agreements are (or at least should be) a matter of applicable law.[100] In this respect, one can identify an emerging formal rule of liberal interpretation on both sides of the Atlantic.

European courts have distanced themselves from a principle of narrow interpretation of arbitration agreements. In the words of the Swiss Federal Tribunal: "[I]f it is established that an arbitration clause exists, there is no reason to interpret that clause restrictively."[101] Similarly, an English court held that "[t]he question is merely one of interpretation, that is of determining the ordinary and natural meaning of the words used, and there is no scope for adopting any particular approach [neither broad and liberal, nor narrow and legalistic] in this regard".[102] The simple search for the true intent of the parties derives directly from the rule of interpretation in good faith.[103]

98. ICC Case No. 1434 (1975), JDI (1976) pp. 978-989.

99. ICC Award No. 6000, 2 ICC Ct. Bull. (1991, no. 2) p. 31at p. 34.

100. It is usually the case that the substantive applicable law of the arbitration agreement and not the procedural law of arbitration governs the question of interpretation of arbitration agreements. *Channel Tunnel Group Ltd v. Balfour Beatty Construction Ltd* [1993] 2 WLR 262; [1993] 1 All ER 664; [1993] AC 334 (Lord Mustill). As a practical matter, courts tend to interpret arbitration agreements by reference to the rules of contract interpretation of the lex fori, while arbitration tribunals rely solely on the parties intentions, without reference to any national law.

101. *Sonatrach v. KCA Drilling Ltd.*, ATF 116 I 56, 15 March 1990.

102. *Overseas Union Insurance Ltd. v. AA Mutual International Insurance Co. Ltd.* [1988] 2 Lloyd's Rep.63 (QBD).

103. See *Fouchard, Gaillard, Goldman*, fn. 6 above, Sect. 1470, p. 825.

On the other hand, the rule of broad interpretation of the scope of arbitration agreements is decades-old in US case law,[104] and is the main expression of the entrenched federal policy in favor of arbitration.[105] Judicial statements of the principle are numerous and cover all aspects of the decision to extend or not to extend. "[A]mbiguities as to the scope of an arbitration clause must be resolved in favor of arbitration."[106] Similarly, "[a] reviewing court examining whether arbitrators exceeded their powers must resolve all doubts in favor of arbitration".[107]

While US case law seems to be ahead of its European counterpart with respect to the extent to which liberal interpretation is admitted, European legislators may be bridging the regulatory gap. The 2006 amendment to the Italian Arbitration Act adopted a general principle of broad interpretation. Art. 808-*quater* provides:

> "In case of doubt, the arbitration agreement shall be interpreted in the sense that the arbitral jurisdiction extends to all disputes arising from the contract or from the relationship to which the agreement refers."[108]

This is cutting-edge normativity and a glimpse of what the future of the regulation of global arbitral justice might look like. The wording "*disputes arising from the contract or from the relationship*" suggests that the broader context of the economic operation should be taken into consideration in the interpretation of the scope of the arbitration agreement, which is not limited to claims arising under the contract.

4. *The Parties: Re-Appropriating Freedom to Arbitrate*

a. *The third phase of arbitral autonomy*

"[T]he right to choose arbitration as a method of dispute resolution"[109] (or jurisdictional autonomy) has expanded significantly in the last decades. Freedom to arbitrate also involves the freedom *not* to arbitrate, that is the right to stay in court, either by selecting a judicial forum, or by abstaining from planning jurisdiction. With the development of pervasive practices of jurisdiction which result in compelling arbitration beyond the formal scope of submission, this second aspect of the parties' freedom to arbitrate has declined. It is a fact of modern arbitral life that international parties have *less* choice to

104. It is also applicable to domestic arbitration. See, for example, *Stein v. Burt-Kuni One, LLC*, 396 F.Supp.2d 1211 (D. Colo. 2005).

105. The Federal Arbitration Act promotes "a liberal federal policy favoring arbitration agreements .... [and] any doubts concerning the scope of arbitrable issues should be resolved in favor of arbitration". *Moses H. Cone Memorial Hosp. v. Mercury Const. Corp.*, 460 U.S. 1, 24-25, 103 S.Ct. 927 (1983).

106. *Mitsubishi Motors v. Soler Chrysler-Plymouth*, 473 U.S. 614, 625 (1985).

107. *Apache Bohai Corp. LDC v. Texaco China BV*, 480 F.3d 397 (5th Cir. 2007), citing *Brook v. Peak Intern., Ltd.*, 294 F.3d 668, 18 I.E.R. Cas. (BNA) 1373, 146 Lab. Cas. (CCH) P 59559 (5th Cir. 2002).

108. "Italian Code of Civil Procedure, Book Four, Title VIII, Arbitration, amended by Legislative Decree of 2 February, 2006, No. 40" in *Handbook*.

109. Peter NYGH, *Choice of Forum and Law in International Commercial Arbitration*, Forum Internationale No. 24 (1997) p. 2.

remain in court. Some have even argued that international parties are increasingly subjected to the mandatory designation of a private judge.[110] It is increasingly more difficult for international parties to shield themselves from an accidental obligation to submit to arbitration, simply by not signing an arbitration clause or by not consenting to arbitrate.

Contemporary practices of jurisdiction mark therefore the third phase in the evolution of the parties' freedom to arbitrate. This freedom was limited, has been expanded, then expanded even more, leading in some cases to a less consensual obligation to arbitrate. The three phases correspond to the phases of modern development of the international arbitral system in general: restriction, development and generalization.

b. *Contractual management of jurisdictional exposure and the calculus of forum shopping*

i. Shifting Focus

With arbitration's universalism, the parties' focus would shift from which jurisdictional option to choose (i.e., whether to arbitrate) to how to *contractually* or *factually* manage the scope of possible exposure to arbitral jurisdiction. The parties may select a place of arbitration which has liberal or restrictive views on the jurisdictional issues which would likely arise. The award creditor may seek enforcement in a more liberal jurisdiction, in particular if enforcement is sought against parent or related entities or with respect to claims arising under related but distinct agreements. This amounts to forum shopping since, as we have seen, national courts typically apply their own lex to issues of extension or consolidation, and therefore a choice of the place of arbitration or enforcement could, in fact, amount to a choice of the law governing jurisdiction.

ii. Management of jurisdiction clauses (MJCs)

A priori, parties may re-exercise their partially expropriated jurisdictional autonomy in ways that would defeat or restrict prevailing extension practices. Signatory entities may wish to restrict the scope of a particular transaction from reaching non-signatory corporate entities or, in the case of State agencies, the State itself. They may do so *via* a restrictive interpretation clause, which would require the tribunal, in case of doubt, to exclude a liberal interpretation of the scope of the arbitration agreement. The parties may also conclude a multiparty arbitration clause which orchestrates the operation of different arbitration clauses contained in a group of contracts or regulates the selection of the tribunal for multiple parties.

The parties may also choose expressly the law applicable to the arbitration agreement, with respect to the *scope* of jurisdiction, and revive their dormant freedom in this respect.[111] The choice of a national law with restrictive views on the particular question of extension that is likely to arise avoids surprise attempts on non-signatories by third parties; but it could tie the hands of the group entities when the need to bring claims

110. See, in this sense, Pierre-Yves GAUTIER, Rev. Arb. (2000) p. 286, Obs. on Cass. Civ. (1st Chamber) 8 February 2000.

111. International parties typically do not choose the law governing the arbitration agreement. See Albert Jan VAN DEN BERG, *The New York Arbitration Convention of 1958* (Kluwer Law International 1981) pp. 126-127.

against the third party contracting with the group arises. The selection of a governing law which provides for liberal solutions gives broader discretion to the tribunal, but increases the exposure of both non-signatory entities and the third party contracting with the group to a possible expansive assertion of jurisdiction.

iii. Their effect in light of the New York Convention

As agreements between signatories, it is likely that management of jurisdiction clauses would not bind non-signatories. A non-signatory company of a group could thus still be able to bring a claim against the third party contracting with the group. In principle, management of jurisdiction clauses would bind the tribunal, since they relate to the exercise of its mandate in ruling on jurisdiction, and to the scope of this mandate. However, the extent to which such contractual arrangements will be given effect to the detriment of equitable or practical considerations that justified extension in the first place is an open question. As a general matter, however, courts should give maximum effect to these clauses, in a spirit of giving back to the parties what is the parties'. Management of jurisdiction clauses also regulate the mandate of the arbitrators and supplement the operation of arbitration clauses. As such, I submit that multiparty clauses, restrictive or liberal interpretation clauses and non-assignability clauses should be entitled to the protection of the New York Convention in the same way ordinary arbitration agreements are.

The Present –

Investment Arbitration as a Governance Tool for Economic International Relations?

The Present – Investment Arbitration as a Governance Tool for Economic International Relations?

Introduction to the Session

*Donald Francis Donovan**

Welcome all.

The evident purpose of today's program is to examine in parallel two discrete but related systems of international arbitration. We spent the first part of the morning discussing international commercial arbitration as a transnational justice system – as a system of international dispute resolution that operates within a structure provided by national and international law, but which no individual state directly operates or supervises. We now want to examine international investment arbitration as a global governance regime. In both cases, we have had as our objective to examine international commercial arbitration and international investment arbitration as *systems*, and to place them in the international legal order.

We don't need to dispute Albert Jan's numbers,[1] or to debate the relative impact of international commercial arbitration and international investment arbitration, in order to recognize the importance of the question we have put to this panel. Just the fact that an organization long and still known as the International Council for Commercial Arbitration did not even think about putting on the program we have organized for today without including investment arbitration on equal footing with commercial arbitration reflects the relatively recent emergence of the system and its import for international dispute resolution today. Yet the topic could hardly have been addressed just a few decades ago.

José Alvarez provides us with a wonderful starting point for our discussion (pp. 137-160). He argues that the international investment arbitration regime may plausibly be described as a form of global governance. He first offers a number of reasons why the system is indeed "global" despite its grounding primarily in bilateral agreements, and then offers four perspectives by which we might understand it as a veritable system of "governance". José concludes by noting that even if international investment arbitration is now plausibly a form of global governance, it is not irreversibly so. He identifies several developments which could undermine the system's "global" and "governance" features.

In response to José, Bruno Simma urges that this nascent regime of global governance be made more human rights-sensitive both by introducing relevant economic and social rights into investment treaties or contracts at the time those agreements are negotiated, and by encouraging arbitrators to engage in more systematic integration into the treaty

---

* Partner, Debevoise & Plimpton LLP; Honorary Vice President and Member of ICCA.

1. See this volume, pp. 15-16.

regime of human rights norms by resort to Art. 31(3)(c) of the Vienna Convention on the Law of Treaties (pp. 161-165). Next, Frank Berman offers a "realist's view" of the system and focuses in particular on the role of the arbitrator (pp. 166-169). He cautions against the substitution of third-party claims and interests over those of the parties to the case, but at the same time recognizes that clarifying, elaborating, and even developing indeterminate and contested areas of the law pursuant to transparent and disciplined interpretive processes lies squarely within the arbitrator's function. Finally, anticipating a re-balancing of interpretive power between states and tribunals, Anthea Roberts charts what she believes is the "next battleground" in investment treaty arbitration, namely, the standards of review by which tribunals assess government conduct alleged to breach investment treaty protections (pp. 170-180).

Recognizing the wealth of wisdom, insight, and experience on the floor, we on the panel have agreed to adhere to strict time limits so that we can be sure to have a full exchange among the panelists and real input from other participants.

So let's start with José.

Is the International Investment Regime a Form of Global Governance?

José E. Alvarez[*]

TABLE OF CONTENTS Page

I. Introduction 137
II. Is It "Global"? 140
III. Is It "Governance"? 149
IV. But Is It Stable? 153
V. Conclusion 158

I. INTRODUCTION

The proposition that the chaotic spaghetti soup of mostly bilateral international investment protection treaties and investor-state arbitral awards is actually a form of "global governance" is counter-intuitive. For this to be true, the motley collection of bilateral investment treaties (BITs), investment chapters of free trade agreements (FTAs), and arbitral decisions emerging in their wake must first be "global"; yet how can it be true that this essentially bilateral regime can generate effects on non-parties to such treaties or to persons not bound by particular investor-state arbitral decisions? Second, even if somehow global rules were to emerge from such a regime, how could a regime – if that is what this diverse set of treaties is – designed merely to provide private investors with a more reliable remedy than old-fashioned diplomatic espousal possibly be a system for *regulating* how states govern themselves?

The assertion that the regime is global and a form of governance does not seem, at first glance, plausible. We know what international schemes for "global governance" look like. They are regimes that, from the outset, seek to achieve universal or nearly universal participation, such as the organizations of the UN system. Global systems for governance, to the extent that they exist at all, have real brick and mortar organizations set up on a tripartite model, with a plenary body for the full membership, a smaller executive organ capable of more expeditious action and international civil servants. Global regimes, established under a single overarching treaty or charter, seek to achieve universal membership. They seek to solve collective action problems or seek to protect the global commons, from securing collective security to avoiding self-destructive economic protectionism. As political scientists have pointed out, these regimes are built on the "pooling" of sovereignty; they seek to secure the benefits of independence and/or centralization.[1] "Independence" might be achieved through reliance on "neutral"

---

* Herbert and Rose Rubin Professor of International Law, New York University School of Law.

1. See Kenneth W. ABBOTT and Duncan SNIDAL, "Why States Act Through Formal International Organizations", 42 J. Conflict Res (1998) p. 3.

international bureaucrats or an independent judiciary for purposes of dispute settlement, such as the International Court of Justice (ICJ) or the WTO Appellate Body. The benefits of "centralization" may be pursued through the pooling of militaries (as in UN peacekeeping) or financial resources (as through the capital uniquely available to the World Bank or the International Monetary Fund (IMF)). Regimes for global governance seek to respond to interests of the "international community" – an imaginary construct, to be sure, but one that lends legitimacy to such efforts and that appears essential to the non-governmental organizations (NGOs) which operate on the periphery of global institutions and represent "international civil society".

Bilateral treaties, on the contrary, have long been seen as the polar opposite of universalistic regimes.[2] Moreover, the proposition that BITs in particular have global effects would seem unlikely given the fact that BITs and FTAs came about precisely because states have repeatedly failed to agree that a multilateral regime was in their collective interests. The bilateral nature of this regime is not an accident. As is well known, today's investment protection treaties were built on the failures of prior efforts to establish multilateral rules for protecting the relevant property rights – and most recently, the unseemly failure of members of the Organisation for Economic Co-operation and Development (OECD) to negotiate a Multilateral Agreement on Investment (the MAI) in 1998. States have repeatedly failed to see the benefits of independence or centralization at least on the global level when it comes to protecting foreign investment and have refused to pool their sovereignties to this end. There would appear to be no "international community" interest at stake with respect to BITs and FTAs – only the respective economic interests of capital-exporting and capital-importing states. The proposition that the approximately 3,000 BITs and FTAs with investment chapters that we have – which exist in the absence of an "investment" organization, a single overarching treaty, or an independent civil service – effectively bind non-parties to such treaties and seek to alter how governments generally conduct their internal affairs would appear to stretch the common-sense meaning of the words "global" and "governance".

Indeed, some would dispute that BITs and FTAs constitute a single "regime" or "system" at all, much less a "global" one.[3] Many scholars, and perhaps some arbitrators, would describe these treaties as lex specialis disconnected from general public international law, as mere treaty-contracts relevant only to the contracting parties, or even as illegitimate "contracts of adhesion" imposed on unsuspecting governing elites who were misled into thinking that concluding a BIT with a rich treaty partner would ensure capital flows from that state.[4] Many would deny that investor-state arbitral awards are globally significant precedents relating to matters of public policy but are instead

---

2. See generally Bruno SIMMA, "From Bilateralism to Community Interest in International Law", 250 *Recueil des Cours de l'Académie de Droit International* (1998) p. 217.
3. For an attempt to describe the distinctive features of the international investment "regime", see Jeswald W. SALACUSE, "The Emerging Global Regime for Investment", 51 Harv. Int'l L. J. (2010) p. 427.
4. But see José E. ALVAREZ, "A BIT on Custom", 42 NY Univ. J. Int'l L. & Pol. (2009) p. 17 at pp. 30-39 (criticizing such views).

mere ad hoc decisions on whether or not a state owes compensation to a particular investor given certain facts. Seeing BITs or their arbitral by-products as a system for global governance certainly would be inconsistent with the leading explanation for how BITs proliferated, namely Andrew Guzman's game theoretical account.[5] As Guzman explains it, lesser developed countries (LDCs) ratified BITs because they were caught in a prisoner's dilemma in which it was impossible for them to act collectively to support their "genuine" interests.[6] For Guzman, those collective interests were epitomized by the General Assembly's efforts to promote the New International Economic Order (NIEO), as represented by such instruments as the G.A.'s 1974 Charter of Economic Rights and Duties of States (which might be described as the "anti-BIT"). As Guzman describes what happened, LDCs simultaneously supported the NIEO as a group while individually defecting by adhering to particular BITs "that hurt them".[7] They did so out of a misplaced effort to advance their own individual interests vis-à-vis rich capital exporters. In this view BITs and FTAs are tit-for-tat deals struck by bilateral sets of states, negotiated on a bilateral basis, directed at achieving purely bilateral gains. Accordingly, these treaties are driven solely by economic not legal motives.[8] Guzman denies the possibility that investment promotion treaties advance "global" law, such as custom.[9] For Guzman, the only truly global law relevant to the regulation of international investment – customary law protecting the rights of aliens such as the Hull Rule in favor of prompt, adequate and effective compensation upon expropriation – had long been undermined prior to the rise of BITs by the LDCs' General Assembly (NIEO) efforts, and their subsequent resort to BITs has done nothing to reinstate those norms.[10] In this view, BITs and FTAs are tit-for-tat deals; that is, efforts whereby capital-importing nations attempt to make credible commitments to capital exporters in the hope of securing more foreign capital from that treaty partner.

In prior work this author has argued that Guzman's historical account of the proliferation of BITs is as erroneous as the conclusions that he draws from it.[11] This Report extends that analysis to describe the many reasons why the international investment regime is quite plausibly described as a form of global governance. At the same time, this Report contends that the effects of the international investment regime are not pre-ordained or unalterable. If the contemporary international investment regime presently constitutes a form of "global governance", that is not the end of history. Both its "global" and "governance" aspects are reversible and being contested by

5. Andrew T. GUZMAN, "Explaining the Popularity of Bilateral Investment Treaties" in Karl P. SAUVANT and Lisa E. SACHS, eds., *The Effect of Treaties on Foreign Direct Investment* (Oxford 2009) p. 73.

6. *Ibid.*, at pp. 76-91.

7. See also Andrew T. GUZMAN, "Why LDCs Sign Treaties that Hurt Them: Explaining the Popularity of Bilateral Investment Treaties", 38 Va. J. Int'l L. (1998) p. 639.

8. A.T. GUZMAN, supra fn. 5, at pp. 93-96.

9. *Ibid.*

10. *Ibid.*

11. See José E. ALVAREZ, "The Once and Future Foreign Investment Regime" in Mahnoush H. ARSANJANI, et. al, eds., *Looking to the Future: Essays on International Law in Honor of W. Michael Reisman* (Martinus Nijhoff 2011) p. 607 at pp. 614-623.

important stakeholders, including some states, arbitrators, NGOs and scholars. Whether the investment regime will long remain a viable form of global governance or splinter into forms of bilateralism may be determined by, among other things, the attitudes of investor-state arbitrators.

II. IS IT "GLOBAL"?

Stephan W. Schill's recent book, *The Multilaterialization of International Investment Law*[12] contains a six-part argument in favor of the international investment regime's global or "multilateral" effects. Schill makes his case, first, by stressing that today's BITs and FTAs share a common historic and multilateral pedigree. He stresses the common intent between such formally bilateral instruments and previous multilateral instruments, including the OECD Draft Convention on the Protection of Foreign Property from 1967, the Convention on the Settlement of Investment Disputes between States and Nationals of Other States (the ICSID Convention), and the Multilateral Investment Guarantee Agency (MIGA).[13] Second, Schill argues that BITs and FTAs were not only intended to produce multilateral effects, they were negotiated on that basis as well and not on a *quid pro quo* basis whereby capital-exporting states attempted to extract purely bilateral concessions. BITs, in short, are not bilateral in function; they advance common, universal interests, as David Ricardo's theory of comparative advantage requires.[14]

Schill's third interlocking argument is that investment protection agreements contain standard general guarantees that put all investors – or at least foreign investors – on the same plane. His fourth contention in favor of "multilaterialization" relies on one of these general principles, namely the most-favored-nation (MFN) clause common to most BITs and FTAs and its generally expansive interpretation by investor-state arbitrators. Schill argues that MFN clauses ratchet up the level of investment protection, locking most states that have at least one BIT in place (which at last count were 180 states) "into the most favorable level of investment protection reached at one point in time and project this level into the future".[15] Fifth, Schill points outs how the broad definition of protected "investment" or "investor" in most of these treaties – which often extend to individual shareholders and not just a company as a whole and may include entities that are incorporated in a BIT party even if this is a mere "paper" presence – has given these agreements a more global ambit. These realities, paired with MFN, encourage treaty beneficiaries to engage in corporate re-structuring to take advantage of the most investor-protective treaty available. Thanks to MFN guarantees and corporate restructuring, BITs and FTAs have become vehicles for the protection of businesses far removed from those that the State Parties to such treaties probably anticipated. Although ostensibly "restricted *ratione personae* to investors that have the nationality of the other contracting party in a bilateral relationship", in reality the third-party beneficiaries of the

---

12. Stephan W. SCHILL, *The Multilateralization of International Investment Law* (Cambridge 2009).
13. *Ibid.*, at pp. 25-49.
14. *Ibid.*, at pp. 96-106.
15. *Ibid.*, at p. 196.

investment regime are, according to Schill, in a comparable position to those who assert *erga omnes* or *erga omnes partes* obligations.[16]

Schill's final argument relies on the multilateralizing impact of investor-state dispute settlement. Granting investors direct access to arbitration becomes an "essential move away from bilateral inter-State compliance toward a multilateral ordering structure" because it "effectively removes the power of States to both unilaterally defect from investment treaties and bilaterally negotiate around the consequences of breaches of such treaties".[17] Schill argues that investor-state arbitral tribunals are empowered by investors' direct right of action, the limited influence of states on the arbitral process, the limited review of arbitral awards and the effective provisions for enforcement of these awards.[18] Schill also points out that most investor-state arbitrators rely on interpretative approaches consistent with a multilateral legal framework, that is, they tend to avoid reliance on treaty-specific negotiation history, privilege systematic over treaty-specific interpretations of commonly accepted treaty provisions and make extensive use of arbitral precedents whether or not these concern the specific treaty at issue. He argues that despite divergent interpretations of some questions, there is an underlying "unity"[19] to the emerging arbitral case law and that a "system"[20] of stable, predictable international investment law has emerged through arbitral interpretation. For Schill, these "multilaterializing" features are exacerbated by adjudicators' needs to fill gaps in the law if only to avoid findings of non-liquet or in order to provide convincing "reasoned" opinions.

There are other reasons, apart from those advanced by Schill, for believing that the investment regime produces multilateral or global effects. If, as Schill indicates, businesses other than those contemplated by BIT drafters are benefiting from such agreements, the realities of political economy help to explain why. As would be predicted by students of Putnam's two-level games,[21] in at least some contexts, states entered into BITs or FTAs due to internal pressures brought by their own national entrepreneurs. National companies may sometimes support treaty rights in favor of foreign investors, even their competitors, if they believe that such rights will benefit them as well. This may be the case, for example, if a country's BIT commitments result in improvements to national laws, administrative or judicial practices stemming from either the implementation of the BIT or the example for the rule of law that it sets. And if national entrepreneurs supported the ratification of BITs, it may become politically impossible for this reason among others for a state to try to limit the benefits of such treaties to only foreign investors. MFN clauses and corporate restructuring are not the only reasons that make it difficult, in a post-BIT world, for countries to restrict BIT benefits to only foreigners from certain BIT signatories. Once a country adheres to even

16. *Ibid.*, at pp. 197-199.
17. *Ibid.*, at p. 242.
18. *Ibid.*, at p. 249.
19. *Ibid.*, at p. 339.
20. *Ibid.*, at p. 357.
21. Robert D. PUTNAM, "Diplomacy and Domestic Politics: The Logic of Two-Level Games", 42 Int'l Org. (1988) p. 427.

a single BIT, for example, it may become less tenable to engage in an expropriatory act that results in less than fair compensation – even if the victim is its own national and not a foreign company – simply because it may be too politically costly to explain to local constituencies why only foreigners are entitled to property rights, the rule of law or politically neutral dispute settlement.

We should also consider how guarantees such as umbrella clauses, treaty-based rights to assert claims in local courts, residual obligations to extend to the investor the "better of" national law or international legal obligations, repeated reliance on customary law (as with respect to the international minimum standard, denial of justice, and full protection and security), assurances to provide "due process" and/or transparency, as well as rights to non-discrimination – *cumulatively or in combination* enhance the prospects for global, and not merely bilateral, rules. This may explain why, as is evidenced by UNCTAD's annual surveys of changes to national laws since 1992,[22] the proliferation of BITs and FTAs has been accompanied by changes to national laws in favor of business interests and liberal capital flows. And to the extent national laws and practices have changed in tandem with the rise of BITs, it appears that most of these efforts do not differentiate between domestic and foreign enterprises or are limited to foreign investors from particular BIT signatories. The evidence suggests that the proliferation of BITs and FTAs in the 1990s reflected and encouraged a global move in favor of the market, deregulation and privatization – as reflected in the influential "Washington Consensus".

There is yet another reason why BITs and FTAs have had global effects: the regulatory actions encouraged by such treaties have been supported by actions of international financial institutions, including the IMF. To the extent that all nations, especially LDCs, have been systematically reforming their laws in favor of liberal capital flows, they were given ample motivation by the pressures imposed under the IMF's structural adjustment conditions. As has been suggested by some, the IMF is, to this extent, itself a global regulator of investment.[23] Governments have also been influenced (and their economies directly impacted) by the "doing business", "good governance" or other indicators supplied by other institutions, like the International Finance Corporation or by market actors.[24] As this suggests, the claim that the international investment regime as a whole lacks "global institutions" is a half truth. While the investment regime lacks a single overarching institution comparable to the WTO, it deploys a number of them – including the international financial institutions, along with ICSID – as supporting players. It is therefore something of a myth to suggest that the international investment

22. See, e.g., UNCTAD, "World Investment Report 2010: Investing in a Low-Carbon Economy" (Geneva 2010) Table III.1, p. 77, at <http://www.unctad.org/templates/webflyer.asp?docid=13423&intItemID=2068&lang=1> (indicating the percentages of national regulatory changes that are both more and less welcoming to foreign investors as a share of national regulatory changes from 2000-2009).

23. See Daniel KALDERIMIS, "IMF Conditionality as Investment Regulation: A Theoretical Analysis", 13 *Social & Legal Studies* (2004) p. 124

24. For a critical review of some of these indicators, see Kevin DAVIS and Michael KRUSE, "Taking the Measure of Law: The Case of the Doing Business Project", 32 Law & Social Inquiry (2007) p. 1095.

regime lacks institutions – or that its aspirations do not include the centralization and independence goals pursued by such institutions.

The thesis that the investment regime has a "global" impact also draws support from considerable interdisciplinary scholarship stressing the "network" or "systems" effects that now regularly occur among state and non-state actors thanks to economic interdependence[25] or "socio-legal" work demonstrating how the interactions between public institutions and businesses generate transnational law.[26] Or consider how the investment regime might be seen from the perspective of those who examine human rights regimes. At the global level, there is no such thing as an international human rights court capable of enforcing human rights. Formally speaking UN human rights treaties are, relative to BITs and FTAs, notoriously weak instruments. States are only subject, after all, to the non-legally binding views uttered from time to time by UN human rights treaty bodies. Yet it is increasingly clear that there is a global system of human rights protection from which no state is wholly immune and that this is true because those treaties operate within a wider web of institutions and non-state actors, including the "mobilizing" and "enforcement" efforts of non-governmental human rights organizations.[27] In the same way, those who examine the impact of BITs, FTAs and investor-state arbitral decisions need to consider not only the complementary regulatory actions of international financial institutions like the IMF but the impact of the market actors whose reactions to state violations may serve as global enforcers of investor rights. The normative ripples of the investment regime – like those of human rights treaties – may extend to innumerable others beyond those immediately subject to a BIT or an investor-state award.

The global impact of BITs, FTAs and investor-state arbitral awards is made more likely to the extent these affect customary international law or general principles of law. In prior work this author has explained how the proliferation of investment protection treaties in all likelihood has affected general public international law.[28] This work needs only brief summary here. The oft-debated issue concerning the impact of BITs on custom needs to consider not only the impact of the proliferation of some 3,000 BITs and FTAs but whether state practice and opinio juris has been affected by corresponding changes in national law and practices. On this score, as is suggested below, it seems probable that what we now expect of governments with respect to how investors are treated has evolved considerably over the course of the twentieth century – and the rise of the investment regime has had something to do with that.

As to whether investor-state arbitral awards themselves play a role in the elaboration of global law, including custom and general principles, it is essential to recognize that

25. See generally Robert O. KEOHANE and Joseph S. NYE, JR., "Introduction" in Joseph S. NYE, JR. and John D. DONAHUE, eds., *Governance in a Globalizing World* (Brookings 2000) p. 1 at pp. 9-12.
26. See, e.g., Gregory C. SHAFFER, "How Business Shapes Law: A Socio-Legal Framework", 42 Conn. L. Rev. (2009) p. 147.
27. See, e.g., Kathryn SIKKINK and Margaret E. KECK, *Activists Beyond Borders* (Cornell Univ. 1998).
28. J.E. ALVAREZ, supra fn. 4. See also Andreas F. LOWENFELD, "Investment Agreements and International Law", 42 Col. J. Transnat'l L. (2003) p. 123.

most BITs and FTAs were designed to affirm, not deviate from, customary protections for investors. Most BITs and FTAs affirm the customary protections accorded to aliens in order to secure an enforceable venue for such rights. They are vehicles for the enforcement of treaty *and* customary rights. With some exceptions, such as treaty provisions that explicitly derogate from the traditional rule requiring exhaustion of local remedies, these treaties should not be seen as lex specialis derogating from the customary rights of investors that predated the rise of BITs. The text of these treaties supports this. Apart from obvious BIT provisions such as the standard US BIT clause that investors "shall in no case be accorded treatment less than that required by international law", or cross-references to custom in connection with such treaties' fair and equitable treatment and expropriation provisions, other US standard BIT clauses such as the clause according investors "effective means of asserting claims" or directing states to make their laws "public", are open-ended invitations to deploy relevant rules of custom or general principles of law. This is so given emerging principles to promote due process, transparency or accountability across a number of regimes, including human rights. For these reasons, those searching for such globally applicable rules tend to resort to investor-state arbitral awards as one of the most readily accessible attempts to give contemporary meaning to such rules.[29]

It is important to recognize that states understood and wanted their investment treaties to reflect and affect customary international law and other non-treaty sources of obligation. Investor-state arbitral decisions' impact on such non-treaty sources of law is not the product of careless or power-mad arbitrators. It results from what those treaties provide or anticipate. At the same time, this means that we should be on guard against claims that the interpretations of custom or general principles issued in the course of investor-state dispute settlement are likely to favor only the interests of investors. The states that affirmed the continued application of such rules can be expected to influence their development and to secure the benefits of such norms. As further noted below, among the general principles of law or rules of custom being affirmed or elaborated within the investment regime are those that respondent states would favor. The impact of investor-state arbitrations on general custom or general principles is a two-way street.

But if general public international law is being shaped by the investment treaty regime, what are tangible examples? What global rules have been affected by the turn to BITs and FTAs?

1. *The Law Relating to Expropriation*

Consider, as one example, the rules of international law governing expropriation and compensation for expropriation considered by the US Supreme Court in its 1964

29. This is all the more the case to the extent the treaty partners insist, as have the NAFTA parties through their joint interpretation of the meaning of the NAFTA's FET provision, that a particular treaty provision is the equivalent of custom. See NAFTA Free Trade Commission, Notes of Interpretation of Certain Chapter 11 Provisions, 31 Jul. 2001, at <http://www.international.gc.ca/trade-agreements-accords-commerciaux/disp-diff/NAFTA-Interpr.aspx?lang+en >. In the wake of that Commission statement, interpretations of the FET clause of the NAFTA by NAFTA arbitrators constitute interpretations of customary law.

decision in *Banco Nacional de Cuba v. Sabbatino*.[30] In that case, as is well known, a majority of that Court found that customary law was so uncertain that it was impossible to conclude that an officially proclaimed nationalization in which the foreign government seized title to alien property and did so in a discriminatory fashion was an internationally illegal taking requiring the payment of compensation. It is highly unlikely that the US Supreme Court would issue the same ruling today. Today, it, along with most international lawyers, would probably agree with the following propositions of international law:

(1) That a state's denial of property rights to an alien (and possibly even to its own national under the customary law of human rights) is not purely a matter of national law or a state's sacrosanct "domestic jurisdiction" but is properly the concern of international law.
(2) That a state's denial of property rights to an alien triggers a number of procedural rights to due process, including, as is suggested by the *Kadi* decision of the European Court of Justice[31] and not only investor-state arbitral decisions, the right to judicial review and the ability to present one's case.
(3) That the "property" of an alien that is subject to customary international law's limitations and constraints may include rights beyond tangible real property but could include at least some forms of vested rights under a contract and, for example, the rights to at least some forms of intellectual property.
(4) That when an expropriation occurs, the person or entity expropriated or the state claiming on that person's behalf has a right to compensation (that is, reparation under the rules of state responsibility) irrespective of whether the property was taken for a public purpose, whether or not it was discriminatory in its effect, and without regard to whether national law provides for such compensation. Today, far more than was true in 1964, as human rights advocates would acknowledge, the right to be compensated for permanent deprivations of one's property is protected under customary law. Moreover, is it widely assumed that custom would require that any such compensation should be commensurate with the value of the property actually taken – and not reflect merely its book value if that value does not reflect the fair market value of the property when it was taken.
(5) That an unlawful expropriation that triggers the procedural and compensation rights mentioned above can take place through "creeping" measures taken by a state at least to the extent these result in a total deprivation of the alien's property interest. It now seems less likely that customary law, and not just the law under a specific BIT, would require the formal issuance by a state of a formal nationalization decree for a finding of an "unlawful" taking to be made.
(6) At the same time, today's conception of custom or general principles of law would also recognize those limitations imposed on the right to property that are now reflected in a number of treaty instruments, including within the European Convention on the

30. *Banco Nacional de Cuba v. Sabbatino*, 376 U.S. 398 (1964).
31. *Kadi & Al Barakaat International v. Council of the European Union*, 3 CMLR 41 (2008) (European Court of Justice).

Protection of Human Rights.[32] It is likely that the general law, and not only the US Model BIT of 2004, would affirm that "except in rare circumstance, non-discriminatory regulatory actions by a Party that are designed and applied to protect legitimate public welfare objections, such as public health, safety, and the environment do not constitute indirect expropriations".[33]

2. *States' Residual Rights to Regulate*

As rule (6) above illustrates, investor-state arbitrators, like their brethren on other international courts or tribunals, are likely to recognize a state's residual right to regulate. At the same time, it is to be expected that general public international law, including rule (6) above, can only provide vague guidance with respect to how adjudicators are supposed to balance the rights to property held by nationals or aliens versus a government's right to regulate. Yet, the fact that neither custom nor general principles, no more than most BITs or FTAs, gives us a clear line between a compensable indirect taking and a non-compensable regulatory act does not mean that such lines do not exist – any more than the comparable lack of clarity with respect to the balance struck by the takings clause in the US Constitution renders that balancing less subject to case-by-case determination.

It is worth noting that recent investor-state arbitral rulings that rely on the state's right to regulate, most notably *Continental Casualty v. Argentina*,[34] do so in the context of treaties that, unlike the GATT-covered agreements' Art. XX,[35] do not elaborate the permissible bases for government regulation or even mention a state's general right to regulate. This is all the more reason for suggesting that the right to regulate must exist as a matter of background rules of general international law. It presumably emerges from the principle of self-determination, and attendant rights of a state to determine its own legal and economic order. Of course, in the *Continental Casualty* case, the arbitrators went further. They found that the "measures not precluded" clause of the US-Argentina BIT, which provides that states are not precluded from taking measures "necessary" to protect their essential security interests, should be read in light of the permissible regulatory measures contained in Art. XX of the GATT-covered agreements and how the word "necessary" is interpreted in trade law.[36] This author has criticized this unnecessary and legally unsupportable finding.[37] Nonetheless, if *Continental Casualty* is a harbinger of things to come, its interpretation may influence how other adjudicators will determine the types of measures states are entitled to take and what kinds of

32. First Protocol to the Convention for the Protection of Human Rights and Fundamental Freedoms, Art. 1 (signed 4 Nov. 1950).
33. US Model BIT 2004, Annex B, 4(b), at <http://www.state.gov/documents/organization/117601.pdf> (last accessed 21 June 2011).
34. *Continental Casualty v. Argentine Republic* (ICSID Case No. ARB/03/9), Award of 5 Sept. 2008.
35. Art. XX, General Agreement on Tariffs and Trade, 30 Oct. 1947, 55 UNTS 194.
36. *Continental Casualty*, supra fn. 34, at paras. 190-192.
37. José E. ALVAREZ and Tegan BRINK, "Revisiting the Necessity Defense" in K.P. SAUVANT, ed., *Yearbook of International Investment Law and Policy 2010-2011* (Oxford).

justifications are acceptable in terms of "good governance". Despite my criticisms of this aspect of that decision, investor-state arbitrations may become vehicles for globalizing trade law – on this or other questions. Thanks to investor-state arbitrations, we may also be in the midst of globalizing law with respect to how states are supposed to "proportionally balance" their sovereign rights to regulate vis-à-vis investor rights.[38]

3. *The International Minimum Standard*

Another example of the impact of the investment regime concerns the "international minimum standard". Most but not all investor-state arbitral decisions have explicitly equated FET treaty guarantees with those under customary law, have assimilated the two standards or at least suggested that an FET treaty guarantee needs to be informed by custom (as would be suggested in any case by application of the traditional rules of treaty interpretation). It is therefore hard to disentangle FET rulings from those based on customary law. A number of tribunals have also suggested that the international minimum standard has evolved over time and it seems likely that its association with the open-ended FET guarantee has something to do with that.[39] We should not be surprised if the international minimum standard is not quite the minimum that it used to be – after all, tribunals are being asked to apply that standard in the context of a treaty that demands that investors be treated "fairly" and "equitably". Even if that standard continues to require "egregious" treatment as was suggested in a 1926 arbitral ruling, it is likely that contemporary investor-state rulings have altered the meaning of what should be deemed "egregious".[40] Much academic ink has been spilled debating whether the elaborate dicta in the *TECMED* or *Waste Management* arbitral decisions on the meaning of FET accurately describe what custom now requires from the national rule of law or whether such requisites, which seem at least as demanding as what sophisticated welfare states require from their administrative agencies, should be seen as part of enforceable "legitimate expectations" of the parties. But whatever one thinks of the legitimate expectations standard for purposes of interpreting FET, it nonetheless seems clear that we now expect more from the national rule of law than we did in the days when the Mexican-US Claims Commission issued its views, as even the arbitral panel that has taken the narrowest view of the meaning of an FET provision has acknowledged.[41] This author would contend that the standard has evolved even since 1959 when Germany concluded its first BIT and that the spread of BITs and FTAs, and all that has accompanied the post-Cold-War turn to the market, has had a great deal to do with the expectations we now have of what "good governance" (and FET) entails.

---

38. See, e.g., Alec Stone SWEET, "Investor-State Arbitration: Proportionality's New Frontier", 4 Law & Ethics of Human Rights (2010) p. 47.

39. See, e.g., *Merrill & Ring v. Canada*, paras. 193 and 209-213 (discussing the evolution of the international minimum standard).

40. See, e.g., *Glamis Gold Ltd. v. United States*, Award, UNCITRAL Arbitration Rules (8 June 2009) at <http://www.state.gov/documents/organization/125798.pdf>, para. 22 (finding that the standard articulated in the 1926 *Neer* case continues to apply to the meaning of FET under the NAFTA but suggesting that what is deemed "egregious" or "shocking" evolves over time).

41. See *Glamis*, supra fn. 40.

Today, most of us would assert, whether in a human rights tribunal or before ICSID, that a state needs to provide some access to a remedy, at least within its courts if not through international arbitration, if it is reneging on a contractual commitment that it made to an investor; that a state cannot assert by way of a defense to such a claim a "secret" or wholly un-transparent law or agency process; that the mere absence of "bad faith" may not remove the taint of illegality from a state's actions; and that any process for adjudicating such a claim that a state provides needs to adhere to basic essentials of due process as affirmed by human rights law and not merely principles drawn from the doctrine of state responsibility to aliens. These propositions can be defended, in my view, even in the absence of an umbrella clause in a BIT.

Custom or general principles of law would also require a state to "ensure" some basic rights of all persons within its jurisdiction, including alien investors. This includes some duties to protect such persons through reasonable police protection from the actions of non-State Parties, such as rioters – even in the absence of a specific "full protection and security" guarantee clause in a BIT (as where a treaty extends fair and equitable treatment or the protections of "international law"). States' duties to respect and to ensure such basic rights – including basic rights to property – equally emerge from regional and some global human rights instruments.[42]

4. *Other General Rules of International Law*

Apart from these substantive rights, investor-state arbitrators – along with other international adjudicators – are applying *and therefore developing* such general principles of law as the meaning of "good faith", the concept of "unjust enrichment" and the general principle against permitting a party from benefitting from its own wrong or being a judge in its own cause. Custom or general principles of law may also emerge and be applied in such disputes to the extent a question arises as to whether state action respects "elementary requirements of the rule of law". Investor-state arbitrators are also frequent users of rules of custom, including those reflected in the Vienna Convention on the Law of Treaties, those codified in the International Law Commission's articles of state responsibility and those dealing with attribution to the customary defense of necessity. While it may be true that these are long-standing rules of custom, even the clearest rule develops once it is applied to concrete facts. The common lawyer does not need to be reminded that law is often made when law meets fact and judges preside over that meeting. Investor-state claims against Argentina have now provided considerable fodder for considering the meaning of the customary defense of necessity, including such matters as which party bears the burden of proof or carries the burden of persuasion, and what the requisites of that defense – "grave peril", "only way" or "significant

42. For a possible example, see the *Kadi* case, supra fn. 31 (finding that the implementation of UN counterterrorist sanctions under European law violated individuals' rights to be heard and rights to non-interference with their property rights).

contribution" – mean.[43] The recent *Enron* annulment committee ruling has now raised additional questions, never previously addressed in these cases, with respect to all of these issues.[44] It may have unsettled not only the law with respect to the meaning of the US-Argentina BIT but also the customary defense of necessity more generally.[45] This may occur, as the *Enron* annulment suggests, even while arbitrators purport to rely on the black-letter codification of that defense provided by the International Law Commission.

5. *International Procedural Rules*

Another category of general law that is probably being affected by investor-state awards is the ostensibly "common law of international procedure" on which these arbitrators, along with other international adjudicators, are relying. We are now seeing considerable discussion of burdens of proof, evidentiary standards more generally or the meaning of vague principles as the "equality of arms". We are also seeing investor-state arbitrators needing to resolve demands for provisional relief, as in the course of recent cases involving Ecuador.[46] These latter demands elicit rulings on such questions as whether such relief requires "irreparable harm" or can be issued merely to avoid aggravating the dispute. It would appear that the question of whether orders of interim relief can be legally binding has migrated from the ICJ – and its rulings in the *Breard-La Grand* line of cases that ICJ orders for provisional relief can indeed be binding –[47] to investor-state arbitrations.[48] It is likely that there will be continued two-way traffic among international courts and tribunals on such procedural questions. As this suggests, how procedural issues are resolved within investor-state cases is likely to have implications at some remove from the underlying rules of ICSID procedure that govern many of them.

III. IS IT "GOVERNANCE"?

The affirmation or production of global law discussed above explains one way that the investment regime has managed to become "multilateral" in some of its effects despite the formally bilateral basis for most of its underlying commitments. Examining the continuing role of custom within this treaty regime is a critical step in seeing that the world of BITs and FTAs has become more than a convenient way for states to avoid gunboat diplomacy or the politicized espousal of investor claims. The investment regime

---

43. For discussion of the relevant cases, see José E. ALVAREZ and Kathyrn KHAMSI, "The Argentine Crisis and Foreign Investors" in K.P. SAUVANT, ed., *Yearbook of International Investment Law & Policy 2008-2009* (Oxford) p. 379.

44. *Enron v. Argentina* (ICSID Case No ARB/01/3), Annulment Decision, paras. 385-393.

45. *Ibid.* See also J.E. ALVAREZ, "The Return of the State", 20 Minn. Int'l L. J. (2011) p. 223 at pp. 248-249.

46. See, e.g., *CEMEX Caracas Investments B.V. and CEMEX Caracas II Investments B.V. v. Boliva* (ICSID Case No. ARB/08/15), Decision of 3 Mar. 2010 on Claimant's Request for Provisional Measures.

47. *LaGrand Case (Germany v. United States)* 2001 ICJ 466 (June 27).

48. See generally Robert VOLTERRA, "Provisional Measures in Investment Treaty Arbitration", Investment Treaty Law. Current Issues III (Br. Institute of Int'l and Comp. Law 2009).

makes general law as it applies international investment law and when it does the latter, some of its effects go global. Once we see that, it becomes easier to recognize that this is also a form of governance. The production of custom and the impact on general principles are ways that BITs/FTAs "regulate" states. The kind of global governance produced – and whether it will endure and is normatively desirable will be debated for years to come.

Those who have argued that the investment regime is, by design or effect, an effort to "regulate" states have characterized this turn to "governance" in different ways. Below are brief descriptions of four of these. [49]

1. *Hegemonic International Law*

For some critics of contemporary international law and its "progress narrative", international investment regulation, whether pursued through investor-state arbitration or the IMF's resort to conditionality, is a species of "hegemonic international law". [50] This characterization is clearest in those who treat the investment regime, along with other multilateral institutions, as part and parcel of an "imperial" state in the making willing to impose the will of powerful interests on those who are in no position to resist. [51] This perspective is also implicit in Guzman's account of how developing states were allegedly forced to conclude BITs that harmed their interests. [52] This view sees investment protection treaties and the issuance of arbitral decisions from a North/South perspective; that is, as law imposed by and through certain hegemonic powers and interests. These critics would appear to agree with Thomas Friedman when he asserts that all states, but particularly those of the Global South, whether they like it or not, are now forced to don what he calls a "Golden Straightjacket" that limits their policy options in order to thrive amidst economic globalization – they just differ from Friedman on whether these limits are normatively desirable. [53] They are also skeptical about whether at least the poorly

49. For a more elaborate description of each of these perspectives, see José E. ALVAREZ, *The Public International Law Regime Governing International Investment* (Martinus Nijhoff 2011). For other approaches to defining forms of global governance, see, e.g., R.O. KEOHANE and J.S. NYE, supra fn. 25 (discussing the concepts of "network" and "system" effects); Thomas G. WEISS, "Governance, Good Governance and Global Governance: Conceptual and Actual Challenges", 21Third World Q. (2000) p. 795 (surveying how governance has been defined or characterized by UN bodies, the OECD, the Commission on Global Governance, among others); Victoria NOURSE and Gregory SHAFFER, "Varieties of New Legal Realism: Can a New World Order Prompt a New Legal Theory?", 95 Cornell L. Rev. (2009) p. 61 at p. 88 (describing the "new governance" approaches of scholars like Charles Sabel).

50. For an introduction to the concept of hegemonic international law, see, e.g., Detlev F. VAGTS, "Hegemonic International Law", 95 Amer. J. Int'l L. (2001) p. 843; José E. ALVAREZ, "Hegemonic International Law Revisited", 97 Amer. J. Int'l L. (2003) p. 873; Nico KRISCH, "International Law in Times of Hegemony: Unequal Power and the Shaping of the International Legal Order", 16 Eur. J. Intl L. (2005) p. 369.

51. See, e.g., Ugo MATTEI, "A Theory of Imperial Law: A Study of U.S. Hegemony and the Latin Resistance" (2003) at <http://works.bepress.com/ugo_mattei/1/>.

52. A.T. GUZMAN, supra fn. 5.

53. Thomas L. FRIEDMAN, *The Lexus and the Olive Tree* (Anchor 2000) at pp. 101-111.

resourced and advised developing states that concluded BITs anticipated the regulatory limits that they would face under such treaties or subsequent arbitral interpretations.

2. *Global Administrative Law*

Other scholars, like my New York University colleague Benedict Kingsbury, have described the international investment regime in less loaded terms, namely as a species of global administrative law (GAL).[54] Global administrative action occurs, in their view, through rule-making, adjudications and other decisions that are neither treaty-making nor simple dispute settlements between states. GAL is not confined to either the processes or the international legal persons of public international law as traditionally understood.[55] GAL scholars focus on regulatory actions taken by formal international organizations, on collective action by transnational networks between national regulatory officials of governments, on distributed administrative arrangements conducted by those officials or hybrid intergovernmental-private arrangements, or action by private institutions with regulatory functions.[56] To authors like Kingsbury, the investment regime shares many of the features of GAL.[57] By accepting the investor guarantees accorded in BITs and FTAs, states have accepted an internal form of supervision. They accept that their own laws, courts and administrative agencies can be judged by objective international standards.[58]

GAL scholars note distinct parallels between the most widely cited interpretation of FET, particularly its more ample interpretation as in *TECMED*, and the standards deployed for judging administrative action under, for example, US administrative law.[59] The *TECMED* standard is effectively a GAL standard. From this perspective, thanks to the "*jurisprudence constante*" produced by investor-state arbitrations, the FET guarantee in particular has emerged as a tool for contesting the legality of governmental action, comparable in scope to demanding that states adhere to the rule of law itself.[60] As the *TECMED* standard suggests, what we ask of investor-state arbitrators is strikingly similar to what we demand from national administrative agencies. Investor-state arbitral tribunals tasked with reviewing whether the actions of governmental agencies are "fair and equitable", are expected to review and control public regulatory actions. Gus Van

---

54. Benedict KINGSBURY and Stephan SCHILL, "Investor-State Arbitration as Governance: Fair and Equitable Treatment, Proportionality, and the Emerging Global Administrative Law" in *El nuevo derecho administrative en América Latina* (2009). See also Benedict KINGSBURY, et al., "The Emergence of Global Administrative Law", 68 Law & Contemporary Problems (2005) p. 15; Gus VAN HARTEN and Martin LOUGHLIN, "Investment Treaty Arbitration as a Species of Global Administrative Law", 17 EUR. J. Int'l L. (2006) p. 121.

55. B. KINGSBURY, supra fn. 54, p. 17.

56. *Ibid.*

57. See B. KINGSBURY and S. SCHILL, supra fn. 54.

58. Campbell MCLACHLAN, "Investment Treaties and General International Law" in A.K. BJORKLUND, *Investment Treaty Law: Current Issues III* (2009).

59. See B. KINGSBURY and S. SCHILL, supra fn. 54, pp. 243-247.

60. See, e.g., C. MCLACHLAN, supra fn. 58, p. 125 (suggesting that the FET principle owes much to the overarching concept of the rule of law).

Harten and Martin Loughlin argue that this is a system akin to national review of administrative action "in that it keeps public authorities within the bounds of legality and provides enforceable remedies to individuals harmed by unlawful state conduct".[61] Investor-state arbitration, along with the actions of international financial institutions, political risk insurers and other market participants, all serve, from this point of view, as a "hybrid", public/private form of "transnational" regulation.

3. *Constitutionalization*

A third description of the investment regime comes from those who believe that the legalization of international investment law has now gone so far that the label of "constitutionalization" may be ascribed to it. For those who define "constitutionalization" as occurring when adjudicators balance the rights of a private party vis-à-vis the state whether through the application of proportionality or other doctrines, investor-state arbitrations are a prime exemplar.[62] Constitutionalists point out that forms of balancing are now apparent with respect to the application of virtually every substantive guarantee contained in investment treaties, from FET to national treatment, and, at least in the views of some arbitrators, with respect to defenses such as "necessity" and the calculation of damages.[63] Constitutionalization may also be one way of describing the fact that some states are now adapting their national constitutional norms in order to make these consistent with their BIT or FTA obligations.[64]

But the "constitutionalism" label has a more radical bite. It is used by some critics of the investment regime as a weapon. In a recent book, David Schneiderman argues that BITs and FTAs institutionalize, as constitutions do, a particular political project, in this instance "neo-liberalism".[65] Investment protection treaties, in his view, force states to recede from the market, restrict their economic functions and limit their redistributionist efforts.[66] Unlike liberal constitutions that empower majoritarian rule while protecting the rights of insular minorities, the investment regime, argues Schneiderman, imposes constraints that insulate economic policy from majoritarian politics by rendering certain options effectively "unconstitutional". He sees the investment regime as "placing ... legal limits on the authority of government, isolating economic from political power, and assigning to investment interests the highest possible

61. G. VAN HARTEN and M. LOUGHLIN, supra fn. 54, p. 149.

62. A.S. SWEET, supra fn. 38.

63. *Ibid.* The *TECMED* tribunal even inquired whether the negative financial impact suffered by the investment was proportional to the public interest protected by the government's regulatory measures and police powers and found these to be reasonable. *Tecnica Medioambientales, TECMED S.A. v. Mexico* (ICSID Case No. ARB/00/2), Award of 29 May 2003, para. 122.

64. See, e.g., MARK TUSHNET, "The Inevitable Globalization of Constitutional Law", 49 Vir. J. Int'l L. (2009) p. 985 (noting the existence of "top-down" and "bottom-up" pressures, including those associated with transnational dispute settlers charged with resolving property disputes and market processes whereby nations necessarily compete for investment, encouraging such change).

65. David SCHNEIDERMAN, *Constitutionalizing Economic Globalization Investment Rules and Democracy's Promise* (Cambridge 2008).

66. See *ibid.*, p. 2.

protection" as part of a pre-commitment strategy to bind future generations.[67] He contends that many of the substantive guarantees in BITs operate in a constitutional fashion and that investor-state jurisprudence, as with respect to its resort to legitimate expectations, borrows heavily from constitutional doctrines used in Europe and in the United States, as with respect to the latter's regulatory takings and substantive due process doctrines.[68]

4. *Humanity's Law*

Ruti Teitel and Robert Howse posit yet another, more optimistic, frame for examining the evolution of international adjudicative mechanisms.[69] Teitel and Howse see signs across divergent international adjudicators – from those judging war crimes to those resolving investment and trade disputes – of a turn to what they call "humanity's law". They define this as an emerging commitment by these diverse international adjudicators to legality itself. They see signs in all of these forums of a growing commitment to interpretation that is sensitive to human rights concerns. For Teitel and Howse, this is suggested by investor-state arbitral outcomes that, as is true of some by the International Criminal Tribunal for the Former Yugoslavia and the WTO Appellate Body, reflect a more "humanity-oriented balance of rights and obligations".[70] Teitel and Howse speculate that this is occurring not because international adjudicators are somehow "above" politics but precisely because they cannot ignore the politics (and the perceived legitimacy) of their own decisions.[71] They suggest that the more humanity-centered investor-state arbitral outcomes stem from a growing awareness that adherence to the traditional "Washington Consensus" is increasingly politically untenable.[72] They argue that hopes for a more human-rights-sensitive international investment regime lie in the professional identity of its adjudicators who, they predict will, over time, increasingly see themselves as agents of the international community and not mere dispute settlers.

IV. BUT IS IT STABLE?

Whether or not one agrees that the investment regime is both "global" and a form of "governance", there is little doubt that the regime is evolving in response to sovereign, NGO and academic backlash. Some of that backlash appears to be emerging precisely because the regime's stakeholders are coming to understand the global governance

---

67. *Ibid.*, p. 4.
68. See, e.g., *ibid.*, p. 107.
69. Ruti TEITEL and Robert HOWSE, "Cross-Judging: Tribunalization in a Fragmented but Interconnected Global Order", 41 NY Univ. J. Int'l L. & Pol. (2009) p. 959.
70. *Ibid.*, p. 981.
71. *Ibid.*
72. *Ibid.*, p. 979.

effects discussed above.[73] While many, perhaps most, states continue to support the basic premises of the international investment regime and continue to negotiate strongly investor-protective BITs, adopt business-friendly laws and regulations, and support international arbitration, others, having seen what the regime has wrought, are having second thoughts.[74]

Adverse or at least more cautious reactions to the governance aspects of the regime are reflected in the actions of some of the states that have fashioned it. Over the course of the last few years a growing number of states from all regions are "re-balancing" their model BITs; passing more restrictive national measures against foreign capital; re-negotiating their older, more investor-protective treaties; suspending BIT negotiations; or, in some cases, even attempting to terminate their existing BITs or their acceptance of ICSID jurisdiction.[75] Today increasing numbers of states are attempting to exercise their "exit and voice" options in respect of the regime. They are chafing at the BIT.

As Stephen Schwebel has noted, the changes to the US Model BIT over time constitute a considerable retrogression from the standpoint of a foreign investor, at least when one's starting point of comparison are the first US BITs negotiated by that country, widely regarded as the most investor-protective in the world.[76] The most recent US BITs and FTAs have reduced the scope of virtually every investor guarantee (including FET) eliminated the umbrella clause guarantee, and shrunk the definition of protected investment; they even assert a self-judging right for states to ignore all investors' rights if this is necessary to protect "essential security".[77] Some of these efforts by the United States – such as its decision in its most recent treaties to restrict the scope of MFN such that its new treaty partners cannot seek to rely on broader investor protections in the United States' older BITs or its efforts to rein in the discretion accorded investor-state arbitrators by binding them to interpretations issued from time to time by the state treaties parties – target precisely those features of the regime that make it plausible to describe it as global in its effects.[78] These changes illustrate how much the erstwhile

73. See generally Osgoode Hall, "Public Statement on the International Investment Regime", 31 August 2010, at < www.osgoode.yorku.ca/public_statement/ > (statement signed by prominent academics expressing "shared concerns" for the "harm done to the public welfare by the international investment regime").

74. See generally José E. ALVAREZ, et al., eds., *The Evolving International Investment Regime* (Oxford 2011).

75. *Ibid.* See also UNCTAD, "World Investment Report 2010", supra fn. 22, at pp. 83-88 (surveying these developments); J.E. ALVAREZ, supra fn. 45.

76. Stephen W. SCHWEBEL, "The United States 2004 Model Bilateral Investment Treaty: An Exercise in the Regressive Development of International Law", 3 Transnational Dispute Management (Apr. 2006, issue 2).

77. See, e.g., José E. ALVAREZ, "The Evolving BIT" in Ian A. LAIRD and Todd WEILER, eds., *Investment Treaty Arbitration and International Law*, Vol. 1 (2010).

78. See, e.g., Kenneth J. VANDEVELDE, "A Comparison of the 2004 and 1994 U.S. Model BITs" in Karl P. Sauvant, ed., *Yearbook International Investment Law & Policy (2008-2009)* (Oxford) p. 283 at p. 301(indicating that since the adoption of the US Model BIT of 2004, the United States has reserved the right to adopt or maintain any measure that accords differential treatment to countries under prior BITs and FTAs, thereby permitting the United States "to provide a lesser level of protection in any agreement in which the reservation appears than under prior agreements,

leader of international investment law has apparently changed its mind since becoming a leading respondent in NAFTA investor-state arbitration. The state that once led the way in toppling the Calvo Clause is now a leader in attempting to "re-calibrate" these treaties to secure greater sovereign "policy space". Other leading BIT/FTA signatories, such as Canada and China, are following suit.[79]

As a result, today's 3,000 BITs and FTAs are a motley group in which strongly investor-protective BITs (modeled on early US models) continue in effect, alongside far more sovereignty-protective ones, including some with open-ended exceptions permitting states to take any and all "prudential" measures under certain circumstances.

Another example of backlash appears with respect to the state that has seen the greatest number of investor-state claims directed against it, Argentina. That state's refusal to comply with investor-state arbitral awards challenges the claim that the investment regime provides an effective bulwark against sovereign override. At the same time, that state's increasing successes before recent ICSID annulment committees undermine the assumption that the investment regime has successfully "depoliticized" the settling of investment disputes.[80] For some, including this author, controversial decisions such as those by annulment committees in *CMS v. Argentina, Sempra v. Argentina* and *Enron v. Argentina* cast doubt on the proposition that political concerns stop at the door to ICSID.[81] These and other arbitral awards also undermine the regime's promise to supply "*jurisprudence constante*". Today, the interpretation of the US BIT's "measures not precluded clause" as well as the customary defense of necessity – as well other prominent issues (such as the definition of "investment" itself) – is probably more uncertain than ever before. The "global law" being produced within the regime is not coherent. If the Argentina decisions are a guide, the regime is not doing a good job of giving states reliable guidance on how they are supposed to govern themselves. Moreover, if Argentina's defiance of ICSID awards spreads to others, frustrated investors may be left with those residual tools associated with "defunct" bilateralism to defend their interests, including negotiating with host states or putting pressure on their home states to engage inter-state countermeasures.

There are many explanations for the backlash against the regime. Some states, such as the United States, may simply be seeking to avoid the threat of continued investor-state litigation. More troubling for the future of the regime is the possibility that its very *raison d'être* is under challenge. To the extent the investment regime is perceived as attempting to codify the "Washington Consensus" mode of governance, that justification has been undermined by its critics, including by prominent US-based economists such

---

notwithstanding the MFN provision").

79. See, e.g., J.E. ALVAREZ, supra fn.77; OECD, "Novel Features in OECD Countries' Recent Investment Agreements: An Overview" (Paris 12 Dec. 2005).

80. For a skeptical view of whether the investment regime has escaped politics, see Martins PAPARINSKIS, "The Limits of Depoliticisation in Contemporary Investor-State Arbitration" in *Select Proceedings of the European Society of International Law, Volume 3, 2010* (Hart Publishing 2012) p. 271.

81. See, e.g., J.E. ALVAREZ, supra fn. 45, at pp. 241-250.

as Joseph Stiglitz and Dani Rodrik.[82] The essence of the Stiglitz/Rodrik critique is that there are many paths to economic development and that no single model fits all. To the extent BITs and FTAs are seen as endorsing a "universal" model for enhancing capital flows and development – a single global model for good governance – this may be, ironically enough, the single greatest threat to the regime's continued viability.

The voices of dissent against the sovereign-constraining aspects of investment protection treaties cast a shadow over the contentions made in Sects. I and II. Today, not everyone believes that all governments should be disempowered, as they would be under many BITs or FTAs, from forcing some foreign investors to participate in joint ventures with local partners or locate in particular regions of the country, transfer their technology, employ local managerial personnel, purchase local content or be compelled to export more than they import. Some believe that forbidding such options to all governments may undermine economic development. Others resist particular aspects of the regime that enhance its "multilateral" effects – such as the conclusion in *Tokios Tokelés v. Ukraine* that a company owned and controlled by nationals of Ukraine that incorporated in a third state precisely to get the benefit of a BIT should nonetheless be able to assert a BIT claim against its own home country.[83] And even erstwhile defenders of the investment regime in North America and Europe worry that some of their investment treaty obligations may limit their options to respond to a serious economic crisis.[84]

The investment regime would not be the first instance in which some of its treaty-makers suffer from buyers' remorse. Indeed, the current backlash against the investment regime resembles prior historical swings between periods characterized by "utopian market liberalism" subsequently met by sovereignty-protective countermovements.[85] As Anthea Roberts has suggested,[86] states have ways to re-assert their sovereign interests. Even schemes for global governance remain creatures of Westphalia. They remain

82. See, e.g., Joseph E. STIGLITZ, *Globalization and its Discontents* (2002) (criticizing the promulgation of the "Washington Consensus"); Dani RODRIK, "Growth Strategies" in P. AGHION and S.N. DURLAUF, eds., *Handbook of Economic Growth* (Amsterdam, Elsevier 2005) available at <http://econ2.econ.iastate.edu/classes/econ502/tesfatsion/GrowthStrategies.DRodrik.GrowthHB2005.pdf> (arguing that pursuit of the Washington Consensus model has not produced economic development as anticipated).

83. But see Stephan W. SCHILL, "The Multilateralization of International Investment Law: Emergence of a Multilateral System of Investment Protection on Bilateral Grounds", 2 Trade, Law and Development Journal (2010, no. 2) p. 59 at p. 75 (defending this conclusion).

84. See generally Anne VAN AAKEN and Jurgen KURTZ, "Emergency Measures and International Investment Law: How Far Can States Go?" in Karl P. Sauvant, ed., *Yearbook International Investment Law & Policy 2009-2010* (Oxford).

85. For an influential account of such a historical dialectic see Karl POLANYI, *The Great Transformation* (2001 edition, originally published in 1944).

86. Anthea ROBERTS, "Power and Persuasion in Investment Treaty Interpretation: The Dual Role of States", 104 Amer. J. Int'l L. (2010) p. 179.

responsive to sovereigns – whose cooperation remains necessary to make such regimes effective and, some believe, legitimate.[87]

As noted, there are signs that some "independent" arbitrators are also receptive to the changing views of states. As is suggested by recent Argentina annulment decisions, some adjudicators charged with enforcing the neutral rule of law may ultimately bend to the will of sovereigns if this seems politically necessary – even at the expense of investors' rights, the ostensibly limited nature of ICSID annulment review and expectations for stable arbitral rulings respectful of precedent.[88]

As the content of BITs and FTAs changes and as some arbitrators react by paying greater deference to respondent states, the regime faces greater risks of internal and external fragmentation. International investment law may become increasingly incoherent internally – if, for example, investors relying on US BITs find themselves subject to an expansive defense of necessity that greatly undermines their rights while investors relying on a UK BIT do not.[89] And, as is suggested by the *Exxon v. Argentina* annulment ruling, international investment law may not cohere externally with customary law as applied elsewhere.[90]

These realities suggest that a description of this regime as a form of global governance is historically contingent. It is too early to say how extensive the current backlash against the regime will be or whether it will prove effective in undermining its "global" or "governance" features. The investment regime is young and the tide of investor-state arbitral rulings even younger, with most of the publicly available awards having been rendered only over the last decade. Like other legal regimes, the investment regime contains features that are relatively autonomous from the power of states. States cannot wholly control the claims that investors bring or what arbitrators will do with them, after all. Irrespective of state concerns, investors will continue to bring investor-state claims if they believe such efforts are worthwhile. And while states can try to withdraw from their treaties, their commitment to international arbitration, or even from complying with awards, not all will be willing and able to do these things. States cannot easily exit from treaties with lengthy termination clauses. The fact that this regime continues to rely on a network of bilateral treaties and not a single multilateral text – as compared to the GATT-covered agreements – presents both opportunities and obstacles to exercising exit and voice. Leaving this regime, escaping its global effects or changing its dimensions is complicated and, especially for the increasing number of states that are both capital

87. See, e.g., Nienke GROSSMAN, "Legitimacy and International Adjudicative Bodies", 41 Geo. Wash. Int'l L. Rev. (2009) p. 107 at pp. 144-148 (arguing that international tribunals' legitimacy turns on, among other things, whether their interpretations are consistent with what states believe the law is or should be).

88. See J.E. ALVAREZ, supra fn. 45, pp. 241-250 (describing how the annulment rulings in *CMS v. Argentina*, *Sempra v. Argentina*, and *Enron v. Argentina* serve to empower the state).

89. Compare *Sempra v. Argentina* (ICSID Case No. ARB/02/16), Annulment Decision of 29 June 2010) to *BG Group and the Republic of Argentina*, UNCITRAL Award (24 Dec. 2007) and *National Grid P.L.C. v. Argentine Republic*, UNCITRAL Award (3 Nov. 2008).

90. See, e.g., *Enron v. Argentina*, supra fn. 44. That annulment ruling implies that the customary defense of necessity may not be the narrow affirmative defense suggested by Art. 25 of the International Law Commission's Articles on State Responsibility.

exporters and importers, not an easy call. Few states have the political will and lawyerly capacity to engage in the piecemeal re-negotiation of numerous bilateral treaties even if they determined that this was on balance in their interests. Moreover, issuing governmental re-interpretations of such treaties, as Roberts suggests ought to be done and as current US BITs and FTAs so provide,[91] still requires the cooperation of treaty partners – not all of whom are likely to agree on precisely the best way to "re-calibrate" their treaty commitments. As Norway has recently discovered, states are also likely to face competing pressures from within about whether or how to re-balance their model BITs.[92] In addition, it is not clear that arbitral bodies will readily accept the binding force of re-interpretations of a BIT issued by its State Parties, especially where these are issued without a clear treaty provision permitting such interpretations and where investors have relied on a different interpretation based on a treaty as originally concluded. There are ambiguities about the extent to which under the positive law (including the customary rules of treaty interpretation) states should be able to change their minds when it comes to treaties that accord rights to third parties who rely on them to their detriment.[93]

Nor can states count on arbitrators being responsive to states' perceived needs to re-calibrate their treaty commitments. Not all arbitrators may be as politically responsive as those who have served on recent ICSID annulment committees involving Argentina. Others may resist pressures to turn those ad hoc committees into a de facto appellate process. It is too early to say how investor-state arbitrators will react to the regime's shifting winds. Some may respond by producing increasingly narrow awards intent on settling the particular dispute before them rather than expansive *jurisprudence constante*. To the extent this occurs, the resulting awards – if published at all – are more likely to resemble those issued in the course of commercial arbitration. Others may respond differently – and attempt to produce all-the-more-reasoned opinions attentive to prior awards to better respond to GAL or other critiques of their legitimacy as de facto global regulators. To the extent investor-state claims continue to be brought, how investor-state arbitrators behave will be an important determinant of the kind of global governance that will result.

V. CONCLUSION

There is room to question whether the world of BITs, FTAs and investor-state arbitral rulings really constitutes a form of global governance. Certainly anyone expecting governance of the kind routinely exercised by reasonably competent governments will

91. A. ROBERTS, supra fn. 86.

92. Norway's 2007/2008 Model BIT was abandoned after complaints from local business groups that a considerably weakened BIT would not be in their interests. The official comments received by the Norway government can be found at <http://www.regjeringen.no/nb/dep/nhd/dok/horinger/horingsdokumenter/2008/horing---modell-for-investeringsavtaler/horingsuttalelser.html?id=496023>.

93. See, e.g., Charles H. BROWER II, "Investor-State Disputes Under NAFTA: The Empire Strikes Back", 40 Colum. J. Transnat'l L. (2001) p. 43 (questioning the enforceability of NAFTA Commission Interpretations particularly if these purport to affect pending arbitrations).

not find comparable institutions at the international level to make, enforce or interpret international investment law. There is no global legislature or administrative agency charged with making investment rules, no collective enforcement arm to enforce such rules, and no international investment court with compulsory jurisdiction. But if these were the requisites for governance, no such scheme would exist at the global level. This has not prevented scholars, UN bureaucrats and many others from describing certain regimes embracing the interaction of states, international organizations, NGOs and the market as involving forms of "governance" distinct from national government.

The international investment regime has a number of features that make it plausible to describe it as a system for global governance. It consists of treaties that, like some others involving trade in goods or human rights, have normative effects on non-signatories, not all of which were contemplated by their drafters. Like some other treaty regimes, its "governance" features are exercised by states themselves, through the passage of conforming national laws or the institutionalization of local practices. Its governance features are also enhanced through the actions of non-state actors, including international organizations and market players. Unlike many other treaties, its enforcement scheme – and consequentially its material effect on how nations behave – is unusually effective.

How one describes the resulting form of governance – as hegemonic law, constitutionalization, GAL or humanity's law – is not just of academic interest. These representations, like others,[94] are fraught with normative and practical implications.

These representations may, for example, frame what investor-state arbitrators do or what they resist doing. Consider the statement in *Total v. Argentina* wherein the arbitrators stress that each ICSID tribunal needs to be guided only by the specific BIT before it in light of the particular facts and may well reach decisions that differ from other tribunals.[95] That tribunal emphasized that its approach to "precedent" was different from that taken in *Saipem S.p.A. v. The People's Republic of Bangladesh*.[96] In *Saipem*, the arbitral panel had indicated that while it was not bound by previous decisions,

> "it must pay due consideration to earlier decisions of international tribunals. It believes that, subject to compelling contrary grounds, it has a duty to adopt solutions established in a series of consistent cases. It also believes that, subject to the specifics of a given treaty and of the circumstances of the actual case, it has a duty to seek to contribute to the harmonious development of investment law and thereby to meet the legitimate expectations of the community of States and investors towards certainty of the rule of law."[97]

94. Compare Emmanuel GAILLARD, *Legal Theory of International Arbitration* (Martinus Nijhoff 2010) (presenting three "representations" of international arbitration and their consequences).

95. *Total S.A. v. Argentina* (ICSID Case No. ARB/04/1), Decision on Liability of 27 Dec. 2010, fn. 187.

96. *Ibid.*

97. *Saipem S.p.A. v. The People's Republic of Bangladesh* (ICSID Case No. ARB/05/07), Decision on Jurisdiction and Recommendation on Provisional Measures, 21 Mar. 2007, para. 67 (quoted in *Total v. Argentina*, supra fn. 95).

The arbitrators in these two cases seem to differ on whether their role is to promote global governance. Some investor-state arbitrators, like those in *Total*, may see their role as not very different from those charged with deciding commercial disputes between private parties, while others, like the ones in *Saipem*, appear more sympathetic to Van Harten's or Kingsbury's views that they are engaged in some form of "public" adjudication attentive to public values.

Conceptualizations of the kind of "governance" that BITs and FTAs impose on states may also influence policy prescriptions for the regime. GAL scholars, for example, have not been reticent about suggesting how GAL principles ought to inform investor-state proceedings as well as the drafting of awards.[98]

Governance views may also influence how disputing parties in investor-state disputes argue as well as how such claims are decided. Alleged North/South inequities – especially those arguably reflected in the texts of BITs or in arbitral rules – are likely to be highlighted by those influenced by the "hegemonic" frame. Constitutionalists are likely to stress the need to "balance" states' regulatory needs with investors' rights. The GAL perspective identifies, among other things, systemic values, such as the need for participation and transparency in the arbitral proceedings themselves, while advocates of humanity's law would support the position, also urged by Bruno Simma, that Art. 31(3)(c) of the Vienna Convention on the Law of Treaties be taken as a license to apply human rights norms in the course of interpreting BITs and FTAs.[99] All of these are contestable propositions – as is the central contention that the investment regime is or will remain a form of global governance.

98. See, e.g., B. KINGSBURY and S. SCHILL, supra fn. 54, at pp. 276-294.

99. See Bruno SIMMA and Theodore KILL, "Harmonizing Investment Protection and International Human Rights: First Steps Towards a Methodology" in C. BINDER, et al., eds., *International Investment Law for the 21st Century: Essays in Honor of Christoph Schreuer* (Oxford, New York 2009) p. 678. See generally Pierre-Marie DUPUY, et. al, ed., *Human Rights in International Investment Law and Arbitration* (Oxford 2009).

Foreign Investment, Human Rights and Global Governance

Bruno Simma[*]

TABLE OF CONTENTS

	Page
I. Human Rights in the Foreign Investment Context	161
II. Achieving Adequate Public Policy Governance	164
III. Conclusion	165

I. HUMAN RIGHTS IN THE FOREIGN INVESTMENT CONTEXT

I wish to focus on a certain issue of governance that is linked to several of the reasons[1] put forward by Professor Alvarez to account for the multilateralization of the international investment regime: that is, first, the multilateralizing impact of investor-State dispute settlement, in other words, its growth into a form of public law adjudication; secondly, the spillovers and interconnections between investment law and other international legal regimes; and, finally, the supporting activities of certain international organizations, such as the "investment regulation" undertaken by international financial institutions and market actors.

Professor Alvarez assures us that the *jurisprudence constante* of investor-State arbitrators will remain an important factor in the scheme for global governance we will have in our field,[2] and I agree with him on that. But what I would instantly add is that for the sake of the legitimacy of the international investment regime the main task of advancing the policies that drive multilateralized governance here should remain with, or be restored to, States and their governments. And in this regard, I have a very specific policy in

---

* Judge at the International Court of Justice.

1. José E. ALVAREZ, "Is the International Investment Regime a Form of Global Governance?", this volume, pp. 137-160. Professor Alvarez enumerates these reasons as follows:

(1) the common historical pedigree of investment protection agreements;
(2) bilateral investment treaties (BITs)/free trade agreements (FTAs) not having been negotiated on a quid pro quo basis;
(3) the common content of BITs/FTAs, including the effects of most favored nation (MFN) clauses;
(4) the globalizing effects of corporate restructuring, also undertaken in order to take advantage of particularly investor-protective BITs (such as those concluded by the Netherlands);
(5) the multilateralizing impact of investor-State dispute settlement (and the impact of arbitral *jurisprudence constante*);
(6) the spillovers and interconnections between investment law and other international legal regimes (including human rights and World Trade Organization law); and
(7) the supporting actions of certain international organizations, such as the "investment regulation" undertaken by international financial institutions and market actors.

2. *Ibid.*, at p. 151.

mind. If I had to place it within the versions of global governance that Professor Alvarez commented upon, it would fit best into the Howse/Teitel formula of "humanity's law".[3]

Let us assume that an investor-State dispute has arisen. In this situation, when what is at issue before a tribunal are the steps that States have taken in the exercise of their public policy authority, I submit that States ought to be prepared to defend such measures not just by reliance on their domestic laws; as the case may be, they ought also to relate these measures to the international obligations to which they have committed themselves. In the context of disputes on foreign investment, such obligations will arise, in the first instance, from international treaties on economic and social rights, like conventions adopted by the International Labour Organization, but above all the principal global treaty in the field, namely the International Covenant on Economic, Social and Cultural Rights of 1966, which at present has been ratified or acceded to by no less than 160 States.[4] Consequently, an overwhelming majority of States Parties to bilateral investment treaties (BITs) and international investment agreements (IIAs) will at the same time be bound by the obligations deriving from the Covenant. The problem is that States are not taking these obligations as seriously as they should, even though more recently there is some progress to be seen. But in our specific field, giving adequate consideration to a host State's international obligations deriving from economic and social human rights has hitherto been the rare exception rather than the rule.

In the ongoing debate over how to define appropriate spaces for public policy regulation vis-à-vis protection of foreign investment, my views are very close to those of Anthea Roberts, who puts strong emphasis on the inherent authority of States to reassert sovereign interests in the international investment regime.[5] Starting from here and then focusing on my agenda of rendering our regime not just less "bilateral" and more "public", but more human rights-sensitive, I see particular traction in exploring both *ex ante* and *ex post* strategies of bringing human rights to bear on foreign investment. What I am aiming at here in practical terms is that we should explore the opening of avenues for human rights discourse in our field in two ways instead of only the one to which we have hitherto given (modest) attention. We should get human rights into the picture not just by encouraging arbitrators to engage in the "systematic integration" of these rights with the help of the Vienna Convention's recently discovered miracle weapon, Art. 31(3)(c).[6] We should start the integration of human rights both earlier and

---

3. See Ruti G. TEITEL, "Humanity's Law: Rule of Law for the New Global Politics", 35 Cornell Int'l L. J. (2001-2002) p. 355; Ruti TEITEL and Robert HOWSE, "Cross-Judging: Tribunalization in a Fragmented but Interconnected Global Order", 41 N.Y.U. J. Int'l & L. Pol. (2009) p. 959.
4. International Covenant on Economic, Social and Cultural Rights, 19 December 1966, United Nations, Treaty Series, vol. 993, p. 3, available at: <www2.ohchr.org/english/law/cescr.htm> (last visited 30 April 2011). For the state of membership of the Covenant, see <http://treaties.un.org/Pages/ViewDetails.aspx?src=TREATY&mtdsg_no=IV-3&chapter=4&lang=en> (last visited 30 April 2011).
5. Anthea ROBERTS, "Power and Persuasion in Investment Treaty Interpretation: The Dual Role of States", 104 AJIL (2010) p. 179.
6. Bruno SIMMA and Theodore KILL, "Harmonizing Investment Protection and International Human Rights: First Steps toward a Methodology" in Christina L. BINDER, Ursula KRIEBAUM, August REINISCH and Stephan WITTICH, *International Investment Law for the 21st Century: Essays in Honour*

more comprehensively, namely by introducing the relevant human rights and respecting and preserving them already at the stage of negotiation of the individual investment contract and at that of the negotiation (or renegotiation) of the international investment agreement.[7]

Here I see a distinct role to be played by national governments in conjunction with the monitoring mechanism for the Economic and Social Covenant institutionalized within the United Nations, that is the Committee on Economic, Social and Cultural Rights (of which I was an expert member from 1987 to 1996 – but I think that the fifteen years that I have since then spent in other, less human rights-focused, bodies of the UN should have erased any *deformation professionelle*). I thus agree with Professor Alvarez's recognition of the inevitability of interconnections between investment law and other international legal regimes.[8] I would simply like to add to these regimes the one on the protection of the human rights relevant in the foreign investment context, particularly in the economic and social rights field. And that is why I suggest that, apart from, and in addition to, the "international investment regulation" already exercised by international financial institutions and various market actors mentioned by Professor Alvarez,[9] the institution of international supervision of the Covenant, particularly the treaty body I have just mentioned, ought to play a substantial role in cooperating with the governments of the States Parties to the Covenant, through its mechanisms of examination of the reports of the parties, the ensuing dialogue and the resulting policy review.[10] The aim of such cooperation would be a human rights-oriented adjustment and contextualization of long-term public policy priorities and programmes vis-à-vis the scope of investment obligations assumed by these States. I would thus suggest an intertwined role for the Covenant Committee, legal advisers in the competent departments of national governments and interested groups in civil society. This role would be to keep States properly informed about their continuing Covenant duties to observe the "progressive realization" of economic and social human rights, and about the ways in which the realization of these rights will be affected by a State's adoption of policies of investment protection.

---

of Christoph Schreuer (2009) pp. 673-707.

7. For details see Bruno SIMMA, "Investment Arbitration: A Place for Human Rights?", Grotius Lecture, March 2011, 60 International & Comparative Law Quarterly (2011) pp. 573-596.
8. *Ibid.*, at p. 8.
9. *Ibid.*, at p. 9.
10. For a detailed summary of the monitoring and review functions of the Committee, see M. Magdalena SÉPULVEDA, *The Nature of the Obligations Under the International Covenant on Economic, Social and Cultural Rights* (2003) at pp. 29-44; Mary DOWELL-JONES, *Contextualising the International Covenant on Economic, Social, and Cultural Rights: Assessing the Economic Deficit* (2004) at pp. 39-58, 127-154, 157-168. See also Robert E. ROBERTSON, "Measuring State Compliance with the Obligation to Devote the 'Maximum Available Resources' to Realizing Economic, Social, and Cultural Rights", 16 Human Rights Quarterly (November 1994, no. 4) pp. 693-714.

II. ACHIEVING ADEQUATE PUBLIC POLICY GOVERNANCE

Global governance, in this sense, could, and should, thus extend beyond the traditionally interested stakeholders and comprise other international institutions that have monitoring and compliance interests affecting the authority of States over, and the scope of, national public policies, like my human rights bodies. To again turn to the Economic and Social Rights Committee, an avenue for such involvement would be for the Committee to include as part of its monitoring guidelines the investment treaty commitments and the impact of existing foreign investment contracts (especially in the field of the provision of basic utilities and services) on the performance of the obligations deriving from the Covenant by the State party under consideration. Another means would be to encourage governments, in the disclosure of regulation relevant to foreign investors, to include their obligations under the Covenant as well as their mid-term/long-term programmes for the realization of economic and social rights. And, of course, the prospective investors' legal teams would have to look into these matters on their part. In the Grotius Lecture that I gave in London in March 2011 I have developed these ideas a little further under the heading of a "human rights audit". Such, what I would call, *ex ante* approaches to the harmonization of investment protection with other interrelated legal regimes particularly that on human rights could, perhaps, abate the further deterioration of investor-State relations beyond the current point.

By this, I don't mean to say that foreign investment arbitration has no substantial role in developing the multilateralization of international investment law, of giving it a public law paradigm – far from it.[11] I believe that each investor-State dispute creates the opportunity for States to address, in Professor Alvarez's terms, the issues of "exit and voice". The manner by which a State devises its public policy defences, negotiates or re-negotiates the key terms and standards of investment agreements, and enforces investment arbitral awards demonstrates how the State "voices" its participation in the increasing "multilateralization" of this regime. The phenomenon of "multilateralization" latent in international investment has not always been self-evident to the State's policy-makers. They have negotiated BITs through a largely insular process.[12] Maybe it was not until the relatively recent outbreak of highly charged investment controversies involving financial crises (such as the nearly fifty arbitrations involving the Argentine crisis), environmental regulation (such as the *Methanex* and *Metalclad* cases), and the delivery of basic services (such as *Aguas del Tunari*), that States have begun to realize the implications of foreign investment arbitration for their own domestic governance capabilities. I share Professor Alvarez's view that investment arbitration involves global governance in crucial ways. But as I am trying to demonstrate in my short contribution, I do so also for an additional reason: at the core of my concern are the State's

11. See Stephan W. SCHILL, "Crafting the International Economic Order: The Public Function of Investment Treaty Arbitration and Its Significance for the Role of the Arbitrator", 23 Leiden J. Intl L. (2010) pp. 401-430.

12. Kenneth J. VANDEVELDE, "A Brief History of International Investment Agreements" in Karl P. SAUVANT and Lisa E. SACHS, eds., *The Effect of Treaties on Foreign Direct Investment: Bilateral Investment Treaties, Double Taxation Treaties, and Investment Flows* (2009) pp. 3-35.

fundamental economic and social obligations under the Covenant – an obviously multilateral international instrument – which, to date, States have not explored, or given a full "voice" to, in investment arbitrations.

The responses of a State to competing issues of compensability to investors versus demands of domestic constituents and citizens also typify the kind of "exit" from this regime that a State may choose to follow. Such responses can vary from outright denunciation of the ICSID Convention (as Bolivia and Ecuador have done); regularly taking arbitral awards to the annulment phase of the proceedings (as Argentina is doing); or renegotiating new standards and more precise formulations to represent a balance of public policy interests and investor demand for the predictability of legal rules (which the 2004 Canada Model BIT / Foreign Investment Protection Agreement (FIPA) appears to have accomplished). Reliance on the crystallization of arbitral precedent, *jurisprudence constante,* might be one way of mediating public policy within such a regime of global governance,[13] but I would also side with Professor Alvarez's understanding of BITs and FTAs as instruments that intentionally and in actual effect constitute efforts "to regulate States".[14] In my view, adequate public policy governance can best be achieved through the continuous development of these instruments, with a purposeful focus on interrelating the State's broad economic and social obligations. Certainly, this is preferable to piecemeal interpretations produced in investment litigation, by unwitting arbitrators who often tend to observe judicial parsimony and resolve disputes as narrowly as possible.

III. CONCLUSION

I suggest that we see the "public policy" interventions I have described as collective efforts that should still be primarily driven by States in the global governance regime of international investment. As I have demonstrated, it is possible for States to look beyond the present architecture of international investment into the wider fabric of international institutions and obligations that, while hitherto not being in the focus of observers, affect States' public policy regulations already – residually but continuously. By the way, the quandary that States face in their attempts to achieve a balance between complying with international obligations and satisfying domestic constituencies is not unique to the international investment regime. When it comes to determining resource priorities in the fulfilment of their economic and social welfare agenda, States are well aware that their coffers – as well as their institutional and regulatory capacities to meet the needs of their population – are in perpetual flux. But the harmonization of financial obligations owed to foreign investors with international economic and social human rights obligations owed to the public should be viewed as part of the same matrix of a State's public policy considerations and objectives of "progressive realization".

13. See Gabrielle KAUFMANN-KOHLER, "Arbitral Precedent: Dream, Necessity, or Excuse?", 2006 Freshfields Lecture, at <www.arbitration-icca.org/media/0/12319143087130/00950001.pdf> (last visited 20 April 2011).

14. *Ibid.*, at p. 5.

The Investment Treaty Arbitrator as Agent of Global Governance

Sir Franklin Berman, KCMG, QC[*]

TABLE OF CONTENTS

	Page
I. Introduction	166
II. How Do Arbitrators Conceive Their Function?	166
III. From Where Do Arbitrators Derive Their Authority?	167
IV. Where Do Arbitrators Find the Material for Their Decisions?	168

I. INTRODUCTION

The problem with this topic is that there is too much to say, so that one has to be selective. My intention is to come down from the conceptual stratosphere, dodging all of the abstract space junk on the way down, and offer a realist's view with both feet firmly on the ground (or even below ground).

The starting point for any analysis is that "governance" is about the exercise of authority, so that it necessarily implies in the first place the *attribution* of authority in some recognizable manner; and equally implies in the second place the existence of forms of *control* over the exercise of that authority. It follows obviously that, if one talks in terms of "global" governance, both the attribution of authority and the control over its exercise would have to operate on a global level. And that means in turn that the agents of governance can only be States, arbitrators and tribunals, and possibly to some extent multilateral organizations as well. My approach will be to look at the issues from the viewpoint of one of that range of agents of governance, the arbitrators and tribunals.

If you wanted, as a *jeux d'ésprit*, to apply one simple-minded criterion to the question, whether international investment arbitration is a form of global governance, you could pose the question in the form: *Where are the women*? The overwhelming predominance of men – starkly evident in the composition of tribunals and International Centre for Settlement of Investment Disputes (ICSID) annulment committees – in and of itself prompts the reflection that we can't be in the presence yet of a developed system of global governance. One that is limping into existence, perhaps, but hasn't yet reached a state of maturity.

II. HOW DO ARBITRATORS CONCEIVE THEIR FUNCTION?

Back, then, to the matter of arbitrators and tribunals, you could start with a different question: How do arbitrators conceive their function? It's probably a bad question, though, one which is too subjective and all too prone to produce the answer that

* Essex Court Chambers; Visiting Professor of International Law, Universities of Oxford and Cape Town; member, Permanent Court of Arbitration.

arbitrators conceive themselves as semi-divine beings dropped to earth by a benevolent providence in order to solve the problems of the world! This may be a caricature, but it does correspond in a way to the old Lauterpachtian conception of the international judge many years ago. Now we take a more realistic view; we see arbitration as a process, and as one among many processes, some of them judicial, some of them not, by which disputing parties arrive at a resolution of their disputes. The Lauterpachtian conception confuses the law with the agents for the implementation of the law. Arbitrators fall among the agents, whose task is to find the law and then to apply it to the case in hand. But to view that twin task as forming part of a developing system of governance may be a useful insight, which helps one to identify what it is that "governance" demands and requires, and how far the institution (for want of a better word) of investment arbitration fulfils that.

III. FROM WHERE DO ARBITRATORS DERIVE THEIR AUTHORITY?

A better starting point might be to pose a question as to the authority possessed by arbitrators. That they exercise authority is not in doubt, but where does it come from? The question attracts a simple answer: they derive their authority from their appointment which – within the field of investment arbitration – has its ultimate root in treaties. You could put the matter another way by asking whether appointment to act as arbitrator should be classed as a private appointment or a public appointment, on the basis that most national systems of law would make a distinction between public and private appointments. Neither categorization would in the present context be problem-free: the nomination, for example, of a party-appointed arbitrator doesn't feel like a public appointment, but conversely, if you take the private analogy too far, you end up with the sort of problem which the UK Supreme Court is currently facing as to whether an arbitrator appointment ought to attract rules applying to an "employee".[1] Could you, on the other hand, regard the *presiding* arbitrator as a public appointment, e.g., if the appointment were made by ICSID or a comparable appointing authority? Perhaps. But the procedures used for appointing presiding arbitrators don't even approximate to those used nationally for public appointments. And the problem lies deeper than that, if you once begin to form the notional picture of a tribunal whose members had different statuses – and therefore perhaps different duties deriving from their different statuses. That would be a most unattractive proposition, out of key with actual practice, and hardly tenable as a model for a systematic structure of investment arbitration.

The consequence is, however, the conclusion that appointment as an arbitrator is a hybrid, resting (in the case of investment arbitration) on a treaty or treaty system. And it follows from that that what arbitrators are appointed to do is to fulfil their duties as laid down by the treaty or treaty system. And it follows further that it is the treaty or

1. *Jivraj v. Hashwani* [2010] EWCA Civ 712. Since this paper was delivered, the Supreme Court has however determined on appeal that the appointment of an arbitrator under a contract is not an "employment" for the purposes of the EU Framework Directive on discrimination in employment or occupation or the corresponding UK Regulations.

treaty system that identifies the material properly at their disposal to fulfil those duties. The classic example is Art. 42 of the Convention on the Settlement of Investment Disputes between States and Nationals of Other States (the ICSID Convention), which lays down the applicable law, namely: the rules of law agreed between the parties and, failing agreement, the law of the Host State, including its conflict of law rules "and such rules of international law as may be applicable". We ought moreover to remind ourselves that a provision of that kind is not merely an aspiration, or a *desideratum*, but a binding requirement, controlled ultimately by the possibility of annulment under Art. 52 of the Convention. And that in turn would be entirely in step with what I described earlier as our starting point, namely that "governance" implies both the attribution of authority and some form of control over its actual exercise.

In other words, one has to bear in mind that the attribution of authority to an arbitrator is necessarily and inevitably subject to limits. You can hardly blame arbitrators in any way if they are constantly very conscious of the limits on their authority and anxious not to exceed them. That is no more than the exercise in good faith of what they have been put there to do – put there either by the parties on their own, or by a combination of the parties and an appointing authority.

IV. WHERE DO ARBITRATORS FIND THE MATERIAL FOR THEIR DECISIONS?

This, however, brings us back to the question of the materials that arbitrators are justified and entitled to make use of in carrying out their essential function, i.e., to reach a formal decision (deliver an award) on the dispute referred to them. This is the question I described earlier in terms of Art. 42 of the ICSID Convention, and it comes back into focus because it often seems to me that the debate wrapped up in this notion of "governance" ultimately revolves around the question "Are arbitrators entitled to, and if so should they, draw in additional materials to inform their judicial decisions – or even on occasion perhaps to play a decisive part in determining how they decide the dispute before them?" If you wanted to situate that in precise terms within the Art. 42 framework, you would no doubt hang it on "and such rules of international law as may be applicable," as that phrase appears at the end of the article.

That brings into the discussion however a whole series of propositions which one often hears advanced, but which – on examination – are different from one another, and often conflict with one another. Propositions such as: tribunals should regard themselves as bound by a *jurisprudence constante*; *or* tribunals should contribute to building up a unified body of law, in the interests of consistency and predictability; *or* tribunals should exercise a creative function in developing the law taking account of submissions put to them by third party *amici*. And so forth.

Let's leave aside for the moment the fact that the first of these propositions begs a very large question: has any of us ever seen a *jurisprudence* that is *less constante*? All of these propositions are directed towards the idea that arbitrators should regard themselves as having a systemic role, one that goes beyond the purely empirical task of deciding the dispute at hand. The argument is an understandable one – particularly so in the case of tribunals appointed within a system such as ICSID, or tribunals considering disputes under multilateral treaties such as the Energy Charter Treaty or NAFTA, but much less so for tribunals of a purely ad hoc character. And even then, this notion of a systemic role has to be balanced against two things. Firstly that tribunals decide cases according to *law*, and (except for cases arising under those multilateral treaties) the substantive law governing the dispute is not automatically the same from one case to another. Secondly – an important factor, this, which is frequently neglected in the academic commentary – the case for decision by a tribunal is *heavily* influenced by the way in which each party has chosen to plead its side of the case. A tribunal's primary duty is to respond to the argument made out before it, not just on the material issues of fact, but on the law as well; *jura novit curia* does not give a tribunal a free hand to dispose of the case on a basis not argued out before it between the parties.

So the systemic role of arbitrators, where it properly exists, is not one that transforms their function into campaigners, or into advocates for a particular world view. Nor is it one that allows them to substitute third-party claims and interests for the claims and interests of the parties, as advanced by them in the course of the proceedings – although it may in appropriate circumstances authorize the arbitrators to take wider factors into account as part of a legitimate interpretative process, for example in the assessment of the "object and purpose" of a treaty instrument. But the most important aspect of a systemic role of that kind is the duty of arbitrators and tribunals to engage with one another's decisions in the debate over areas of international law that may not be clear or settled, or may be in a state of significant development. That, I think, is part of the function of a responsible tribunal which transcends a very narrow view of the function as confined exclusively to the contours of the case before it, but does not in and of itself affect the basis on which it is called on to decide that particular case. The process is one of clarifying and elaborating – and even developing – indeterminate or contested areas of law, by applying the relevant rules to particular cases, and is a well-recognized aspect of the judicial function. But it has to be done openly. To engage consciously in it, though, demands of arbitrators that they should take particular care over their reasoning, over their explanation and analysis of the basis on which they are deciding the instant case. And it demands of arbitrators that they should engage with how other arbitrators have handled similar or comparable questions in other cases, even while respecting the inescapable fact that some prior decisions are good ones, entitled therefore to respect, while others are bad ones, and are therefore not to be followed.

So if my remarks appear sceptical or astringent, they are not intended to be negative, but to map out a reasonable role for arbitrators in the slow march towards what may ultimately amount one day to a form of global governance.

The Next Battleground: Standards of Review in Investment Treaty Arbitration

Anthea Roberts[*]

TABLE OF CONTENTS | Page

I.	Introduction	170
II.	Moving Beyond the Commercial Arbitration Paradigm	173
III.	Calls for Judicial Restraint Under the Public Law Paradigm	175
IV.	The Appropriateness and Limits of the Public Law Paradigm	177
V.	Conclusion	180

I. INTRODUCTION

Investment treaty arbitration involves a balance of governance powers between States and arbitral tribunals. By entering into investment treaties with broad and vague substantive provisions and by permitting investors to bring claims directly before arbitral tribunals, States have delegated authority to investment tribunals not only to resolve investor-State disputes but to interpret, apply and thereby develop investment treaty law. Individually, tribunals have the authority to review legislative, executive and judicial actions of respondent States, including the power to adjudicate upon the balance struck between investor rights and other public interests, such as protection of the environment, human and labour rights, and the economy. Collectively, these tribunals are helping to define certain global governance standards because investment awards frequently become publicly available and are then cited by other tribunals and participants within the investment treaty field as persuasive (though non-binding) authority on the meaning of investment treaty protections.

In this way, investment treaty arbitration represents a form of global governance because it involves the review of governance functions of respondent States and the exercise of governance functions by arbitral tribunals.[1] Yet, as José Alvarez notes, the extent to which the field represents a system of global governance is both unstable and currently undergoing a process of contestation.[2] As part of this process, Bruno Simma

* Department of Law, London School of Economics and Political Science.

1. Benedict KINGSBURY and Stephan W. SCHILL, "Investor-State Arbitration as Governance: Fair and Equitable Treatment, Proportionality, and the Emerging Global Administrative Law" in Albert Jan VAN DEN BERG, ed., *50 Years of the New York Convention*, ICCA Congress Series no. 14 (2009) p. 5, also available as Institute for International Law and Justice Working Paper 2009/6 (Global Administrative Law Series) at <http://iilj.org/publications/documents/2009-6.Kingsbury Schill.pdf>.
2. José ALVAREZ, "Is the International Investment Regime a Form of Global Governance?", this volume, pp. 137-160.

has called for certain powers associated with global governance to be restored to States.[3] Meanwhile Frank Berman contends that both States and tribunals can be "agents of governance", but has focussed on the governance role that arbitrators and tribunals play in investment treaty arbitration.[4] I agree with Berman's premise, but my focus is on the appropriate balance of power between States, on the one hand, and arbitral tribunals, on the other hand. I contend that part of the process of destabilization that Alvarez identifies comes from attempts by States to recalibrate this balance of power, with States re-asserting their rights as both treaty parties and sovereigns.

States are attempting to re-assert their interpretive rights as treaty parties through various means. As Alvarez notes, we are witnessing a growing level of specificity in a new breed of investment treaties (see, e.g., the 2004 US Model Bilateral Investment Treaty (BIT) and the 2004 Canada Model BIT) where States are spelling out the extent and limits of many of their treaty provisions. By increasing the specificity of their commitments, States are playing a greater role in defining their investment treaty obligations and, correspondingly, the breadth of interpretive authority delegated to arbitral tribunals is being reduced. Some States are also asserting their ongoing interpretive role as treaty parties through the use of subsequent agreements and practice.[5] The Notes of Interpretation issued by NAFTA's Free Trade Commission represents a prominent example, but other examples exist and can be expected to increase over time. Again, the more active treaty parties are in defining their investment treaty commitments, the less flexibility tribunals will have in interpreting those provisions.

States are also seeking to recalibrate their interpretive balance of power with tribunals by re-asserting their rights as sovereigns. A number of new investment treaties and model BITs contain clauses in which States expressly reserve the right to regulate in the public interest, including regulations designed to protect the environment, human and labour rights, and the economy. Some also include self-judging clauses that permit States to determine whether investor protections need to be compromised in order to achieve certain essential interests. Beyond these substantive carve-outs, we are witnessing growing calls by States, academics and NGOs for investment arbitral tribunals to recognize that they are engaged in a form of international judicial review and thus should adopt appropriate levels of deference when reviewing the legislative, executive and judicial acts of respondent States. Some draw on domestic public law comparisons, arguing that tribunals should adopt deferential standards of review when adjudicating upon governmental conduct. Others rely on international comparisons, invoking notions such as the margin of appreciation doctrine that some international courts adopt when reviewing State actions for conformity with international obligations.

---

3. Bruno SIMMA, "Foreign Investment, Human Rights and Global Governance", this volume, pp. 161-165.
4. Sir Franklin BERMAN, "The Investment Treaty Arbitrator as Agent of Global Governance", this volume, pp. 166-169).
5. Anthea ROBERTS, "Power and Persuasion in Investment Treaty Interpretation: The Dual Role of States", 104 American Journal of International Law (2010) p. 179.

It is this aspect – the appropriateness of investment treaty tribunals adopting deferential standards of review – that I believe represents the next battleground for those who conceptualize investment treaty arbitration as a form of global governance. Accordingly, my comments in response to Alvarez's presentation will focus on this issue.

Standards of review are important because they help to determine how interventionist or deferential tribunals will be in assessing the actions and decisions of respondent States. As investment provisions are broad and vague, tribunals have considerable scope to determine how to interpret and apply these provisions in concrete cases. They can choose to take a very interventionist approach by, for example, applying exacting standards to determine whether governmental actions are the only or best means of achieving certain policy goals. For instance, the tribunal in *CMS Gas Transmission v. Argentina* asked whether the measures taken by Argentina to respond to its economic crisis were the "only steps available" to it.[6] Or tribunals can take a more deferential approach by, for example, giving states wider latitude to determine what policy goals they wish to achieve and how best to achieve them. For instance, the tribunal in *Continental Casualty v. Argentina* asked whether Argentina's action was the "least restrictive measure reasonably available" to protect its economy.[7]

Exercising judicial restraint or deference does not amount to a failure to review governmental conduct, nor does it necessitate a finding of no liability in investor-State arbitrations. Domestic courts and international courts and tribunals, such as the European Court of Human Rights and the World Trade Organization (WTO) Appellate Body, routinely exercise deferential review whilst still finding government agencies or States liable in appropriate cases. Instead, the degree of deference adopted is relevant to determining how strictly tribunals will scrutinize governmental conduct and how readily they will substitute their own views for those of respondent States. For example:

– If a State regulatory agency decides that a chemical is harmful and should be banned, despite the negative impact that this will have on foreign investors, when should arbitral tribunals second-guess these questions of science and policy?
– If a State legislature decides to enact measures to protect the environment or its economy, even though these measures will harm foreign investors, when should arbitral tribunals sit in judgment of the appropriateness of these policy goals or the measures enacted to achieve them?
– If a national court has made certain determinations of fact or given certain interpretations of national law, should arbitral tribunals consider these issues afresh if they are implicated in an investor-State dispute?

Deference is not an all or nothing concept; rather, deference or judicial restraint is a concept measured by degrees that has a direct impact on the balance of governance powers between States and tribunals. The greater the level of deference, the more

6. *CMS Gas Transmission Co. v. Argentine Republic* (ICSID Case No. ARB/01/8), Award of 12 May 2005, para. 324.
7. *Continental Casualty Co v. Argentine Republic* (ICSID Case No. ARB/03/9), Award of 5 Sept. 2008, paras. 192-195.

latitude States will have to exercise their governance functions; the lower the level of deference, the more power tribunals will assume and the greater will be their governance functions. That is why, in Santiago Montt's words, "standards of review adopted by arbitral panels directly reflect – or more precisely, define – the distribution of powers that must inevitably exist between those tribunals and the national bodies under [their] control".[8]

To those who view investment arbitration as another species of international (commercial) arbitration, the notion that arbitral tribunals should adopt deferential standards when reviewing the conduct of one disputing party is unfamiliar at best and an outrage at worst. Yet the failure of some arbitral tribunals to recognize the public nature of investment treaty arbitration, and to allow States a sufficient margin to determine and implement various policy goals, has contributed to the legitimacy crisis in which the investment treaty system currently finds itself.[9] As investment treaty arbitration involves the review and exercise of governance functions, more attention needs to be paid to standards of review as a crucial mechanism for calibrating the balance of governance powers between States and tribunals.

II. MOVING BEYOND THE COMMERCIAL ARBITRATION PARADIGM

To the extent that investment treaty arbitration is understood as simply another form of international commercial arbitration, the idea of tribunals according deference to one of the disputing parties could be viewed as anathema. A central tenet in international commercial arbitration is "equality of arms" between the disputing parties,[10] while concepts such as "deference" and "standards of review" do not even appear in the main international commercial arbitration treatises and awards.[11] Understanding why deferential standards of review are alien to international commercial arbitration yet central to investment treaty arbitration requires an appreciation of the differences between these systems.

---

8. Santiago MONTT, *State Liability in Investment Treaty Arbitration: Global Constitutional and Administrative Law in the BIT Generation* (Hart Publishing 2009) p. 15.
9. Michael WAIBEL, Asha KAUSHAL, Kyo-Hwa Liz CHUNG and Claire BALCHIN, eds., *The Backlash Against Investment Arbitration: Perceptions and Reality* (Kluwer Law International 2010).
10. Thomas W. WALDE, "Procedural Challenges in Investment Arbitration Under the Shadow of the Dual Role of the State: Asymmetries and Tribunals' Duty to Ensure, Pro-actively, the Equality of Arms", 26 Arbitration International (2010) p. 3; Thomas W. WALDE, "'Equality of Arms' in Investment Arbitration: Procedural Challenges" in Katia YANNACA-SMALL, ed., *Arbitration Under International Investment Agreements: A Guide to the Key Issues* (Oxford University Press 2010) p. 161.
11. Stephan W. SCHILL, "Rethinking the Substantive Standards of Protection Under Investment Treaties: How Much Deference Should Investment Treaty Tribunals Pay to the Regulatory or Judicial Acts of Host States?" in *Flaws and Presumptions: Rethinking Arbitration Law and Practice in a New Arbitral Seat: The Proceedings of the Mauritius International Arbitration Conference 2010* (forthcoming, 2012).

International commercial arbitration is a form of private dispute resolution between private parties concerning their private rights and obligations only. The disputing parties are treated as equals – both substantively in terms of their contractual relations (equal contracting parties) and procedurally in terms of their dispute resolution status (equal disputing parties). This is true even when one party is a State as States are generally considered to be acting in their private capacities when they enter into and breach commercial contracts. International commercial arbitral tribunals are thus called upon to resolve private contractual disputes rather than to adjudicate upon public governance functions. Their awards tend to remain confidential and thus are unlikely to form a body of persuasive precedents as to the meaning of common obligations. As a result, international commercial arbitrations generally have a relatively contained effect, directly impacting upon the disputing parties but rarely having significant broader consequences.

Investment treaty arbitration, by contrast, is better understood as a form of public law adjudication because States act in their public capacity when entering into and breaching treaty obligations.[12] Investment treaty disputes often implicate matters of public concern, particularly where liability turns on an underlying regulatory act, the dispute concerns the provision of important public services that have been privatized or contracted out by the government, the claim implicates the appropriate balance between investor rights and other public interests, or the damages claim is large enough to have serious implications for the public purse.[13] As in international commercial arbitration, States and investors are equal disputing parties. But unlike commercial arbitrations, which are based on private contracts entered into by equal contracting parties, the substantive relationship between States and investors underlying the investment treaty system is a hierarchical one of super- and subordination as governor and governed.[14] Investment arbitral tribunals are thus not adjudicating upon the contractual rights and obligations of private parties, but the public obligations of sovereign States.

The governance role of arbitral tribunals also differs between international commercial and investment arbitration. While commercial arbitration often turns on the interpretation of one-off contracts, investment arbitration frequently concerns the interpretation of common treaty terms. The governing law in commercial arbitrations varies considerably, whereas investment treaties are interpreted against and contribute to the creation of public international law. While commercial arbitral awards tend to remain confidential, investment awards frequently become publicly available and are recognized as a subsidiary means for the determination of public international law. All of these factors contribute to investment awards building a body of persuasive precedents

---

12. Gus VAN HARTEN and Martin LOUGHLIN, "Investment Treaty Arbitration as a Species of Global Administrative Law", 17 European Journal of International Law (2006) p. 121; Gus VAN HARTEN, *Investment Treaty Arbitration and Public Law* (Oxford University Press 2007) pp. 45-71.

13. See generally José E. ALVAREZ, Book Review: *Investment Treaty Arbitration and Public Law*, 102 American Journal of International Law (2008) p. 909 at pp. 911-912; International Institute for Sustainable Development, "Transparency in Investor-State Arbitration", p. 3 (draft paper on file with author).

14. Stephan W. SCHILL, "International Investment Law and Comparative Public Law: An Introduction" in Stephan W. SCHILL, ed., *International Investment Law and Comparative Public Law* (Oxford University Press 2010) p. 3 at p. 15

that provide shape and contours to investment treaty law in a way that is not replicated in the commercial arbitration field. Instead of simply passively finding and applying the law, investment treaty tribunals are "actors in their own right who impact, concretize and further develop international investment law through their jurisprudence".[15] In these ways, investment arbitral tribunals not only review governance functions, but also engage in governance through their own role in law creation.

III. CALLS FOR JUDICIAL RESTRAINT UNDER THE PUBLIC LAW PARADIGM

If both States and investment arbitral tribunals play a role in governance, it becomes important to consider how governance powers are and should be shared between them. Should investment tribunals subject governmental regulations to in-depth de novo review or should they accord governments some level of deference or a margin of appreciation in which to act? To what extent should investment tribunals be interventionist and prepared to substitute their view of good governance and appropriate public policy for that of respondent States and to what extent should they exercise judicial restraint? From those who view investment treaty arbitration as a form of public law adjudication instead of private dispute resolution, we can expect to hear increasing calls for investment arbitral tribunals to embrace deferential standards of review based on analogies with domestic public law and international human rights and trade adjudication.

Some contend that investment tribunals are performing a judicial review function analogous to that performed by domestic courts and, accordingly, appropriate guidance on standards of review should be drawn from a comparative public law approach.[16] Stephan Schill, for example, argues that investment tribunals should exercise some deference to the regulatory actions of defendant States as "courts in virtually all domestic legal orders exercise some degree of deference *vis-à-vis* the acts of the legislator and acts of domestic regulatory agencies".[17] Domestic systems frequently recognize different levels of scrutiny – such as strict scrutiny, intermediate scrutiny and rational basis review – with the appropriate level for a particular case depending on a number of factors, including the nature of the individual right, the purpose of the governmental measure and the relative expertise of the governmental decision-makers and adjudicatory body tasked with reviewing its decision

Others, such as William Burke-White and Andreas von Staden, call for deferential standards of review by investment tribunals based on comparisons with international adjudication in other areas, such as trade and human rights.[18] Unlike the domestic context, where standards of review concern the allocation of law-making power between

15. S.W. SCHILL, *op. cit.*, fn. 11.

16. *Ibid.*; S. MONTT, *op. cit.*, fn. 8, pp. 22-23.

17. S.W. SCHILL, *op. cit.*, fn. 11.

18. William W. BURKE-WHITE and Andreas VON STADEN, "Private Litigation in the Public Law Sphere: The Standard of Review in Investor-State Arbitrations", 35 Yale Journal of International Law (2010) p. 284.

different arms of government, review standards in the international context concern the allocation of authority between States and international tribunals. Such deference may be particularly appropriate where, as in the investment, human rights and trade contexts, adjudicatory bodies are asked to review domestic regulations and actions occurring within a State's borders.

In the trade context, the GATT and WTO Agreements contain no express provision on general standards of review, but the Appellate Body has prescribed a standard based on the requirement in Art. 11 of the Dispute Settlement Understanding that panels make an "objective assessment" of the matters before them.[19] Recognizing that the standard of review adopted "must reflect the balance established ... between the jurisdictional competences conceded by the Members to the WTO and the jurisdictional competences retained by the Members for themselves",[20] the Appellate Body endorsed a middle level of review that did not amount to either de novo review (where the panel could substitute its findings for those of national authorities) or total deference (where the panel totally deferred to the findings of national authorities).[21]

In the human rights context, the European Convention on Human Rights also contains no express provision on review standards, but the European Court of Human Rights has developed the margin of appreciation doctrine for assessing governmental conduct. This doctrine embodies two principles: *judicial deference*, meaning that international tribunals should exercise a certain degree of judicial restraint when evaluating the actions of national authorities, giving some deference to their decisions rather than undertaking full, de novo evaluations; and *normative flexibility*, meaning that some international norms are sufficiently open-ended or uncertain that they can be met in a variety of ways, giving States a certain "zone of legality" in which they are free to act.[22]

---

19. WTO European Communities—Measures Concerning Meat and Meat Products, Appellate Body Report (13 Feb. 1998) WT/DS26/AB/R, paras. 116, 118-119.
20. *Ibid.*, para. 115.
21. See generally Stefan ZLEPTNIG, "The Standard of Review in WTO Law: An Analysis of Law, Legitimacy and the Distribution of Legal and Political Authority", 6 European Integration Online Papers (no. 17); Mads ANDENAS and Stefan ZLEPTNIG, "Proportionality and Balancing in WTO Law: A Comparative Perspective", East Asian International Economic Law & Policy Programme, Policy Paper No. 2 (Nov. 2006); Matthias OESCH, *Standards of Review in WTO Dispute Resolution* (Oxford University Press 2004); James P. DURLING, "Deference, But Only When Due: WTO Review of Anti-Dumping Measures", 6 Journal of International Economic Law (2003) p. 125; Steven P. CROLEY and John H. JACKSON, "WTO Dispute Procedures, Standard of Review, and Deference to National Governments", 90 American Journal of International Law (1996) p. 194; Claus-Dieter EHLERMANN and Nicolas LOCKHART, "Standard of Review in WTO Law", 7 Journal of International Economic Law (2004) p. 493; Michael M. DU, "Standard of Review Under the SPS Agreement After EC-Hormones II", 59 International & Comparative Law Quarterly (2010) p. 441.
22. Yuval SHANY, "Toward a General Margin of Appreciation Doctrine in International Law", 16 European Journal of International Law (2005) p. 907 at pp. 909-910.

IV. THE APPROPRIATENESS AND LIMITS OF THE PUBLIC LAW PARADIGM

Some are likely to reject outright the public law paradigm and calls for judicial restraint or deference. For example, during discussions following this panel, certain audience members raised the following objections:

– How could investment tribunals exercise deference in the face of a State expropriating an investor's property as that would result in a State being found not liable, which goes against the very purpose of investment treaties, i.e., to protect foreign investments? This question confuses judicial restraint and deferential standards of review with the absence of review. Investment tribunals can exercise judicial restraint and still find States liable in appropriate cases – as, indeed, do many domestic and international courts. Most cases these days do not fall into the clear-cut category of direct expropriations, where there may be little room for deference, but instead turn on harder to define standards, such as indirect expropriation and fair and equitable treatment. The latter will often require an assessment of governmental policies and regulations, in which deferential standards of review may be particularly appropriate. And while investment treaties are designed to protect the interests of foreign investors in order to promote foreign investment, this policy goal was not designed to trump all other public policy goals.

– Where do these standards of review come from given that they are not expressly set forth in the investment treaties? As a general matter, neither strict nor deferential standards of review are prescribed in investment treaties. There are exceptions, such as self-judging clauses that require arbitral tribunals to not enquire into certain determinations or to assess them against a relatively low threshold of good faith. But, outside these provisions, any court or tribunal called to adjudicate upon governmental functions must have some conception of the standard they are employing as this is part of the judicial function. Numerous international courts and tribunals (including the European Court of Human Rights and the WTO Appellate Body) have established deferential standards of review when adjudicating upon governmental conduct without standards of review or deference being explicitly addressed in their underlying treaties. Instead, deference is seen as a mechanism for ensuring the appropriate balance of governance powers between States and international courts and tribunals.

– Is the public law paradigm appropriate given that investment tribunals merely award damages and do not strike down governmental legislation or regulation? As is evident from the reaction of States that are parties to investment treaties, States do not view investment arbitral awards as not impacting upon their sovereignty merely because the remedy awarded is generally damages. The possibility of future investor claims could have a chilling effect on governmental conduct by preventing governments from adopting certain courses of action for fear of future liability.[23] And where damages are awarded, this follows from a judgment that a State is responsible for having violated its public treaty obligations. Thus damages awards implicitly involve judicial review, which

23. G. VAN HARTEN and M. LOUGHLIN, *op. cit.*, fn. 12, p. 131.

explains why other domestic and international regimes view damages actions arising out of governmental conduct as a form of State or public law liability.[24]

– Could it be that deferential standards of review might be appropriate for *standing* international courts and tribunals whilst being inappropriate for ad hoc investment treaty tribunals? The ad hoc or standing nature of a tribunal does not change the fact that it must decide how interventionist or deferential to be in reviewing governmental conduct in the case before it. Ad hoc awards are only binding on the disputing parties, as is the case with the decisions of many standing international courts.[25] But, as with other international judgments, there is an established pattern of these awards becoming public and contributing to an emerging jurisprudence about the meaning of investment treaty provisions, which means that awards may have effects far beyond the individual case. And while the ad hoc nature of arbitral tribunals would make attempts to formulate a coherent approach to standards of review more difficult, a general approach could still be developed just as certain levels of agreement are coalescing around substantive standards and procedural questions within the investment treaty field.

However, even if one accepts that the investment treaty system establishes a system of public law adjudication, one may still have questions about the appropriateness and limits of the public law analogy with respect to deferential review standards. From this perspective, I raise the following concerns.

First, the domestic justification for deferential standards of review is derived from and justified by the constitutional law concept of separation of powers. For example, domestic courts exercise deference to the acts of the legislature where the latter is better placed to represent the will of the demos. But to what extent is this rationale applicable in relations between States and international tribunals? Certainly, investment tribunals lack strong claims to democratic legitimacy,[26] but so do many of the States that appear before them as respondents. Is this justification for deferential review applicable when dealing with States that are not robust democracies? If not, would deference result in a differential approach that subjected some States to intense scrutiny and others to mild review according to their internal political structure? Such an approach would play into concerns about investment treaty arbitration applying different standards to Western and non-Western States and sits awkwardly with the traditional public international law approach of treating all States as equal regardless of their internal political constitution.

Second, even when dealing with robust democracies, is the rationale for deference applicable when investment treaties are designed to protect foreign investors who may not be adequately protected through domestic political processes? In *SD Myers*, the tribunal noted that it did not have an "open-ended mandate to second-guess government

24. S. MONTT, *op. cit.*, fn. 8, pp. 137-138; G. VAN HARTEN and M. LOUGHLIN, *op. cit.*, fn. 12, pp. 131-133.

25. See, e.g., Statute of the International Court of Justice, Arts. 38(1)(d) and 59. On the role of international courts in developing international law, see Alan BOYLE and Christine CHINKIN, *The Making of International Law* (Oxford University Press, Oxford 2007) p. 268.

26. S. MONTT, *op. cit.*, fn. 8, pp. 127, 133-137.

decision-making" because governments have to make many potentially controversial choices and the "ordinary remedy ... for errors in modern governments is through internal political and legal processes, including elections".[27] But domestic courts, particularly constitutional courts, often play a role in protecting minority rights that might otherwise be infringed by legislative and executive action under the sway of majoritarian politics. Should investment tribunals defer to legislative acts on the basis that the legislature better reflects the wishes of the majority of the host State's population, or should they act like constitutional courts tasked with ensuring that investor rights, like minority rights, are protected from majoritarian wishes?

Third, are the justifications offered for deference appropriate in the investment treaty context? For instance, Burke-White and von Staden argue that investment tribunals should exercise deference because arbitrators rarely have public law expertise (so they lack institutional capacity when adjudicating upon public law issues) and are not embedded within the national environment in which these decisions are made (so they lack a full appreciation of the dispute's context and their decisions may be viewed as illegitimate by and within the host State).[28] But respondent States may be well versed in public law issues without having expertise in whether their actions offend investment treaty protections. In such cases, respondent States and investment tribunals have different areas of expertise, making it difficult to apply a concept of deference when a finding of liability requires domestic policy goals and international legal protections to be weighed. And having arbitrators that are not embedded within the national context may be important in ensuring disinterested adjudication and protecting the rights of foreigners that might not be particularly valued within the national environment.

Finally, the issue of deference is complicated by the dual roles that States play as treaty parties and sovereigns, on the one hand, and respondents, on the other hand.[29] Host States and investors have a hierarchical substantive relationship (as between governor and governed) but a horizontal procedural relationship (as between equal disputing parties). Investment tribunals are both agents of the treaty parties in one sense, suggesting a subordinate role to these States, and trustees charged with impartially adjudicating upon the merits of investor-State disputes, suggesting a superior role to respondent States.[30] There are strong arguments for investment tribunals according sovereign States some measure of deference, particularly when it comes to adjudicating upon governmental decision-making. But States may wish to pursue their own interests without being found liable in investor-State disputes, which may make them less than impartial when striking a balance between investor rights and other interests and concluding that their actions are in accordance with their international legal obligations. Calls for deference, then,

27. *SD Myers Inc v. Canada*, UNCITRAL/NAFTA, First Partial Award (13 Nov. 2000) para. 261.

28. W.W. BURKE-WHITE and A. VON STADEN, *op. cit.*, fn. 18, pp. 329-333.

29. A. ROBERTS, *op. cit.*, fn. 5.

30. *Ibid.*, pp. 185-187. On the differences between delegating to agents and trustees, see Karen J. ALTER, "Agents or Trustees? International Courts in Their Political Context", 14 European Journal of International Relations (2008) p. 33 at pp. 38-39; Karen J. ALTER, "Delegation to International Courts and the Limits of Re-contracting Political Power" in Darren G. HAWKINS, David A. LAKE, Daniel L. NIELSON and Michael J. TIERNEY, eds., *Delegation and Agency in International Organizations* (Cambridge University Press 2006) p. 312 at pp. 326-329.

must be tempered by the need for procedural equality between the disputing parties, protection of previously agreed upon investor rights and impartial decision-making by investment tribunals.

V. CONCLUSION

As investment treaty arbitration comes to be understood as a form of public law adjudication, we can expect to see an increasing focus on standards of review as a key mechanism through which the balance of interpretive power between States and arbitral tribunals is calibrated. Walking this tightrope will be difficult. If investment arbitral tribunals afford too much deference to States, they are likely to undermine the utility of investment protections from the perspective of investors, which may compromise some of the system's essential aims. If they afford States too little deference, investment tribunals are likely to undermine their own legitimacy in the eyes of States, which may pose a threat to the continuation of the investment treaty system. Attempts by States to adjust this balance represent part of the current process of destabilization that Alvarez has identified, but these efforts will hopefully lead to a new – and better – equilibrium of power in the future.

The Future –

What Will Change?

Round Table*

Gabrielle Kaufmann-Kohler: I hope you all had a good lunch. Now that we have dealt with where we are this morning, we will move on to where we are going, to the future; obviously we touched on the future this morning already.

We will structure the debate around two propositions about changes that the future may bring. For each proposition there will be one or two proponents who will set out their views about the evolution, and others will then comment.

Once we have dealt with the two propositions, we will open the floor discussion and you will be able to ask questions or make your own comments about both propositions at the same time.

We will then end the debate with a question: How should ICCA address the changes that will have been identified?

This morning we introduced the speakers by simply referring you to the CVs in the materials. This afternoon, I will briefly introduce the different panellists by drawing your attention to the special expertise of each one, because this is why they were chosen to contribute to our debate, with a view to giving as wide a picture as possible about the future.

Guillermo Aguilar Alvarez is with King & Spalding. He was the principal legal counsel to the government of Mexico for the negotiation and implementation of NAFTA [North American Free Trade Agreement] and other free trade agreements. It is this perspective from the government that we will be interested in.

Karl-Heinz Böckstiegel obviously needs no introduction. He is presently Chairman of DIS [*Deutsche Institution für Schiedsgerichtsbarkeit* – German Institution of Arbitration]. A lot could be said about him. Let me stress today that he will contribute from his very broad and long-standing experience and expertise in both commercial and investment arbitration, as we will cover both types of arbitration.

Justice Croft has practiced extensively commercial law and was an arbitrator and mediator. Now – and this is the reason why we are interested in his views – he is in charge of international and domestic arbitration in the Supreme Court of Victoria, Australia. He will tell you about his experience in a specialized arbitration court and what influence the existence of a specialized court may have on the evolution of arbitration.

Chris Drahozal is a professor at the University of Kansas Law School and an associate reporter for the Restatement of US arbitration law. He has published a number of empirical studies on commercial arbitration. This is the area on which we would like to hear him in particular.

Peter Goldsmith is presently with Debevoise & Plimpton in London. We are interested in his views because previously he was the Attorney General for the United Kingdom. He will thus bring a state perspective to the debate.

By contrast, Beat Hess was, until earlier this year, the Legal Director and a member of the Group Executive Committee of Shell. Prior to that, he was General Counsel of

* Verbatim transcript of Briault Reporting Suisse SARL.

ABB and he is presently on the board of Nestlé. He obviously will contribute a business perspective to this debate.

Catherine Kessedjian is a professor at University of Paris II. She is also Global Professor at New York University. She has written extensively about the issues that we will discuss. She is known for voicing critical views, not mainstream views; that is what we would like to hear this afternoon.

Campbell McLachlan is a professor at Victoria University of Wellington and an arbitrator. He is well known for his publications in private international law, commercial arbitration and investment law as well. He will contribute his very broad perspective that spans over private and public law.

Renaud Sorieul is a Director of the UN Office of Legal Affairs and the Secretary of UNCITRAL, which he joined in 1989. He has a long-standing experience of the works of UNCITRAL and we are interested in knowing how UNCITRAL sees the evolution from its unique platform.

Ariel Ye is with King & Wood in Beijing. She has twenty years of experience in PRC litigation and arbitration. She will bring to the debate an Asian or more specifically Chinese perspective, in the awareness that the world is changing and that international arbitration must integrate the views and the demands of emerging countries.

Having said that, I would suggest that we now turn to the debate and to our first proposition. The first proposition deals with the actors of arbitration. Among the actors, we will focus on the users. While other actors – arbitrators, institutions, courts – are involved as well, arbitration is here to meet the needs of the users. The first proposition is rather general: The needs and expectations of the users of arbitration are changing.

The first proponent will be Guillermo. Guillermo will speak about the needs and expectations of states from his governmental perspective. We have heard this morning about re-calibration of the demands or re-balancing, and that is what we would like to further explore now. Guillermo, you have the floor.

Guillermo Aguilar Alvarez: Thank you, Gabrielle. Generally speaking, states can only be respondents to investment arbitration cases. States win cases by not losing them. However, without the consent of the states to submit investment disputes to arbitration, there would be no investment arbitration and we would be back to the years when ICCA was founded, to the times of diplomatic protection and the Calvo doctrine.

Proposition number 1 focuses on the perception among some states that arbitrators chosen from the international commercial arbitration bar have a natural tendency to side with the investor.

The question I ask is whether the problem is really with the arbitrators and whether we should not take a look at rules that the arbitrators interpret and apply. The reason I ask this question is because some countries appear to have a better track record defending investment arbitration cases with arbitrators that are largely drawn from exactly the same pool of international commercial arbitrators. So, I think it behoves upon us to ask ourselves how that legal norm that arbitrators apply is developed. I would submit that there appears to be a correlation between the intensity with which those legal norms are negotiated by the sovereigns and balance in the outcome of cases.

Let me use NAFTA as an example. The blueprint for the negotiation of NAFTA was the US Argentina bilateral investment treaty (BIT) which had been signed roughly as we were getting ready to wrap up the NAFTA negotiations. It was heavily negotiated and eventually became Chapter 11 of the NAFTA. If you compare the two texts, you will notice that there are some significant differences. I will refer to some of those differences just as an example.

The definition of investment is a *numerus clausus*. It is not an including definition. The definition of investment tells you what does not constitute an investment, for example short-term debt. There is no umbrella clause. The state may consolidate in one arbitration different cases that arise out of the same measure, placing investors in a difficult position and avoiding harassment by litigation. Lastly, but most importantly, the State Parties preserve the authority to interpret the NAFTA and the NAFTA provides that interpretations by the State Parties are binding on arbitration tribunals.

This was the NAFTA party's response to the risk that the ebb and flow of arbitral wisdom would not put fences around some of the more generally defined standards in NAFTA. Again, this was the State Party's response and there was no discussion of deference to the state in the exercise of its regulatory authority.

What else can the states do to preserve the system? Some states see these treaties as a very useful internal tool to freeze certain market economy policies and avoid their modification by subsequent political change. Other states judge the system by keeping score of wins and losses. That, of course, fuels opposition by local constituencies and the kind of backlash that we talked about this morning.

Looking ahead, long-term sustainability of the system may be compromised but I would submit that pressure is coming from the quality and the definition of the rules rather than from their application by arbitrators as drafted, and that pressure is also coming from the degree of support that the system gets from the states, both capital importing and capital exporting.

That is proposition number 1.

Gabrielle Kaufmann-Kohler: Beat, would you like to supplement the proposition as a second proponent, but now from the standpoint of the needs of business?

Beat Hess: I am probably a strange animal here, representing the oil and gas industry. I have been told that I have a maximum of five minutes to talk. That is already a challenge after lunch – to keep the audience awake for five minutes! I will do my best.

Of course, almost all of my forty years as in-house counsel in the energy business, I was much confronted with arbitration, first as general counsel of ABB and later as general counsel of Shell, and as a member of the Executive Committee.

If you allow me, I will just share a few thoughts of what the big-ticket litigation and arbitration issues are in our industry and then also what kept me awake at night when I was involved in arbitration.

First, just a few words about the big-ticket litigation issues. There is oil and gas in the ground for the next 300 years. So, don't worry, there is enough around! That means that the oil and gas industry in particular will continue with heavy investments and big projects.

For example, Shell invests about US$ 35-40 billion every year in exploration activities or you have plants that are in the US$ 20-30 billion project cost. We have one in Qatar where we manage in-house 2,500 contracts and I can assure you that many of these contracts will run into disputes and will end up in arbitration. So, there is a huge potential for arbitration around large projects. That is really the first area of big-ticket issues under arbitration.

The second is a very serious one. I call it local legal instability. I have observed over the last few years an increasing disrespect for the rule of law and the old Roman principle of *pacta sunt servanda* seems no longer to exist in many parts of the world. So, of course, investment arbitration has become very popular and what we call stability clauses in our contracts have become increasingly popular topics of our arbitration issues.

Our business is a very long-term business. So, stability of the legal environment is absolutely key. We will know in ten, fifteen, twenty years from now whether what we invest today – US$ 10-20 billion in a project – was a good investment. So, we really have to be able to rely on a stable legal environment.

If you are in the lollipop business, you can just pack up and go. If you are in the oil and gas business certain rulers will tell you, "You know what, Shell or Exxon, the oil is here", and sooner than you would like to you end up in investment arbitration.

The third big-ticket issue that I want to mention that will increasingly be in arbitration is technology and licensing of technology. In our business, we say the easy oil is gone or will soon be gone. So, exploration activities become more and more sophisticated and complex. For example, we measure the behaviour of waves in the Gulf of Mexico by satellite and conclude on the long-term behaviour of waves whether there is oil or not or we send nanobots into reservoirs and measure reservoirs so that we know the exact extent.

Of course, there are many other topics. I mentioned just three now. I heard this morning that environmental matters might be dragged into investment arbitration, and human rights matters might be dragged into investment arbitration. Well, if that happens, I can tell you, who are in the arbitration business, you will have Christmas every day again, there will be a lot of arbitration activity going on and large companies will fight it tooth and nail.

I should probably stop right here and tell you a bit later what, in this arbitration environment, kept me and actually still keeps me awake at night. That will be the second part.

Gabrielle Kaufmann-Kohler: Would you not want to say now what kept you awake at night? It would allow others to react right away.

Beat Hess: I can say right now what kept me awake at night. Of course, first is the quality of the arbitrators. I have been involved in dozens of arbitrations, both in ABB and Shell, and it always amazed me how big the difference between arbitrators can be. What we need in our environment is arbitrators who understand a large global business, understand the inner workings of a large global company and understand how a large global company is ticking.

The second issue is clarity of procedural rules and guidance by the tribunal and counsel, of course, where the rules are unclear. I have often encountered hesitation, for example, from the corner of the chair of an arbitration tribunal to give clear guidance on the proceedings.

The third issue is speed, speed, speed. Large global companies – probably I should not say that and you should forget it right away – are not worried about the cost of arbitration. So, forget that. Please do not quote me. But they are worried about clarity, they are worried about speed, they are worried about headlines, about reports around the arbitration and they are certainly worried about reputation. Whether you are in a normal court or in arbitration, bad headlines around the case are not what large companies want to have.

Then, together with speed, I have observed an increasing creeping up of practices that we really dislike and that is the whole issue of discovery. And today as we are in the electronic world, electronic discovery. We send out document preservation notices, very sophisticated. I have observed that we are not far away, in many arbitration cases, from US-style – no offence to our American friends here – discovery procedures. We do not want that. We think that civil countries with a civil law background have other rules of evidence, you cannot just compare the two systems, and we are very reluctant and hesitant to accept this style of discovery.

Fifth –

Gabrielle Kaufmann-Kohler: Is the further point also on procedure? If this is so, we could move it to the second proposition? As for the discovery part, I think you will get a lot of support here.

Beat Hess: The other part is about enforceability.

Gabrielle Kaufmann-Kohler: Then we can move this to the second proposition that deals with the proceedings.

Beat Hess: Let's stop here, then.

Gabrielle Kaufmann-Kohler: Thank you so much. There was a lot contained in these two expositions of the first proposition.

Reactions? Peter, would you like to react more from a government perspective?

Lord Goldsmith QC: Thank you. Normally I like to start a presentation with a joke. Beat, you had five minutes; I have three. So, that will have to do for the joke – and there is a risk that, if I don't get on, that will have to do for my three minutes as well!

The perspectives that I wanted to bring to this are partly my experience in government, though, of course, coming from the United Kingdom – which is a capital-exporting country rather than a capital-importing country – it has a very different perspective on investment arbitration. Together with Eduardo Silva Romero – who I think is in the audience – I have been chairing a task force on state and state entities arbitration in the International Chamber of Commerce [ICC]. That has given us some insight particularly into the way that states view arbitration. It is in the context of a particular institution but I think some of the lessons from it are relevant.

I want to use that to comment on some of the points that have been made in the proposition. There are really five points I want to make.

First of all, it is a mistake for us to think that states are only involved in arbitration in investment disputes, whether it is treaty or bilateral or multilateral or domestic laws which have investment rules. If you take the ICC, not surprisingly, when we did a statistical analysis of the number of cases in which states and state entities have been involved, the vast majority of the cases – and there were quite a number, over 500 in the period we looked at, which I think was twenty years – were, of course, commercial cases and not investment arbitration cases, because the ICC is not the natural place for those to be dealt with. There were some investment treaty cases but predominantly they were commercial disputes. So I think it is very important, when one is considering a government's response, that it is not simply from the investment point of view. They have an interest, as others do, in the proper working of commercial arbitration in relation to construction contracts, long-term supply contracts and those other areas.

Second – we touched on the arbitral process – states, we discovered, so we believe from the researches we did, do have particular issues with the way that arbitrators may be appointed. Jan Paulsson, who is here and, indeed, other chairmen, may not like it being said that they are more interested in being able to choose their own arbitrators than having anyone else, including an arbitral institution, choose them. So, we had discussions which we have looked at in the context of the ICC rules of default appointments and appointments of chairpersons of tribunals – the issues which states have about how much confidence they have in arbitrators who are appointed, for example, on the recommendation of a national committee or have come from countries where they may think that the cultural and legal background is not the same. That gives rise to a special issue about arbitrators.

Third, there are special problems always for states because of the public nature of the work that they do and it gives rise, we have discovered, to particular areas like confidentiality, which is a double-edged sword as far as states are concerned. On the one hand sometimes they quite like having their disputes dealt with behind closed doors. Sometimes, on the other hand, as they clamour for their tax payers and for others to know what is going on, which confidentiality can give rise to, there are issues about the involvement of others in cases in which the states are involved. That gives rise, for example, to the question of should amicus briefs be possible because there are issues of public interest. It gives rise to issues in relation to the transparency of challenges to arbitrators and the reasons that are given for them where states may have to do more in terms of explaining to the public why someone has decided something against them where there were issues about that person's impartiality.

Fourth, there are issues in relation to emergency procedures. We think states would have much more concern about arbitral institutions having the ability effectively to provide interim measures, particularly in the context of investment cases. It is an inconvenience for commercial parties to have to go to court because an arbitral tribunal has not been composed. It may make it impossible in state cases actually to achieve any interim measures in those circumstances.

Finally, because I want to stick to my brief, I just want to pick up the point that Beat made about speed, simply to say that I think this may well be an area where, because on the whole states tend more often to be respondents, even in commercial cases, than claimants, they may be less concerned about speed than others. Indeed, there is a general perception that defendants in litigation and arbitration are surprisingly unenthusiastic about getting to the end result unless there are reasons like a clog on a balance sheet (which does not affect states) or a need to merge with another company which, save in certain specific federalist circumstances, do not apply to states as well.

I will stop at that moment.

Gabrielle Kaufmann-Kohler: Chris, would you like to comment? You have written about the "flight from arbitration"; what about the flight from arbitration and any other thoughts that may be inspired by what was said?

Christopher R. Drahozal: Certainly. There have been some suggestions, although we have not heard them today, that there is a "flight" from arbitration, not just domestically in the United States but also internationally. The suggestion is that users have become fed up with some things about arbitration and have decided to move away from it. I have a few empirical comments on that point.[1]

One way you might measure flight is by looking at the number of case filings. If that is the measure you use, in recent years arbitration has been a resounding success. Lumping together the filings for a number of arbitration institutions, total case filings increased by over 60 per cent between 2005 and 2009, although they dropped off a little bit in 2010.[2]

The problem with that measure, of course, is that it is affected by factors other than simply how users perceive arbitration. In this case, an increase in the number of disputes is likely causing the increase in filings. With the financial crisis, the economic downturn and so forth, it is not surprising that the number of disputes would go up, even if parties were becoming dissatisfied with arbitration. So, the number of cases filed is not a great measure.

A better measure, from my perspective, would be to look at the actual use of arbitration clauses in contracts and to see how that has changed.

The phrase "flight from arbitration" comes from a paper by a couple of American law professors, Ted Eisenberg and Geoff Miller, who found, in their words, a "surprisingly low" use of arbitration clauses in international contracts.[3] Barely twenty per cent of the international contracts they studied included arbitration clauses. It turns out that those results are driven largely by the sample of contracts they looked at; they got their data from US securities law filings, which means they were looking at things like merger agreements, complex financing arrangements and so forth, contracts that usually you would not expect to have arbitration clauses. So, it really is not that surprising, to me, anyway, that they found a low use of arbitration clauses.

Others have picked up on their study and ultimately concluded – incorrectly – that arbitration just cannot compete any more. To actually evaluate that question (this is

1. For more detailed discussion, see Christopher R. DRAHOZAL, "Disenchanted? Business Satisfaction with International Arbitration", 2 World Arb. & Med. Rev. (2008, no. 5) p. 1.
2. See Hong Kong International Arbitration Centre, "Statistics", at <www.hkiac.org/show_content.php?article_id=9> (last accessed 8 June 2011).
3. Theodore EISENBERG and Geoffrey P. MILLER, "The Flight from Arbitration: An Empirical Study of Ex Ante Arbitration Clauses in the Contracts of Publicly Held Companies", 56 DePaul L. Rev. (2007) p. 335.

really a call for data) it would be nice to be able to find similar samples of a broader array of international contracts. We cannot just look at contracts in cases that have been filed with arbitration institutions because, by definition, those contracts almost always have arbitration clauses. To measure the flight from arbitration, if any, we need some sort of base line and right now we do not really have that.

The main thing we have now is surveys. Queen Mary does its biannual survey (first with Pricewaterhouse, now with White & Case).[4] In 2008 the survey found what it described as a high degree of satisfaction with arbitration, which immediately led to choruses of protests from corporate counsel who were not so well satisfied.

Actually, I think the numbers from the survey itself are not that overwhelming. Most of the respondents were corporate counsel who were "fairly satisfied", not "very satisfied", with arbitration. The respondents were not "disappointed" but they were only fairly satisfied, suggesting to me kind of a lukewarm response.

To follow up on Beat's comment, one of the criticisms of arbitration reported in the Queen Mary surveys was that it was too slow; the respondents were concerned about the speed of the process. I will say, though, that the number one criticism was expense. So, maybe those doing the survey did not talk to in-house counsel at oil companies.

At some point, disenchantment with arbitration can turn into flight; if people get too fed up with arbitration, they may decide to move away from arbitration all together.

Finally, let me offer one friendly amendment, perhaps, to proposition 1. What we are discussing here are the expectations of users. But it seems to me we should also look at the expectations of potential users, people who are not using arbitration now but who might.

A co-author and I did a study of franchisors in the United States where there had been reports of a flight from arbitration.[5] We found that, in fact, looking at contracts, yes, there were franchisors who had stopped using arbitration. But we also found that other franchisors which had not previously used arbitration had now started using it. Essentially, it was a wash – there had been a change in the composition of the franchisors using arbitration but the overall use of arbitration clauses had not changed.

I hope we would consider ways not just to keep people who currently use arbitration satisfied with the process or to make them more satisfied but also to see if there are ways we can make people who do not use arbitration currently perhaps more interested in doing so.

---

4. School of International Arbitration, Queen Mary, University of London and White & Case, *2010 International Arbitration Survey: Choices in International Arbitration*, available at <http://www.arbitrationonline.org/docs/2010_InternationalArbitrationSurveyReport.pdf> (last accessed 8 June 2011); School of International Arbitration, Queen Mary, University of London and PricewaterhouseCoopers, *International Arbitration: Corporate Attitudes and Practices 2008*, available at <www.arbitrationonline.org/docs/IAstudy_2008.pdf> (last accessed 8 June 2011); School of International Arbitration, Queen Mary, University of London and PricewaterhouseCoopers, *International Arbitration: Corporate Attitudes and Practices 2006*, available at <www.arbitrationonline.org/docs/IAstudy_2006.pdf> (last accessed 8 June 2011).
5. Christopher R. DRAHOZAL and Quentin R. WITTROCK, "Is There a Flight from Arbitration?", 37 Hofstra L. Rev. (2008) p. 71.

Gabrielle Kaufmann-Kohler: Thanks. Ariel, would you like to tell us how the needs are seen from your part of the world?

Lu Ariel Ye: Yes. Although I had my first international commercial arbitration in 1997, when I was a first-year associate in a state-owned law firm, I would say China is still a newcomer to international commercial arbitration, simply because in the past two or three decades China has been one of the most favoured destinations for foreign investment; that is, an enormous amount of money goes into China. At that stage, most of the joint ventures, almost all the joint venture contracts, have arbitration clauses because of the recommendation of the government. The majority of them are using CIETAC [China International Economic and Trade Arbitration Commission] arbitration.

In the last four or five years, we have also seen an explosion of outbound investments. As a result, there are substantial flows of money both ways, inbound and outbound. Chinese private-owned companies and state-owned companies are aggressively engaging in international expansion.

I will share one story with you which I learned from a friend of one of my clients. He told us that about two years ago he acquired some business from London; he bought a pharmaceutical company and the entire deal closed within one week. He asked the other side's lawyers to draft the documents and he did not hire any lawyer at all to even look at the contract. He just flew to London and presented a cheque of about US$ 40 million followed by a handshake. I did not dare to ask him what kind of a dispute resolution clause he had in the contract! I do not think he would have had an answer to that question.

In recent days, we do see many Chinese companies, when they do business outside China, using international arbitration. We see ICC arbitration, Stockholm arbitration and, very frequently and more and more, Hong Kong arbitration and Singapore arbitration. It is quite common now for a Chinese company, if it does business with its Asian neighbours, to choose Singapore for arbitration. Very often, when Chinese companies are doing business with their business partners outside Asia, initially they insist on CIETAC arbitration and then they settle on Hong Kong arbitration. It is becoming quite common now.

One of the frustrations we have learned from all our Chinese clients is regarding the disclosure or discovery or production of documents. That is something we do not have in our system, that is something CIETAC arbitration does not have, and that is something where Chinese companies experience frustration.

In an AAA [American Arbitration Association] arbitration I had in the year 2005, it was such a burden to produce an enormous amount of documents that the Chinese client withdrew from the case and then received a default award against it, for the sole reason that they could not afford to go through this very painful process of document production.

Or in a Stockholm arbitration, when it came to the production of documents, our clients were asked to produce copies of vouchers and invoices which amounted to 300,000 pages, about thirty-something boxes.

In my view, this type of process does not help to find the truth. Maybe international arbitration tribunals could exercise some sort of control over this to help parties to appreciate whether it is worthwhile engaging in such an exercise or not. To me, 300,000 pages of paper produced and copied and sent over to the other side – which did not look at it – is an environmental disaster.

Gabrielle Kaufmann-Kohler: Some may say that technology may assist here. Nevertheless, I note the environmental disaster caused by document production. Document production is apparently not only an arbitrator's nightmare!

The comments so far have brought to light many aspects; some are recurrent. Let me first highlight the concern about the long-term sustainability. In investment arbitration, the correlation between the wording of the treaty and the outcome clearly has a say in the acceptability of the mechanism.

Then we heard about legal instability and the search for a better implementation of the rule of law. That may have something to do, at least in investment arbitration, with the ad hoc nature of the tribunals and the issue that we discussed this morning – no precedent, no *stare decisis*, no *jurisprudence constante*.

We have heard also about the quality of the arbitrators. That is a point that has been raised by several panellists. The appointment of the arbitrators – who appoints, how, what is expected from a good arbitrator; clarity of the proceedings as well; the same type of search, if you want, as the stability of the legal framework. It is only human nature; human nature wants clear rules and clear guidance.

We heard also about speed, several times from very different angles. We have heard about document production, which we might or might not come back to later on.

Let me see who else wants to react to this initial proposition and comments on proposition 1.

Catherine Kessedjian: As I was listening to what was said at the beginning of this session, I was wondering whether the needs and expectations of the participants, of the users of arbitration, are changing or whether their needs and expectations are exactly the same as they were centuries ago but it is the practice itself which has changed.

Users have a dispute and they want that dispute to be resolved fairly, as rapidly as possible and as inexpensively as possible. I think that is the basic need.

What we have been doing, all of us within the legal profession and those who have been involved in arbitration, is importing more and more in arbitration processes, rules and procedures that, at some stage, were only applied in courts.

As to discovery, when I started arbitration many years ago, we never discussed it because discovery was not used. There was a tacit understanding that it was not to be used. I guess that the founders of ICCA in 1961 did not think about those kind of issues because the practice had not developed then. It is because the practice of arbitration has changed – and I think we lawyers are to be blamed – that we have seen users reacting to what the practice has become in the arbitration world.

My second comment goes to the general concept of "users". I really wonder whether we can speak of users in general, users' needs and expectations in general. We have all witnessed a dramatic increase in the matters for which arbitration is used nowadays, in ways that did not exist before. Arbitration was left to large transactions, big corporations. Nowadays it is not seldom that you face a dispute for a fairly small amount where you wonder why the parties have agreed to arbitrate and whether arbitration is indeed the proper means of dispute resolution.

I think we have to consider all of that before we jump to conclusions that users indeed have different needs and expectations.

Gabrielle Kaufmann-Kohler: Point taken. Karl-Heinz, you wish to comment?

Karl-Heinz Böckstiegel: I would say one word, really. We have heard slightly different comments on the relevance of costs of arbitration. Of course, we are all used to the general statement that arbitration has become too expensive and all of that.

I am looking at Diana and quite a few in this room who were at the IFCAI Conference in Berlin just before this meeting here, where we discussed costs for a day and a half.

Let me make just one point from that Conference. It became clear from the discussion in Berlin that if you look at costs of a case, 82-90 per cent of these costs are for the representation of the parties. That is what you can see from cost claims that come at the end of a procedure. Two to 4 per cent are normally the charges of the institution and then something in the range of 16 to 10 per cent is the fees and costs of the arbitrators.

Therefore, when we are discussing a reduction of costs, we are really, if you want to be relevant, discussing: is it possible to reduce costs for the representation of the parties? As soon as you know that, you start realizing how difficult it will be, because the more complex the procedures become the more the parties will need time and work. I just want to make it clear that this is really the difficult issue in that context.

Thank you.

Gabrielle Kaufmann-Kohler: Are there any other comments on these issues? Are the expectations, are the needs changing? What really strikes me is a point that Catherine flagged. Are the needs and expectations unchanged, namely speed, clarity, maybe costs/maybe not; getting to a resolution according to clear rules in as short a time as possible. Have we distanced ourselves more and more from these unchanged expectations as we went along during the last decades? Is *that* the problem? Let us leave the first proposition with this question and move on.

The second proposition is about the proceedings. We have touched on a number of issues about the proceedings already because it is difficult to draw a very clear line between the different aspects.

The proposition is: The proceedings are changing. Arbitration is moving from a process to a system. What does this mean? Arbitration was an exception to the rule, the rule being judicial dispute resolution. Today it has become the rule and, being the rule, it develops into a system.

Campbell, you are the one to express these ideas.

Campbell McLachlan QC: Thank you very much. In the eight minutes generously allotted to me by Gabrielle, I just want to put before you a single question, which is: Has international arbitration moved from being a process to a system and, if so, what are the implications for the future? That is not simply an academic question. In fact, as I will try to show, it has highly practical implications for the way we might envision our work in the future.

Since we are celebrating here the five-decade anniversary of ICCA, in answering that question I shall divide my answer to that question into five short sections.

Firstly, process. Obviously arbitration as a process, as an alternative form of dispute resolution to a legal system, is at least as old as Justinian, if not older, in both commercial and in inter-state disputes. But I suggest to you that throughout the life of ICCA, the last fifty years, we have been engaged in the progressive unshackling of international arbitration as a process from the control of national legal systems.

In the elegant and erudite written version of this paper which you have in your materials, Professor Reisman describes this as an "anarcho-capitalist fantasy".[6] I am not sure that that view would be entirely accepted by the Supreme Court of Canada who, in the *Dell Computer* case in 2007, found that "[a]rbitration is part of no state's judicial system.... The arbitrator has no allegiance or connection to any single country.... In short, arbitration is a creature that owes its existence to the will of the parties alone."[7]

The truth is that the triple benefits of flexibility, neutrality and enforceability have facilitated the colonizing of whole areas of human activity which we could never have envisioned even on the founding of ICCA. I speak, of course, of investment treaty arbitration but also the very widespread use of arbitration as the predominant means of resolving sports disputes and even, in a ground-breaking way, intra-state peace and boundary disputes – the *Abyei* case before a tribunal constituted under the aegis of the Permanent Court of Arbitration [PCA].[8]

I am not saying that this means that arbitration has no connection with state legal systems; that the seat of the arbitration is irrelevant or that state support and enforcement are not vital to its operation. But the question that I want to put before you as a proposition for discussion is whether the result of this progressive unshackling and this widening of activity has been to create something more than merely a dispute settlement system which is an alternative to a legal system but rather to create a system in itself.

For the second part of the proposition, on "system", what I suggest is that arbitration has, in many fields of international dispute settlement, today become the dominant form of dispute resolution. It has moved from being the exception to the rule. That has also entailed an extension of the core concept of consent on which all arbitration is founded, from the consensus *ad idem* paradigm of the contract to standing consent, as we see in investment treaties; as we see in the sports field; and as we see in many contracts of adhesion, transnational consumer contracts.

The third element of this movement to system is a movement from thinking about arbitration as being purely an exercise in comparative law to seeing arbitration as we very much heard discussed this morning as being an exercise in the elaboration of international rules and principles – guided, of course, by the great pillar of the 1958 New York Convention and also by the work of UNCITRAL and the IBA [International Bar Association].

---

6. Michael REISMAN and Brian RICHARDSON "Tribunals and Courts: an Interpretation of the Architecture of International Commercial Arbitration", this volume, p. 17.
7. *Dell Computer Corp v. Union des consommateurs* 2007 SCC 34, (2007) 284 DLR (4th) 577, [51].
8. *Government of Sudan and The Sudan People's Liberation Movement/Army (the Abyei Arbitration)*, Final Award of 22 July 2009, available at <www.pca-cpa.org/upload/files/Abyei%20Final%20Award.pdf>.

One can see a similar trend in investment treaty arbitration, from the original creation of ICSID [International Centre for Settlement of Investment Disputes], which was designed to be simply a facilitation of a process of arbitration, to the emergence, as José Alvarez suggested to us this morning, through the litigation of treaty disputes of a much more substantively cohesive system, even if there are substantial doctrinal disagreements within it.[9]

That has led to the kind of grand claims made by Emmanuel Gaillard this morning[10] and also by Gary Born, of there being a common corpus of international arbitration law, an *ordre juridique arbitral*.

I do not think we should accept these claims uncritically, whether as an accurate description or normatively as to what the law ought to be; but I do think we need to think a little about what the implications of those claims might actually be.

A third part of the proposition is that "systemic pressures emerge". If we are going to start thinking about arbitration as a system, then it falls to be judged by the ways in which we commonly judge legal systems. These are not simply on measures of efficacy. They are also on measures of legality and "normativity".

In a thought-provoking article just published in the excellent new Journal of International Dispute Settlement by Thomas Schultz from the Graduate Institute here in Geneva,[11] Schultz takes up this idea and pursues the various measures by which we normally assess the rule-of-law status of a legal system. By some of those measures, arbitration struggles somewhat.

For example, as we discussed this morning, if there is no regular means of reporting arbitration awards, how can one operate a system of precedent?

Professor Reisman deals with that by saying therefore we should ascribe a very low law-generative power to arbitral awards. But the question I would ask is that, if large areas of commercial activity have actually been shifted out of judicial systems and are being dealt with predominantly in arbitration, is that really satisfactory? We still need to be able to develop substantive international commercial law.

Second, there is the public law challenge, discussed by José Alvarez in the context of investment arbitration this morning, but very much alive in commercial arbitration as well (for example in the debate about the impact of competition law within commercial arbitration disputes).

Third, there is the pressure for more transparency, which has been a huge element in the investment field.

Fourth, there is the notion of an increasing development of free-standing ethical rules within international arbitration, both for arbitrators and for counsel.

---

9. José E. ALVAREZ, "Is the International Investment Regime a Form of Global Governance?" this volume, pp. 137-160.

10. Emmanuel GAILLARD, "International Arbitration as a Transnational System of Justice", this volume, pp. 66-73.

11. Thomas SCHULTZ "The Concept of Law in Transnational Arbitral Legal Orders and Some of Its Consequences" 2 (2011) JIDS p. 59.

Finally, there is the issue of jurisdictional coordination, *lis pendens* and consolidation, between arbitration tribunals.[12] That is not because a one-size-fits-all approach is going to work. But we need to be concerned with overlap and conflicts between tribunals handling very similar or related disputes.

Those are some of the systemic pressures which I submit that the system is encountering.

Before I close by suggesting some alternative possible routes to the future, I just want to qualify what I have said by just recognizing very briefly some inherent limitations which arise out of the very nature of arbitration itself, all of which will be well known to you.

First, all arbitration is based upon consent. However we seek to broaden that concept, we cannot get away from it.

Second, all arbitration ultimately requires state forebearance and support.

Third, arbitration continuously relies upon national law to provide the content of many of the substantive rules that are applied. Not all of them. After all, the United Nations Convention on Contracts for the International Sale of Goods 1980 [CISG] and other international legal codes have been very substantial and important developments towards greater international uniformity. But still national law has the predominant role in substantive law, at least in commercial arbitration.

Fourth, confidentiality, which is a very important factor in commercial arbitration, acts as a brake upon the emergence of a system of ascertainment and precedent.

Finally, there is the "world-is-flat" notion of arbitration – the horizontality of the system – often expressed in the proposition that tribunals are sovereign. Of course, expressed in that way, this claim is too broad. States are sovereign. Tribunals merely have that power of decision with which the parties have invested them. Nevertheless, they have within that ambit an independent power of decision.

Those are some of the limitations.

What are the alternative routes to the future?

It seems to me that there are three possible ways in which international dispute settlement could go in the future. They are not necessarily mutually exclusive.

The first is increasing fragmentation and specialization. In various ways, I think Catherine Kessedjian and also Renaud Sorieul are going to develop that notion that even within arbitration we are getting increasingly specialized.

The second possibility is that we are in a transition stage towards some kind of international judicialization. After all, that happened in World Trade Law. We moved from a system which was largely arbitration-like for many years under the GATT [General Agreement on Tariffs and Trade] to a full-scale judicial system of standing tribunals. It is happening to some extent in the commercial field as well.

The third possibility, which does not, I think, risk juridification, is simply that we go back to the founding notion of what arbitration was about and the founding concept, indeed, of this Council. That is the notion of the development of common principles which it is both the promise and the responsibility of arbitration to find and elucidate –

12. Campbell MCLACHLAN, *Lis Pendens in International Litigation*, 336 *Recueil des Cours* (2008) 199, Ch. II.

those fundamental rules of procedure which connect arbitration with the much larger concept of due process and which ensure that, so far from being anarchic, it can help to fulfil the enlarged responsibility which it now carries in international dispute resolution.

Thank you very much. [Applause]

Gabrielle Kaufmann-Kohler: No doubt we will come back on a number of your points, especially your three ways ahead, but first of all I would like to give Catherine the floor for her reaction to these proposals.

Catherine Kessedjian: When we were preparing for this panel you asked me to say a few words about the evolution we are facing right now about harmonization, unification and diversity. The kind of developments in the arbitration rules that we are facing is actually quite surprising in a way and perhaps worrisome in another way.

At the same time, I will try to answer or comment on what Campbell just said so eloquently.

First of all, on the concept that we are in a transitory period. It seems to me that we are always in a transitory period. The world is changing, we are changing, our activities are changing. It is the nature of the game. We have to be flexible and, after all, arbitration is about flexibility. We have to adapt what we are doing as arbitrators and as counsel to what the activities in dispute call for.

My second point would be on the arbitration system. It is very fanciful, in a way, to say what Emmanuel Gaillard and others are describing as a self-standing transnational system; I do not think it describes perfectly the system which exists right now.

Right now the world is more complex. Yes, there are a number of rules which have reached a level of uniformity. That is, if we are talking about procedural rules, if we are talking about the process, I have very little difficulty in saying that, indeed, there is an arbitration practice that is developing and that practice is more and more uniform. There are best practices developing and therefore there is a lex arbitri that is more and more transnational. Hence, left to procedural issues, I would accept that proposition.

My concern is about developing this transnational world of arbitration as a privatization of most of the disputes arising in our societies. I stop for a minute to emphasize the plural, "societies". Indeed, I am one of the people who have much difficulty accepting the idea there is only one international community, be it of states or corporations or other bodies or institutions. Particularly in commercial dealings I do not think we have one single community but we have several communities that have to live together and coordinate their activities. What I am worried about is that we probably have not studied enough – empirical studies are difficult, as we heard before – the impact on the development of the substantive legal norm of the trend to privatize dispute resolution. I was talking about procedural on one side; now I am talking about the substantive legal norm. I think by increasingly privatizing our dispute resolution mechanisms we are probably losing out in the development of legal norms. However, the world may need that development. We probably need to be more careful about that and, particularly we, as arbitrators, need to be conscious of the role we play in that respect.

My last point deals with the tension between unification and diversity. I am puzzled by the fact that we hear a description of our world as favouring a transnational uniform arbitration process at the very same time we are seeing countries, regions, trying to develop different kinds of rules in order to compete with one another.

Let's take Europe. We are faced with the proposal by one institution in the European Union to include for the first time arbitration rules in an instrument that has nothing to do with arbitration (namely Regulation 44/2001 also known as Brussels I). What are we doing there? Do we want to develop regional systems? What does that mean? Can we start to develop a regional system without having a clear idea of the kind of policy we want to have behind that system? I think we are putting the chicken before the egg. This is why I want to air a word of caution. Do not prepare rules at a time when we do not really know what kind of policy we want to have, at least regionally.

Gabrielle Kaufmann-Kohler: We have understood to whom this message is addressed! It is true that for the last fifty years arbitration has moved towards uniformity. Is the clock now ticking the other way? If so, it may be linked to what happens in the world in general, with more regulation, more nationalistic approaches as opposed to the global approach that we had seen for years. This may be the result of the financial and economic crisis. Be this as it may, one would think that it would be in line with the nature of international arbitration that these developments occur on a global level rather than on regional levels, as is currently happening in Europe.

That leads me directly to Renaud Sorieul. It might be good if you could address the diversification issue. Then I will turn to Justice Croft.

Renaud Sorieul: Thank you very much, Gabrielle. I also thank the organizers for making it possible for me to be here today.

I have three minutes to discuss UNCITRAL, its role and where it is going in the field of arbitration, which is difficult, particularly since there is more of UNCITRAL in the room than at this podium. I note that former Secretaries of UNCITRAL are present but also many among those active delegates who make the policy of the UNCITRAL Working Group on Arbitration. So, the best I can do is simply to open a perspective from the Secretariat's standpoint.

Over the past fifty years, the United Nations at large and UNCITRAL in particular have been designing a system of arbitration law based on generic rules. For example, you may remember that we have been very cautious to maintain this generic approach in our recent revision of the UNCITRAL Arbitration Rules. This illustrates a traditional understanding of the original mandate of UNCITRAL to further the progressive harmonization of the law of international trade. Differences between legal systems are bridged by establishing an overarching framework of rules operating at a high level of generality.

In the specific field of arbitration, we have now moved on to discussing one aspect of investment arbitration: transparency in treaty-based investor-State arbitration. Here again, we started from the idea that our approach should be as generic as possible. We are looking at the possibility of reaching consensus on a set of rules that would ultimately constitute the message of the United Nations to the world regarding transparency in investment arbitration. Thus, we are not trying to create rules for exclusive use within the framework of the UNCITRAL Arbitration Rules.

However, we are aware that tensions may occur between our harmonization activity and another goal of UNCITRAL, that of modernizing the law of international trade. Consistent with what has been noted by previous speakers, such a tension may oppose our generic approach to rule-making and the call we hear from various circles for more specific tools.

For example, we increasingly hear that there is a need for arbitration rules or standards in the field of insolvency (insolvency also happens to be one area where UNCITRAL has worked extensively in the past). We also hear that we should give specific attention to arbitration in the field of procurement (where we are finalizing the revision of the UNCITRAL Model Law on Procurement of Goods, Construction and Services). Here, there is little room for arbitration in the context of the procurement process itself but we are encouraged to study the specific aspects of contract administration in the phase that follows the award of the procurement contract.[13]

We are also considering dispute settlement in the field of electronic commerce. Here I would draw your attention to the existence of another UNCITRAL body, Working Group III (On-line Dispute Resolution), which will be meeting next week [23-27 May 2011] in New York. That working group is looking at a cross-section of electronic commerce issues and alternative dispute resolution issues, including arbitration. I would specifically draw your attention to that aspect of our work, which might be considered by some in this room as somewhat unworthy of their attention because it deals with low-value transactions concluded in a very specific context relying on the use of specific technology.

I should point out that we are also discussing in that working group the possible creation of arbitration mechanisms. It may very well involve the drafting of specific rules and specific enforcement mechanisms. We even hear views about the use of the New York Convention and the possible need to adapt it as an enforcement tool for decisions to be rendered in that context. At this stage, no decision has been to move in that direction. I am not saying this is happening or should happen, but this is certainly one of the issues that is being discussed and that would benefit from the active involvement of arbitration specialists.

Finally, we heard at an UNCITRAL Colloquium on financial inclusion a presentation on arbitration in the area of microfinance (based on an existing experience in Peru). It may be useful to highlight that trend in particular in the context of the question on how to address the challenges for the next fifty years.

To conclude with a remark on the occasional tension between private sector and State players in negotiations held at UNCITRAL, I would say we have recently witnessed, as was also noted by previous speakers, an increased willingness of states to re-establish or reclaim some control over what is essentially an inter-governmental process. As we consider possible refinement to the international framework for arbitration, it is not surprising that we are confronted with consequences of the success of arbitration,

---

13. See Don WALLACE, Jr."Public Procurement, Long-term Government Contracts and Dispute Settlement: the Need for National Systems to Prevent and Resolve Disputes Between Regulators and Private Operators of Infrastructure and Providers of Public Services" in *Modern Law for Global Commerce Proceedings of the Congress of the United Nations Commission on International Trade Law Held on the Occasion of the Fortieth Session of the Commission*, Vienna, 9-12 July 2007, p. 358 et seq.

particularly where we envisage transplanting it into areas where it was previously unknown. Arbitration may become victim of its own success where the perception of the public interest at stake differs from that generally encountered in commercial arbitration.

With this, my time is probably exhausted. I would simply recall that contribution by ICCA has been essential to the completion of certain UNCITRAL projects (as demonstrated by the *travaux préparatoires* of the 1976 UNCITRAL Arbitration Rules) or to the implementation of parts of the mandate of UNCITRAL (such as the ICCA publications of case law on UN texts regarding arbitration). I look forward to continuing and amplifying cooperation between our two institutions in the future.

Gabrielle Kaufmann-Kohler: We note your point on claims for more state control. It is something very different from what we have seen in the last five decades. It may indicate a turning point or it may not. We will have to think about it.

There is one aspect we have not touched on so far this afternoon, but which we addressed extensively this morning: The role of the courts. Thinking about changes in the needs, in the proceedings, one should ask: Should the courts change as well? On the aspect of the court's role in a changing landscape, I would like to give the floor to Justice Croft from Australia, who can tell us about an experiment particularly relevant in our context.

The Hon Justice Clyde Croft: Thank you. I turn now to look at the role of the courts in harmonization or diversification. Recently there have been significant efforts by individuals and organizations, public and private, to encourage and develop arbitration in Australia, to encourage innovation and diversity in arbitration and dispute resolution generally. These include efforts by the judiciary to create and promote the services of specialist lists and judges, significant legislative changes, and the development of new rules, services and education programmes by arbitral institutions and centres.

Arbitral institutions are also playing their role as promoters, educators, innovators and guardians of ethical standards. The aim of Australia's present arbitration reinvigoration process is to increase the use of both international and domestic commercial arbitration, in significant part by making its legal infrastructure as modern and facilitative as possible and clear to both international and domestic eyes.

The aim is to apply uniform internationally understood and accepted arbitration legislation and, through the flexibility of that legislation, combined with specialist and supportive courts, materially assist parties in the development and application of flexible arbitration arrangements substantively and procedurally. Flexibility and diversity of this kind will only thrive in a known, certain and supportive legal environment, all of which is necessary to drive innovation and cost effectiveness.

As a result of its reviews in relation to international and domestic commercial arbitration, Australia enacted the International Arbitration Amendment Act 2010 which amended the existing International Arbitration Act. At a state level, the Australian Uniform Commercial Arbitration Act 2010 will apply to domestic arbitration.

This legislation makes and will make Australia and its respective states and territories one of the few jurisdictions to implement, with amendments, the 2006 revisions to the Model Law. These include a more modern form requirement for arbitration agreements, a prescribed appointing authority and provisions which govern, more comprehensively, the grant of interim measures of protection.

The judiciary plays an essential role in supporting and promoting arbitration. The Supreme Court of Victoria has comprehensive jurisdiction to assist in all aspects of international and domestic commercial arbitration. On 1 January 2010 the new arbitration list in the Commercial Court of the Victoria Supreme Court began its operation. All arbitration matters brought in the Victoria court are heard in the arbitration list and its operation is set out or explained in some detail in the practice note which I have attached to my paper, which examines matters in further detail.[14]

The theme or the thrust of the practice note is to emphasize the court's supportive role. The guidelines are flexible and non-prescriptive. Innovation, flexibility and diversity are positively encouraged in a known procedural environment.

It is clear that there are substantial benefits that flow from providing a specialist list with a specialist judge or judges. A court that has established an arbitration list is likely to be more aware of the specific issues that arise in the arbitration context. Also, a consistent body of arbitration-related decisions can be developed by judges that have an interest and expertise in arbitration. This is also essential to assist in developing sound arbitration law expertise, not only to promote Australia's reputation as an arbitration-friendly jurisdiction but also to provide an environment that is in harmony with international arbitral law and thinking and which will promote innovation, flexibility, diversity and efficiency in dispute resolution. This process is also assisted by a close liaison with arbitration users – arbitrators, counsel, parties – and arbitral institutions, which is possible with a specialist list.

I suppose the theme of my comments is that, whilst on one view one might see the development in Australia and other jurisdictions of standardized Model Law provisions and standardized court procedures as limiting, in my view, the legal certainty of that environment provides the basis for encouraging innovation and diversity in arbitration itself.

Thank you.

Gabrielle Kaufmann-Kohler: Karl-Heinz would you like to react to the different comments that we heard? We have a few more minutes before we open the floor to the audience.

Karl-Heinz Böckstiegel: I have just three points which I would like to make shortly regarding future development.

The first is the question: Will the institutions change? Indeed, I think they may, at least the distribution of cases among the institutions.

I have noticed recently, in three different cases, what I would call an outsourcing of domestic commercial arbitration. I cannot go into the details. But the reasons seem to be simply that the parties to these disputes felt uncomfortable with their own domestic arbitration system and therefore outsourced their dispute to foreign national institutions. When I saw this the third time, I thought I would mention it as a possible pattern.

14. "Supreme Court of Victoria, Practice Note No. 2 of 2010, Arbitration Business", annexed to Clyde CROFT, The Development of Australia as an Arbitral Seat – A Victorian Supreme Court Perspective", this volume, p. 227 at pp. 255-259.

Further, as far as investment arbitration is concerned, I do see some changes already now. In addition to the traditional bodies for investment arbitration – ICSID, NAFTA, CAFTA [United States-Dominican Republic-Central America Free Trade Agreement] – I see more uses of what used to be or still are the institutions for commercial arbitration being now used also for investment arbitration. I think Peter Goldsmith mentioned already that this is true for the ICC, even though the ICC has many other commercial cases with states which are not investment arbitrations. I see this also with the Stockholm Chamber of Commerce. This seems to happen particularly as soon as parties go to the UNCITRAL Rules to be applicable in investment disputes – and I have the impression they do this more and more. In such a context, quite often the parties or the arbitrators suggest an administration by the PCA, which is having a growing number of cases, for good reason, because it is a very efficient institution as I know from my own experience.

Even for inter-government disputes, as some certainly know in this room, we have a certain shift. The *Softwood Lumber* cases in which I was involved have been publicized and present an example. As you know, they are disputes between the two governments of the United States and Canada that went to LCIA [London Court of International Arbitration] arbitration. All this seems to show that the role of institutions will change perhaps even more in the future.

The second question: Will the proceedings change? Here I see, and probably that will continue, a shift from confidentiality to – to put it positively – transparency. In commercial arbitration, where obviously confidentiality is supposed to be one of the assets, the institutions like the ICC are pressed to at least publish sanitized awards so that people can recognize patterns in what actually has been decided. Also, in commercial cases, I see a rather negligent way – to put it cautiously – of dealing with confidentiality: It seems to happen more and more that, if a party or if counsel finds it helpful for whatever purpose, suddenly the award or the proceedings appear on the internet.

Of course, this trend goes much further in investment arbitration, as I think we heard already this morning. If I recall it correctly, the CAFTA Rules provide that hearings are public, and in NAFTA cases a similar approach has been taken in practice recently. Often the parties' briefs are on the internet, as we heard this morning. In ICSID cases, the tribunals have sometimes accepted to have, to a great extent, public hearings or at least much more transparency beyond what the Rules provide for. And, again, in the *Softwood Lumber* cases – we had absolutely public hearings, which, as I have experienced from my own involvement, considerably changes the pattern of behaviour of counsel and tribunals, because they want to make sure that the attending public does not misunderstand though it is less familiar with the case.

As a personal note, let me add that I was astonished how many people came to these hearings. We had one room for 100 and then we had an overflow room for another 100. I had expected only a few students to come, but most of the people were well-dressed ladies and gentlemen and they spent the day there obviously because their interests or those of other institutions were involved.

My third point is a reaction to what I heard from the second panel this morning on governance. I strongly believe that arbitrators and tribunals should decide the case, no less but also no more. Obviously that includes reasoning and in that reasoning you will look at what other decisions tribunals have made in comparable cases, but you should not go beyond that.

Arbitrators have not been selected – and, let's face it, they are selected by parties or institutions for a particular dispute – to develop the law of the world. Being a professor myself, I may say I think we have too many professors in arbitration who feel they have to do just that.

Obviously, once you issue an award, that will have an impact, hopefully, if it is a good award, for future development. But to draw these consequences should be left to the commentators or future tribunals. Proposals for the development of the law can be made and are made, by state organs, like the International Law Commission or UNCITRAL, or by NGOs like the IBA or ILA [International Law Association]. That is where law should be developed and those forums are better fit for that function. Of course, if states really want a change, they can change their national legislation, they can change their treaties or conclude new treaties. They are the ones who should develop international law or relevant national law, but that is not the mandate of arbitrators who are selected to decide a particular case.

That is all I have to say.

Gabrielle Kaufmann-Kohler: I suggest we open the floor now and the panellists will then have opportunities to respond. Many issues have been raised, of different importance, different types of issues, about proceedings, about the expectations of users. No doubt there are questions and comments.

Laurence Craig: This is a question that is addressed principally to Beat Hess, who talks about being oppressed by the arbitral system in respect to confidentiality or lack thereof, and discovery, but it builds upon Catherine Kessedjian's comment that we should be hesitant to talk about one group of users or one kind of party, that it is a very vast system of arbitration.

I also build upon Campbell McLachlan saying that commercial arbitration is principally a product of contract and it represents a kind of privatization of justice that develops into a kind of arbitration system. It is this system which Beat Hess says is going the wrong way because the users want confidentiality and no or very limited document production.

My question is, if the parties to the contract of arbitration, the agreement of arbitration, want that, why don't they provide that in their contract, particularly when we are dealing with sophisticated users, such as large corporate users?

Gabrielle Kaufmann-Kohler: I suggest we take a number of questions and then we can proceed to the answers.

Diana Droulers: I wanted just to make a comment on expectations and uniformity. The world does not expect uniformity. We have generic rules, which I think is an assessment that the world is completely different, it is unbalanced, and that the development of countries, and the development of arbitration in different areas of the world, is different.

I think the expectation is to have clear rules and some sort of predictability. If you take into account – and that comes for the institutions that you were mentioning – the amount of money that is being fought over before the institutions, if you add the number of all the cases that the ICC has and from there on mention all institutions of the world, it is enormous; and they are there by choice because parties decided to take them to arbitration. So, I think one thing that people most expect is clearness, not only in the writing of the rules but clearness in the conditions for exercising their right to go to arbitration.

The proof that it is spreading all over the world is not only the system of international law that one might talk about; it is also all the institutions that are dedicated to arbitration, dedicated to study arbitration, to help train people who are working in arbitration, to making ethical rules and so on in a lot of places.

So, I do not think we are going the wrong way, unlike Laurence Craig said; we are just going different ways, because, in order to stay the same, we have to keep changing all the time.

Gabrielle Kaufmann-Kohler: While I turn to the next speaker, can I ask you and those who will follow you to please state your name and to try to be brief so we can give the floor to as many as possible.

Koorosh Ameli: My name is Ameli of Ameli International Arbitration. I have two questions or points. One is with regard to the appointment of party-appointed arbitrators when they resign. Under the revised UNCITRAL arbitration rule there is a very good improvement that if a party-appointed arbitrator resigns the original system that appointed him will not be operational but the appointing authority will make the appointment. I believe that is a very good improvement. To some extent already the ICC has applied this rule since 1988.

Perhaps another improvement in this direction could be the appointment of non-nationals in the arbitration system for party-appointed arbitrators. This has been in practice. Of course it has to be part of the arbitration clause. Perhaps this could be a good step for the future.

My second point –

Gabrielle Kaufmann-Kohler: Could I remind you of my request to brief. We take your point on nationality. We have not discussed it here but the nationality requirements for arbitrators may soon be dead. That is something we have to consider.

Koorosh Ameli: That is why I raised it.

Gabrielle Kaufmann-Kohler: Could I ask you to be very brief on your last point. Then I would like to turn to someone else.

Koorosh Ameli: Yes. The second point refers to class action, which again the participants discussed. This is for the future. Class actions are being discussed in Belgium and in the European Commission. Perhaps it is an area to be considered for the future.

Gabrielle Kaufmann-Kohler: Absolutely. It is being practiced in the United States – we heard about it this morning – but is not yet considered with serious prospects for Europe.

Michael Schneider: Michael Schneider, Lalive, in Geneva. I would like to pick up the first point of Catherine Kessedjian. What has changed, she said, is not so much the needs of the users, it is how we deal with them.

I think what is significant is the composition of this panel. You have one user and nine people – derivatives, so to speak – who live off arbitration. In the discussion, there was very little said about the challenge that Beat put to us. Very few responded to it. You are developing systems, and I think it is quite preoccupying.

One of the messages Campbell had, we have in our system; in order for the system to work, we need more cases. Arbitrations are confidential, so arbitration is not that good for solving disputes. I am paraphrasing a little bit. In fact, that was part of the early English legislation, that you excluded a certain area because it did not produce cases for developing the law.

So, I think one thing we should do, we should be more responsive to what Beat is telling us and discuss more how to we respond to these questions.

One of the problems I see about developing more rules, there are problems perceived and by solving the problems we create new problems.

One of the other problems is all this arbitration training. There are so many people being trained in arbitration, much more than I think can find a job in arbitration. So, what are they going to do? They are going to become professors. [Laughter] They are going to write rules and guidelines and all kinds of things and Beat is sitting there waiting for the answer. [Applause]

Gabrielle Kaufmann-Kohler: Point taken!

Nagla Nassar: Nagla Nassar, from Cairo, Egypt. I have a comment on what Catherine Kessedjian said.

Really, the expectations of the party or of the users of arbitration are driven by the advisers, not really by the end-users of arbitration. From practice you can see what a user expects is what advice he gets from his advisers. If a legal community does not have a vision where arbitration should be going and what is the policy underneath it, then we have to face what we are facing now.

Gabrielle Kaufmann-Kohler: Good comment. Can I give the floor to the panellists who have been expressly called upon and to whomever else on the panel wants to react to the questions and comments we have just heard?

Beat you were certainly called upon.

Beat Hess: I will react. Actually, I was sitting here and I was thinking exactly what you [indicating Michael Schneider] said. So, thank you for that.

I was tempted to intervene and say, "Guys, let's come back to basics." I ask myself why do I want to see arbitration rules in my contracts, the many contracts that I did for Shell? It is simple. First, it is speed and certainty. Second, it is confidentiality, except that in investment arbitration you can forget about confidentiality; the government will make of it what it thinks is in its interest. Thirdly, it is the familiarity of the arbitrators with the issues under dispute. Those are really the key issues why we want to have arbitration clauses.

Where have we gone? What do I say to my board when we have a case in arbitration? These are exactly the issues that my board wants to know: How long does it take; how about the certainty; and are the arbitrators familiar with our business. Then they will ask what about enforceability and, in investment disputes, they will ask what does that mean for our relationship with the host government? Those are really the key issues.

I am a bit blunt now. You can discuss as long as you want about future rules and where arbitration should go. As long as these basic requirements – that I am sure my colleagues from many other industries will share – are not taken into consideration you will drift away from what were and still should be the benefits of arbitration.

Gabrielle Kaufmann-Kohler: We heard it and will remember it.

Campbell McLachlan QC: The point which I had understood Beat to make in his initial intervention was that what he required was a clarity of procedural rules. That does not mean endless further complexity of procedural rules. What it does mean, however, is some kind of assurance – which I would take, frankly, as the sort of fundamental starting point before anything else goes on top – that the procedure which one is entering is going to be to provide a fair and just means of resolving the dispute. It is not always the case that one can simply make that up on the back of an envelope. There are a number of questions, very important questions, out there, where I think this organization, rather in the same way as the IBA Committee has done on a number of issues, could show the lead in informally developing a consensus which, whether or not it finds its way into binding rules, nevertheless would make a very valuable contribution to that kind of clarity of procedure.

Gabrielle Kaufmann-Kohler: Thank you. Who else wants to react to the different comments? If there are no immediate further observations from the panel, let me turn again to the audience. Yes, please, Justice Kaye.

Judith Kaye: My name is Judith Kaye. First of all, thank you so much, it has really been a wonderful programme.

What I found of particular interest this afternoon was your two wing men on the panel. I note that you [indicating Beat Hess] did not answer the question that was put by the gentleman in the front row there [indicating Laurence Craig] which is: All of these things that are so important to you as a user, why don't you take a moment or two in the dispute resolution clause to say what it is you are looking for? Don't we need really to do more of that rather than criticize in retrospect that things did not quite work out as you had hoped? There is so much opportunity for users – these are, after all, agreements – to put more of what you expect out of a proceeding in the dispute resolution clause.

Then I want to comment on the other wing man. I was so pleased to see a member of the judiciary. We have noticed so many things happening but probably over the fifty years the presence of the judiciary in arbitration proceedings at every stage has been one of the developments. Maybe very negative, very positive, but the judiciary is in not only at the end for enforcement but at the beginning and so many other places. There are so many opportunities, as our speaker judge noted, for the judiciary, which has administrative powers in addition to the decision-making powers, to help improve the process. We have heard a few of them today. I think conferring with judicial colleagues, bringing them into the conversation, is perhaps a lesson of the past half century.

Gabrielle Kaufmann-Kohler: Thank you.

Beat Hess: Could I just answer the question here?

Gabrielle Kaufmann-Kohler: I think you have to!

Beat Hess: I am eager to do that! It is a fair push-back but I will push back as well.

The arbitration community developed the ICC Rules and the UNCITRAL Rules and the AAA Rules and you name it. Now what I hear is, "Well, you can't really rely on these rules; you guys should tell us what you want." Yes, ok, we relied on these rules, and on the simplicity of these arbitration clauses, and we felt that these arbitration clauses give us speedy, reliable arbitration proceedings. Now you are telling us "in your negotiations you should be much more detailed".

I am sure many of you have negotiated arbitration clauses in large contracts and, if you go into negotiating beyond, say, for example, the ICC Arbitration Rules, well, I wish you good luck with many of your counterparts going into this kind of detail.

That is my comment on what I consider to be a fair comment, but I give it back.

Gabrielle Kaufmann-Kohler: Justice Croft?

The Hon Justice Clyde Croft: Thank you [to Judith Kaye] for that intervention. That prompts me to mention another aspect of the role or the effect of the judiciary in terms of expectations.

Arbitration is commonly criticized – I suppose I am speaking more about domestic arbitration – as emulating and simply following the procedures of court litigation.

The comment I would make about that is, if you look at well-managed, modern, commercial courts, where cases are case-managed by a judge with a docket, that is not old-style litigation, it is very expeditious litigation, often so expeditious the parties find it a bit too fast, and certainly domestically, because you do not have the enforcement problems with domestic commercial arbitration.

I would be very surprised if a well-managed commercial court could not provide a very competitive service with anything that the arbitration field can provide. I think there has been an ongoing healthy competition between the courts and arbitration.

We saw arbitration become much more cost effective, then the commercial courts came along and picked up some of the processes. So, you have this sort of leap-frogging effect, which I think is very healthy and feeds into the expectations of commercial parties, who are really quite sophisticated, they know what sort of dispute resolution they really want.

It is a matter of who is providing the best service.

Gabrielle Kaufmann-Kohler: Undoubtedly. Sir Frank?

Sir Franklin Berman: I was delighted to see the balance that is coming back to this discussion as we engage with the real issues about the arbitral process. So, let's add the final bit of the picture. Aren't we entitled also to hear what are the arbitrators entitled to expect from the parties?

Here is my little list – which has no reference at all to current cases on which I happen to be sitting.

First, can we please have some adequate guarantee which appears on the surface that the client is in charge of the case and not counsel? [Applause]

Second, can we please see the parties and their representatives using particularly the written procedure in the case as a way of narrowing the issues that they are really in dispute about instead of as an excuse for broadening?

Thirdly, when, under these simple systems of procedure, the tribunal expects the parties to agree so far as they possibly can on procedural issues, under the overall authority of the tribunal, they should do so, thus reducing the amount on which the tribunal has to rule.

Fourthly, please stop demanding for the hearings unreasonable periods of time which leads a tribunal to have to put off the prospective date of the arbitration for another year and then to hear complaints about how long the process takes. [Applause]

Unknown Questioner: I would like to briefly go back to the point introduced by Ms. Kaye. We heard about educating the parties. Your comments reminded me of a recent experience I had in Serbia, training Serbian judges. I think I can say honestly that there are now more trained judges in arbitration in Serbia than there are in the Netherlands! As a consequence of the financing of Member States or potential Member States of the EU, one of the – almost – conditions is that the judiciary is trained in a number of subjects, including arbitration. I realized, as I was flying to Belgrade, how absurd this was, in a way, that I was teaching this subject, which I would love to teach in the Netherlands, but which is not a compulsory or even a voluntary subject for the Dutch judiciary. So, I think that is an area that should definitely be picked up in connection with further points addressed by the others.

Gabrielle Kaufmann-Kohler: That comment is a perfect transition to our last question. And before we go over that last question, I should say that – while Pierre Tercier will close the debate for the day – the intent of this roundtable is not to reach definitive conclusions. So I will not ask each panellist to conclude.

This debate is meant to raise questions and show possible avenues more than anything else. It is meant as food for thought. The idea is not to give final answers, just to be aware of the problems and think about possible solutions. When you speak about the future, there are in any event no definitive answers.

That leads us now to the final point. Each panel participant may, in one minute – that is the rule of the game – give one idea of what ICCA could do to address the changes and deficiencies we have discussed now, in order for us to gather ideas. I am sure there are many ideas in the audience as well, but this time we will just hear the roundtable participants. Who wants to start with ideas?

Catherine Kessedjian: I think one of the ideas is the difficulty we are having now with the way ICCA is actually structured. I think that anything that ICCA would want to tackle and take up would require a different structure and, particularly you need a membership. My experience comes from the American Law Institute where you indeed have a Council but you have a membership. So when the American Law Institute approves rules, they are approved by the entire membership even though they have been prepared by rapporteurs, with a close monitoring by the Council.

So, if we want to see an increased role for ICCA, we have to think in terms of a different structure. I would see two potential roles that ICCA could take in the future. Sponsor empirical studies. We are definitely in need of more empirical studies. Whatever we are able to do either through universities or through Queen Mary-type studies is not enough. We do not know enough about the practice.

Second – somebody alluded to this earlier – we have to think in terms of developing some rules, notably about accountability and ethics. I think that is a major issue and I am wondering whether ICCA could have a role there.

Gabrielle Kaufmann-Kohler: Thanks for raising accountability. We have not really touched on accountability, while it was on our list of issues. We have chosen other topics. Let's remember accountability and let's take note of your other suggestions.

Who else has a suggestion?

Lord Goldsmith QC: One of the things that this discussion has demonstrated is that the absence of clarity as to what an arbitration is going to do does not seem to stop people from choosing it.

It is a bit like the word "table". When you mention the word table some people may think of a do-it-yourself piece of Formica from Sweden, some may think of it as a Louis XV object with sixteen chairs and inlaid ivory. Still it is a table.

Maybe the point is that people do not care, actually, when they are choosing it, otherwise they would spend more time putting them into their dispute resolution clauses. Either they do not care that much about what the result is as long as it functions as a table, or there is a great confidence trick that we are running at the moment, giving the impression to the user world that arbitration is a single thing.

Maybe what ICCA needs to do is to help provide that predictability so people know what it is they are getting when they choose arbitration. Maybe the precise content of that does not matter nearly as much as those of us who talk about this a lot – and please don't stop inviting me to talk about it – think it does matter.

Gabrielle Kaufmann-Kohler: And what is your proposal for ICCA?

Lord Goldsmith QC: The proposal is: find a way of producing predictability as to what arbitration is going to mean but without focussing quite so much on refinement of the rules because I strongly suspect that does not matter nearly as much as we say it does.

Gabrielle Kaufmann-Kohler: Further proposals? Campbell?

Campbell McLachlan QC: One minute, three sub-proposals. First, expand on a more systemized basis the reporting of the reasoning in arbitral awards, on substantive law issues as well as on procedural issues. Second, take up the mandate in Art. II(2) of the Statement of Purpose of the ICCA Council on a more organized basis to elucidate fundamental rules of procedure. I concur with Catherine's suggestion that an initial area would be ethical duties. Third, taking up a point made by Johnny Veeder last night, hold a conference in Africa.[15]

Gabrielle Kaufmann-Kohler: Chris?

Christopher R. Drahozal: Catherine took mine when she suggested sponsoring and doing more empirical research. I agree completely with that point. I do want to note that there are various types of empirical research – not just surveys – such as experiments and simulations as well as observational studies, which might include counting awards and things like that.

Another possibility that ICCA might consider is to spend more time educating judges. I have to admit that I have been very disappointed with the US Supreme Court and some of its arbitration decisions lately. The Court can be a "bull in a china shop" with its treatment of arbitration law in trying to reach a particular bottom line. The new *ICCA's Guide to the Interpretation of the 1958 New York Convention* is a good start,[16] but there may be some value in getting a broader understanding in the judiciary as to what arbitration law is and why it is the way it is.

Gabrielle Kaufmann-Kohler: Justice Croft?

The Hon Justice Clyde Croft: I would certainly like to urge ICCA to encourage governments to develop and sponsor programmes to educate judges in relation to commercial arbitration but also to encourage governments to establish specialized arbitration courts so that the sort of expertise and advantages that I have outlined might spread around the world.

Gabrielle Kaufmann-Kohler: Renaud?

Renaud Sorieul: We are already very grateful to ICCA for the material it provides to us by way of analysis of case law on some of our texts. We are in the process of also trying to expand our training activity, not exactly in Serbia but in some other parts of the world where the need seems to be quite obvious. In that process, we are trying to prepare a guide to enactment of the New York Convention, which is not exactly prepared in the same spirit as a document recently prepared by ICCA, but obviously we will look forward to future cooperation in gathering materials for that document.

---

15. V.V. VEEDER, "Gala Dinner Address: Memories from ICCA's First Fifty Years", this volume, pp. 5-10.

16. Available at <www.arbitration-icca.org>.

Gabrielle Kaufmann-Kohler: Guillermo, what should ICCA do?

Guillermo Aguilar Alvarez: Perhaps take the lead in going back to basics, to paraphrase Beat, and promote best practices to achieve speed, certainty and enforceability, some of the issues that he raised as a matter of concern for the users of the system.

Gabrielle Kaufmann-Kohler: Are there any other suggestions?

I may give just one about a point that struck me listening to the debate. It will show that we are taking Beat's comments seriously. We need more business people involved in ICCA to have a better understanding of the repercussions of what we are doing here.

I will not repeat the proposals; you have heard them; they will be reported in the proceedings, and we will all be able to work on them for the next fifty years!

That allows me to close this debate and thank all the panellists wholeheartedly for participating in a difficult exercise. Difficult, because they had very little time available and nevertheless managed to make a wealth of very substantive points.

Now I will turn to Pierre Tercier to close the scientific part of the day and then to Jan to close the conference. [Applause]

Pierre Tercier: Good afternoon, ladies and gentlemen. My role is to draw a conclusion. What is a conclusion? It is certainly the last intervention. Be sure it will be the last one.

It has to be short. Be sure it will be short.

What should the content of a conclusion be? Should it be a summary of the essence of what has been said? It would be totally illusory and pretentious to think that I would be able, in five minutes, to summarize such a brilliant day filled with extremely interesting presentations. What I can do, however, is express a few thoughts – based on today's presentations and input – about what the future of arbitration could be.

Who is best to speak about such future? The young generation, of course. Therefore, following the suggestion of Jan [Paulsson], I will give the floor to two representatives of the very young generation of future arbitrators. They will give their own view of the future. You have their CVs in your materials and I have the pleasure to give the floor first to Ndanga for her presentation. Please, Ndanga? [Applause]

Ndanga Kamau:[17] Thank you very much, Professor Tercier. Contrary to what the conference programme suggests, I have not come back from the future to tell you what ICCA will be like. I am simply here to give you my current perspective, the perspective of a young practitioner who has just started out, based in Houston. In doing this, I would like to focus on an aspect that has not received much attention over the course of the Conference, that is, the arbitration practitioner.

Those of you who were at the gala dinner last night will have heard Johnny Veeder say that there has come into existence an elite group of international arbitration practitioners;[18] these are the so-called animals, to borrow Judge Bruno Simma's analogy.

---

17. Member, International Arbitration Practice Group and Foreign Legal Consultant, Houston Office, King & Spalding.

18. V.V. VEEDER, "Gala Dinner Address: Memories from ICCA's First Fifty Years", this volume, pp. 5-10.

When you visit a zoo, you are likely to want information about the animals' habitat, diet and activities. Let us then examine the international arbitration practitioner in similar terms.

If you ask an international arbitration practitioner where they are based, they will answer Geneva, London, New York, Paris; increasingly also Dubai, Hong Kong or Singapore. If you ask them who their clients are, they will tell you sovereign states, energy companies, telecom companies and so forth. But if you ask them where their clients are from, you may well find that you have to reach for your Smartphones to locate the answer. Where exactly are Luanda, Bishkek, Bamako, Riga? No territory is too remote.

The arbitration practitioner cuts a bold and fearless figure, travelling across the world to anywhere an arbitration agreement may exist, armed only with an iPhone with access to Google Translate. It is no wonder that many young lawyers want to join this elite corps of practitioners – perhaps there are too many of us, as Michael Schneider lamented today.

But there is an elephant in the room that we don't talk about and that is the lack of inclusiveness in this profession. If you are an arbitrator or a member of a dispute settlement group in a major law firm you are probably not that concerned about it because your bottom line is quite good, or you know that you have a lot of arbitral appointments. But if we are to consider arbitration in the way ICCA would like us to – as a system of dispute settlement which should spread and grow around the world, then let us ask ourselves this: how long will the more "exotic" parties that we represent continue to submit to a process in which they do not recognize themselves? Not just physically, but in terms of their ideas and approaches to dispute settlement?

In the last session, we heard a lot about rule-making and about refining the processes by which disputes are settled. If we want arbitration to continue and thrive, if we want ICCA 100 to be an opportunity for the celebration of the diversity and growth of this process that started 50 years ago with a small band of men, then we need to think about how we who are present today can make this process more inclusive. In that vein I would like to extend the idea proposed by Campbell McLachlan for a Congress in Africa and suggest that ICCA 2014 should be held in Africa.

Thank you very much for listening.

Pierre Tercier: Thank you very much, Ndanga. Now, Patrick, it is your turn to give us your view of our future.

Patrick Miller:[19] My name is Patrick Miller. I am originally from Michigan and I was fortunate enough to study international arbitration at the University of Miami. A few weeks ago, I began my professional life in Paris.

Unlike most of you who've benefited from – in some cases – as much as fifty years of experience, whose hard work and dedication have brought this field to where it is today, I still have much to learn. I have only modest questions and suppositions. And I thank you for the opportunity to evoke with you an idea which is of concern to many in my

19. Stagiare, International Arbitration Group, Freshfields Bruckhaus Deringer, Paris.

generation. I would like to put this in the form of a question, which I believe all of us, young and old, must address over the next fifty years.

The authority of arbitrators stems from the notion that their decisions will be seen as legitimate in the eyes of the wider community. And legitimacy depends in large part on the openness and accountability of the arbitral system as a whole. Without this essential feature of legitimacy, international arbitration would cease to serve its valuable function – to settle international disputes peacefully, to minimize disruption to the international transactions on which the global community depends.

If we look to the other side of the coin, the perception of illegitimacy is the consequence, notably, of opacity and entrenchment of personal influence in the functioning of the system of international arbitration – once they have convinced the parties to grant them the power of arbitral authority.

So I'd like to ask this. Will those who develop arbitral rules and institutions see themselves as working for the professional benefit of a few arbitrators and lawyers? Is their enterprise the establishment of networks of personal influence? Or will they understand that arbitration's great advances will be reversed unless the broader community can see and understand what they are doing, and be convinced that they are indeed pursuing the general interest?

We, the neophytes, perhaps take for granted the conscious and patient efforts, you, our predecessors, have made to establish arbitration's legitimacy in the international community. But we do understand, or at least we should understand, that it is the responsibility of our generation to be on the right side of this equation – and for this too, we will continue to need you to set the good example.

Thank you so much for listening.

Pierre Tercier: Ladies and gentlemen, if you allow one of the representatives of a bit less young generation to also give his view on the future, I would like to highlight three points, three different sequences of the history of how Geneva and International Commercial Arbitration happened to meet. Three acts.

Act 1: Geneva 1923-1927. It is in this city that a small number of eminent lawyers had the bright idea to imagine a Protocol and a Convention on Recognition and Execution of foreign awards (the so-called Geneva Convention). This was an incredible step, an incredible idea. They were real visionaries, they were real pioneers. Why? Because they imagined to prepare, under the auspices of the League of Nations (the predecessor of the UN) an Act that would later on lead to the globalization of the dispute resolution system worldwide. Indeed, if the Geneva Convention has not had a very important practical influence because it was only ratified by a small number of states, it was really the first step made in favour of the birth of modern arbitration. Its influence has been huge, and ultimately led to the New York Convention and its incredible success.

Act 2: Geneva 1961. In this city, again, a small number of eminent lawyers had another bright idea – create a forum, our ICCA. Why? As we heard yesterday from Johnny [Veeder]: in order to have a think tank to find the real features of the baby. It was certainly not the only or the first institution interested in international arbitration. But, at that time they were the first to decide to create a totally independent body of people who were preparing what could be the future of international arbitration. It was an informal group, independent from any state or any other institution, devoted only to the development of the doctrine of international arbitration. It has had a huge influence on many approaches that are nowadays generally recognized.

Act 3: Geneva 2011. Again, in this city a small number of lawyers decided that we should celebrate the fiftieth anniversary of ICCA. This is again a very important step. Why? We all know that arbitration has changed drastically in the last twenty years: in my view, a change of paradigm. Why? Arbitration was first and for a long time more or less limited to a certain number of countries or states, especially Europe and other western countries. Now it is really international, we have heard it now, with the entry of Asia, of Latin America and of Africa. It is a total and deep change. Arbitration was for a long time a system reserved to large companies able to offer themselves the luxury of submitting their dispute to a small body of respected lawyers. Now arbitration is generalized, standardized, banalized. It has become the common method of dispute resolution on the international level. Perhaps not the only one, but probably, for the time being, the preferred one. The arbitrators are still chosen by the parties for the adjudication of a case and not more, but the fact their decision may have a large impact, in the development of international law. The role of the arbitrators is changing and the role of the arbitral institutions is growing. In the absence of any legislative body at an international level and of real international tribunals, the arbitrators, the institutions, and to some extent the courts that control them are playing a new role that exceeds their primary mission. Today's presentations and discussions reflected perfectly this change in the role of arbitration. We hope that they contributed to the considerations for the future of this institution.

Arbitrators have to play a role as part of the exercise of justice; this is a very presumptuous and difficult task. Therefore, I am convinced – as you, I hope – that ICCA is and will remain one of the key figures for the indispensable existence and development of a system that must remain independent, flexible, efficient, and above all trustful.

Ladies and gentlemen, you may have seen that I was co-chair of the committee that organized this event. Normally the co-chair is not allowed to address thanks to the members of the committee to which he belongs, but in this case it is possible. Why? Because my function was actually very limited. Except for one or two ideas, I had nothing to do and I was merely copied in all letters and e-mails that were exchanged! This gives me good opportunity to testify that the group that has prepared this event was absolutely excellent. It is a group of young lawyers, from Geneva mostly, but also from Lausanne, Bern and Zurich. You will find their names in the leaflet. They did a great job: in particular, they found our sponsors who supported this event, they prepared the brochure, they prepared the organization. I would like to thank them warmly for everything they have done for the success of this meeting. [Applause]

I would like, of course, to thank again our speakers, our panellists, for a very outstanding event. I am sure that I am not speaking only on my behalf. We really had a great day.

Last, but not least, and before giving the floor back to our Chairman, I would like to address our gratitude to the person who was really the key leader of this event: Gabrielle, you have really done everything that was possible in order to make this a success. I think you are the only person who was able to do it. Besides some other occupations sometimes! [Laughter] You have led this with efficiency, with diligence, with calm and charm. You have prepared the programme, you have convinced the authorities, our speakers, you have conducted it from the very beginning to the end. For all that we are extremely grateful. Thank you very much again, Gabrielle. [Applause]

Ladies and gentlemen, again, thank you, all of you, for being present and for your participation. We know how difficult it is to realize an event that brings something to each and every participant, as different as they may be. I have the impression, shared by most of those to whom I had an opportunity to speak, that it was a success, that it was in the style of "*l'esprit de Chambésy*" and we have now to pursue that beautiful endeavour.

Thank you very much and have a safe journey home. [Applause]

Jan Paulsson: Cultural adaptability is important in international arbitration and, as proof of the cultural adaptability of ICCA, we are – in the land of the clocks, on the minute, on the dot – on time.

It remains for me to seize an occasion possibly to exercise my ambitions as a demagogue because I speak to release you, ladies and gentlemen, but I hope I release you with a feeling that you still have an appetite for more and that you leave with lots of ideas in your mind, things that you agree with and, better yet, things that you disagree with and wish to improve and things you will keep in your minds until we meet again in 2012 in Singapore.

May I, Pierre, answer your question: You hoped that we are content. When you confide in the Swiss and you count on them to organize an event, your expectations are very high, and they were exceeded.

So, thank you from us as well. From ICCA to you, the participants, thank you so much for your participation here today and see you soon. Thank you. [Applause]

Appendices

APPENDIX I

A Brief History of ICCA

ICCA 50 Organizing Committee[*]

TABLE OF CONTENTS

	Page
I. 50th Anniversary of ICCA	219
II. The Beginning	219
III. Purpose and Impact of ICCA on the Development of Arbitration Laws	222
IV. ICCA Conferences and Congresses	224
V. ICCA Publications	225

I. 50TH ANNIVERSARY OF ICCA

In 1961, on the occasion of the negotiations of the European Convention on International Commercial Arbitration, the International Council for Commercial Arbitration (ICCA) was founded in Geneva.

Since 2011 marks the 50th anniversary of ICCA, it seems only natural to host a Conference on "Arbitration – The Next 50 Years" and celebrate this remarkable event.

For the last half century, ICCA has been devoted to the promotion and improvement of arbitration, conciliation and other forms of international commercial dispute resolution. ICCA is an international not-for-profit organization and maintains official status as a non-governmental United Nations accredited organization.

ICCA is not an arbitral institution, nor does it administer arbitrations or act as an appointing authority. Rather, ICCA's activities include convening international arbitration congresses and conferences, sponsoring authoritative dispute resolution publications and promoting the harmonization of arbitration and conciliation rules, laws, procedures and standards.

II. THE BEGINNING

1. *Informal Gatherings of Friends*

ICCA was the result of informal gatherings of friends that took place in 1961. Several years prior, friendships had been formed when a group of delegates assembled to assist in the drafting of the New York Convention of 1958.

* Excerpt from the Brochure "ICCA 50th Anniversary, Geneva 2011", published by the ICCA 50 Organizing Committee.

In April 1961, certain delegates of this group again reassembled to negotiate and draft the European Convention on International Commercial Arbitration. That spring, the drafting sessions took place in Geneva at the *Office europeén*, as it then was, of the United Nations.

At the end of the sessions, a group of delegates, including Jean Robert, Pieter Sanders, Niel Pearson, Eugenio Minoli, would fall into the habit of meeting at Relais de Chambésy, a café near the offices of the international organizations.

Pieter Sanders recalls that "the atmosphere was perfect" at Relais de Chambésy. It created an ideal environment to discuss the development of arbitration and arbitration law. It is there that the founders of ICCA agreed to organize an international congress devoted to raising awareness of, and improving international commercial arbitration.

"The whole ICCA started with a club of old friends who knew each other very well; in this club of Chambésy, which was elaborating the Convention of 1961 of Geneva, there was the feeling that what was really needed for international commercial arbitration were conferences."
(Pieter Sanders)

"ICCA was the very first forum having this purely international idea; "a special purpose was the exchange of experiences, of practical experiences and the discussion of theoretical problems; it promotes understanding; it brings together the practices of different countries ... to create a bridge ... between people of various nationalities and various countries." (Pierre Lalive)

ICCA has its origins in these informal gatherings of people, who at the time launched the first international congress of its kind. In 1975, the original "Statement of Purposes and Procedures" of ICCA was adopted. It was later amended in 1994, 2007 and 2009. "Howard Holzmann drafted the statutes in Paris with Jean Robert," remembers Pieter Sanders.

2. *The First Congress*

The first Congress took place in May 1961 in Paris under the auspices of the Comité Français de l'Arbitrage and it has been "enriched by the spontaneous creation of ICCA at the initiative of those whose friendship was born when drafting the New York Convention".[1]

The aim of the first Congress was to improve the legal framework and the functioning of international arbitration. One of the ambitions of the congress was formulated in the following terms (and in French!):

> "*Notre ambition est de dégager quelques notions communes et de faire ressortir la nécessité de réformes portant sur des textes législatifs anachroniques et sur des pratiques procédurières incompatibles avec la bonne foi qui devrait être à la base de tout règlement arbitral*"[2]
>
> ["Our ambition is to identify some common notions and to highlight the necessity of reforms concerning outdated legislative texts and dilatory tactics incompatible with the principle of good faith, which should be the basis of any arbitral resolution."]

The first Congress was a success and was followed by many others.

1. Bertrand MOREAU, "Welcoming Address, Paris 1998 Congress" in *Improving the Efficiency of Arbitration Agreements and Awards: 40 Years of Application of the New York Convention*, ICCA Congress Series no. 9 (1998) p. 7.
2. Charles CARABIBER, Rev. arb. (1961) p. 45.

III. PURPOSE AND IMPACT OF ICCA ON THE DEVELOPMENT OF ARBITRATION LAWS

ICCA is devoted to developing international commercial arbitration, conciliation and other methods of dispute resolution. In particular ICCA is committed to promoting "harmonization of rules, laws, procedures and standards" and improving the processes of conciliation, arbitration and other means of preventing and resolving international commercial disputes and difficulties.

> "*Art. 2 of the Statement of Purposes and Procedures*:
> 1. ICCA shall continue its activities for (i) the preparation and conduct of international arbitration congresses and conferences, (ii) the preparation and publication of authoritative texts, (iii) the performance of its functions as a non-governmental organization recognized by the United Nations, and for cooperation with other international bodies, and (iv) shall undertake any other activities in connection with the further development of international commercial arbitration, conciliation and other methods of dispute resolution
> 2. ICCA shall continue to develop and provide a means by which arbitrators, conciliators, practitioners, users, scholars and arbitration organizations in various parts of the world may cooperate in activities related to international commercial dispute prevention and resolution, including inter alia:
>
> – promoting research
> – exchanging information and sharing knowledge
> – encouraging or sponsoring publications
> – promoting harmonization of rules, laws, procedures and standards
> – carrying out any other activities for promoting the use and improving the processes of conciliation, arbitration and any other means for preventing and resolving international commercial disputes and difficulties.
>
> 3. Arbitration organizations in various parts of the world and other interested bodies and individuals may be invited to participate in congresses and other activities sponsored by ICCA, Each arbitration organization which participates in the activities of ICCA shall retain its own autonomy and independence, ICCA may cooperate with organizations of the United Nations, with other international bodies and with various interested organizations in carrying out projects related to international commercial arbitration, conciliation and other means of dispute resolution."

In 1993, Lord Mustill expressed the purposes of ICCA in these words:

> "The Council is the prime forum for the strengthening and development of the law and practice of commercial arbitration. It has a pivotal role in maintaining intellectual and professional contacts between those who in many countries can influence the present conduct and the future growth of international commercial

> arbitration. In this field, inconsistency, fragmentation, misunderstanding and even hostility are constant dangers."[3]

ICCA has been successful in these objectives. In particular, ICCA has actively participated in the preparation and amendments of the work of UNCITRAL, as well as in the discussion of topics of significant importance for the development of international arbitration law.

Cooperation with UNCITRAL began in the early days when the latter invited ICCA to establish a representative group for consultation as part the preparation of the 1976 UNCITRAL Arbitration Rules. Following extensive consultation with this group, a preliminary draft was issued and was made available for consultation and discussion during the Vth ICCA Congress in New Delhi in 1975.

ICCA has been at the forefront of the development of the law and has contributed to the elaboration of the main texts that shape international arbitration:

- In 1975, ICCA discussed the UNCITRAL Arbitration Rules, which were adopted in 1976;
- In 1984, ICCA discussed the UNCITRAL Model Law on International Commercial Arbitration, which was adopted in 1985;
- In 1994, ICCA discussed the project for improving planning of arbitral proceedings, which resulted in the UNCITRAL Notes on Organizing Arbitral Proceedings;
- In 2002, ICCA discussed the UNCITRAL Model Law on Conciliation, which was adopted in 2002;
- The same year, ICCA discussed the proposed amendments to the UNCITRAL Model Law on International Commercial Arbitration, later adopted in 2006;
- In 2008, ICCA discussed the revision of the UNCITRAL Arbitration Rules, adopted in 2010.

> "One of the reasons for the world-wide acceptance of the UNCITRAL Arbitration Rules and the Model Law was that UNCITRAL has from the very beginning sought advice from practitioners and users before the projects were finalized. Once can say that ICCA's International Arbitration Congresses and Conferences have played an important clearing-house function: Working Party I of ICCA's Vth International Arbitration Congress in New Delhi, January 1975, commented on the draft UNCITRAL Arbitration Rules, and ICCA's Third Interim Meeting in Lausanne, May 1984, was exclusively devoted to the discussion of the UNCITRAL's project for a Model Law on International Commercial Arbitration."[4]

---

3. Lord Michael MUSTILL, "Keynote Speech, Bahrain 1993 Conference" in *International Arbitration in a Changing World*, ICCA Congress Series no. 6 (1993) p. 13.
4. Werner MELIS, "Opening Address, Vienna 1994 Congress" in *Planning Efficient Arbitration Proceedings and The Law Applicable in International Arbitration*, ICCA Congress Series no. 7 (1994) p. 9.

ICCA has also dealt with fundamental principles of international arbitration law, which have become widely recognized in this field, such as the concept of international public policy or the capacity of states to arbitrate. In addition, ICCA has worked towards improving the efficiency of the processes available for settling international disputes.

More recently, ICCA discussed a possible revision of the New York Convention.

IV. ICCA CONGRESSES AND CONFERENCES

An important activity of ICCA is the preparation and conduct of international arbitration congresses.

An ICCA congress or conference is usually held every other year for the purpose of presenting and discussing papers on different aspects of international dispute resolution. These meetings attract a large number of participants from all parts of the world and have made significant contributions to the development of dispute resolution theory and practice.

From the outset, it was announced that ICCA Congresses would be designed to work actively and seriously: "*Notre Congrès sera plutôt un congrès de travail qu'un congrès où en dine et danse.*" ["Our Congress will be a congress of work rather than one of dining and dancing."][5]

In keeping with the universal ambit of its activities and of international commercial arbitration, ICCA convened its congresses and conferences in all regions of the world. The congresses or conferences were held regularly from 1961 in the following cities:

Ist Congress	Paris, France	1961
IInd Congress	Rotterdam, the Netherlands	1966
IIIrd Congress	Venice, Italy	1969
IVth Congress	Moscow, Russia	1972
Interim Meeting	London, United Kingdom	1974
Vth Congress	New Delhi, India	1975
Interim Meeting	Vienna, Austria	1976
VIth Congress	Mexico City, Mexico	1978
Interim Meeting	Warsaw, Poland	1980
VIIth Congress	Hamburg, Germany	1982
Interim Meeting	Lausanne, Switzerland	1984
VIIIth Congress	New York, United States	1986
IXth Congress	Tokyo, Japan	1988
Xth Congress	Stockholm, Sweden	1990
XIth Conference	Bahrain	1993

5. Pieter SANDERS, Rev. arb. (1961) p. 15.

XIIth Congress	Vienna Austria	1994
XIIIth Conference	Seoul, South Korea	1996
XIVth Conference	Paris, France	1998
XVth Conference	New Delhi, India	2000
XVIth Congress	London, United Kingdom	2002
XVIIth Conference	Beijing, China	2004
XVIIIth Congress	Montreal, Canada	2006
XIXth Conference	Dublin, Ireland	2008
XXth Congress	Rio Brazil	2010
50th Anniversary Conference	Geneva, Switzerland	2011
XXIst Conference	Singapore	2012

V. ICCA PUBLICATIONS

Contributing to the development of legal scholarship through the publication of books and articles is a long-standing tradition at ICCA. These publications are prepared with the assistance of the Permanent Court of Arbitration and published in cooperation with Kluwer Law International. ICCA's publication offices are located at the Peace Palace in The Hague.

1. *Yearbook Commercial Arbitration*

In 1975, during the Vth Congress in New Dehli, ICCA resolved that it would issue a "Yearbook", for the purpose of providing "a central medium for the international dissemination of the fruits of arbitration research".

Since 1976, the *Yearbook Commercial Arbitration* has been a major source of information concerning international arbitration jurisprudence. Published under the guidance of the General Editor, Albert Jan van den Berg, and with the assistance of the Permanent Court of Arbitration, the *Yearbook* provides an annual update on key developments which include: institutional and ad hoc arbitral awards, court decisions on arbitration from around the world, court decisions on major multilateral arbitration conventions, commentary on the court decisions on the New York Convention 1958, updates on developments in arbitration law and practice, an investment treaty awards and decisions digest and a bibliography of the latest texts.

2. *International Handbook on Commercial Arbitration*

The *International Handbook on Commercial Arbitration* details the arbitral law and practice in over seventy countries and is an essential tool for anyone practicing international arbitration across multiple jurisdictions. Published under the leadership of General Editor, Jan Paulsson, and with the assistance of the Permanent Court of Arbitration, the *Handbook* contains authoritative country reports prepared by leading arbitrators, academics and practitioners on national arbitral practice, as well as the relevant national legislation.

3. Congress Series

Since the first conference in 1961, ICCA conferences and congresses have provided a platform for exchange and discussion on all aspects of international arbitration, including: emerging ideas in the field, fundamental principles and contentious topics of the day. In 1982, in Hamburg, ICCA's Council decided that ICCA would take charge of publishing its congresses and interim meetings. This was done in order to "free the organizers of these meetings from the burden of preparing such publications and their distribution". ICCA Publications began presenting the papers from its conferences and congresses in the Congress Series.

The Congress Series contains the resolutions, reports and communications presented during the congress or conference.

APPENDIX II

The Development of Australia as an Arbitral Seat – A Victorian Supreme Court Perspective

Clyde Croft[*]

TABLE OF CONTENTS

	Page
I. Introduction	227
II. Australian Model Law Arbitration Legislation	229
III. An Attractive Arbitral Seat	231
IV. The Specialist Arbitration List of the Commercial Court of the Supreme Court of Victoria	234
V. Key Legislative Provisions – The International Arbitration Act 1974 (as Amended in 2010) and the Commercial Arbitration Act 2010	240
VI. Conclusion	254
Annex I: Supreme Court of Victoria, Practice Note No. 2 of 2010 – Arbitration Business	255

I. INTRODUCTION

Commercial arbitration continues its global growth – with very significant increases in the number of disputes initiated, as well as in the monetary sums in dispute. This strong trend can be partially attributed to developing and rapidly industrializing economies, particularly those in Asia, and the consequent increase in business opportunities and ensuing disputes. No doubt the impact of long-established arbitral jurisdictions, such as New York, London, Paris and other European centres, has also played a part. However, given that international arbitration generally relies on mutual consent, businesses and legal practitioners must have been satisfied at the time of contracting that dispute resolution by arbitration was fair, efficient and enforceable. Contracting parties must first have had a favourable disposition towards arbitration, and also been able to understand the specific factors and decisions to be made which influence the particular ways in which an arbitration may be conducted. Surveys such as the *2010 International*

* B Ec LLM (Monash), PhD (Cambridge), LFACICA, LFIAMA, JFAMINZ, FCIArb; Judge in charge of the Commercial Court Arbitration List, Supreme Court of Victoria.

I would like to thank Mr. David Markham, B.Com LLB (Hons)(Monash), my Senior Associate, and Mr. Drossos Stamboulakis, my Associate, for their invaluable assistance in the preparation of this paper.

Arbitration Survey: Choices in International Arbitration[1] show that parties do consider various factors in choosing a favourable seat or law to govern the contract.

Given the sophistication of the corporations that utilize international arbitration, there is a certain level of competition between arbitral jurisdictions. Potential seats take active measures to promote their approach to arbitration; otherwise they risk marginalization in the competitive global marketplace. Failing to present attractively may have significantly adverse consequences, particularly in terms of the development of a jurisdiction's international legal expertise, and the involvement of its legal and other professionals in international trade and commerce.

Success in this respect is, of course, not only dependent on arbitrators and arbitration practitioners. The whole process must be well supported by arbitral institutions and, importantly, the courts. All concerned must play their part in maintaining the quality of arbitral processes and outcomes, and in reducing delay and expense. Courts, whether they be supervising or enforcing, must understand and support arbitration in all these respects – and they must be impartial and efficient. This is particularly important in an atmosphere of concern, internationally and domestically, at the incidence of delay and expense. Also of fundamental importance is the state of the arbitration law, the legislation regulating both domestic and international arbitration.

Australia has not developed a high volume of commercial arbitration business. This is in contrast to the outstanding success seen in Europe and the United States, for example. There are many reasons for this, which no doubt include the role and impact, both perceived and real, of the national and state legislatures, courts, and arbitral bodies.

Recently, there have been significant efforts made by individuals and organizations, public and private, to encourage and develop arbitration in Australia. These include efforts by the judiciary to create and promote the services of specialist lists and judges, significant legislative changes, and development of new rules, services and education programs by arbitral institutes and centres. Arbitrators, arbitration practitioners, arbitral institutes, governments and courts involved or interested in arbitration are, with this momentum, utilizing the opportunities to bolster and reinforce both domestic and international arbitral regimes. Arbitral institutions are also playing their part as promoters, educators and guardians of ethical standards.[2]

The aim of the present arbitration reinvigoration process is to increase the use of both international and domestic commercial arbitration in Australia. International experience indicates that countries that have been successful in establishing busy international arbitration centres and attracting significant international arbitration work also have significant and active domestic arbitration sectors. The two feed off each other. The vibrant domestic arbitration sector provides significant experience for its arbitrators – and also for its courts. It is all the more so where the domestic arbitration law is based

1. Queen Mary, University of London, School of International Arbitration, *2010 International Arbitration Survey: Choices in International Arbitration*, sponsored by White & Case LLP (hereinafter *QM Survey*).
2. Including the Australian Centre for International Commercial Arbitration (ACICA), the Chartered Institute of Arbitrators (Australian Branch) and the Institute of Arbitrators and Mediators Australia (IAMA).

on an international regime, such as the UNCITRAL Model Law on International Commercial Arbitration (the Model Law)[3] – as is the emerging position in Australia.

This paper discusses these issues with reference to the international and domestic arbitration environment in Australia, and particularly the role of the specialist Arbitration List in the Commercial Court of the Supreme Court of Victoria.

II. AUSTRALIAN MODEL LAW ARBITRATION LEGISLATION

There has been significant legislative activity in the Asia-Pacific region. Perhaps most prominently, the governments of Australia, Singapore and Hong Kong independently reviewed their respective arbitration legislation. These efforts were directed to updating, modernizing and clarifying existing arbitration law and practice, as well as promoting the individual jurisdiction as an attractive seat for future arbitrations.

As a result of its reviews in relation to international and domestic commercial arbitration, Australia chose to adopt the majority of the 2006 amendments to the Model Law, bringing it into line with Singapore and Hong Kong. All three jurisdictions now have provisions largely consistent with the 2006 Model Law, including provisions modernizing the form requirement for an arbitration agreement, designating a prescribed appointing authority and governing the grant of interim measures. Nevertheless, with the exception of these jurisdictions, the enactment of the *International Arbitration Amendment Act* 2010 made Australia one of few countries to implement (with amendments) the 2006 revisions to the Model Law.[4]

The revised *International Arbitration Act* in both Australia and Singapore came into effect on 6 July 2010 and 1 January 2010, respectively. The updated Hong Kong Arbitration Ordinance commenced operation on 1 June 2011. The Australian uniform *Commercial Arbitration Bill* 2010, which will apply the Model Law provisions, with some adaptations, to domestic commercial arbitration is to be implemented in all states and territories. New South Wales was the first state to adopt the new uniform commercial arbitration legislation in the *Commercial Arbitration Act 2010* (NSW), which commenced operation on 1 October 2010. The *Commercial Arbitration Act 2011* (Vic) was assented to on 18 October 2011 and came into operation on 17 November 2011.

As indicated, and as will be discussed, the Model Law, as amended in 2006, forms the basis of both the *International Arbitration Act* 1974 (Commonwealth of Australia) (the

3. United Nations Commission on International Trade Law (UNCITRAL), Model Law on International Commercial Arbitration 1985 (as adopted by UNCITRAL on 21 June 1985). Adopted by the UN General Assembly 11 December 1985 (General Assembly Resolution 40/72), with revisions (as amended by UNCITRAL and adopted on 7 July 2006) adopted by the UN General Assembly on 4 December 2006 (General Assembly Resolution 61/33).

4. Only Georgia, Hong Kong, Ireland, Mauritius, New Zealand, Peru, Rwanda, Singapore, Slovenia and Florida (US) have implemented the 2006 version. For current adoption status, see UNCITRAL website: <www.uncitral.org/uncitral/en/uncitral_texts/arbitration/1985Model_arbitration_status.html>.

IAA), as amended in 2010,[5] and the soon to be adopted uniform *Commercial Arbitration Acts* (the CAA). The position that the IAA, which provides for international arbitration,[6] and the CAA, which provides for domestic arbitration, are national legislation in the first instance and state and territory legislation in the second does, to a great extent, reflect the realities of the division of legislative powers in the Australian federation – a notion that may cause a degree of puzzlement to those who live and work in unitary states.[7] The use of the amended Model Law as the basis of both the international and domestic commercial arbitration legislation in Australia provides legislation which is based on current international consensus and accepted practice and which is well understood internationally. Consequently the Australian legislation, at both levels, becomes immediately accessible and understood internationally – particularly as it is expected that it will be interpreted and administered by the Australian courts on the basis of accepted international jurisprudence. In terms of substance, the Model Law is an internationally drafted and accepted arbitration regime that is very supportive of commercial arbitration. It has been enacted in over sixty nation states. It allows parties the freedom to decide how they want their disputes resolved with minimal court intervention, but with maximum court support. Consequently, the Model Law is the arbitration law against which all other arbitration laws tend to be judged.

The choice of the Model Law as the basis for the CAA will assist with achieving a great deal of uniformity between the international and domestic regimes. As both the IAA and the CAA apply the Model Law provisions, with some additions and adaptations to accommodate their particular contexts, judgments under one regime can and will inform judgments under the other. State and Territory Supreme Court judges, when making decisions under the CAA, will need to be more aware of the impact of their judgments

5. Extensive amendments were made by the International Arbitration Amendment Act 2010 as a result of the review of the then existing Australian international arbitration legislation, the International Arbitration Act 1974. In relation to the review, see Commonwealth of Australia Attorney General's Department "Review of the International Arbitration Act 1974, Discussion Paper", November 2008.

6. As Sect. 16 of the IAA applies the Model Law, as amended in 2006, arbitration is "international" if the provisions of Art. 1(3) of the Model Law are applicable. As to the meaning of "commercial" in the context of the expression "international commercial arbitration" as used in Art. 1(1) of the Model Law, reference should be made to *UNCITRAL Model Law on International Commercial Arbitration 1985 – With amendments as adopted in 2006* (United Nations, Vienna, 2008) p. 1, fn. 2 (available at <www.uncitral.org/pdf/english/texts/arbitration/ml-arb/07-86998_Ebook.pdf>).

7. Consequently it may assist to clarify some points arising from this federal structure. The IAA is national legislation of the national (federal) parliament, the Parliament of the Commonwealth of Australia. The CAA is national uniform legislation but is, nevertheless, the legislation of the individual state and territory parliaments. The reference to "the territories" in this paper is a reference to the mainland territories only (i.e., The Australian Capital Territory (ACT) and the Northern Territory of Australia (NT)); though the IAA does apply throughout Australia and all its territories, mainland and external (see IAA, Sect. 16). Reference to "Australian legislation" is a more general reference to both the national and the state and territory legislation operating within Australia. Similarly a reference to "Australian courts" is a general reference to the Federal Court of Australia and to the state and territory Supreme Courts.

on the interpretation of the IAA, as they have jurisdiction under both regimes.[8] Additionally, international and domestic parties are likely, and entitled, to assume that a decision on similar or identical provisions under one regime will be found to apply with equal force under the other regime. Consequently, decisions under the CAA will also be considered in determining whether Australia is an attractive seat for international arbitrations. Given that, at least initially, it is likely that there will be more decisions under the CAA than the IAA, it would seem that Australia's Model Law jurisprudence will be developed, at first, by the State and Territory Supreme Courts, as the Federal Court of Australia, which has jurisdiction under the IAA has no jurisdiction in the domestic regime. There was some controversy surrounding the question whether the Federal Court should be given exclusive jurisdiction under the IAA during the process of review which led to the amending legislation.[9] At the time this issue was being discussed the only context was the proposed amendments to the IAA and not the effect of applying the Model Law domestically in terms of the CAA, which raises the variety of additional considerations to which reference has been made.

Similarly, the Hong Kong Arbitration Ordinance provides for a unitary regime, removing the distinction between domestic and international arbitrations. Singapore, however, continues to maintain a distinction between domestic and international arbitrations, the former operating under the Arbitration Act (Chapter 10), and the latter under Singapore's International Arbitration Act (Chapter 143A). Nonetheless, Singapore's domestic Arbitration Act relies heavily on Model Law provisions, and thus the provisions of the domestic Act are largely similar to those of the international regime.

III. AN ATTRACTIVE ARBITRAL SEAT

The *QM Survey* provides a "checklist" for assessing the attractiveness, or otherwise, of a jurisdiction as a seat for arbitrations. The *QM Survey* found that the most important factor influencing the choice of the seat for arbitration was the "formal legal infrastructure" at the seat.[10] The passage of the Model Law-based legislation enhances Australia's position in this respect. Australia, like other attractive international arbitration seats, has stable government institutions. With these legislative reforms the "arbitration friendliness" of Australia has improved significantly. As discussed below in Sect. IV, the Arbitration List in the Victorian Supreme Court was established to facilitate efficient arbitration proceedings by providing constantly accessible and efficient court processes to support arbitration proceedings at all stages – and to ensure the absence of delay in the hearing of urgent applications. According to the *QM Survey* these are considerations in determining the convenience, hence the attractiveness, of a seat.

8. A position which is reinforced, and required, by Sect. 2A of the CAA (see below).
9. The issue was raised in the Commonwealth of Australia Attorney General's Department "Review of the International Arbitration Act 1974, Discussion Paper", November 2008 in Sect. H.
10. *QM Survey*, p. 17.

The governing law of the contract is also an important factor in selecting an arbitral seat –and the two may coincide. While Australian law is obviously not as frequently specified as the law of the contract as, for example, English or New York law, it may be seen as a useful option. It is based on English common law and its own developed jurisprudence is regularly cited and applied in other jurisdictions. Of course, arbitrations in Australia can and do apply English law with relative ease; or, similarly, New York, Singapore or Hong Kong law if that is desired. The effect of the choice of seat on enforceability of the arbitral award is also a serious matter – and one to be considered carefully. The choice of a jurisdiction where neutrality and impartiality are questionable may invite enforcement problems. Australia does not, of course, present any such problem.

Additionally, according to the *QM Survey*, a critical factor in choosing the governing law is the neutrality and impartiality of the legal system – and Australian law and Australia cannot be faulted on that score.

Arbitral institutions and their rules are another factor that may influence the choice of the seat. The Australian Centre for International Commercial Arbitration (ACICA) provides a choice of modern arbitration rules – its rules of general application to international arbitrations and an expedited set of rules tailored for smaller disputes. ACICA has played a leading role in raising the profile of arbitration in Australia, supporting the process and educating arbitrators.

There is also the important question of cost (arbitrators', experts' and lawyers' fees). In this context steps might be taken to limit or control fee structures which do not encourage efficiency, such as time costing, and which may cut across the aim of legislatures, courts and arbitrators to promote speed and cost-effective processes.[11]

It would, of course, be counterproductive to gloss over the fact that, at times, there has been a perception that the Australian courts have hindered effective commercial arbitration, both by intervening too much in the arbitral process and by interpreting the arbitral law in an interventionist rather than a supportive way. This perception, as well as many other factors, was one of the reasons that Australian commercial arbitration legislation required attention; though the domestic legislation had also become very dated as a result of developments in legislation elsewhere.[12] Prior to the enactment of

---

11. And see, in the litigation context, Justice Clyde CROFT, "*AON* and Its Implications for the Commercial Court", a paper presented at the Commercial Court CPD and CLE – "*Aon Risk Services Australia Ltd v. ANU* [2009] HCA 27: What Does This Mean for Litigation and How Will It Affect Trial Preparation?" seminar on 19 August 2010, available at <www.supreme court. vic.gov.au/wps/wcm/connect/justlib/supreme+court/home/library/supreme+-+aon+and+its+implications+for+the++commercial+court>.

12. The domestic commercial arbitration legislation, prior to the enactment of the Commercial Arbitration Act 2010 in New South Wales was uniform (or substantially uniform) legislation which flowed from the work of the Standing Committee of Attorneys-General (SCAG – see fn. 45 below) in the late 1970s and early 1980s which was based on the then new and innovative legislative developments in England which resulted in the enactment of new legislation in the form of the Arbitration Act 1975 (Eng) and, principally, the Arbitration Act 1979 (Eng). Victoria was the first State to enact the legislation SCAG had developed, in the form of the Commercial Arbitration Act 1984. New South Wales followed shortly afterwards as, in due course, did the other States and the Territories. Apart from in New South Wales, as a result of its enactment of

the then new, uniform, domestic commercial arbitration legislation in the mid-1980s commercial arbitration had been constrained very significantly by the case-stated procedure which could be used, in effect, to force a retrial of the issues in an arbitration in the reviewing court. Naturally, the cost, expense and delay involved had the effect of making commercial arbitration very unattractive.

There were great hopes for the uniform legislation, based on the English experience. For example, it was expected that the new constrained appeal and review provisions, based as they were on the 1979 English legislation, would lead Australian courts to adopt the same "hands-off" approach which came to be expressed by Lord Diplock in the, so-called, *Nema* guidelines.[13] With the hindsight of history we know that this did not occur, at least not uniformly, and a good deal of uncertainty resulted which did not assist the development of commercial arbitration.

In defence of the courts it might be said that the legislatures could have included the *Nema* guidelines in the new Acts if this had been the legislative intent, but given the provenance of the legislation and the English case law I think it would have to be conceded that there were some "unfortunate" decisions. There were some problems with over-intervention in the arbitration process by way of judicial review of awards and as a result of an increasing tendency for parties to challenge awards on the basis of, what is generally best described as, "technical misconduct". This should not, however, overshadow the very effective and useful work of the courts in expediting and supporting arbitration through very "arbitration friendly" decisions on the operation of the arbitration legislation, and more generally. This is unsurprising and consistent with the approach of the common law over a long period of time. In this respect it is, in my view, worth noting that the common law courts were as far back as the eighteenth century, extraordinarily supportive of commercial arbitration as Professor James Oldham's account of the work of Lord Mansfield in the latter part of that century illustrates.[14] More recently, the English, Singapore and Hong Kong courts, for example, have been very supportive, as many of our courts have been, and continue to be.

Also of concern has been the actual performance of arbitration itself. Although the education programs of the arbitral institutions seek to develop and promote innovative techniques which save time and cost, all too often arbitration as practiced in Australia has tended to replicate traditional litigation. I say "traditional litigation" as for many years the Commercial Courts in this and other countries have embraced aggressive case management and time-saving techniques which have made "innovative litigation" far more attractive than domestic commercial arbitration in many instances.

In more recent times this healthy competition and the example provided by these courts has fed into arbitration processes and emboldened arbitrators to be more robust in applying active case management and more innovative techniques. This process has

---

the Commercial Arbitration Act 2010, this is the domestic commercial arbitration legislation still in force in Australia.

13. See *Pioneer Shipping Ltd v. BTP Tioxide Ltd ("The Nema")* [1982] AC 724 at 742; and see J.A. SHARKEY and J.B. DORTER, *Commercial Arbitration* (LBC 1986) pp. 268-274.

14. J. OLDHAM, *English Common Law in the Age of Mansfield* (University of North Carolina Press 2004) pp. 68-72.

also been assisted by cross-fertilization from international arbitration where innovation in arbitration processes has tended to be in advance of domestic arbitration, if only because of very significant time, cost and logistical constraints applying to the former. Interestingly the approach of international arbitrators has also assisted the courts and we now see the application of such techniques as "chess clock" time management being used by the courts. Other positive influences include the very successful special reference procedures available and applied extensively by the Supreme Court of New South Wales – which provide, in effect, an expedited, supervised, commercial arbitration process with minimal appeal potential and no enforcement problems. These provisions are now being applied more frequently in the Supreme Court of Victoria.

IV. THE SPECIALIST ARBITRATION LIST OF THE COMMERCIAL COURT OF THE SUPREME COURT OF VICTORIA

The Supreme Court of Victoria is vested with supervisory, supportive and enforcement jurisdiction over both domestic and international commercial arbitration. As noted previously, the Federal Court of Australia only has jurisdiction with respect to international arbitration, as defined in the Commonwealth IAA, as amended in 2010.

On the 1 January 2010, the new Arbitration List of the Commercial Court in the Victorian Supreme Court began operation. I am pleased to be the judge in charge of the list, which is the only specialist arbitration list in Australia.[15]

The popularity of specialist arbitration lists or courts is growing in the region. In August 2010, Bombay's High Court announced the creation of a court dedicated to arbitration-related applications. In China, a similar practice has arisen where a lower court decision not to enforce an award is, in practice, automatically referred to a higher court to review, and if not enforced it must, consequently, be reviewed by the Supreme People's Court. All of these efforts are aimed at ensuring that specialization in the resolution of arbitral disputes leads to consistent and predictable outcomes in line with global arbitration jurisprudence and international conventions and obligations. The Court of First Instance of the High Court of Hong Kong and the High Court of Singapore have been achieving these results for some time. The Dubai International Financial Centre Court has similar goals and has a good relationship with the DIFC-LCIA Arbitration Centre.

1. *The Operation of the List*

All arbitration matters brought in the Victorian Supreme Court are to be heard in the Arbitration List of the Commercial Court. Arbitration matters are exempt from the usual Commercial Court fee, which applies because of the managed list and expeditious processes which are available. The operation of the arbitration list is set out in *Practice*

15. The Federal Court of Australia has a panel of judges available to hear arbitration matters, but it has not established a separate list.

Note 2 of 2010 – Arbitration Business.[16] The Practice Note sets out procedural information as well as useful guidelines for those considering an application. Parties are encouraged to communicate directly with my Associates before commencing an application at the Registry. There are a number of advantages to this approach. First, the parties can seek to clarify any procedural or administrative issues. Second, enquiries are made with Associates who have experience in handling arbitration-related enquiries. Third, and most importantly, parties are given a very early opportunity to suggest when the application should be heard. This is essential given the expedition of matters that the Arbitration List aims to achieve. In fact, given the priority put on hearing arbitration-related matters quickly, the parties have often asked for a more relaxed timetable than has been offered to them.

There are also more substantive benefits that flow from providing a specialist list, with a specialist judge or judges. A court that has established an arbitration list is likely to be more aware of the specific issues that arise in the arbitration context. Also, a consistent body of arbitration-related decisions can be developed by judges who have an interest or expertise in arbitration. This is especially important in the early days of Australia's new arbitration regime when each new decision is potentially going to have an impact on the interpretation of the Model Law provisions in Australia as well as on the reputation of Australian courts in dealing with arbitration. Consistent interpretation and application of the IAA and the CAA, and which conforms with international thinking having regard to the Model Law base of both pieces of legislation, is leading to the minimum amount of court intervention necessary, as well as providing support for the arbitration process when required.

An important area that the courts need to ensure is clear and easily accessible is the procedure to be applied with respect to the making of and dealing with applications under the IAA and the CAA. In this context, procedure must also include listing procedures and expedition.[17] Specialist courts with arbitration lists assist in this respect. The procedural approach to applications under the IAA and the CAA will have a major impact on the way that Australian arbitration law is viewed. For example, staying court proceedings in favour of an arbitration is a pro-arbitration step, but if it takes an excessive time for the stay application to be heard and determined, the arbitration process has probably been thwarted anyway. Procedural consistency and expediency is far more likely to be achieved when there are specialist arbitration lists and judges; as the experience in leading commercial arbitration centres such as London, Singapore and Hong Kong shows. Specific arbitration practice notes and rules are essential to this process.

16. See Annex I to this Paper, pp. 255-259.

17. Noting in this respect that the Victorian Supreme Court Arbitration List (List G) is available twenty-four hours per day, seven days per week and hearings can and do take place outside court hours as required.

2. Liaison Between Courts and with Arbitration Users

If the objectives of the IAA and the CAA[18] are to be fully realized, the courts need to communicate with and receive feedback from commercial arbitration stakeholders. Specialist courts with arbitration lists are particularly well placed to do this as they are in contact with the relevant parties and practitioners to the greatest extent possible. An Arbitration Users' Group for the Supreme Court of Victoria is being established. I expect that this Users' Group will be especially useful in discussing and developing the procedures for commencing and disposing of applications under the IAA and the CAA. This consultation may lead to further improvements to the Arbitration Business Practice Note.[19] I would expect that other courts will establish similar consultative mechanisms.

The courts in a federal state like Australia, where the jurisdiction is spread between a number of different courts, need to liaise with each other to develop and share their arbitration expertise. The existence of specialist arbitration lists will help in this regard by directing arbitration business to particular judges within a court who can then share their knowledge and experience with the arbitration judges from other courts. This consultation between judges of the Federal Court and the judges of the State and Territory Supreme Courts will be essential if, as I expect, the majority of Model Law decisions are initially made under the CAA. This process is being assisted by the ACICA Judicial Liaison Committee which was established in late October 2010. This Committee is chaired by a former Chief Justice of the High Court of Australia, the Hon Murray Gleeson AC. The Committee includes the judges hearing arbitration-related cases from the Supreme Courts and the Federal Court, as well as representatives from ACICA. It aims to promote uniformity in the rules and procedures relating to arbitration in Australia – particularly concerning the enforcement of arbitration agreements and awards, as well as the appointment of arbitrators, and the provision of interim measures or other assistance in support of arbitration.

3. Raising the Expectations on Arbitrators and Practitioners

In order to achieve the general objectives discussed, courts need, and value, assistance from parties and their representatives. Solicitors and counsel are able to provide significant assistance to the courts in applying the Model Law provisions, as applied by the IAA or as adopted by the CAA, in a manner consistent with international and domestic jurisprudence. Assistance by reference to commentaries and case law in submissions informed by comprehensive research, including consideration of the broader policy considerations underlying the legislation – policy considerations which may have an international dimension, for the purposes of both the IAA and the CAA – is essential. The existence of a specialist arbitration list with a specialist judge or judges can provide a focus for arbitrators and arbitration practitioners, both for the purpose of educating arbitrators and practitioners in this respect and providing an understood level of knowledge and expectation having regard to the expertise of the court.

---

18. See below, Sect. V.*1*.

19. Practice Note No. 2 of 2010 – Arbitration Business (Annex I to this Paper, pp. 255-259).

4. *Decisions in the Arbitration List*

The Arbitration List has attracted a significant amount of work since it began operation nearly eighteen months ago. During that time I have handed down judgments in six arbitration matters,[20] some quite significant, and dealt with a variety of other applications. Each case that has gone to judgment has raised a different issue regarding the extent to which the Court can intervene or assist in arbitration decisions or processes, including enforcement – both those of procedure and substance. Four of the decisions were made under the Victorian Commercial Arbitration Act 1984, which is the domestic commercial arbitration legislation. However, the principles in those cases are still very relevant in examining the relationship between the Court and arbitration more generally. *Arnwell Pty Ltd v. Teilaboot Pty Ltd & Ors*[21] raised issues regarding court intervention in procedural decisions made by an arbitral tribunal. *Oakton Services Pty Ltd v. Tenix Solutions*[22] was a successful application to stay court proceedings in favour of arbitration as there was an arbitration agreement in place. *Thoroughvision Pty Ltd v. Sky Channel Pty Limited & Anor*[23] involved an application for leave to appeal an arbitral award under Sect. 38 of the Commercial Arbitration Act and an application to set aside an award for misconduct under Sect. 42 of that Act on the basis of insufficient reasons provided in the award. I found that there was no manifest error of law on the face of the award for the purposes of Sub-sect. 38(5)(b)(i) and that there was no misconduct on the part of the arbitrator for the purposes of Sect. 42 on the basis asserted. This required examination of the quality of reasons required of an arbitrator under Sub-sect. 29(1)(c) of the Commercial Arbitration Act 1984 in the context of a decision of the Victorian Court of Appeal[24] and a recent decision of the New South Wales Court of Appeal[25] in that area. The *Thoroughvision* decision was referred to (though not named) in an article in the legal section of the *Australian Financial Review*[26] on 30 April 2010 which said that I suggested the New South Wales Court of Appeal approach in relation to the quality of reasons that an arbitrator must give was preferable. This is something of an oversimplification because clearly the Victorian decision is binding in Victoria within the ambit of the issues decided. Consequently, it may be helpful to set out what I did say in *Thoroughvision*:[27]

---

20. *Arnwell Pty Ltd v. Teilaboot Pty Ltd & Ors* [2010] VSC 123; *Thoroughvision Pty Ltd v. Sky Channel Pty Limited & Anor* [2010] VSC 139; *Oakton Services Pty Ltd v. Tenix Solutions IMES Pty Ltd* [2010] VSC 176; *Winter v. Equuscorp Pty Ltd* [2010] VSC 419; *Altain Khuder LLC v. IMC Mining Inc & Anor* [2011] VSC 1; *Altain Khuder LLC v. IMC Mining Inc & Anor (No 2)* [2011] VSC 12.
21. [2010] VSC 123.
22. [2010] VSC 176.
23. [2010] VSC 139 (*Thoroughvision*).
24. *Oil Basins Ltd v. BHP Billiton Ltd* (2007) 18 VR 346.
25. *Gordian Runoff Ltd v. Westport Insurance Corporation* [2010] NSWCA 57.
26. James EYERS, "Battle for Arbitration Continues", Australian Financial Review (30 April 2010) p. 42.
27. *Thoroughvision Pty Ltd v. Sky Channel Pty Limited & Anor* [2010] VSC 139 at [54]-[58].

"54. In my opinion, it is clear from the authorities that a principle of proportionality applies with respect to the nature and extent of reasons which an arbitrator is obliged to provide in an arbitration award. An example of a case in which very extensive and comprehensive reasons were required is *Oil Basins Ltd v. BHP Billiton Ltd.*[28] This was, however, an arbitration that involved 15 hearing days, an arbitral tribunal of three, conflicting and substantive expert evidence and substantial submissions. The present arbitration is, on the other hand, an arbitration confined with respect to the proper construction of the MOU. Further, as indicated, the Deed of Arbitration requires that the arbitration be conducted in accordance with the overriding objective referred to in that Deed, adopting procedures suitable to the determination of the type of issues involved and at the same time avoiding unnecessary delay and expense so as to provide a fair, expeditious and cost effective process for the determination of these issues.

55. It is well established that the reasons need show only that the arbitrator grasped the main contentions advanced by the parties, and communicated to the parties, in broad terms, the reasons for the conclusions reached.[29] The reasoning process must be exposed so that the reader of the award can understand how and why the conclusion was reached;[30] It is clear that reasons need not be elaborate or lengthy, provided that these requirements are met.[31] The decision of the Court of Appeal in *Oil Basins Ltd v. BHP Billiton Ltd*[32] confirms that an arbitrator must address each issue raised for decision within the scope of the arbitration agreement.[33] However it does not follow that the position outlined on the basis of the authorities to which reference has been made is rendered any different, or that the nature and extent of reasons is not to be fashioned by reference to the nature of the matters in dispute and, proportionately, having regard to the complexity of the issues, the importance, monetary or otherwise, of the arbitration proceedings and the nature of the arbitral proceedings, expeditious or otherwise, as agreed between the parties.

(....)

58. The present arbitration is, as indicated, to be distinguished from the very substantial, complex and lengthy arbitration proceeding the subject of the *Oil Basins* appeal. Additionally, this is not a case where, as in *Oil Basins*, the Arbitrator has omitted to deal with an entire and substantial issue, possibly, of critical significance to the arbitration. In this context I do not take the view that there is any relevant inconsistency for present purposes in the decisions of the Victorian

---

28. (2007) 18 VR 346 at 367, [57] (Buchanan, Nettle and Dodds-Streeton JJA).
29. See *UCATT v. Brain* [1981] IRLR 224 at 228 (Donaldson LJ); and see *Oil Basins Ltd v. BHP Billiton Ltd* (2007) 18 VR 346 at 364-368 [50]-[59] (Buchanan, Nettle and Dodds-Streeton JJA); and *Gordian Runoff Ltd v. Westport Insurance Corporation* [2010] NSWCA 57.
30. *Davidson v. Fish* [2008] VSC 32 at [12] (Pagone J); and see *Rashid v. Minister for Immigration and Citizenship* [2007] FCAFC 25 at [18] (Heerey, Stone and Edwards JJ).
31. See *Stefan v. General Medical Council* [1999] 1 WLR 1293 at 1304.
32. (2007) 18 VR 346.
33. See (2007) 18 VR 346 at 364 (Buchanan, Nettle and Dodds-Streeton JJA).

and New South Wales Courts of Appeal in *Oil Basins* and *Gordian Runoff*, respectively."[34]

Winter v. Equuscorp[35] was an unsuccessful attempt to appeal from a domestic commercial arbitration award.

The two most recent decisions were made under the IAA. These were the two judgments in *Altain Khuder LLC v. IMC Mining Inc &Anor*,[36] judgments which are significant for a number of reasons. First, the case involved the interpretation of the requirements of Sects. 8 and 9 of the IAA (as amended in 2010) for enforcement of a foreign arbitral award (provisions which reflect Arts. V and IV, respectively of the 1958 New York Convention).[37] The legislation, as amended, had not been interpreted in this respect previously.[38]

Second, it was a determination on the basis of various authorities from other jurisdictions, as reviewed (including *Dallah v. Government of Pakistan* in the Supreme Court of the United Kingdom) that the party seeking enforcement need only comply with the formal requirements of Art. IV of the New York Convention (reflected in Sect. 9 of the IAA) without any burden of proving the substantive elements of these formal requirements. The argument in *Khuder* was that the plaintiff bore the burden of establishing that one of the parties against which enforcement was sought was a party to the arbitration agreement – though not formally named as such. The judgment was significant in finding that in the particular circumstances of the case the burden lay, rather, on the party resisting enforcement to establish one or more of the defences to enforcement provided for in Sect. 8 of the IAA (provisions which apply the defences provided for in Art. V of the New York Convention); and similarly in relation to public policy issues.

Third, there was a discussion of principles such as *Kompetenz-Kompetenz* and the applicable or proper law to be applied in relation to various issues in the context of the application.

Fourth, the judgment confirmed procedural aspects of an application for enforcement in the context of arguments by the defendant resisting enforcement that an initial ex parte proceeding was not appropriate and that there had been lack of candour on the part of the plaintiff in its application ex parte. The initial ex parte application was for procedural orders which, if not responded to by the defendant, the award debtor, would result in an order for enforcement, by default.

---

34. I am strengthened in this view by the conditional language adopted by Allsop P with respect to the extent of inconsistency between these decisions (see [2010] NSWCA 57 at [222] and [224]).

35. [2010] VSC 419.

36. [2011] VSC 1 and [2011] VSC 12.

37. United Nations Convention on the Recognition and Enforcement of Foreign Arbitral Awards, opened for signature 10 June 1958, 330 UNTS 38 (entered into force 7 June 1959) (New York Convention).

38. The enforcement provisions of the IAA have subsequently been interpreted by Foster J of Federal Court of Australia in *Uganda Telecom Limited v. Hi-Tech Telecom Pty Ltd* [2011] FCA 131 (22 February 2011) and *Uganda Telecom Limited v. Hi-Tech Telecom Pty Ltd* (No. 2) [2011] FCA 206 (11 March 2011).

Fifth, in relation to costs, I considered and applied various Hong Kong High Court decisions to the effect that a party successfully seeking enforcement of a foreign arbitral award is entitled to full indemnity costs.[39] This was the first time that the issue had been determined in this way in Australia.

The unsuccessful party in the *Altain Khuder* cases, the award debtor, appealed the decisions to the Victorian Court of Appeal.[40]

5. *Government Support*

August 2010 saw the opening of the Australian International Disputes Centre, based in Sydney. Funded by the Australian and New South Wales governments and ACICA it offers modern purpose-built hearing facilities akin to its counterpart in Singapore, and also houses leading ADR providers in Australia – including ACICA, the Australian Branch of the Chartered Institute of Arbitrators and the Australian Commercial Disputes Centre (ACDC). It is envisaged that other Australian states, including Victoria, will also follow suit, acting in conjunction through a "grid" of co-ordinated centres throughout Australia to offer services to domestic and international parties alike.[41]

V. KEY LEGISLATIVE PROVISIONS – THE INTERNATIONAL ARBITRATION ACT 1974 (AS AMENDED IN 2010) AND THE COMMERCIAL ARBITRATION ACT 2010

The IAA applies the Model Law, as amended in 2006, to international commercial arbitrations and the CAA applies this version of the Model Law domestically – with some optional provisions (internationally) and adaptations (domestically).[42]

1. *Interpretation*

a. *Interpretation provisions*

Clearly, if the Supreme Courts of the States and Territories and the Federal Court do not interpret the Model Law, as applied by the IAA and the CAA consistently and in accordance with the legislative purpose and the provenance of the provisions, the present legislative reforms will not be successful in promoting and developing international and domestic commercial arbitration in Australia. The interpretation provisions of the Acts should, however, help in this respect, and it is to these that I now turn.

---

39. See cases such as *A v. R* [2009] 3 HKLRD 389.

40. After the time of writing, the appeal was allowed on 22 August 2011 in *IMC Aviation Solutions Pty Ltd v. Altain Khuder LLC* [2011] VSCA 248.

41. The Hon. Marilyn WARREN AC, Chief Justice of Victoria, "Victoria's Commitment to Arbitration Including International Arbitration and Recent Developments", remarks at the Australian Centre for International Commercial Arbitration reception at the Melbourne Office of Mallesons Stephen Jacques on 13 May 2010.

42. See above, fn. 7.

i. International Arbitration Act – matters to which the court must have regard – objects of the Act

A court or authority in exercising the functions and powers listed in Sub-sect. 39(1) must, in doing so:[43]

> "have regard to:
> (a) the objects of the Act; and
> (b) the fact that:
> (i) arbitration is an efficient, impartial, enforceable and timely method by which to resolve commercial disputes; and
> (ii) awards are intended to provide certainty and finality."

The extensive list in Sub-sect. 39(1) seems to cover most, if not all, situations where a court or authority[44] will be applying or interpreting the IAA, the Model Law, the New York Convention or arbitration agreements and awards. A court or authority is directed to have regard to the objects of the IAA rather than obliged to apply the objects of the Act or the other considerations. Nevertheless, this probably makes little practical difference.

The objects of the IAA are set out in Sect. 2D, as follows:

> "The objects of this Act are:
> (a) to facilitate international trade and commerce by encouraging the use of arbitration as a method of resolving disputes; and
> (b) to facilitate the use of arbitration agreements made in relation to international trade and commerce; and
> (c) to facilitate the recognition and enforcement of arbitral awards made in relation to international trade and commerce; and
> (d) to give effect to Australia's obligations under the Convention on the Recognition and Enforcement of Foreign Arbitral Awards adopted in 1958 by the United Nations Conference on International Commercial Arbitration at its twenty-fourth meeting; and

---

43. IAA, Sect. 39(2).

44. See IAA Sect. 18:

> "(1) A court or authority prescribed for the purposes of this subsection is taken to have been specified in Article 6 of the Model Law as a court or authority competent to perform the functions referred to in Article 11(3) of the Model Law.
> (2) A court or authority prescribed for the purposes of this subsection is taken to have been specified in Article 6 of the Model Law as a court or authority competent to perform the functions referred to in Article 11(4) of the Model Law."

The functions referred to in Art. 11(3) and (4) of the Model Law are the appointment of arbitrators. ACICA has now been prescribed as an "authority" for the purpose of these provisions. See Sect. V.*4.a.*, "Relevant Courts", below for further details.

(e) to give effect to the UNCITRAL Model Law on International Commercial Arbitration adopted by the United Nations Commission on International Trade Law on 21 June 1985 and amended by the United Nations Commission on International Trade Law on 7 July 2006; and
(f) to give effect to the Convention on the Settlement of Investment Disputes between States and Nationals of Other States signed by Australia on 24 March 1975."

The Parliamentary intention and objective is made quite clear by the combination of both Sects. 39 and 2D – the efficient settlement of disputes by encouraging the use of arbitration in the context of international trade and commerce. Regard should also be had to Art. 2A of the Model Law as amended in 2006 which provides:

"(1) In the interpretation of this Law, regard is to be had to its international origin and to the need to promote uniformity in its application and the observance of good faith.
(2) Questions concerning matters governed by the Law which are not expressly settled in it are to be settled in conformity with the general principles on which this Law is based."

ii. Commercial Arbitration Act[45] – Paramount object of Act

The paramount object of the CAA "to facilitate the fair and final resolution of commercial disputes without unnecessary delay or expense" is an addition to the Model Law. The CAA is to be interpreted "so that (as far as practicable) the paramount object is achieved".[46] While this section is aimed more at parties and arbitrators it is also a reminder to judges interpreting and applying the Act that one of the main advantages of commercial arbitration, in the domestic context, is the ability of parties and arbitrators to tailor arbitration procedures for the most efficient resolution of the dispute. Sometimes parties will want an arbitration that is just as formal as a court proceeding and sometimes they will want a "look and sniff" arbitration, and between these extremes lies the spectrum of possible arbitration procedures. If parties agree to procedures, which are less formal than court proceedings, courts should not interfere with this choice. The same applies if the parties have clearly agreed to procedures which replicate full, traditional, litigation. The problems always arise when there is a mismatch of expectations and reality, where a party or parties and the arbitrator see themselves at different points on the "spectrum". This is an issue to which arbitrators must direct their attention, and is a matter which many arbitration rules specifically require that they do give their attention and ensure that procedures are appropriate to the nature and value

45. References to sections in the CAA are to SCAG's Model Bill unless otherwise stated. SCAG is a committee comprising the Attorneys-General of the Commonwealth of Australia and each of the six states and two mainland territories (the Act and the NT). One of the roles of SCAG is the development of national uniform legislation, such as the CAA.

46. CAA, Sect. 1AC(2)(b).

of the dispute.[47] This is also an issue addressed in the IAA as a matter to which the courts must have regard.

b. Consistency in the interpretation of the IAA and the CAA

The most important provision for the achievement of consistency between interpretation of the CAA and the IAA is found in Sect. 2A of the CAA:

> "2A (1) Subject to section 1AC, in the interpretation of this Act, regard is to be had to the need to promote so far as practicable uniformity between the application of this Act to domestic commercial arbitrations and the application of the provisions of the Model Law (as given effect by the *International Arbitration Act 1974* of the Commonwealth) to international commercial arbitrations and the observance of good faith.
>
> ....
>
> (3) Without limiting subsection (1), in interpreting this Act, reference may be made to the documents relating to the Model Law of:
>
> (a) the United Nations Commission on International Trade Law, and
>
> (b) its working groups for the preparation of the Model Law."

Even if this provision did not contain this express exhortation, the courts would nevertheless be expected to interpret the two Acts consistently unless there was a good reason not to do so.

c. Having regard to the international origin and the need to promote uniformity

Consistency of interpretation is important, but only if the interpretation is both consistent and in accordance with accepted international jurisprudence with respect to the Model Law. As indicated previously it is critically important that the IAA and CAA are not treated as stand-alone pieces of legislation devoid of the international jurisprudence.[48]

The IAA and the CAA apply or are based on the Model Law that has been adopted in over sixty countries. The Model Law and the New York Convention, are, by their very nature, international. They are instruments which have been drafted internationally and which were intended by the drafters to apply to international disputes, between entities from different countries. Arbitrations are usually seated in a neutral country, and the arbitration award may be sought to be enforced in any country where the party liable, the award debtor, has assets; though far more easily if that country is a party to the New York Convention. Without uniformity of application, the international commercial arbitration system would not be a system at all. It would encounter similar difficulties as arise when trying to resolve international commercial disputes in national courts and, ultimately, seeking to enforce judgments internationally. It is beneficial to all countries

---

47. See, for example, Australian Centre for International Commercial Arbitration Expedited Arbitration Rules, Rule 3 "Overriding Objective" and Rule 13.1.

48. And see Sect. 2A of the CAA, set out above, which requires this approach from the CAA perspective.

which have adopted the Model Law (or similarly supportive arbitration laws) and the New York Convention if a harmonized system is maintained.

In a practical sense, this means that Australian courts should have regard to decisions of overseas courts applying and interpreting the Model Law. In my view, the CAA and the IAA encourage this approach as the interpretative provisions specifically direct judges to have regard to the international origins of the provisions applied by the IAA, and to the desirability of the uniform application of these provisions internationally.[49] The same result is contemplated with respect to the Model Law provisions adopted in the CAA provisions.[50]

d. Principle of comity

The High Court of Australia in *Farah Constructions Pty Ltd v. Say-Dee Pty Ltd* reaffirmed the principle that:[51]

> "Intermediate appellate courts and trial judges in Australia should not depart from decisions in intermediate appellate courts in another jurisdiction on the interpretation of Commonwealth legislation or uniform national legislation unless they are convinced that the interpretation is plainly wrong."[52]

This principle would appear to apply to both the CAA as uniform national legislation and the IAA as national legislation. The application of this principle is likely to be important in the international commercial arbitration context because of the dearth of High Court authority under the IAA and in relation to the Model Law provisions. It is also important in the domestic arbitration context and will assist further in the development of international arbitration jurisprudence as decisions on the CAA provisions feed interpretation of the IAA and the Model Law provisions generally, as discussed previously.

2. Model Law Covers the Field

The previous Sect. 21 of the IAA allowed parties to agree to have their dispute settled in accordance with a law other than the Model Law. This allowed parties to opt out of the Model Law. The 2010 amendments to the IAA repealed this section; particularly with the objective of making it clear that when parties choose arbitral rules they are not automatically opting out of the operation of the Model Law. In other words arbitral rules and the Model Law can coexist. This clarification was made necessary by the decision in *Eisenwerk v. Australian Granites Ltd* [2001] 1 Qd R 461.

However, by repealing Sect. 21 the IAA may compromise party autonomy by not allowing parties to opt out of the Model Law in favour of another law. Parties wishing

49. See IAA, Sect. 2D.

50. See CAA, Sect. 2A.

51. (2007) 230 CLR 89 at 150 per Gleeson CJ, Gummow, Callinan, Heydon and Crennan JJ.

52. *Australian Securities Commission v. Marlborough Gold Mines Ltd* (1993) 177 CLR 485 at 492 per Mason CJ, Brennan, Dawson, Toohey and Gaudron JJ.

to conduct an international commercial arbitration in Australia may want to apply another law or rely on a set of arbitration rules which exclude the Model Law. There seems little reason to inhibit them from doing this. In some situations such a choice will create an extra level of complexity, but arbitrators in international arbitrations are often required to apply laws from more than one country and from a variety of sources.

Sect. 21 of the IAA also makes it clear that when the IAA applies to an arbitration the State and Territory acts have no residual operation.

3. *Writing Requirement*

The 1985 Model Law provides that "an arbitration agreement shall be in writing".[53] The writing requirements for an arbitration agreement are relaxed in the 2006 Model Law where two options are provided for the formal requirements of an arbitration agreement.[54] Option I still requires the arbitration agreement to be in writing, but this can include a contract that is formed orally (or by other means) and only evidenced in writing. Option II only requires an agreement between the parties and seemingly requires no formalities. The IAA adopts Option I. Consequently, an arbitration agreement must be in writing or evidenced in writing.[55] This is a more liberal approach than the current writing requirement in the IAA and is more liberal than most of the countries that have not adopted the 2006 Model Law.

Art. II of the New York Convention is also important when considering formal requirements. An award that does not comply with these formal requirements may suffer difficulties in enforcement as the New York Convention will not apply. Art. II of the New York Convention requires an arbitration agreement in writing. This can be interpreted in a number of ways, but at its most strict could require a signed written agreement. Even if this interpretation of the New York Convention is adopted, parties seeking to enforce an arbitration award in Australia based on an arbitration agreement only evidenced in writing may ask for the more liberal approach in the IAA to be applied under Art. VII(1) of the New York Convention. Art. VII(1) allows a party to rely on a provision of law in the country where enforcement is sought if it is different to the New York Convention.[56] In the present example, a party could possibly rely on the more liberal writing requirement.

Arbitration clauses often form a part of long, detailed, highly negotiated contracts. Consequently, formal requirements are usually satisfied. However, issues of formality may be more likely to arise when parties agree, separately to the main contract, that arbitration will be used.

---

53. 1985 Model Law, Art. 7.
54. 2006 Model Law, Art. 7.
55. See Sub-sects. 3(1) and 3(4) of the IAA.
56. In this respect reference should also be made to the *Explanatory Note by the UNCITRAL Secretariat on the Model Law on International Commercial Arbitration,* being the Recommendation regarding the interpretation of article II, paragraph 2, and article VII, paragraph 1, of the [New York Convention], contained in Part Three of the *Model Law on International Commercial Arbitration 1985 – with amendments as adopted in 2006* (United Nations, Vienna, 2008), pp. 39 and 40 (available at <www.uncitral.org/pdf/english/texts/arbitration/ml-arb/07-86998_Ebook.pdf>).

Domestically, the CAA also adopts Option I for formal validity. It does not suffer from complications of enforcement discussed above as the New York Convention is not required for the enforcement of domestic commercial arbitration awards.

4. Court Assistance and Supervision

a. Relevant courts

Courts are given certain functions under the Model Law. The functions include the appointment of arbitrators (Art. 11(3) and (4)), the removal of arbitrators (Arts. 13(3) and 14), decisions on arbitral jurisdiction (after the tribunal has already decided) (Art. 16(3)) and the setting aside of arbitral awards (Art. 34(2)).

Under Sect. 18 of the IAA these functions can be performed by the relevant state or territory Supreme Court or by the Federal Court. This gives parties a choice of forum and will place pressure on the courts to provide efficient court procedures. As discussed above, the Arbitration List of the Supreme Court of Victoria is designed to provide an efficient and expeditious service in support of commercial arbitration; domestic and international. It has been argued that giving jurisdiction to multiple courts will create inconsistency in interpretation of national legislation. This should be able to be avoided by courts having regard to the interpretation provisions of the IAA in the context of the international character of the Model Law, by the establishment of specialist arbitration lists and with the assistance of the ACICA Judicial Liaison Committee.

There is provision in Sect. 18 of the IAA for an authority to be prescribed for the purpose of appointing arbitrators under Art. 11(3) and (4) of the Model Law. ACICA has been prescribed as the sole default appointing authority in relation to Art. 11(3) and (4).[57] In my opinion this is a very desirable development as courts are not necessarily well placed for deciding which arbitrator will be best suited to a particular dispute. It is a decision desirably left to the parties themselves or, in the absence of agreement, a professional body like ACICA, which has a greater knowledge of arbitrators and their expertise. It also saves the parties the cost of applying to a court to appoint an arbitrator when third-party assistance is required. It is a step towards the systems in place in the popular arbitration centres of Hong Kong[58] and Singapore.[59]

In relation to domestic arbitrations, the Supreme Court of the relevant state or territory is the court appointed to perform the various facilitative and supervisory functions under the CAA.[60] Other courts can be given jurisdiction to perform these functions if the parties agree. In New South Wales both the District Court and the Local Court are available to the parties if they agree either before or after their dispute has arisen.

57. International Arbitration Regulations 2011 (Commonwealth of Australia).

58. The Hong Kong International Arbitration Centre is appointed under Sect. 34C(3) Arbitration Ordinance (Hong Kong).

59. The Chairman of the Singapore International Arbitration Centre is appointed under Art. 8(2) International Arbitration Act (Singapore).

60. CAA, Sect. 6.

b. Stay of court proceedings

If parties have agreed to arbitrate their disputes, they should be held to that agreement. Under Art. 8 of the Model Law if a party to an arbitration agreement files a claim in a court the other party has a right to apply for a stay of the court proceedings in favour of arbitration. A court will grant a stay unless the arbitration agreement is "null and void, inoperative or incapable of being performed". If there is a valid arbitration agreement the court must grant a stay.

The IAA applies these Model Law provisions internationally,[61] as does the CAA domestically.[62]

c. Specific court assistance provisions

i. International Arbitration Act – additional provisions

The IAA Amendment Act adds to the list of optional provisions available in Division 3 Part III (Optional Provisions) of the IAA. The optional provisions are:

– Sect. 23 Parties may obtain subpoenas;
– Sect. 23A Failure to assist arbitral tribunal;
– Sect. 23B Default by party to an arbitration agreement;
– Sect. 23C-23G Disclosure of confidential information;
– Sect. 23H Death of a party to an arbitration agreement;
– Sect. 23J Evidence;
– Sect. 23K Security for costs;
– Sect. 24 Consolidation of arbitral proceedings;
– Sect. 25 Interest up to making of award;
– Sect. 26 Interest on debt under award;
– Sect. 27 Costs.

All of the optional provisions supplement the Model Law and are generally facilitative of arbitration. Most of them apply on an opt-out basis. This is important because parties may not give specific thought to the optional provisions when drafting the arbitration agreement, and they may be unwilling to give more power to the arbitral tribunal once a dispute has arisen. The confidentiality provisions (Sects. 23C to 23G) only apply on an opt-in basis; as do the provisions concerning consolidation of arbitral proceedings (Sect. 24).

ii. Commercial Arbitration Act

There are a number of ways in which the court can assist the parties and the arbitral tribunal in reaching an efficient resolution of the dispute. Under Sect. 27 of the CAA the court may assist the arbitral tribunal in taking evidence if requested by the arbitral tribunal or a party with approval from the arbitral tribunal. Under Sect. 27A of the

61. IAA, Sect. 16.
62. CAA, Sect. 8.

CAA, the court may also issue subpoenas requiring a person to attend to give evidence or to produce documents to the arbitral tribunal. If an arbitral tribunal has ordered a person to attend to give evidence or provide documents, and that person has failed to comply, the court may order that person to comply with the arbitral tribunal's orders.

d. Interim measures

i. International Arbitration Act

Prior to the 2010 amendments, the IAA adopted Art. 17 of the 1985 Model Law, which states that the arbitral tribunal may "order any party to take such interim measure of protection as the arbitral tribunal may consider necessary in respect of the subject-matter of the dispute".

The fundamental problem with this provision was that there is no procedure within the Model Law for a party to have an interim measure granted by an arbitral tribunal enforced by a court. Enforcement provisions under the 1985 Model Law only apply to "awards", which, at the very least, must finally determine some of the issues in dispute.

In practice, interim measures ordered by an arbitral tribunal are often complied with as it is not prudent tactics to ignore the arbitral tribunal that is to decide the issues of substance, and also because the same interim measure can be applied for from a court under Art. 9 of the Model Law. The latter option may raise res judicata issues if it puts the court in the position of having to determine something already dealt with by the arbitral tribunal. Parties may be better off avoiding this possible complication and applying directly to a court, rather than applying to the arbitral tribunal.[63] This means, however, that parties would not be able to have the entire matter dealt with by an arbitral tribunal.

The 2006 amendments to the Model Law avoid these complications by the creation of an enforceable interim measure regime. The IAA adopts all these amendments in relation to interim measures apart from Art. 17B, which gives arbitral tribunals the power to grant ex parte interim measures. Art. 17H(1) allows interim measures to be enforced by a court subject to the limited grounds for refusing enforcement set out in Art. 17I. Sect. 18B of the IAA specifically prevents arbitral tribunals from making ex parte interim measure orders, known as preliminary orders, under Art. 17B of the Model Law. The major criticism of ex parte orders in arbitration is that they run counter to the consensual nature of arbitration. This criticism may be overstated as Art. 17B of the Model Law is an opt-out provision, which can be excluded by party agreement. Under the Model Law, if parties do not wish to have the option of ex parte preliminary orders available then, consistently with the principle of party autonomy, they can exclude them.

63. Clyde CROFT and Bronwyn LINCOLN, "The Role of the Courts; Enforcement of Arbitration Awards and Anti-arbitration Injunctions" in K.E. LINDGREN, ed., *International Commercial Litigation and Dispute Resolution* (2010) p. 76.

ii. Commercial Arbitration Act

Although parties to an arbitration agreement are not to make substantive claims in court, they can still apply to a court for an interim measure of protection. The types of interim measures sought are usually injunctions to preserve the status quo, freezing orders, etc. Arbitral tribunals, under Sect. 17, also have the power to order interim measures. Under Sect. 17H interim measures made by an arbitral tribunal are enforceable by the court. Enforcement can only be refused on the limited grounds provided for in Sect. 17I. Parties to an arbitration are likely to comply with interim measures ordered by the arbitral tribunal as they risk costs consequences in court in the event that such recourse is made necessary by non-compliance.

e. Appointment of and challenge to arbitrators and arbitrators unable to act

The Model Law provides parties with broad autonomy in making provision for the appointment of arbitrators, by agreement directly or through an agreed procedure. The position is similar with respect to challenges. In these respects reference should be made to Arts. 11 to 13 of the Model Law, provisions which are applied to international arbitrations by the IAA. Nevertheless, a party wishing to avoid arbitration has an incentive to avoid or delay the appointment or challenge process, or processes. In order to avoid any resulting deadlock the court, or possibly an "other authority" such as ACICA, as discussed above, is given a supervisory role when agreement is not reached or when arbitrators are challenged – together with power to appoint or to decide any challenge. Similar provisions apply under Art. 14 of the Model Law where an arbitrator becomes de jure or de facto unable to perform his or her functions or for other reasons fails to act without undue delay. These provisions are applied by the IAA.[64] Similar provisions, which are taken from the Model Law, apply under the CAA.[65]

f. Determination of preliminary point of law by the Court – domestic arbitrations only

Commercial Arbitration Act

Sect. 27J of the CAA, which is an addition to the Model Law, allows a party to apply to the court for a determination on a preliminary point of law. This can only occur with the consent of the arbitrator or all the other parties; so it is not a provision likely to be abused. Delays may arise, however, if the determinations made by the court are appealed on a regular basis; but this is unlikely under the new legislative regime.

g. Setting aside and appealing awards – domestic arbitrations only

Commercial Arbitration Act

Sect. 34 of the CAA, which is based on the Model Law, sets out the very limited grounds under which a party can apply to have an award set aside. The grounds do not cover

64. See IAA, Sect. 16, which applies the Model Law.

65. See Sects. 11 to 15 of the CAA; which also contain specific provisions to the effect that decisions by the court in this respect, within its powers, are final.

errors of law or fact by the arbitral award, but rather deal with situations were there was no power to issue the award in the first place. Among other things an award can be set aside because the dispute is not covered by the arbitration agreement; there is not a properly constituted tribunal; the arbitration agreement is void; or the award is in conflict with the public policy of the state. The grounds are very narrow, and are unlikely to be successfully relied upon on a frequent basis. Similar grounds apply under the enforcement provisions in Sect. 36 of the CAA.

In the domestic context the grounds in Sect. 34 of the CAA (based on Art. 34 of the Model Law) were thought, at least potentially, to be too narrow. Consequently there is a broader appeal right given under Sect. 34A of the CAA. This section is an addition to the Model Law provisions, which are reflected in Sect. 34 of the CAA. Sect. 34A of the CAA allows an appeal on a question of law if the parties agree that such an appeal may be made and the court grants leave. This section is the high point of the court's supervisory role and goes further than the grounds set out in Sect. 34. Although Sect. 34A does go further than Sect. 34, the appeal right is still restricted. Determinations of fact cannot be subject to appeal, but, of course, there is often difficulty in separating law from fact. The decision of the tribunal must be "obviously wrong" or the question must be one of "general public importance" and the arbitral decision is open to "serious doubt". These tests are somewhat similar to those under the Commercial Arbitration Act 1984 (Vic), but they appear to be more constrained and should be seen as at least incorporating the more restrictive approach to appeals contained in the *Nema* guidelines.[66]

For completeness, it is noted that in relation to international arbitrations there is no appeal right conferred under the IAA over and above any right with respect to court supervision provided for in the Model Law.

5. *Confidentiality*

a. *International Arbitration Act*

The optional provisions added by the IAA Amendment Act in Sects. 23C to 23G were directed at addressing a perceived deficiency in Australia in relation to the confidentiality of arbitral proceedings as a result of the decision in *Esso Australia Resources Ltd v. Plowman*,[67] where the High Court of Australia decided that arbitrations were private but not confidential.

Sect. 23C prohibits parties and the arbitral tribunal from disclosing confidential information[68] except as provided for by the Act. Sect. 23D specifies the situations when confidential information can be disclosed such as by consent of all the parties, for the purpose of obtaining professional advice or when required to disclose by a court. Sect.

---

66. See *Pioneer Shipping Ltd v. BTP Tioxide Ltd ("The Nema")* [1982] AC 724 at 742; and see J.A. SHARKEY and J.B. DORTER, *Commercial Arbitration*, fn. 13 above, pp. 268-274.

67. (1985) 183 CLR 10.

68. Confidential information is defined in Sub-sect. 15(1) of the IAA. In summary, it includes information relating to the arbitral proceedings such as pleadings, evidence, transcripts, submissions, rulings and awards.

23E gives the arbitral tribunal the power, on application of a party, to allow disclosure of confidential information in circumstances outside Sect. 23D. Sects. 23F and 23G give the court the power to prohibit disclosure or allow disclosure, respectively, after an application under Sect. 23E has already been made.[69] The court must apply a public interest test – does the public interest lie in preserving confidentiality or in disclosure?

These sections give some protection, but considering the international perception of the treatment of confidentiality in Australia it may have been desirable to adopt a more comprehensive approach such as that adopted in Sects. 14A to 14I of the *Arbitration Act 1996* (New Zealand). The IAA confidentiality provisions are based on Sects. 14B to 14E of the New Zealand Act. However, the New Zealand provisions go further and make the distinction between privacy and confidentiality. Under Sect. 14A arbitrations must be private. In Sects. 14F to 14I the New Zealand Act sets up a regime which allows for the possibility of court proceedings relating to an arbitration being conducted in private. A party must apply for the court proceedings to be conducted in private (Sub-sect. 14F(2)(a)) and state their reasons for doing so (Sect. 14G). The court needs to balance the public interest and must consider the factors set out in Sect. 14H. These are:

(a) the open justice principle;
(b) the privacy and confidentiality of arbitral proceedings;
(c) any other public interest considerations;
(d) the terms of any arbitration agreement between the parties to the proceedings; and
(e) the reasons stated by the applicant under Sect. 14G(b).

As Australia has no private arbitral appeal mechanism[70] provisions that allow private court proceedings would be beneficial.

Considering that confidentiality has always been one of the most important claimed benefits of commercial arbitration it seems surprising that the confidentiality provisions of the IAA are applied on an opt-in rather than an opt-out basis. Nevertheless, any problems with confidentiality can be alleviated by practitioners being aware of these problems and making sure the parties opt in to the confidentiality provisions and also choose arbitration rules that provide for confidentiality and deal with confidentiality issues in a reasonable and practical way.

b. Commercial Arbitration Act

Confidentiality is one of the key benefits for parties choosing domestic arbitration. For this reason, it was important that specific confidentiality provisions be added to the Model Law provisions which are adopted domestically by the CAA. Again, this is especially the case in Australia given the concerns about confidentiality as a result of the decision in *Esso Australia Resources Ltd v. Plowman.*[71] The confidentiality provisions in Sects.

---

69. If the arbitral tribunal's mandate has finished then a party can apply directly to the court – Sect. 23G(3)(a) IAA Amendment Act.
70. Such as the private Arbitration Appeal Tribunal system established by the Arbitrators' and Mediators' Institute of New Zealand.
71. (1985) 183 CLR 10.

27E to 27I of the CAA apply, crucially, on an opt-out basis. The court can make orders allowing or disallowing disclosure of confidential arbitral information if the mandate of the arbitral tribunal is terminated or the arbitral tribunal has already ruled on the disclosure of the information.

6. *Reasonable Opportunity to Present Case*

Art. 18 of the Model Law states "... each party shall be given a *full* opportunity of presenting his case" (emphasis added). In situations where a party seeks to delay arbitration proceedings it may rely on this provision to argue that it can present evidence and submissions no matter how costly, lengthy and unnecessary they may prove to be. Although it might be said, and with considerable force, that this view conflicts with the objectives and approach of the Model Law and the IAA, it is at least arguable, particularly before an arbitral tribunal.

To remove doubt the IAA[72] and the new CAA[73] "amended" the "full opportunity" provision in the Model Law to provide for a "reasonable opportunity". This will encourage parties to consider the flexibility of arbitral procedure. Clearly there needs to be proportionality between the complexity of the dispute and the procedures adopted.

7. *Enforcement of Foreign Awards*

Sub-sect. 8(1) of the IAA states that "[s]ubject to this Part, a foreign award is binding by virtue of this Act for all purposes on the parties to the arbitration agreement in pursuance of which it was made". Sub-sect. 8(3A) of the IAA now provides, specifically, that the court may only refuse to enforce a foreign award if the circumstances mentioned in Sub-sects. 8(5) or 8(7) of the IAA apply. These sub-sections are based on Art. 34(2) of the Model Law and Art. V of the New York Convention. Thus the only basis upon which a court can refuse enforcement of a foreign award is on a ground or grounds set out in Sub-sects. 8(5) and 8(7). As discussed above in relation to the *Khuder* judgments (pp. 239-240 above), there is no onus on the enforcing party to prove anything other than the formal requirements under Art. IV of the New York Convention; provisions which are reflected in Sect. 9 of the IAA. It is then for the party resisting enforcement to establish, affirmatively, that any of the defensive provisions of Sub-sects. 8(5) or 8(7) apply. It follows that the burden of proof in this respect falls on the resisting party, the award debtor.

Under Arts. 34(2)(b)(ii) and 36(1)(b)(ii) of the Model Law an award may be set aside or refused enforcement, respectively, if an award is in conflict with public policy. This position is reflected in Sub-sect. 8(7)(b) of the IAA which provides for the refusal of enforcement when enforcement would be contrary to public policy.

Sub-sect. 8(7A) of the IAA provides that:

---

72. Sect. 18C.
73. Sect. 18.

> "To avoid doubt and without limiting paragraph [8](7)(b), the enforcement of a foreign award would be contrary to public policy if:
> (a) the making of the award was induced or affected by fraud or corruption; or
> (b) a breach of the rules of natural justice occurred in connection with the making of the award."

This formulation is also applied to *Part II – Enforcement of Foreign Awards* of the IAA, and also the enforcement of interim measures under Art. 17I(1)(b)(ii) of the Model Law.[74]

These provisions would not, however, appear to add a great deal to the interpretation of the provisions of either the Model Law or the New York Convention insofar as they relate to enforcement and public policy. Nevertheless it does appear that Sub-sect. 8(7A) and Sect. 19[75] of the IAA are narrow rather than expansive provisions. Having regard to these provisions, and also to Sect. 2D of the IAA, which sets out the objectives of the IAA, it would appear that "public policy" is likely to be defined, and applied, narrowly in Australia.

8. *Immunity of Arbitrators*

The IAA has adopted a similar approach to that found in Sect. 74 of the English Arbitration Act 1996. Sect. 28 provides:

> "(1) An arbitrator is not liable for anything done or omitted to be done by the arbitrator in good faith in his or her capacity as arbitrator.
> (2) An entity that appoints, or fails or refuses to appoint, a person as arbitrator is not liable in relation to the appointment, failure or refusal if it was done in good faith."

This immunity of arbitrators for acts or omissions done in good faith is broader than previous immunity given to arbitrators in Australia.[76] The protection also extends to entities that appoint arbitrators (e.g., a nominating or appointing body such as ACICA). This is a move in line with international practice and will be a factor considered in the choice of Australia as an arbitral seat.

Immunity is provided for domestically in Sect. 39 of the CAA. These provisions are to substantially the same effect as the proposed Sect. 28 of the IAA; but the immunity also extends to the arbitrator acting as a "mediator, conciliator or other non-arbitral intermediary".

---

74. IAA Sect. 19.

75. Sect. 19 of the IAA contains provisions similar to Sub-sect. 8(7A) with respect to interim measures of protection.

76. C.f., Sect. 51 of the Commercial Arbitration Act 1984 (Vic).

VI. CONCLUSION

As has been discussed, parties entering into arbitration agreements consider a variety of factors before choosing on the arbitral seat.

The recent legislative reforms in Australia add to its attractiveness in this respect. These reforms also make arbitration an attractive option for disputes that are domestic rather than international in character.

The importance of impartial, efficient, accessible, supportive and "arbitration friendly" courts cannot be overstressed. In this context the creation of a specialist arbitration list like the Arbitration List in the Supreme Court of Victoria is very significant.

Annex I

Supreme Court of Victoria, Practice Note No. 2 of 2010 – Arbitration Business

Court Support for Arbitration

1. The Court is supportive of the wishes of disputants to resolve all or part of their dispute by arbitration and will assist parties in a variety of ways, including –
   (a) assistance and support for the arbitration process (e.g. subpoenas to witnesses or for production of documents, interim measures of protection (injunctive relief or otherwise) and orders with respect to the constitution of the arbitral tribunal);
   (b) determination of discrete questions of law which arbitrators or parties are able to refer to the Court (depending on the statutory or other basis of the arbitration process);
   (c) expeditious hearing and determination of appeals from the arbitration process (to the extent permitted under the statutory or other basis of the arbitration process);
   (d) enforcement of arbitration awards and orders of arbitral tribunals (to the extent permitted under the statutory or other basis of the arbitration process); and
   (e) referring a proceeding or a question to arbitration under Chapter I Rule 50.08.
2. Court assistance is provided for all arbitration proceedings, international or domestic, and whether conducted under the *International Arbitration Act 1974* (Cth) or the *Commercial Arbitration Act 1984* (Vic). Enforcement or other proceedings with respect to arbitration conducted under these statutory provisions or under legislation in other jurisdictions (international and other Australian jurisdictions) are also available in the Court, subject to the provisions of the *International Arbitration Act 1974* or the *Commercial Arbitration Act 1984*, to the extent applicable.

International Arbitration

3. The *International Arbitration Act 1974* (s 18) confers jurisdiction on the Court to provide assistance with respect to the matters specified in Article 6 of the United Nations Commission on International Trade Law ("UNCITRAL") *Model Law on International Commercial Arbitration 1985* ("the *Model Law*") –
   (a) appointment of a sole or presiding arbitrator failing agreement by the parties or co-arbitrators (Article 11(3));
   (b) appointment of an arbitrator or arbitrators where the appointment procedure agreed by the parties fails (Article 11(4));
   (c) deciding on challenges to an arbitrator or arbitrators (Article 13(3));
   (d) termination of the mandate of an arbitrator as a result of a failure or impossibility to act (Article 14);

(e) determining whether the arbitral tribunal has jurisdiction (Article 16); and
(f) setting aside arbitral awards on the limited grounds specified in Article 34.

4. In addition to providing assistance under Article 6 of the *Model Law*, the *International Arbitration Act 1974* confers jurisdiction on the Court to –
   (a) enforce foreign arbitral agreements by staying a proceeding or part of a proceeding that is before the Court which invites the determination of a matter capable of settlement by arbitration which is subject to such an agreement (section 7(2));
   (b) make interim or supplementary orders for the preservation of the rights of the parties or in relation to any property for the purpose of providing effective enforcement of arbitration agreements (section 7(3)); and
   (c) enforce foreign arbitral awards to which the *Convention on the Recognition and Enforcement of Foreign Arbitral Awards* 1958 ("the New York Convention") applies (section 8).
5. It is noted that the jurisdiction of the Court to provide interim measures of protection (e.g. interlocutory injunctive relief for the preservation of assets or evidence, *Mareva* injunctions, search orders and the like) in partnership with the arbitration process is recognised in Article 9 of the *Model Law*.

Domestic (Australian) Arbitration

6. Domestic (Australian) arbitration is currently subject to the operation of the uniform commercial arbitration acts. The Victorian legislation is contained in the *Commercial Arbitration Act 1984*.
7. The *Commercial Arbitration Act 1984* confers jurisdiction on the Court to provide assistance to the arbitration process in a variety of matters and circumstances, including –
   (a) appointment or removal of arbitrators (sections 8, 10, 11, 13 and 44);
   (b) ordering the attendance of witnesses or the production of documents (sections 17 and 18);
   (c) consolidation of arbitration proceedings in some circumstances (section 26);
   (d) correction of arbitration awards (section 30);
   (e) enforcement of arbitration awards (section 33);
   (f) taxation of any costs of an arbitration that are directed to be paid by an award and which are not taxed or settled by the arbitrator (section 34);
   (g) assessment of the arbitrator's fees and expenses (section 35);
   (h) orders in relation to the costs of an abortive arbitration (section 36);
   (i) review of awards where there is a manifest error of law on the face of the award or there is strong evidence of an error of law where determination of the question dealt with by the award may add or be likely to add substantially to the certainty of commercial law (section 38);
   (j) determination of a preliminary point of law with the consent of the arbitrator or of all the parties (section 39);
   (k) setting aside an award where there has been misconduct by the arbitrator or setting aside the award in whole or in part where the arbitrator has misconducted the arbitration proceedings (section 42);

(l) remitting any matter for reconsideration by the arbitrator (section 43);
(m) termination of arbitration proceedings and, possibly, removing the dispute to the Court in the event of undue delay (section 46);
(n) the making of interlocutory orders for the purposes of and in relation to arbitration proceedings, to the same extent as may be done for the purposes of and in relation to proceedings in the Court (section 47);
(o) extension of time periods under the *Commercial Arbitration Act 1984* or the arbitration agreement (section 48); and
(p) staying Court proceedings to allow the arbitration to proceed (section 53).

Procedural Matters

8. Applications under the *International Arbitration Act* 1974 (Cth) must be commenced by originating motion. In determining whether an arbitration is international, reference should be made to the provisions of the *International Arbitration Act 1974* and also to the UNCITRAL *Model Law* (which the provisions of this Act apply) – particularly, Article 1 of the *Model Law*. Applications under the *Commercial Arbitration Act 1984* (Vic) must also be commenced by originating motion and must comply with Chapter II, Order 9.
9. Parties seeking to bring an application must first consult with the Associate to the Judge managing Commercial Court, List G – Arbitration proceedings, to establish a hearing date and to appoint a Judge or Associate Judge to hear the application. The Prothonotary will only accept a summons with a return date authorised by this Associate.
10. An application to enforce a foreign award pursuant to the *International Arbitration Act 1974* (section 8), should, as far as possible, comply with the requirements of Chapter II, Rules 9.04 and 9.05. An application to enforce a domestic (Australian) award pursuant to the *Commercial Arbitration Act 1984* must comply with the requirements of Chapter II, Rules 9.04 and 9.05.
11. An application to set aside a foreign award pursuant to Article VI of the New York Convention or Article 34 of the *Model Law* (see Part II and sections 16 and 20 of the *International Arbitration Act 1984*) should, as far as possible, comply with the requirements of Chapter II, Rules 9.04 and 9.05.
12. An application for leave to appeal against an arbitrator's award under the *Commercial Arbitration Act 1984* must comply with the requirements of Chapter II, Rule 9.06 and Chapter I, Rules 4.06 and 4.07.
13. Subject to any direction of the Judge or Associate Judge hearing the application, practitioners must deliver to the Judge or Associate Judge, not less than two clear days before the time appointed for the hearing of the application, a copy of all affidavits including exhibits together with a brief outline of argument in support of the application.
14. From time to time urgent interlocutory applications arise in the course of arbitrations. The Court will be available on very short notice to hear and promptly determine these applications. The following provisions shall apply to applications which are accepted by the Judge managing Commercial Court, List G, as urgent.

(a) The applicant should deliver to the Associate to this Judge at the time of seeking to bring the application a copy of the application and of all affidavits including exhibits and a brief outline of argument in support of the application.
(b) The practitioner for the respondent should as soon as practicable and in any event on the day prior to the hearing of the application (if possible in all the circumstances) deliver to the Associate to the Judge or Associate Judge appointed to hear the application, a copy of all affidavits including exhibits filed in opposition together with a brief outline of argument.
(c) If all parties to the application so request, the judicial officer appointed to hear the application may agree to determine the application within 24 hours of the completion of argument provided that in such a case no reasons for the decision will be provided at the time of determination. Any party requiring reasons must so advise the judicial officer at the time of the determination and the judicial officer will provide reasons, but they will be in short form. Reasons in short form will be simply statements, without elaboration, of the findings of fact and principles of law which lead to the determination.
(d) If the application is one that is properly made ex parte, this should be clearly stated in all communications with the Associate to the Judge. Such communications need not be copied to the respondent until the interim determination of the application.
(e) Where an application for an interlocutory order offers, or the court accepts, or an order or other Court document records the giving of "the usual undertaking as to damages", this shall be taken to mean the following undertaking given to the Court:

> To abide by any order which this Court might make as to damages, in case this Court shall be of the opinion that any person shall have sustained any loss, by reason of this order, which the party giving the undertaking ought to pay.

15. These procedural arrangements will apply notwithstanding the Commercial Court Practice Note No. 1 of 2010. Otherwise, the Commercial Court Practice Note is applicable.

Commercial Court – Arbitration Proceedings

16. The Chief Justice has appointed the Hon. Justice Croft to manage Commercial Court, List G – Arbitration proceedings. All arbitration proceedings, any applications in arbitration proceedings, and any urgent applications with respect to arbitration matters, should be directed to His Honour's Associate (telephone: 03.9603 7731).
17. Arbitration matters arising in proceedings already allocated to the Technology, Engineering and Construction List (TEC List) will continue to be managed within that List by the Hon. Justice Vickery, though they may be transferred to List G in accordance with the usual practice applied in the Commercial Court with respect

to the transfer of matters between lists in that Court. The same position applies with respect to the possibility of transfer of arbitration matters from List G to the TEC List.

18. Any changes in these arrangements will be notified from time to time on the Commercial Court website – <www.commercialcourt.com.au>.
19. This Practice Note takes effect on and from 1 January 2010.
20. This Practice Note is in substitution for Practice Note No. 7 of 2006 which is hereby revoked.

Vivienne Macgillivray
Executive Associate to the Chief Justice
17 December 2009

ICCA 50 GENEVA CONFERENCE LIST OF PARTICIPANTS

Argentina

Tawil, Guido Santiago
Member of ICCA
M & M Bomchil
Suipacha 268, 12th Floor
C1008AAF Buenos Aires

Australia

Bonnell, Max
Mallesons Stephen Jacques
Governor Phillip Tower, Level 61
1 Farrer Place
Sydney, NSW 2000

Croft, Hon. Justice Clyde
Supreme Court of Victoria
210 William Street
Melbourne, Victoria 3000

Kovacs, Robert
Clayton Utz
Level 18, 333 Collins Street
Melbourne, Victoria 3000

Megens, Peter
Mallesons Stephen Jacques
Level 50, 600 Bourke Street
Melbourne, Victoria 3000

Pryles, Michael
Member of ICCA
Level 18, 333 Colins Street
Melbourne, Victoria 3000

Rana, Rashda
Lend Lease
The Bond 30 Hickson Road
Millers Point, NSW 2000

Austria

Baier, Anton
Baier Boehm Attorneys at Law
Kaerntner Ring 12
1010 Vienna

Boehm, Erhard
Baier Boehm Attorneys at Law
Kaerntner Ring 12
1010 Vienna

Hauser, Wulf Gordian
Hauser Partners Rechtsanwälte
Seilerstätte 18-20
1010 Vienna

Hempel, Karl
University of Vienna
Rotenturmstrasse 12
1010 Vienna

Herrmann, Gerold
Honorary President of ICCA
Reimersgasse 16 B2
1190 Vienna

Horvath, Günther
Freshfields Bruckhaus Deringer
Seilergasse 16
1010 Vienna

Riegler, Stefan
Baker & McKenzie
Schottenring 25
1010 Vienna

Sekolec, Jernej
Pyrkergasse 31/13
1190 Vienna

Sirakov, Kamen
ENWC Attorneys at law
Schwarzenbergplatz 7
1030 Vienna

Sorieul, Renaud
UNCITRAL Secretariat
Vienna International Centre
PO Box 500
A-1400 Vienna

Steindl, Barbara Helene
Brauneis Klauser Praendl
Bauernmarkt 200
1010 Vienna

Willheim, Johannes
Willheim Muller Rechtsanwälte
Rockhgasse 6
1010 Vienna

Bahrain

Al Aradi, Ali
BCDR-AAA
Suite 401, Park Plaza
Bldg 247 Road 1704
Diplomatic Area
Manama

Al Khalifa, Shaikh Khalid Bin Ali
BCDR–AAA
Suite 401, Park Plaza
Bldg 247 Road 1704
Diplomatic Area
Manama

MacPherson, James
BCDR-AAA
Suite 401, Park Plaza
Bldg 247 Road 1704
Diplomatic Area
Manama

Belgium

Bassiri, Niuscha
Hanotiau & van den Berg
IT Tower, 9th Floor
Avenue Louise 480
1050 Brussels

Dieux, Xavier
Willkie Farr & Gallagher
Avenue Louise 480/3B
1050 Brussels

Hanotiau, Bernard
Member of ICCA
Hanotiau & van den Berg
IT Tower, 9th Floor
Avenue Louise 480
1050 Brussels

Lefebvre, Paul
Hanotiau & van den Berg
IT Tower, 9th Floor
Avenue Louise 480
1050 Brussels

Matray, Didier
Matray, Matray & Hallet
Rue des Fories 2
4020 Liège

Matray, Gautier
Matray, Matray & Hallet
Allée du Cloître 7
1000 Brussels

Olofsson, Rolf
White & Case LLP
Rue de la Loi 62
1040 Brussels

Stein, Erica
Hanotiau & van den Berg
IT Tower, 9th Floor
Avenue Louise 480
1050 Brussels

Van Houtte, Vera
Stibbe
Loxumstraat 25
1000 Brussels

Van den Berg, Albert Jan
General Editor of ICCA
Hanotiau & van den Berg
IT Tower, 9th Floor
Avenue Louise 480
1050 Brussels

Verbruggen, Caroline
DLA Piper
106 Avenue Louise
1050 Brussels

Bermuda

Elkinson, Jeffrey
Conyers Dill & Pearman
Clarendon House
2 Church Street
PO Box HM 666
Hamilton HM CX

Bolivia

Wayar, Bernardo
University of Geneva

Brazil

Abbud, André
Barbosa, Müssnich & Aragào
Av. Presidente Juscelino Kubischeck, 1455
11° andar
São Paulo 04543-011

Barros, Octavio
Barbosa, Müssnich & Aragào
Av. Almirante Barroso, 52, 31° andar
Rio de Janeiro 20031-000

Braghetta, Adriana
L.O. Baptista Advogados
Av. Paulista, 1294, 8° andar
São Paulo 01310-100

Campos Soares, Patricia
University of Geneva

Costa, Pedro
Barbosa, Müssnich & Aragào
Av. Almirante Barroso, 52, 31° andar
Rio de Janeiro 20031-000

Fernandes de Andrade, Gustavo
Sergio Bermudes Law Firm
Praça XV de Novembro, 20, 8° andar
Rio de Janeiro 20010-010

Gandelman, Marcelo
Barbosa, Müssnich & Aragào
Av. Almirante Barroso, 52, 31° andar
Rio de Janeiro 20031-000

Gonçalves, Eduardo
Mattos Filho, Veiga Filho, Marrey Jr.
e Quiroga Advogados
Al. Joaquim Eugênio de Lima, 447
São Paulo 01403-001

Grion, Renato
Pinheiro Neto Advogados
Rua Hungria, 1100
São Paulo 01455-906

Harel-Grion, Nathalie
Trench, Rossi, Watanabe
(Baker & McKenzie)
Av. Dr. Chucri Zaidan, 920, 13° andar
São Paulo 04583-904

Laudares Pereira, Fernando
University of Geneva

Müssnich, Francisco
Barbosa, Müssnich & Aragào
Av. Almirante Barroso, 52, 31° andar
Rio de Janeiro 20031-000

Nehring Netto, Carlos
Advisory Member of ICCA
Nehring & Associados
Av. Paulista, 1294, 12° andar
São Paulo 01310-915

Ribas, Marcel Alberge
Rua João Américo de Oliveira, 177
Curitiba 80035-060

Soares, Rafael Vicente
L.O. Baptista Advogados
Av. Paulista, 1294, 8° andar
São Paulo 01310-100

Soares Maciel, Pedro
Veirano Advogados
Av. das Nações Unidas, 12.995, 18° andar
São Paulo 04578-000

Straube, Frederico
Camara de Comercio Brasil Canada
Rua do Rocio, 220, 12° andar, cj. 121
Villa Olimpia
São Paulo 04552-000

Canada

Antaki, Nabil N.
University of Montreal
90 Willowdale, Apt. 303
Outremont QC H3T 1E9

Barin, Babak
BCF
25th Floor
1100 René–Levesque Boulevard West

Suite 250000
Montréal QC H3B 5C9

Fortier, Yves
Member of ICCA
1 Place Ville Marie, Suite 2822
Montréal QC H3B 4R4

Lalonde, Marc
Advisory Member of ICCA
1155 René–Levesque Boulevard West
Suite 3320
Montréal QC H3B 3V2

Leon, Barry
Perley–Robertson, Hill & McDougall
1400 – 340 Albert Street
Ottawa ON K1R 0A5

McDougall, Andrew
Perley–Robertson, Hill & McDougall
1400 – 340 Albert Street
Ottawa ON K1R 0A5

McLaren, Richard
McKenzie Lake Lawyers
300 Dundas Street
London ON N6B 1T6

Ouimet, Eric
BCF
25th Floor
1100 René–Levesque Boulevard West
Montréal QC H3B 5C9

Weiler, Todd
#19-2014 Valleyrun Boulevard
London ON N6G 5N8

Chile

Jimenez, Dyalá
DJ Arbitraje
Av. Vitacura, 2939, Piso 10
Las Condes Santiago

Orrego Vicuña, Francisco
Member of ICCA
Av. El Golf No. 40, Piso 6
Santiago 7550107

China PR

Jiang, Caroline
University of Geneva

Liu, Yalan
University of Geneva

Ma, Arthur (Zhihua)
Fangda Partners
21/F, China World Tower
No. 1, Jian Guo Men Wai Avenue
100004 Beijing

Rowland, James
King & Wood PRC Lawyers
40th Floor, Tower A, Fortune Plaza
7 Dongsanhuan Zhonglu, Chaoyang
100020 Beijing

Ye, Ariel (Lu)
King & Wood PRC Lawyers
40th Floor, Tower A, Fortune Plaza
7 Dongsanhuan Zhonglu, Chaoyang
100020 Beijing

Colombia

Prado, Elizabeth
University of Geneva

Cyprus

Athanasiou, Maria
University of Geneva

Czech Republic

Lokajova, Maria
Squire, Sanders & Dempsey
Václavské náměstí 57/813
110 00 Prague 1

Makarius, Vit
Havel, Holasek & Partners s.r.o.
Týn 1049/3
110 00 Prague

Pekar, Rostislav
Squire, Sanders & Dempsey
Václavské náměstí 57/813
110 00 Prague 1

Trapl, Vojtech
Advokati s.r.o.
Dvorecka 2a/1162
147 00 Prague

Denmark

Gernaa, Henriette
Gorrissen Ferderspiel
H.C Andersens Boulevard 12
1553 Copenhagen V

Schiersing, Niels
Horten
Philip Heymans Alle 7
PO Box 191
2900 Hellerup, Copenhagen

Ecuador

Arroyo, Veronica
University of Geneva

Egypt

Matar, Amir
Hafez Avocats
5 Ibrahim Naguib Street
Garden City
11451 Cairo

Nassar, Nagla
Nassar Law
39, Kasr El- Nil Street
11211 Cairo

Eritrea

Sereke, Wegahtabrhan
University of Geneva

Ethiopia

Yimer, Bahakal
University of Geneva

Finland

Mattson, Robert
Robert Mattson Attorneys at Law
Ehrensvardintie 21A
00150 Helsinki

Möller, Gustaf
Arbitration Institute
Chamber of Commerce of Finland
PO Box 1000
00101 Helsinki

Saarikivi, Aapo
Roschier
Keskuskato 7A
00100 Helsinki

France

Banifatemi, Yas
Shearman & Sterling
114, avenue des Champs-Elysées
75008 Paris

Beechey, John
ICC International Court of Arbitration
38, cours Albert 1er
75008 Paris

Bernard, Patrick
Bernard Hertz Béjot
8, rue Murillo
75008 Paris

Betto, Jean-Georges
Hogan Lovells International
6, avenue Kléber
75116 Paris

Bonnard, Sebastien
Lacourte Balas & Associés
55, avenue Kléber
75016 Paris

Bühler, Michael
Jones Day
2, rue Saint Florentin
75001 Paris

Castello, James
King & Spalding
65-67, avenue des Champs-Elysées
75008 Paris

Craig, W. Laurence
Orrick, Herrington & Sutcliffe
31, avenue Pierre 1er de Serbie
75782 Paris cedex 16

Degos, Louis
K&L Gates
78, avenue Raymond Poincaré
75116 Paris

Delanoy, Louis Christophe
Bredin Prat
130, rue du Faubourg Saint-Honoré
75008 Paris

Dupeyre, Romain
BOPS
47, rue Dumont d'Urville
75001 Paris

Dupeyron, Carine
August & Debouzy
8, avenue de Messine
75008 Paris

Errera, Marie
Gide Loyrette Nouel
26, cours Albert 1er
75008 Paris

Fathallah, Raed
Bredin Prat
130, rue Faubourg Saint-Honoré
75008 Paris

Gaillard, Emmanuel
Member of ICCA
Shearman & Sterling
114, avenue des Champs-Elysées
75008 Paris

Garaud, Jean-Yves
Cleary Gottlieb
12, rue de Tilsitt
75008 Paris

Gelinas, Paul-A.
Cabinet Paul-A. Gelinas
69, avenue Victor Hugo
75116 Paris

Goldsmith, Aren
Cleary Gottlieb
12, rue de Tilsitt
75008 Paris

Gouiffes, Laurent
Hogan Lovells International
6, avenue Kleber
75116 Paris

Heitzmann, Pierre
Jones Day
2, rue Saint-Florentin
75001 Paris

Honlet, Jean-Christophe
Salans
5, boulevard Malesherbes
75008 Paris

Kaplan, Charles
Herbert Smith
66, avenue Marceau
75008 Paris

Kessedjian, Catherine
Université Panthéon-Assas Paris II
12, Place du Panthéon
75005 Paris

Kiffer, Laurence
Cabinet Teynier Pic & Associés
56, rue de Londres
75008 Paris

Kleiman, Elie
Freshfields Bruckhaus Deringer
2, rue Paul Cézanne
75008 Paris

Le Lay, Hervé
Gide Loyrette Nouel
26, cours Albert 1er
75008 Paris

Leboulanger, Philippe
Cabinet Leboulanger
5, rue de Chaillot
75116 Paris

Lecuyer-Thieffry, Christine
Thieffry & Associés
29, rue de Lisbonne
75008 Paris

Legum, Barton
Salans
5, boulevard Malesherbes
75008 Paris

Lemaire, Gillian
Hafez
51, avenue Raymond Poincarré
75116 Paris

Manassyan, Armine
Salans
5, boulevard Malesherbes
75008 Paris

Mayer, Pierre
Dechert
32, rue de Monceau
75008 Paris

Mireze, Philippe
International Chamber of Commerce – ICC
38, cours Albert 1er
75008 Paris

Munoz, Alexandra
Gide Loyrette Nouel
26, cours Albert 1er
75008 Paris

Peterson, Patricia
Linklaters
25, rue de Marignan
75008 Paris

Petrochilos, Georgios
Freshfields Bruckhaus Deringer
2, rue Paul Cézanne
75008 Paris

Pinsolle, Philippe
Shearman & Sterling
114, avenue des Champs-Elysées
75008 Paris

Pinsolle, Olivier
University of Geneva

Polkinghorne, Michael
White & Case
19, Place Vendôme
75001 Paris

Poloni, Flore
August & Debouzy
8, avenue de Messine
75008 Paris

Secomb, Matthew
White & Case
19, Place Vendôme
75001 Paris

Seraglini, Christophe
White & Case
19, Place Vendôme
75001 Paris

Silva Romero, Eduardo
Dechert
32, rue de Monceau
75008 Paris

Stern, Brigitte
Université Paris I Panthéon-Sorbonne
7, rue Pierre Nicole
75005 Paris

Stoyanov, Marie
Freshfields Bruckhaus Deringer
2, rue Paul Cézanne
75008 Paris

Thieffry, Patrick
Thieffry & Associés
29, rue de Lisbonne
75008 Paris

Turner, Peter
Freshfields Bruckhaus Deringer
2, rue Paul Cézanne
75008 Paris

Vagenheim, Alexandre
Castaldi Mourre & Partners

73, boulevard Haussmann
75008 Paris

Van Leeuwen, Mélanie
Loyens & Loeff
1, avenue Franklin D. Roosevelt
75008 Paris

Wetmore, Todd
Shearman & Sterling
114, avenue des Champs-Elysées
75008 Paris

Williams, Jonathan
Gide Loyrette Nouel
26, cours Albert 1er
75008 Paris

Ziade, Roland
Cleary Gottlieb
12, rue de Tilsitt
75008 Paris

Germany

Böckstiegel, Karl-Heinz
Member of ICCA
Parkstrasse 38
51427 Bergisch-Gladbach

Bredow, Jens
German Institution for Arbitration (DIS)
Beethovenstrasse 5-13
50674 Cologne

Busse, Daniel
Allen & Overy
Taunustor 2
60311 Frankfurt am Main

Eiser, Julia
University of Geneva

Elemenler, Muhammed
University of Geneva

Gantenberg, Ulrike
Heuking Kühn Lüer Wojtek
Georg-Glock-Strasse 4
40474 Dusseldorf

Hunter, Robert
Hogan Lovells International
Untermainanlage 1
60329 Frankfurt am Main

Kaczor, Tobiasz
Universities of Tübingen & Geneva
Koslinerstrasse 3
75181 Pforzheim

Krapfel, Claudia
Gleiss Lutz
Maybachstrasse 6
70469 Stuttgart

Kreindler, Richard
Shearman & Sterling
Gervinusstrasse17
60322 Frankfurt am Main

Laffargue-Haak, Tanneke
EPO
Bayerstrasse 34
80335 Munich

Nacimiento, Patricia
White & Case
Bockenheimer Landstrasse 20
60323 Frankfurt am Main

Niedermaier, Tilman
CMS Hasche Sigle
Nymphenburgerstrasse 12
80335 Munich

Raeschke-Kessler, Hilmar
Rechtsanwalt beim Bundesgerichtshof
Am Dickhaeuterplatz 18
76275 Karlsruhe-Ettlingen

Reeg, Axel
Reeg Rechtsanwälte
R 3 , 4-5
68161 Mannheim

Schäfer, Erik
Cohausz & Florack
Patent- und Rechtsanwälte
Bleichstrasse 14
40211 Dusseldorf

Schardt, Ramone
Siemens AG
Werner-von-Siemens-Strasse 50
91052 Erlangen

Triebel, Volker
Hogan Lovells International
Kennedydamm 24
40476 Dusseldorf

Von Schlabrendorff, Fabian
Clifford Chance
Mainzer Landstrasse 46
60325 Frankfurt am Main

Wilske, Stephan
Gleiss Lutz
Maybachstrasse 6
70469 Stuttgart

Greece

Amro, Ihab
Athens Law School
Student Dormitory, Oulwf palme 2-4, Ilisia
157 71 Athens

Chalkias, Panagiotis
University of Geneva

Dimolitsa, Antonias
A. Dimolitsa & Associates
11 Merlin Street
106 71 Athens

Tsifopoulou, Eirini
University of Geneva

Vassardanis, Aphrodite
A. Vassardanis & Partners
30 Vassilissis Olga Street
151 24 Maroussi Athens

Vassardanis, Ioannis
A. Vassardanis & Partners
30 Vassilissis Olga Street
151 24 Maroussi Athens

Hong Kong SAR

Bao, Chiann
Hong Kong International Arbitration Centre
38/F Two Exchange Square
8 Connaught Place

Bateson, David
Mallesons Stephen Jacques
13/F Gloucester Tower
The Landmark
15 Queens Road
Central

Cheng, Teresa
Vice President of ICCA
Des Voeux Chambers
38/F Gloucester Tower
The Landmark
Central

Gearing, Matthew
Allen & Overy
9th Floor, Three Exchange Square
Central

Kaplan, Neil
Member of ICCA
Mallesons Stephen Jacques
13/F Gloucester Tower
The Landmark
15 Queens Road
Central

Li, Justin
38/F Gloucester Tower
The Landmark
Central

Moser, Michael
Level 8, Two Exchange Square
8 Connaught Place
Central

Rooney, Kim
Gilt Chambers
8/F Far East Finance Centre
16 Harcourt Road
Hong Kong

Wong, Kwai Huen
Hong Kong International Arbitration Centre
38/F Two Exchange Square
8 Connaught Place

Hungary

Horváth, Eva
Pázmány Peter Catholic University
Szentkiralyi u. 28-30
1088 Budapest

Kecskés, László
Arbitration Institute of The Hungarian Chamber of Commerce & Industry
Kossuth tér 6-8
1055 Budapest

Kelemen, Judit
Squire, Sanders & Dempsey
Roosevelt tér 7-8
1051 Budapest

Szász, Iván
Honorary Vice President of ICCA
Squire, Sanders & Dempsey
Roosevelt tér 7-8
1051 Budapest

India

Dave, Dushyant
Member of ICCA
'Atlantis' Building
43, Prithviraj Road
New Delhi 110011

Dholakia, Shishir
Supreme Court of India
97, Lawyer's Chambers
New Delhi 110001

Donde, Rahul
University of Geneva

Kachwaha, Sumeet
Kachwaha & Partners
1/6 Shanti Niketan
New Delhi 110021

Nariman, Fali S.
Honoray President of ICCA
F-21/22 Hauz Khas Enclave
New Delhi 110016

Rai, Kumar Sumit
University of Geneva

Ireland

Bridgeman, James
The Law Library
Four Courts, Inns Quay
Dublin 9

Bunni, Nael
Member of ICCA
Bunni & Associates
42 Thormanby Road
Dublin

Collins, Michael
Law Library
4 Arran Square, Arran Quay
Dublin 7

Maguire, Roderick
Four Courts
Dublin 7

Ó hOisin, Colm
158 Church Street
Dublin

Reichert, Klaus
Brick Court Chambers
145-151 Church Street
Dublin 7

Italy

Azzali, Stefano
Milan Chamber of Arbitration
Palazzo Turati, Via Meravigli, 9/B
20123 Milan

Bariatti, Stefania
Chiomenti Studio Legale
Via Verdi, 2
20121 Milan

Mechelli, Stefano
McDermott Will & Emery
Via Dei Bossi, 4/6
20121 Milan

Radicati di Brozolo, Luca G.
Bonelli Erede Pappalardo Studio Legale
Via Barozzi 1
20100 Milan

Rubino-Sammartano, Mauro
Bianchi Rubino-Sammartano & Associati
Viale Cassiodoro, 1
20145 Milan

Santoboni, Danilo
Bocconi School of Law
Via Sarfatti, 25
Milan

Jamaica

John, Omar
University of Miami

Japan

Naito, Junya
Momo-O, Matsuo & Namba
Kojimachi Diamond Building 6F
4-1 Kojimachi, Chiyoda-ku
Tokyo 102-0083

Taniguchi, Yasuhei
Advisory Member of ICCA
Matsuo & Kosugi
Fukoku Seimei Building, 18th Floor
2-2-2 Uchisaiwai-cho, Chiyoda-ku
Tokyo 100-0011

Kenya

Njoroge, Chege
Lesinko & Njoroge Advocates
Development House, Moi Avenue
PO Box 17643-00100
Nairobi

Korea

Chung, Kyongwha
Bae, Kim & Lee LLC
647-15 Yoksam-dong, Kangnam-gu
Seoul 135-723

Doh, Jae Moon
The Korean Commercial Arbitration Board
43rd FL, Trade Tower
Seoul 135-729

Kim, Kap - You (Kevin)
Secretary General of ICCA
Bae, Kim & Lee LLC
647-15 Yoksam-dong, Kangnam-gu
Seoul 135-723

Kim, Min-Kyoo
The Koream Commercial Arbitration Board
43rd FL, Trade Tower
Seoul 135-729

Morrison, James
Bae, Kim & Lee LLC
647-15 Yoksam-dong, Kangnam-gu
Seoul 135-723

Lebanon

Comair Obeid, Nayla
Obeid Law Firm
Makarem Building, Sami El Solh Avenue
BP 116/2234 Law Courts
Beirut 1109 2020

Najjar, Nathalie
Ibrahim Najjar Law Firm
11 Madrasset El Salam Street Samaha 2
Beirut 116 2270

Obeid, Ziad
Obeid Law Firm
Makarem Building, Sami El Solh Avenue
BP 116/2234 Law Courts
Beirut 1109 2020

Sakr, Marwan
Hennaoui & Sakr
Sodeco Buildings, Block 8
590 Petro Trad Street
Beirut 116 2230

Lithuania

Audzevicius, Ramunas
Motieka & Audzevicius
Gyneju street 4
01109 Vilnius

Smaliukas, Andrius
Lawin Lideika, Petrauskas, Valiunas
Jogailos g 9/1
01116 Vilnius

Traceviciute, Aiste
Apprenticeship programme,
Anthony Canham, London

Malaysia

Abraham, Cecil
Member of ICCA
Zul Rafique & Partners
D3-3-8, Solaris Dutamas
No. 1, Jalan Dutamas 1
50480 Kuala Lumpur

Mauritius

Hossen, Rashid
Employment Relations Tribunal
Level 18, Newton Tower
Sir Williams Newton Street
Port Louis

Soopramanien, Shalini
University of Geneva

Mexico

Franco Rodriguez, Francisco
University of Geneva

Jaimes, Ana
University of Geneva

Netherlands

Ameli, Koorosh
Ameli International Arbitration
PO Box 1052
2240 BB Wassenaar

Bier, Lyda
L. Bier B.V.
Baroniesingel 32
5262KB Vught

Borelli, Silvia
ICCA Publications
Peace Palace
Carnegieplein 2
2517 KJ The Hague

Bosman, Lise
ICCA Publications
Peace Palace
Carnegieplein 2
2517 KJ The Hague

Daly, Brooks
Permanent Court of Arbitration
Peace Palace
Carnegieplein 2
2517 KJ The Hague

De Ly, Filip
Erasmus University
c/o Johan Buziaulaan 33
3584 ZT Utrecht

de Vries, Gwen
Wolters Kluwer Law & Business
Zuidpoolsingel 2
2408 ZE Alphen aan den Rijn

Levine, Judith
Permanent Court of Arbitration
Peace Palace
Carnegieplein 2
2517 KJ The Hague

Meijer, Gerard
NautaDutilh
Weena 750
3014 DA Rotterdam

Pulkowski, Dirk
Permanent Court of Arbitration
Peace Palace
Carnegieplein 2
2517 KJ The Hague

Quinn, Catherine
Permanent Court of Arbitration
Peace Palace
Carnegieplein 2
2517 KJ The Hague

Schofield, Garth
Permanent Court of Arbitration
Peace Palace
Carnegieplein 2
2517 KJ The Hague

Simma, Bruno
International Court of Justice
Peace Palace
Carnegieplein 2
2517 KJ The Hague

van Baren, Willem
Allen & Overy
Barbara Strozzilaan 101
1083 HN Amsterdam

van Haersolte-van Hof, Jacomijn
HaersolteHof B.V.
Tobias Asserlaan 5
2517 KC The Hague

van Hees, Floris
Clifford Chance
Droogbak 1A
1013 GE Amsterdam

van Houtte, Hans
Iran-US Claims Tribunal
Parkweg 13
2585 JH The Hague

van Leyenhorst, Max
Legaltree
Hogedijk 92
2861 GD Bergambacht

van Rooij, Rene
NAI
Aert van Nesstraat 25 J-K
3012 CA Rotterdam

Verschoor, Vincent
Wolters Kluwer Law & Business
Zuidpoolsingel 2
2408 ZE Alphen aan den Rijn

von Hombracht-Brinkman, Fredy
NAI
Aert Van Nesstraat 25 J-K
3012 CA Rotterdam

New Zealand

McLachlan, Campbell, QC
Victoria University of Wellington Law School
PO Box 600
6140 Wellington

Williams, David
Member of ICCA
Bankside Chambers
Level 22, The Lumley Centre
88 Shortland Street
PO Box 405
1140 Auckland

Nigeria

Biachi, Patricia
ARCSSTE-E
African Regional Centre for Space Science and Technology Education-English
OAU Campus
234 Ile-Ife

Eleodimuo, Christopher
University of Lagos
Akao
Lagos

Ojo, Christopher
Bayo Ojo & Co
4th Floor, ITF House
6 Adetokunbo Ademola Crescent
Wuse II
FCT Abuja

Osuagwu, Ugochukwu Emmanuel
St. Francis Xavier Solicitors & Advocates
38 Mambolo Street
Wuse II
23409 Abuja

Oyekunle, Tinuade
Honorary Vice President of ICCA
Sonotina Chambers
17 Olujobi Street

Gbagada, Phase 1, (Near Anthony Bus Stop)
1234 Lagos

Norway

Thommesen, Nina
University of Geneva

Pakistan

Naeem Khan, Muhammad
Muhammad Akram & Son
Trading & Investment
PO Box No. 1029
Rawalpindi 46000

Sarwana, Ahmed
Abraham & Sarwana
Mezzanine Floor, PIDC House
Dr Ziauddin Road
Karachi 75530

Poland

Chojecki, Pawel
Łaszczuk & Partners
Plac Pilsudskiego 2
00-073 Warsaw

Kruzewski, Bartosz
Clifford Chance
ul. Lwowska 19
00-660 Warsaw

Krzywosz, Przemyslaw
Przemyslaw Krzywosz Kancelaria Prawna
Marconich 11/5
Warsaw

Michalowska, Katarzyna
Soltysinski & Szlezak
ul. Wawelska 15B
02-034 Warsaw

Nowaczyk, Piotr
Salans
Rondo ONZ 1
00-124 Warsaw

Szpara, Justyna
Łaszczuk & Partners
Plac Pilsudskiego 2
00-073 Warsaw

Wardynski, Tomasz
Wardynski & Partners
Al. Ujazdowskie 10
00-478 Warsaw

Portugal

Anselmo Vaz, Teresa
Afra Associados – Sociedade de Advogados
Rua Castilho, 32, 4° andar
1250-070 Lisbon

Borges, Carla
Linklaters
Av. Fontas Pereira de Melo, 14, 15° andar
1050-121 Lisbon

Júdice, José Miguel
PLMJ – A. M. Pereira, Sáragga Leal, Oliveira Martins, Júdice e Associados
Av. da Liberdade, 224
1250-148 Lisbon

Lousa, Nuno
Linklaters
Av. Fontas Pereira de Melo, 14, 15° andar
1050-121 Lisbon

Romania

Baias, Flavius
The Court of International Commercial Arbitration
2 Octavian Goga Blvd., 3rd District
030982 Bucharest

Leaua, Crenguta
The Court of International Commercial Arbitration
2 Octavian Goga Blvd., 3rd District
030982 Bucharest

Russian Federation

Khvalei, Vladimir
Baker & McKenzie
Sadovaya Plaza, 12th Floor
7, Dolgorukovskaya Street
127006 Moscow

Komarov, Alexander
Vice President of ICCA
International Arbitration Court
of the Russian Federation
6, Ilynka Street
109012 Moscow

Lebedev, Sergei
Honorary Vice President of ICCA
Maritime Arbitration Commission at the Chamber of Commerce and Industry of the Russian Federation
6, Ilynka Street
109012 Moscow

Singapore

Cavinder, Bull
Singapore International Arbitration Centre
32 Maxwell Road
Singapore 69115

Hwang, Michael
Member of ICCA
Michael Hwang S.C.
1 Finalayson Green #14-02
Singapore 18989

Lau, Christopher
Maxwell Chambers
32 Maxwell Road #02-04
Singapore 069115

Spain

Arias, David
Perez-Llorca
Alcalá, 61
28014 Madrid

Cainzos Fernandez, Jose Antonio
Clifford Chance
Paseo de la Castellana, 110
28046 Madrid

Cremades, Bernardo M.
Member of ICCA
B. Cremades y Asociados
Calle Goya 18, planta 2
28001 Madrid

De Los Santos, Carlos
J&A Garrigues
Calle de Hermosilla, 3
28001 Madrid

Diez-Picazo Gimenez, Ignacio
Herbert Smith
Paseo de la Castellana, 66
28046 Madrid

Fernández-Armesto, Juan
Armesto & Asociados
General Pardiñas, 102
28006 Madrid

Fernández-Ballesteros, Miguel Ángel
Fernández-Ballesteros
Serrano, 22
28001 Madrid

Malaga, Francisco
Linklaters
Calle Zurbarán, 28
28010 Madrid

Pombo, Fernando
Gomez-Acebo & Pombo
Castellana, 216
28046 Madrid

Temboury Redondo, Miguel
Court of Arbitration
Madrid Chamber of Commerce
Ribera del Loira, 56-58
28042 Madrid

Sweden

Almelöv, Jörgen
Setterwalls Advokatbyrå AB
Arsenalsgatan 6
101 39 Stockholm

Bagner, Hans
Frank Advokatbyrå AB
Regeringsgatan 20
103 87 Stockholm

Bergman, Linn
Arbitration Institute of the Stockholm Chamber of Commerce
PO Box 16050
103 21 Stockholm

Dandenell, Helena
Frank Advokatbyrå AB
Regeringsgatan 20
103 87 Stockholm

Danelius, Johan
Hamilton Advokatbyrå
PO Box 715
101 33 Stockholm

Ericson, Johannes
Hamilton Advokatbyrå
PO Box 715
101 33 Stockholm

Franke, Ulf
Honorary Secretary General of ICCA
Chapmansgatan 2
112 36 Stockholm

Gernandt, Johan
Vinge
Smålandsgatan 20
PO Box 1703
111 87 Stockholm

Johansson, Tom
Hamilton Advokatbyrå
PO Box 715
101 33 Stockholm

Kadelburger, John
Advocat John Kadelburger AB
Engelbrektsgatan 9-11
114 32 Stockholm

Knuts, Gisela
Roschier
PO Box 7358
103 90 Stockholm

Magnusson, Annette
Arbitration Institute of the Stockholm Chamber of Commerce
PO Box 16050
103 21 Stockholm

Öhrström, Marie
Setterwalls Advokatbyrå AB
Arsenalsgatan 6
101 39 Stockholm

Persson, Kristoffer
Frank Advokatbyrå AB
Regeringsgatan 20
103 87 Stockholm

Ragnwaldh, Jakob
Mannheimer Swartling Advokatbyra AB
Box 1711
111 87 Stockholm

Soederlund, Christer
Vinge
Smålandsgatan 20
PO Box 1703
111 87 Stockholm

Waering, Christina
Setterwalls Advokatbyrå AB
Arsenalsgatan 6
101 39 Stockholm

Switzerland

Aebi, Martin
Lenz & Staehelin
Bleicherweg 58
8027 Zurich

Ah Choon, Feodora
Python & Peter
9, rue Firmin-Massot
1206 Geneva

Akikol, Diana
Lenz & Staehelin
Route de Chêne 30
1211 Geneva 17

Allen, Brooks
Sidley Austin

139, rue de Lausanne
1202 Geneva

Arfazadeh, Homayoon
Python & Peter
8, avenue Jules-Crosnier
1206 Geneva

Arroyo, Manuel
Bär & Karrer AG
Brandschenkestrasse 90
8027 Zurich

Baizeau, Domitille
Lalive
35, rue de la Mairie
1211 Geneva 6

Bajrai, Deena
Permanent Mission of Singapore in Geneva
Avenue du Pailly 10
1219 Châtelaine Geneva

Bangert, Jan
Böckli Bodmer & Partners
St. Jakobs-Strasse 41, PO Box 2348
4002 Basel

Barnett, Jonathan
Homburger AG
Weinbergstrasse 56
8042 Zurich

Bärtsch, Philippe
Schellenberg Wittmer
15bis, rue des Alpes
1211 Geneva 1

Beffa, Luca
Baker & McKenzie
Rue Pedro-Meylan 5
1208 Geneva

Benevenuto, Rachel
Nobel & Hug
Dufourstrasse 29
8032 Zurich

Berger, Bernhard
Kellerhals Attorneys at Law
Effingerstrasse 1
3001 Bern

Bersheda, Tetiana
Bersheda Avocats
15, rue Général Dufour
1204 Geneva

Biesel, Eric
Geneva Chamber of Commerce
4, boulevard du Théâtre
1204 Geneva

Biggart, John
Deloitte AG
General Guisan-Quai 38
8022 Zurich

Blessing, Marc
Bär & Karrer AG
Brandschenkestrasse 90
8027 Zurich

Boisson de Chazournes, Laurence
University of Geneva
40, boulevard du Pont d'Arve
1211 Geneva 4

Bonnan, Régis
Lévy Kaufmann-Kohler
3-5, rue du Conseil Général
PO Box 552
1211 Geneva 4

Boog, Christopher
Schellenberg Wittmer
Löwenstrasse 19
8021 Zurich

Bösch, Michael
Thouvenin Rechtsanwälte
Klausstrasse 33
8034 Zurich

Brown-Berset, Dominique
Brown Page
37-39, rue de Vermont
1202 Geneva

Brunoni, Brenno
Fédération Suisse des Avocats
Marktgasse 400
PO Box 8321
3001 Bern

Burckhardt, Thomas
Simonius Pfrommer & Partner
Aeschenvorstadt 67
4010 Basel

Casserly, David
Lévy Kaufmann-Kohler
3-5, rue du Conseil Général
PO Box 552
1211 Geneva 4

Catelli, Cinzia
Niederer Kraft Frey AG
Bahnhofstrasse 13
8001 Zurich

Christie, Konstantin
Python & Peter
9, rue Firmin-Massot
1206 Geneva

Courvoisier, Maurice
Wenger Plattner
Aeschenvorstadt 55
4010 Basel

Cremades, Anne-Carole
Schellenberg Wittmer
15bis, rue des Alpes
1211 Geneva 1

Dallafior, Roberto
Nater Dallafior
Hottingerstrasse 21
8032 Zurich

Dasser, Felix
Homburger
Weinbergstrasse 56
8042 Zurich

De Castro, Ignacio
WIPO Arbitration and Mediation Center
34, chemin des Colombettes
1211 Geneva 20

De Werra, Jacques
University of Geneva
Department of Commercial Law
40, boulevard du Pont d'Arve
1211 Geneva 4

Dickenmann, Philipp J.
CMS von Erlach Henrici AG
Dreikönigstrasse 7
PO Box 2991
8022 Zurich

Dodge, Kirstin
Homburger
Weinbergstrasse 56
8042 Zurich

Duteil, Perrine
Tavernier Tschanz
11bis, rue Toepffer
1206 Geneva

Ehle, Bernd
Lalive
35, rue de la Mairie
1211 Geneva 6

Favre-Bulle, Xavier
Lenz & Staehelin
Route de Chêne 30
1211 Geneva 17

Fellrath, Isabelle
Tavernier Tschanz
11bis, rue Toepffer
1206 Geneva

Frey, Harold
Lenz & Staehelin
Bleicherweg 58
8027 Zurich

Frick, Joachim
Baker & McKenzie
Holbeinstrasse 30
8034 Zurich

Gallego, Jaime
Lalive
35, rue de la Mairie
1211 Geneva 6

Geisinger, Elliott
Schellenberg Wittmer
15bis, rue des Alpes
1211 Geneva 1

Genton, Pierre Michel
PMG Consulting Engineers & Economists
72, rue du Centre
1025 St-Suplice / Lausanne

Giovannini, Teresa
Lalive
35, rue de la Mairie
1211 Geneva 6

Graenicher, Dieter
Wenger Plattner
Aeschenvorstadt 55
4010 Basel

Gunter, Pierre -Yves
Python & Peter
6, rue François-Bellot
1206 Geneva

Habegger, Philipp
Walder Wyss Ltd
Seefeldstrasse 123
PO Box 1236
8034 Zurich

Hargrove, James
Eversheds
20, rue du Marché
1204 Geneva

Hasler, Erika
Lévy Kaufmann-Kohler
3-5, rue du Conseil Général
PO Box 552
1211 Geneva 4

Hehenberger, Patrick
7, route de Crassier
1262 Eysins

Heiskanen, Veijo
Lalive
35, rue de la Mairie
1211 Geneva 6

Hess, Beat
Kilchbergstrasse 164
8038 Zurich
Switzerland

Hirsch, Laurent
Hirsch Kobel
8, rue Eynard
1205 Geneva

Hochstrasser, Daniel
Bär & Karrer AG
Brandschenkestrasse 90
8027 Zurich

Hoffmann, Anne K.
Python & Peter
9, rue Firmin-Massot
1206 Geneva

Hofmann, Dieter
Walder Wyss Ltd.
Seefeldstrasse 1236
PO Box 123
8034 Zurich

Imhoos, Christophe
Jean-Pierre et Christophe Imhoos & Partners
1 Place du Port
1204 Geneva

Inaudi, Matteo
Ming Halperin Burger & Inaudi
5, avenue Léon Gaud
1206 Geneva

Jahnel, Werner
Lalive
Löwenstrasse 2
8021 Zurich

Jermini, Cesare
Bär & Karrer SA
Via Vegezzi 6
6901 Lugano

Johnson, Alexandra
Python & Peter
9, rue Firmin-Massot
1206 Geneva

Jolles, Alexander
Schellenberg Wittmer
Löwenstrasse 19
8021 Zurich

Joory, Marc
Python & Peter
9, rue Firmin-Massot
1206 Geneva

Kälin-Nauer, Claudia
Lavaterstrasse 98
8002 Zurich

Kaiser, François
Carrard & Associes
Place Saint-François 1
PO Box 7191
1002 Lausanne

Kalnina, Ieva
Lévy Kaufmann-Kohler
3-5, rue du Conseil Général
PO Box 552
1211 Geneva 4

Kaufmann-Kohler, Gabrielle
Member of ICCA
Lévy Kaufmann-Kohler
3-5, rue du Conseil Général
PO Box 552
1211 Geneva 4

Karrer, Pierre A.
Lavater-Strasse 98
8002 Zurich

Kellerhals, Franz
Kellerhals Attorneys at Law
Effingerstrasse 1
3001 Berne

Kessler, Didier
Kessler & Associates
Chemin des Crets de Champel 3
1206 Geneva

Knoepfler, François
Courtils 49
2016 Cortaillod

Knoll, Joachim
Brown & Page
37-39, rue de Vermont
1202 Geneva 20

Kobel, Pierre
Hirsch Kobel
8, rue Eynard
1200 Geneva

Koch, Christopher
Landolt & Koch
17, rue du Mont-Blanc
1201 Geneva

Koenig, B. Gino
Lustenberger Glaus & Partner
Wiesenstrasse 10
PO Box 1073
8032 Zurich

Krausz, Nora
ZPG
2, rue Bovy-Lysberg
1211 Geneva

Laborde, Gustavo
Lévy Kaufmann-Kohler
3-5, rue du Conseil Général
PO Box 552
1211 Geneva 4

Lalive, Pierre
Advisory Member of ICCA
Lalive
35, rue de la Mairie
1211 Geneva 6

Landolt, Phillip
Landolt & Koch
17, rue du Mont-Blanc
1201 Geneva

Lauterburg, Bernhard
Prager Dreifuss AG
Schweizerhof-Passage 7
3001 Bern

Lawson, David
Bonnard Lawson
11, rue du Général-Dufour
1204 Geneva

Legler, Thomas
Python & Peter
6, rue François-Bellot
1206 Geneva

Leimbacher, Elisabeth
Lévy Kaufmann-Kohler
3-5, rue du Conseil Général
PO Box 552
1211 Geneva 4

Lenggenhager, Fadri
Lenz & Staehelin
Bleicherweg 58
8027 Zurich

Lévy, Laurent
Lévy Kaufmann-Kohler
3-5, rue du Conseil Général
PO Box 552
1211 Geneva 4

Liatowitsch, Manuel
Schellenberg Wittmer
Löwenstrasse 19
8021 Zurich

Macmillan, Rory
Macmillan Keck
72, boulevard Saint Georges
1205 Geneva

Marceau, Gabrielle
WTO
154, rue Lausanne
1211 Geneva 21

Marguerat, Jean
Froriep Renggli
4, rue Charles-Bonnet
1211 Geneva 12

Marugg, Daniel
Gloor Sieger
Utoquai 37
PO Box 581
8024 Zurich

Marzolini, Paolo
Lenz & Staehelin
Route de Chêne 30
1211 Geneva 17

Mazuranic, Alexandre
Schellenberg Wittmer
15bis, rue des Alpes
1211 Geneva 1

Meier, Andrea
Wartmann & Merker
Fraumünsterstrasse 29
8022 Zurich

Menz, James U.
Schellenberg Wittmer
Löwenstrasse 19
8021 Zurich

Meyer, Bernhard
MME Partners
Kreuzstrasse 42
8008 Zurich

Min, Eun-Joo
WIPO Arbitration and Mediation Center
34, chemin des Colombettes
1211 Geneva 20

Morand, Pierre- Andre
Mentha & Partners
4, rue de l'Athénée
1211 Geneva 12

Mosch, Ruth
University of Geneva
Chemin de Bonvard 67
1222 Geneva

Nessi, Sebastiano
Lenz & Staehelin
Route de Chêne 30
1208 Geneva 17

Noel, Anna
Bureau du Prof. Pierre Tercier
5, chemin Guillaume Ritter
1700 Fribourg

Paris, Marion
University of Geneva

Patocchi, Paolo Michele
Lenz & Staehelin
Route de Chêne 30
1208 Geneva 17

Pedrazzini, Matteo
LHA Avocats
100, rue du Rhône
PO Box 3403
1211 Geneva 3

Peregrina, Daniel
Baker & McKenzie
5, rue Pedro Meylan
1208 Geneva

Perret, François
Perret
17, boulevard des Philosophes
1205 Geneva

Peter, Wolfgang
Python & Peter
9, rue Firmin-Massot
1206 Geneva

Petti, Angelina
Schellenberg Wittmer
15bis, rue des Alpes
1211 Geneva 1

Philippe, Arnaud
Niederer Kraft Frey AG
Bahnhostrasse 13
8001 Zurich

Potesta, Michele
University of Geneva

Preti, Philippe
Mentha & Associés
4, rue de l'Athénée 4
1211 Geneva 12

Raha, Joya
CCIG
4, boulevard du Théâtre
1204 Geneva

Raneda, Julie
Schellenberg Wittmer
15bis, rue des Alpes
1211 Geneva 1

Rattray, Adam
WIPO Arbitration and Mediation Center
34, chemin des Colombettes
1211 Geneva 20

Recordon, Pierre-Alain
BRS Avocats
9, boulevard des Philosophes
1205 Geneva

Reichert, Douglas
1, rue Etienne Dumont
PO Box 5327
Geneva 11

Reilly, Louise
Court of Arbitration for Sport
Château de Béthusy
2, avenue de Beaumont
1012 Lausanne

Rentsch, Noelle
Lévy Kaufmann-Kohler
3-5, rue du Conseil Général
PO Box 552
1211 Geneva 4

Rigozzi, Antonio
Lévy Kaufmann-Kohler
3-5, rue du Conseil Général
PO Box 552
1211 Geneva 4

Rochat, Jean Philippe
Carrard & Associés
Place Saint-François 1
PO Box 7191
1002 Lausanne

Rohner, Thomas
Pestalozzi
Löwenstrasse 1
8001 Zurich

Roud, Sophie
Python & Peter
9, rue Firmin-Massot
1206 Geneva

Rubeli, Guy-Philippe
Lachenal & Le Fort
65, rue du Rhône
1211 Geneva

Sacco, Sabina
Lévy Kaufmann-Kohler
3-5, rue du Conseil Général
PO Box 552
1211 Geneva 4

Sambeth Glasner, Birgit
Altenburger
11bis, rue Toepffer
1206 Geneva

Scherer, Matthias
Lalive

35, rue de la Mairie
1211 Geneva 6

Schlaepfer, Anne Veronique
Schellenberg Wittmer
15bis, rue des Alpes
1201 Geneva

Schmid, Ernst F.
Niederer Kraft Frey
Bahnhofstrasse 13
8001 Zurich

Schneider, Michael
Lalive
35, rue de la Mairie
1211 Geneva 6

Schnyder, Sabine
Sidley Austin
139, rue de Lausanne
1202 Geneva

Schramm, Dorothee
Schellenberg Wittmer
Löwenstrasse 19
8021 Zurich

Schultz, Thomas
Iheid, Geneva University Law Faculty
Villa Moynier
120B, rue de Lausanne
1202 Geneva

Stirnimann, Franz
Lalive
35, rue de la Mairie
1211 Geneva 6

Stutzer, Hansjoerg
Thouvenin Rechtsanwälte
Klausstrasse 33
8034 Zurich

Tercier, Pierre
Member of ICCA
5, ch. Guillaume Ritter
1700 Fribourg

Touchard, Cendrine
République et Canton de Genève
PO Box 3964
1211 Genève

Tran Thang, Nhu-Hoang
Bersheda Avocats
15, rue Général Dufour,
1204 Geneva

Veit, Marc
Walder Wyss Ltd.
Seefeldstrasse 123
PO Box 1236
8034 Zurich

Vermeille, François
PMG Consulting Engineers & Economists
72, rue du Centre
1025 Saint-Suplice/Lausanne

Vock, Dominik
MME Partners
Kreuzstrasse 42
Zurich

Von Wunschheim, Clarisse
WunschARB GmbH
c/o Baumgartner Mächler
Löwenstrasse 2
PO Box 2121
8022 Zurich

Voser, Nathalie
Schellenberg Wittmer
Löwenstrasse 19
8021 Zurich

Wehrli, Daniel
Gloor Sieger
Utoquai 37
PO Box 581
8024 Zurich

Wenger, Werner
Wenger Plattner
Aeschenvorstadt 55
4010 Basel

Wicki, Jodok
CMS von Erlach Henrici AG
Dreikönigstrasse 7
8022 Zurich

Wiebecke, Martin
Anwaltsburo Wiebecke
Kohlrainstrasse 10
8700 Zurich

Wuelher, Norbert
IOM
7, Place des Perrières
1296 Coppet

Xoudis, Julia
Python & Peter
9, rue Firmin-Massot
1206 Geneva

Yasseen, Rabab
Mentha & Partners
4, rue de l'Athénée
1211 Geneva 12

Zarate, Paz
Lévy Kaufmann & Kohler
3-5, rue du Conseil Général
PO Box 552
1211 Geneva 4

Tunesia

Kemicha, Fathi
Member of ICCA
Kemicha Legal Consulting KLC
PO Box 27
Les Berges du Lac
1053 Tunis

Turkey

Balkaya, Bennar
Balkaya & Balkaya Attorneys At Law
Kocayol Cad. Kozyatagi Sok. Yavuzlar
Apt. No:23/27 K:8
34742 Kozyatagi/Istanbul

Ukraine

Drobot, Elena
Viza
Karla Marxa Avenue 27
49000 Dnepropetrovsk

Iavorskyi, Maksym
University of Geneva

Osadcha, Mariia
Viza
49027 Dnepropetrovsk

United Arab Emirates

Al-Khatib, Abdulla
UAE University
UAE University Islamic Institution
Al-Ain

Al Tamimi, Essam
Al Tamimi & Company
Dubai International Financial Centre
Building 4 East, 6th Floor
Sheikh Zayed Road
PO Box 9275
Dubai

Emmerson, Alec
Clyde & Co
Level 15, Rolex Tower
Sheikh Zayed Road
PO Box 7001
Dubai

Farhad, Alain
Freshfields Bruckhaus Deringer
Al Fattan Currency Tower, 20th floor
Dubai International Financial Centre
PO Box 506 569
Dubai

United Kingdom

Alexander, Jay
Baker Botts
41 Lothbury
London EC2R 7HF

Alvey, Nicki
Chartered Institute of Arbitrators
12 Bloomsbury Square
London WC1A 2LP

Baruti, Rukia
Suite 15124
Lower Ground Floor
145-157 St. John Street
London EC1V 4PY

Bentham, Jayne
Simmons & Simmons
Ropemaker Street
London EC2Y 9SS

Berkeley, Andrew
49 Arden Road
London N3 3AD

Berkeley, Iona
8 New Square
Lincoln's Inn
London WC2A 3QP

Berman, Sir Franklin, KCMG QC
Essex Court Chambers
24 Lincoln's Inn Fields
London WC2A 3ED

Boesch, Bruno
Froriep Renggli
17 Godliman Street
London EC4V 5BD

Brennan, Lorraine
JAMS International
70 Fleet Street
London EC4Y 1EU

Brynmor Thomas, David
39 Essex Street
London WC2R 3AT

Burn, George
Salans
Millenium Bridge House
2 Lambeth Hill
London EC4V 4AJ

Carroll, Ben
Linklaters
One Silk Street
London EC2Y 8HQ

Carlson, Hugh
K&L Gates
One New Change
London EC4M 9AF

Caulfield, Christopher
Squire, Sanders & Dempsey
2 Park Lane
Leeds LS3 1ES

Cohen, Paul
12 Gray's Inn
12 Gray's Inn Square
London WC1R 5JP

Cooling, Thomas Liam
Freshfields Bruckhaus Deringer
65 Fleet Street
London EC4Y 1HS

Davies, David
Essex Court Chambers
24 Lincoln's Inn Fields
London WC2A 3EG

Davison, Michael
Hogan Lovells International
Atlantic House
Holborn Viaduct
London EC1A

Dundas, Hew
1st Colme Street
Edinburgh EH3 6AA

Escobar, Alex
Baker Botts
41 Lothbury
London EC2R 7HF

Foden, Timothy
Allen & Overy
One Bishops Square
London E1 6AD

Freeman, James
Allen & Overy
One Bishops Square
London E1 6AD

Garibaldi, Oscar
Covington & Burling
265 Strand
London WC2H 1BH

Goldsmith, Lord (Peter)
Debevoise & Plimpton
Tower 42
Old Broad Street
London EC2N 1HQ

Griffith, Gavan
Essex Court Chambers
24 Lincoln's Inn Fields
London WC2A 3ED

Heilbron, Hilary
Brick Court Chambers
7-8 Essex Street
London WC2R 3LD

Hirst, Peter
Clyde & Co
51 Eastcheap
London EC3M 1JP

Hodges, Paula
Herbert Smith
Exchange House
Primrose Street
London EC2A 2HS

Holloway, David
41 Indigo Mews
London N16 9AE

Hunter, J. Martin
Member of ICCA
Essex Court Chambers
24 Lincoln's Inn Fields
London WC2A 3EG

Khan, Hussain
K&L Gates
One New Change
London EC4M 9AF

Lamb, Sophie
Debevoise & Plimpton
Tower 42
Old Broad Street
London EC2N 1HQ

Landau, Toby
Essex Court Chambers
24 Lincoln's Inn Fields
London WC2A 3EG

Leanez, Alejandro
WilmerHale
49 Park Lane
London W1K 1PS

Leaver, Peter
Essex Court Chambers
One Essex Court Temple
London EC4Y 9AR

Miles, Wendy
Wilmer Cutler Pickering Hale & Dorr
49 Park Lane
London W1K 1PS

Morgan, Simon
Simmons & Simmons
Ropemaker Street
London EC2Y 9SS

Nadar, Aisha
Nadar Consulting
1 Hans Place
London SW1X 0EU

Noury, Sylvia
Freshfield Bruckhaus Deringer
65 Fleet Street
London EC4Y 1HS

O'Callaghan, Kieron
Hogan Lovells International
Atlantic House
Holborn Viaduct
London EC1A 2FG

Oputa, Adaora
Freshfields Bruckhaus Deringer
65 Fleet Street
London EC4Y 1HT

Parker, Chris
Herbert Smith
Exchange House
Primrose Street
London EC2A 2HS

Parratt, David
Advocates Library
Parliament House
Royal Mile
Edinburgh EH1 1RF

Pullen, Andrew
Allen & Overy
One Bishops Square
London E1 6AD

Quirk, Iain
Essex Court Chambers
24 Lincoln's Inn Fields
London WC2A 3EG

Rawding, Nigel
Freshfields Bruckhaus Deringer
65 Fleet Street
London EC4Y 1HS

Roberts, Anthea
Law Department
London School of Economics
Houghton Street
London WC2A 2AE

Ruff, Deborah
Dewey & LeBoeuf
1 Minster Court
Mincing Lane
London EC3R 7YL

Runeland, Per
SJ Berwin
10 Queen Street Place
London EC4R 1BE

Sheppard, Audley
Clifford Chance
10 Upper Bank Street
London E14 5JJ

Smith, Michael Forbes
Chartered Institute of Arbitrators
12 Bloomsbury Square
London WC1A 2LP

Stevez Sanz, Marlene
SJ Berwin
10 Queen Street Place
London EC4R 1BE

Style, Christopher
Linklaters
One Silk Street
London EC2Y 8HQ

Taylor, Eleanor
Wolters Kluwer Law & Business
250 Waterloo Road
London SE1 8RD

Tevendale, Craig
Herbert Smith
Exchange House
Primrose Street
London EC2A 2HS

Veeder, V.V.
Member of ICCA
Essex Court Chambers
24 Lincoln's Inn Fields
London WC2A 3ED

Verhoosel, Gaetan
Covington & Burling
265 Strand
London WC2R 1BH

Vinovrski, Nicola
Clyde & Co
51 Eastcheap
London EC3M 1JP

United States

Aguilar-Alvarez, Guillermo
Vice President of ICCA
King & Spalding
1185 Avenue of the Americas
New York, NY 10036

Ali, Arif
Crowell & Moring
1001 Pennsylvania Avenue, NW, 10th Floor
Washington, DC 20004

Amirfar, Catherine
Debevoise & Plimpton
919 Third Avenue
New York, NY 10022

Arsanjani, Mahnoush
The American Society of International Law
2223 Massachusetts Avenue, NW
Washington, DC 20008

Astigarraga, José
Astigarraga Davis
701 Brickell Avenue, 16th Floor
Miami, FL 33131

Barkett, John
Shook Hardy & Bacon

3200 Miami Center
201 S. Biscayne Boulevard
Miami, FL 33131-4332

Cheek, Marney
Covington & Burling
1201 Pennsylvania Avenue, NW
Washington, DC 20004

Chinn, Christopher
150 Norman Avenue, Apt 2R
Brooklyn, NY 11222

Coe, Jack
Pepperdine University
1370 Southwind Circle
Westlake Village, CA 91361

Day, Peter
Mercer Island Arbitration
Chambers International
6915 SE 33rd Street
Mercer Island, WA 98040-3323

Digon, Rocio
King & Spalding
1185 Avenue of the Americas
New York, NY 10036

Donovan, Donald Francis
Honorary Vice President of ICCA
Debevoise & Plimpton
919 Third Avenue
New York, NY 10022

Drahozal, Christopher
University of Kansas School of Law
Green Hall, Room 502
1535 W. 15th St
Lawrence, Kansas 66045

Fantechi, Massimo
590 Madison Avenue, 21th Floor
New York, NY 10022

Freedberg, Judith
University of Miami School of Law
1311 Miller Drive, D345
Coral Gables, FL 33124-8087

Frischknecht, Andreas
Chaffetz Lindsey
505 Fifth Avenue, 4th Floor
New York, NY 10017

Gardiner, John
Skadden, Arps, Slate, Meagher & Flom
4 Times Square
New York, NY 10036

Gimblett, Jonathan
Covington & Burling
1201 Pennyslvania Avenue, NW
Washington, DC 20004

Gonzalez, Daniel
Hogan Lovells International
Mellon Financial Center
1111 Brickell Avenue, Suite 1900
Miami, FL 33131

Hosking, James
Chaffetz Lindsey
505 Fifth Avenue, 4th Floor
New York, NY 10017

Johnson, Thomas
Covington & Burling
1201 Pennsylvania Avenue, NW
Washington, DC 20004

Kamau, Ndanga
King & Spalding
1100 Louisiana Street, Suite 4000
Houston, TX 77019

Kaye, Judith
Skadden, Arps, Slate, Meagher & Flom
4 Times Square
New York, NY 10036

Kessler, Philip
Thompson & Knight
900 Third Avenue
New York, NY 10022-4728

Landy, Burton
Akerman Senterfitt
One Southeast Third Avenue
25th Floor
Miami, FL 33131

Lindsey, David
Chaffetz Lindsey

505 Fifth Avenue, 4th Floor
New York, NY 10017

Matthews, Joseph
Colson Hicks Eidson
255 Alhambra Circle, Penthouse
Coral Gables, FL 33134

McGarry, Brian
University of Geneva

Naimark, Richard
International Centre for Dispute Resolution
1633 Broadway, 10th Floor
New York, NY 10019-6708

Nelson, Timothy
Skadden, Arps, Slate, Meagher & Flom
4 Times Square
New York, NY 12572

Paulsson, Jan
President and General Editor of ICCA
University of Miami School of Law
1311 Miller Drive
Coral Gables, FL 33146

Paulsson, Marike
University of Miami School of Law
1311 Miller Drive
Coral Gables, FL 33146

Pierce, John
Wilmer Cutler Pickering Hale & Dor-
399 Park Avenue
New York, NY 10022

Reed, Lucy
Freshfields Bruckhaus Deringer
520 Madison Avenue, 34th Floor
New York, NY 10022

Reisman, W. Michael
Yale Law School
127 Wall Street
New Haven, CT 06511

Richardson, Brian
Yale Law School
109 Church Street, Apt. 312
New Haven, CT 06510

Slate, Debora
1855 St. Francis Street
Reston, VA 20190

Slate, William K., II
Member of ICCA
American Arbitration Association
1776 Eye Street, NW, Suite 850
Washington, DC 20006

Wang Sheng Chang
Member of ICCA
262 North Cottage Road
Sterling, VA 20164

West, Briana
University of Geneva

Whitesell, Anne- Marie
Dechert
1775 L Street, NW
Washington, DC 20006-2401

Venezuela

De Jesus O., Alfredo
Venezuelan Arbitration Committee
Centro Lido, Torre C, Piso 7, Oficina 73-C
Avenida Francisco de Miranda El Rosal
Caracas 1060

Droulers, Diana
International Federation of Commercial Arbitration Institutions (IFCAI)
PO Box 2835
Caracas 1101

Tejera Perez, Victorino
University of Geneva

Zimbabwe

Dumbutshena, Inviolata
University of Technology, Sidney;
presently Malawi-based

INTERNATIONAL COUNCIL FOR COMMERCIAL ARBITRATION (ICCA)

Correspondence address:
Mr. Kap-You (Kevin) Kim
Secretary General ICCA
Bae, Kim & Lee LLC
647-15 Yoksam-dong
Kangnam-gu
Seoul 135-723
Korea
Phone: +1-822 3404 0333
Fax: +1-822 3404 7306
E-mail: kevin.kim@bkl.co.kr

LIST OF OFFICERS AND MEMBERS

March 2012

OFFICERS

Honorary Presidents

THE HON. GIORGIO BERNINI (Bologna, Italy)
Former Minister of Foreign Trade and Member of Parliament; Former Member, Italian Antitrust Authority; Professor, University of Bologna, Chair of Arbitration and International Commercial Law; President, Association for the Teaching and Study of Arbitration and International Trade Law (AISA); Member, Executive Committee, Italian Arbitration Association; Senior Partner, Studio Bernini e Associati

DR. GEROLD HERRMANN (Vienna, Austria)
Former Secretary, United Nations Commission on International Trade Law (UNCITRAL); Honorary Professor, University of Vienna

MR. FALI S. NARIMAN (New Delhi, India)
President Emeritus, Bar Association of India; Honorary Member, International Commission of Jurists; Past President, Law Association for Asia and the Pacific (LAWASIA); Member of the Court, London Court of International Arbitration (LCIA); Past Vice Chairman, International Court of Arbitration of the International Chamber of Commerce (ICC); Past Co-Chair, Human Rights Institute of the International Bar Association (IBA); Senior Advocate, Supreme Court of India

PROF. PIETER SANDERS (Schiedam, The Netherlands)
Honorary President, Netherlands Arbitration Institute; Professor Emeritus, Faculty of Law, Erasmus University, Rotterdam

President

PROF. JAN PAULSSON (Paris, France)
General Editor, ICCA *International Handbook on Commercial Arbitration*; Michael Klein Distinguished Scholar Chair, University of Miami School of Law; Centennial Professor of Law, London School of Economics; Judge and Past President, World Bank Administrative Tribunal; President, Administrative Tribunal, European Bank for Reconstruction and Development; Past President, LCIA

Honorary Vice Presidents

MR. DONALD FRANCIS DONOVAN (New York, USA)
Adjunct Professor, New York University School of Law; Former Vice President, American Society of International Law; Former Chair, Institute for Transnational Arbitration; Former Chair, US National Committee, ICC International Court of Arbitration; Board of Directors, Human Rights First

JUDGE HOWARD M. HOLTZMANN (New York, USA)
Honorary Chairman of the Board, American Arbitration Association; Substitute Judge, Iran-United States Claims Tribunal, The Hague

PROF. SERGEI LEBEDEV (Moscow, Russian Federation)
Former President, Maritime Arbitration Commission (1972-2011); Member of the Presidium, International Commercial Arbitration Court of the Russian Federation Chamber of Commerce and Industry; Professor, Moscow Institute of International Relations (University); Former Commissioner, UN Compensation Commission;

Expert to various UNCITRAL projects, including the Working Group on Arbitration (since 1970)

DDR. WERNER MELIS (Vienna, Austria)
Honorary President, International Arbitral Centre of the Austrian Federal Economic Chamber, Vienna; Past Vice President, LCIA

MS. TINUADE OYEKUNLE (Lagos, Nigeria)
Barrister and Solicitor of the Supreme Court of Nigeria; Arbitrator and Notary Public; Member, Association of Arbitrators of Nigeria; Fellow, Chartered Institute of Arbitrators, London; Member, Arbitration Committee of the Lagos Chamber of Commerce; Chartered Arbitrator; Member, Panel Membership Group (PMG), Chartered Institute of Arbitrators, London; Former Chairman, Education & Training Committee of the Chartered Institute of Arbitrators, London; Former Member, Board of Management of the Chartered Institute of Arbitrators, London; Regional Representative for Promotion of Arbitration in the West African Region; Past Chairman, Chartered Institute of Arbitrators, Nigeria Branch; Former Member, London Court of International Arbitration; Correspondent of UNIDROIT

Vice Presidents

MR. GUILLERMO AGUILAR-ALVAREZ (New York, USA)
Past General Counsel, ICC International Court of Arbitration; Principal Legal Counsel for the Government of Mexico for the Negotiation and Implementation of NAFTA; Visiting Scholar, Yale Law School; Partner, King & Spalding

MS. TERESA CHENG, GBS, SC, JP (Hong Kong)
Senior Counsel; Vice President, ICC International Court of Arbitration; Vice Chair, Hong Kong International Arbitration Centre; Past President, Chartered Institute of Arbitrators; Visiting Professor, Tsinghua University; Adjunct Professor, Hong Kong University and Hong Kong Polytechnic University

PROF. ALEXANDER S. KOMAROV (Moscow, Russian Federation)
Honorary Chairman, ICC Russia National Committee, Arbitration Commission; Professor, Head of International Private Law Chair, Russian Academy of Foreign Trade; Member of the Presidium, International Commercial Arbitration Court at the Russian Federation Chamber of Commerce and Industry

Honorary Secretaries General

MR. ULF FRANKE (Stockholm, Sweden)
Past Secretary General, ICCA; Past Secretary General, Arbitration Institute of the Stockholm Chamber of Commerce; Past President, International Federation of Commercial Arbitration Institutions (IFCAI)

MR. ANTONIO R. PARRA (Washington, DC, USA)
Past Secretary General, ICCA; Past Deputy Secretary-General and Legal Adviser, International Centre for Settlement of Investment Disputes (ICSID); Fellow, Chartered Institute of Arbitrators; Consultant, World Bank

Secretary General

MR. KAP-YOU (KEVIN) KIM (Seoul, Korea)
Head of Arbitration Group, Bae, Kim & Lee LLC; Senior Advisor, Korea Commercial Arbitration Board (KCAB); Vice President, Korean Council for International Arbitration (KOCIA); Member, ICC International Court of Arbitration; Member, LCIA; Board Member, American Arbitration Association; Panel of Arbitrators, ICSID; Editorial Board Member, Global Arbitration Review; Part-time Professor, Judicial Training and Research Institute, Supreme Court of Korea; Visiting Professor, Sung Kyun Kwan School of Law

MEMBERS

MR. CECIL ABRAHAM (Kuala Lumpur, Malaysia)
Head of Dispute Resolution Practice Group, Zul Rafique & Partners; Fellow, Chartered Institute of Arbitrators; Member, ICC Commission on Arbitration; Member, Advisory Council, Singapore International Arbitration Centre; Member, Advisory Panel, Kuala Lumpur Regional Centre for Arbitration; Past President, Inter-Pacific Bar Association; Past Chairman, Chartered Institute of Arbitrators, Malaysia Branch; Past Vice President, Asia Pacific Regional Arbitration Group (APRAG); Past Deputy President, Malaysian Institute of Arbitrators; Past Member, LCIA Court; Past Vice Chair, Committee D of the International Bar Association

PROF. DR. ALBERT JAN VAN DEN BERG (Brussels, Belgium)
General Editor, ICCA *Yearbook Commercial Arbitration*; Past President, Netherlands Arbitration Institute; Professor of Arbitration Law, Erasmus University, Rotterdam; Visiting Professor, University of Miami School of Law

PROF. DR. PIERO BERNARDINI (Rome, Italy)
Past Professor of Arbitration Law, LUISS University, Rome; President, Italian Arbitration Association; Past Vice-President, ICC International Court of Arbitration

PROF. DR. KARL-HEINZ BÖCKSTIEGEL (Bergisch-Gladbach, Germany)
Professor Emeritus of International Business Law, University of Cologne; Chairman, German Institution of Arbitration (DIS); Past Patron, Chartered Institute of Arbitrators; Past President, International Law Association (ILA); Past President, LCIA; Past President, Iran-United States Claims Tribunal, The Hague

PROF. DR. NAEL G. BUNNI (Dublin, Ireland)
Past President, Chartered Institute of Arbitrators; Member, Board of Trustees and Chairman, Executive Committee, Dubai International Arbitration Centre; Past Member, LCIA Board of Directors; Visiting Professor in Construction Law and Contract Administration, Trinity College, Dublin; Chartered Engineer and Chartered Registered Arbitrator

PROF. BERNARDO M. CREMADES (Madrid, Spain)
Professor, Faculty of Law, Madrid University; Member of the Madrid Bar

MR. DUSHYANT DAVE (New Delhi, India)
Senior Advocate at the Supreme Court of India; Member of the Board, American Arbitration Association; Former member, LCIA Court; Vice Chair, Arbitration Committee, IBA; Former member, National Legal Services Authority of India (NALSA)

M[E] YVES DERAINS (Paris, France)
Past Secretary General, ICC International Court of Arbitration; Chairman, ICC Institute of World Business Law; Member of the Paris Bar

MR. L. YVES FORTIER, CC, QC (Montréal, Canada)
Former Chairman Emeritus and Senior Partner, Ogilvy Renault Montreal; Past President, LCIA; Former Ambassador and Permanent Representative of Canada to the United Nations; Judge *ad hoc*, International Court of Justice; Member, 20 Essex Court Chambers

PROF. DR. EMMANUEL GAILLARD (Paris, France)
Professor of Law, University of Paris XII; Chairman, International Arbitration Institute; Past Member, LCIA Court; Past Chairman, International Arbitration Committee, ILA

PROF. DR. BERNARD HANOTIAU (Brussels, Belgium)
Member, Brussels and Paris Bars; Professor of International Dispute Resolution, University of Louvain; Former Vice-President, LCIA; Former Vice-Chairman, Institute of Transnational Arbitration and CEPANI (Belgium)

PROF. MARTIN HUNTER (London, United Kingdom)
Barrister; Professor Emeritus, Nottingham Trent University; Visiting Professor, Central European University Budapest, King's College London and University of Miami; Chairman, Dubai International Arbitration Centre; Honorary Dean of Postgraduate Studies, T.M.C. Asser Instituut, The Hague

MR. MICHAEL HWANG, SC (Singapore)
Former Acting High Court Judge, Singapore; Advocate and Solicitor, Singapore; Member, Permanent Court of Arbitration; Chartered Arbitrator; Adjunct Professor, National University of Singapore; Former Vice Chair Committee D, International Bar Association; Former Vice Chair, ICC International Court of Arbitration; Council Member, International Council of Arbitration for Sport (ICAS); Member, LCIA; Chief Justice, Dubai International Financial Centre Court; Former President, Law Society of Singapore; Non-Resident Ambassador of Singapore to Switzerland

MR. NEIL KAPLAN, CBE, QC (Hong Kong)
Former Judge, High Court, Hong Kong; Chairman, Hong Kong International Arbitration Centre (1991-2004); Past President, Chartered Institute of Arbitrators; Honorary Professor, City University of Hong Kong

PROF. DR. GABRIELLE KAUFMANN-KOHLER (Geneva, Switzerland)
Professor, Geneva University Law School; Director, Geneva Master in International Dispute Settlement (MIDS); Partner, Lévy Kaufmann-Kohler; Honorary President, Swiss Arbitration Association (ASA)

DR. FATHI KEMICHA (Tunis, Tunisia)
Avocat à la Cour, Member of the Bars of Paris and Tunisia; Former Chair and Member, World Bank Group Sanctions Board; Former Member, International Law Commission of the United Nations; Member, Board of Trustees and Executive Committee, Dubai International Arbitration Centre; Former Vice President, London

Court of International Arbitration and ICC Commission on Arbitration; first appointed Secretary General of the Constitutional Court of the Kingdom of Bahrain (January 2003 - December 2005)

MR. ARTHUR MARRIOTT, QC (London, United Kingdom)
Barrister

PROF. FRANCISCO ORREGO VICUÑA (Santiago, Chile)
Professor of Law, Heidelberg University Center for Latin America and Honorary Director of the LL.M. on Investments, Trade and Arbitration offered jointly by the University of Heidelberg and the Max Planck Institute; Judge *ad hoc*, International Court of Justice; Former Judge and President, Administrative Tribunal of the World Bank; Judge, International Monetary Fund Administrative Tribunal; Former Vice President, LCIA; Member, Latin American Committee of Arbitrators of the ICC; Arbitrator in ICSID, ICC, PCA, UNCITRAL and other arbitration centers and rules

PROF. WILLIAM W. PARK (Cohasset, USA)
Professor of Law, Boston University; General Editor, Arbitration International; President, LCIA; Past Chairman, American Bar Association Committee on International Commercial Dispute Resolution

PROF. DR. MICHAEL PRYLES (Melbourne, Australia)
Chairman, Singapore International Arbitration Centre; Member, Board of Trustees, Dubai International Arbitration Centre; Former President, Australian Centre for International Commercial Arbitration; President, Asia Pacific Regional Arbitration Group; Former Commissioner, United Nations Compensation Commission; Court Member, LCIA Court

MR. WILLIAM K. SLATE II (Washington, DC, USA)
President and Chief Executive Officer, American Arbitration Association; Founder, Global Center for Dispute Resolution Research; Member, Arbitrator and Mediator, Panels of the International Court of Arbitration for Sport (Switzerland); Member, International Commercial Arbitration Court at the Ukraine Chamber of Commerce and Industry; Member, China International Economic and Trade Arbitration Commission (CIETAC)

PROF. DR. GUIDO SANTIAGO TAWIL (Buenos Aires, Argentina)
Professor of Law, University of Buenos Aires School of Law; Chairman, Latin American Arbitration Association (ALARB); Former Co-Chair, IBA Arbitration Committee; Council Member, IBA Legal Practice Division; Member, LCIA;

Member, Institute for Transnational Arbitration Academic Council; Member, ICC Latin American Arbitrators Committee; Member, ICC Institute of World Business Law; Attorney at Law, Partner, M. & M. Bomchil

PROF. PIERRE TERCIER (Fribourg, Switzerland)
Honorary Chairman, International Court of Arbitration of the International Chamber of Commerce; Professor Emeritus, Law Faculty, University of Fribourg; Former Chairman, Swiss Antitrust Commission

MR. V.V. VEEDER, QC (London, United Kingdom)
Vice President, LCIA; Council Member, ICC Institute of World Business Law and of the Arbitration Institute of the Stockholm Chamber of Commerce; Visiting Professor on Investment Arbitration, King's College, University of London

THE HON. S. AMOS WAKO, F.C.I.ARB, SC (Nairobi, Kenya)
Attorney General, Republic of Kenya; Former Chairman, Arbitration Tribunal, Kenya Chamber of Commerce and Industry; Arbitrator, Vienna Convention on Law of Treaties, Centre for Settlement of Investment Disputes; Former Vice President, LCIA-Africa Region; Former Chairman, Law Society of Kenya; Former Member, International Advisory Committee of WIPO Centre for Settlement of Disputes; Former Commission Member, International Commission of Jurists; Former Deputy Secretary General, IBA; Former Secretary General, African Bar Association; Former President, Asian-African Legal Consultative Organisation; Member, International Law Commission (2007-2011); Former Senior Partner, Kaplan & Stratton

DR. WANG SHENG CHANG (Ashburn, USA)
Former Vice Chairman and Former Secretary General, CIETAC; Former Vice Chairman, China Maritime Arbitration Commission (CMAC); Professor of Law, University of International Economics and Business, Beijing; Director, CBJ International LLC

MR. DAVID A.R. WILLIAMS, QC (Auckland, New Zealand)
Former Judge of the High Court of New Zealand; Former Chief Justice of the Cook Islands; Justice of the Cook Islands Court of Appeal; Judge, Court of Dubai International Financial Centre; Past President, Arbitrators and Mediators Institute of New Zealand; Former Member, ICC Court of International Arbitration; Former Member, LCIA; Board of Directors, American Arbitration Association; Honorary Professor of Law, University of Auckland, New Zealand; Barrister, Member of New Zealand and English Bars

Advisory Members

MR. ROBERT COULSON (Riverside, USA)
Former President, American Arbitration Association

PROF. DR. RADOMIR DJUROVIČ (Belgrade, Serbia)
Former President, Arbitration Court of Yugoslavia; Professor of International Commercial Law, Belgrade University

DR. MAURO FERRANTE (Rome, Italy)
Secretary General, Italian Arbitration Association; Managing Director, ICC-Italy

PROF. AHMED S. EL-KOSHERI (Cairo, Egypt)
Former Professor of International Economic Law and Former President, International University for African Development; Member, *Institut de Droit International*; Partner, Kosheri, Rashed & Riad Law Firm

PROF. DR. DR. HC. PIERRE LALIVE D'EPINAY (Geneva, Switzerland)
Honorary President, ASA; Professor Emeritus Geneva University; Honorary Chairman, ICC Institute of International Business Law and Practice; Member and Former President (1989-1991), *Institut de Droit International*; Attorney at Law, Lalive, Geneva

THE HON. MARC LALONDE (Montréal, Canada)
Former Judge *ad hoc*, International Court of Justice; Former Minister of Justice and Attorney General; Former Minister of Energy, Mines and Resources; Former Minister of Finance; Former President, LCIA North American Users Committee; Member, Institute of International Business Law and Practice

MR. MARK LITTMAN, QC (London, United Kingdom)
Barrister

M[E] CARLOS NEHRING NETTO (São Paulo, Brazil)
Former Member, ICC International Court of Arbitration; Member, London Court of International Arbitration

MR. ALAIN PLANTEY (Paris, France)
Président d'honneur, ICC International Court of Arbitration; Former Member of the *Conseil d'État*; Member and Former President, *Institut de France*; Member and Former President, Academy of Moral and Political Sciences (*Institut de France*); Former Ambassador of France; Former Professor of Law, University of Paris I

THE HON. ANDREW JOHN ROGERS, QC (Sydney, Australia)
Former Chief Judge, Commercial Division, Supreme Court of New South Wales; Chairman, National Dispute Centre, Sydney; Adjunct Professor, University of Technology, Sydney

DR. JOSÉ LUIS SIQUEIROS (Mexico City, Mexico)
President, Inter-American Bar Association; Past President, Mexican Academy of International Commercial Arbitration; Past Chairman, Inter-American Juridical Committee (OAS)

PROF. TANG HOUZHI (Beijing, People's Republic of China)
Honorary Vice Chairman, CIETAC; Vice Chairman, CCPIT/CCOIC Beijing Conciliation Centre; Professor, Law School of the People's University of China; Visiting Professor, Amoy University School of Law; Arbitration Adviser, UN International Trade Centre; Fellow and Chartered Arbitrator, Chartered Institute of Arbitrators; Former Court Member, LCIA; Honorary Professor, Hong Kong City University School of Law; Vice President, IFCAI

PROF. YASUHEI TANIGUCHI (Tokyo, Japan)
Former Member, Appellate Body of the World Trade Organization Dispute Settlement Body; Professor Emeritus, Kyoto University; President, Japan Association of Arbitrators; Special Advisor to the Japan Commercial Arbitration Association; Of Counsel, Matsuo & Kosugi